*Man and his world*

ISBN 0-460-93180-6

*Typography and binding designed by Arnold Rockman, M.T.D.C.*

*Printed and bound in Canada by The Bryant Press Limited*

# Man and his world

*studies in prose*

*selected and edited by* **Malcolm Ross**, M.A., PH.D., F.R.S.C.,
*Professor of English Literature*
*at Trinity College, University of Toronto,*
*and* **John Stevens**, M.A., *formerly Head*
*of the Department of English, Don Mills Collegiate Institute*

*J. M. Dent & Sons (Canada) Limited, Toronto*

# Contents

# Preface

A book of this kind must have quality. It must also have range. Accordingly, the editors have sought to bring to student and teacher stories and essays of intrinsic interest and permanent value. But it will be noticed at once that these stories and essays are of very different sorts and conditions. Do the stories by Joyce and Thurber and Maugham really belong together in the same literary family or type? Can the term "essay" be used without qualification and apology to describe the pieces by writers as different in tone and manner and intention as Charles Lamb and Bertrand Russell? One might even wonder if the essay and the short story are always separate and distinct literary types. Is not the Leacock essay, "My Remarkable Uncle", teetering on the edge of becoming a short story?

The book, in other words, has range. It has been prepared and edited in the conviction that a rigid understanding and use of the terms "short story" and "essay" can be most misleading. The short story is not just a dwarfed novel composed in equal parts of "theme", "plot", and "character". The editors have indeed included stories with a nice and recognizable balance of "theme", "plot", and "character". But there are stories here (and very good stories, too) with almost no plot, stories with little or no characterization, stories which are close in effect to lyric poetry, and stories which argue a point in the way that essays sometimes do.

Similarly, the essays in this book range from the "informal" and "familiar" style of writers like Thackeray and Beerbohm to careful exercises in persuasion, such as the essay by C. S. Lewis. Then, there will be found essays of reminiscence and nostalgia, satirical essays written in controlled anger, essays which are little meditations on the meaning of life, and essays which turn our eyes now inward, now outward. Here are spoken essays, taking their tone and shape from the radio instead of the page; here are essays which seem to have grown up and out from the newspaper column and the editor's latest crusade.

In both the essay and short story forms, the range of theme and style is almost endless. Precise definition is therefore difficult if not impossible to achieve. The essay *is* a brief composition in prose. The short story, relatively speaking, *is* short. But essays may be lyrical, didactic, formal, or familiar. So may short stories. Both (or either) may be philosophical, theological, psychological, or sociological. Or almost anything else! Certainly it is not helpful to read or judge either an essay or a story in terms of some blanket definition of what the "type" is *supposed* to be. In a sense, each essay and each story deserves a critical approach proper to itself. Each has its own secret, its own "whatness". For this reason, the editors, by means of questions appended to each selection in the book, have attempted to direct the student's attention to the peculiar tone, form, technique, and effect of the work under study. In each of the three parts of the book, one essay and one story have been given rather intensive critical treatment. These "sample" critical approaches by the editors are not meant to settle dogmatically questions of interpretation, or to provide an infallible guide as to how a story or essay should be read. The intention has been to suggest various ways of "entering" a work of art. It is hoped (and expected) that both the questions and the critiques will inspire counter-questions and counter-critiques. In short, the editors have tried to ask some of the relevant questions and to suggest a few hypothetical answers. Every hypothesis must be tested — and tested against the student's own experience of the story or essay. Nor is it uncommon, after the testing, for an hypothesis to be discarded. . . . It is hoped that both the questions and the critiques will provoke meaningful exploration and debate, not only in the classroom, but also in the course of the student's private study of the stories and essays.

Of course, each story and essay in this collection ought to be considered primarily by itself and for itself. But art, like life, presents contrasts and invites comparisons. The first critiques in parts One and Three of the book do draw tentative lines of comparison between essays within the section, and some of the questions throughout the book make the same attempt; but the teacher and student are invited to seek further differences and similarities. For instance, Hugh MacLennan's "Remembrance Day, 2010 A.D." and Charles Lamb's "Juke Judkins" are both ironic monologues. What are their differences in theme and development? Compare H. G. Wells' use of fantasy in "The Door in the Wall" with D. H. Lawrence's use of it in "The Rocking-Horse Winner". Compare the writers' treatment of courage in the two stories, "The Firing Squad" and "Pax Britannica". These are but a few of the possibilities. And such comparisons are no mere idle exercise; they deepen the reader's understanding of each of the stories or essays compared.

Brief biographies and bibliographies are given for each of the authors included. The notes, placed in the appendix, do not pretend to usurp the functions of a standard dictionary and atlas.

# Part one

*William*

*Faulkner*

# On receiving the Nobel Prize

*William Faulkner (1897- 1962) was born in New Albany, Mississippi, of a family once powerful and wealthy, but impoverished by the Civil War. During the First World War, he flew with the Royal Flying Corps in Europe. After the war, he attended the University of Mississippi, but did not graduate. After drifting about the United States and Europe, he returned to the town of Oxford, Mississippi, where he worked as a carpenter, did farm work, and wrote. Beginning with* The Sound and the Fury *(1929), he produced a cycle of novels and stories set in an imaginary county in Mississippi. Some of these are* Sartoris *(1929),* Sanctuary *(1931),* Light in August *(1932),* Absalom, Absalom! *(1936),* Unvanquished *(1938),* The Hamlet *(1940),* Go Down Moses *(1942),* Intruder in the Dust *(1948), and* Requiem for a Nun *(1951). He considers* A Fable *(1954), a religious allegory paralleling Christ's Passion, to be the most important work of his life. In 1950 Faulkner gave the following eloquent address in Stockholm on the occasion of his receiving the Nobel Prize in literature.*

I FEEL THAT this award was not made to me as a man but to my work — a life's work in the agony and sweat of the human spirit, not for glory and least of all for profit, but to create out of the materials of the human spirit something which did not exist there before. So this award is only mine in trust. It will not be difficult to find a dedication for the money part of it commensurate with the purpose and significance of its origin. But I would like to do the same with the acclaim, too, by using this moment as a pinnacle from which I might be listened to by the young men and women already dedicated to the same anguish and travail, among whom is already that one who will some day stand here where I am standing.

Our tragedy today is a general and a universal physical fear so long sustained by now that we can even bear it. There are no longer problems of the spirit. There is only the question: When will I be blown up? Because of this, the young man or woman writing today has forgotten the problems of the human heart in conflict with itself which alone can make good writing because only that is worth writing about, worth the agony and the sweat.

He must learn them again. He must teach himself that the basest of all things is to be afraid; and, teaching himself that, forget it forever, leaving no room in his workshop for anything but the old verities and truths of the heart, the old universal truths lacking which any story is ephemeral and doomed — love and honor and pity and pride and compassion and sacrifice. Until he does so he labors under a curse. He writes not of love, but of lust, of defeats in which nobody loses anything of value, of victories without hope and worst of all without pity or compassion. His griefs grieve on no universal bones, leaving no scars. He writes not of the heart but of the glands.

Until he relearns these things he will write as though he stood among and watched the end of man. I decline to accept the end of man. It is easy enough to say that man is immortal simply because he will endure; that when the last ding-dong of doom has clanged and faded from the last worthless rock hanging tideless in the last red and dying evening, that even then there will still be one more sound: that of his puny inexhaustible voice still talking. I refuse to accept this. I believe that man will not merely endure: he will prevail. He is immortal, not because he alone among creatures has an inexhaustible voice, but because he has a soul, a spirit capable of compassion and sacrifice and endurance. The poet's, the writer's, duty is to write about these things. It is his privilege to help man endure by lifting his heart, by reminding him of the courage and honor and hope and pride and compassion and pity and sacrifice which have been the glory of his past. The poet's voice need not merely be the record of man, it can be one of the props, the pillars to help him endure and prevail.

*Waldemar*
*Kaempffert*

# Man and his world

━━━━━━━━━━━━━━━━━━━━

*Waldemar Kaempffert (1877-1956), American science editor
and author, was born and educated in New York city, graduating
from City College in 1897 and continuing graduate studies at
New York University.* From 1897 to 1915, *he was at first
assistant editor and then managing editor of the* Scientific
American, *and from 1915 to 1920, he edited* Popular Science
Monthly. *In 1927, after several years as a free-lance writer, he
became science editor of the* New York Times, *a position which
he held for the remainder of his life. His special fields of interest
were the history of invention and the study of how science and
technology have affected human society. Some of his numerous
essays have been collected in* Explorations in Science *(1953),
and in an earlier volume* Science Today and Tomorrow *(copyright 1939 by Waldemar Kaempffert), from which the following essay is reprinted by permission of The Viking Press, Inc.*

━━━━━━━━━━━━━━━━━━━━

MAN RUSHES through the air in passenger planes at speeds of more
than 150 miles an hour and dreams of rocket ships that will whisk
him across the Atlantic between breakfast and luncheon. He
rises miles into the stratosphere, where oxygen must be inhaled
from a tank if he is to retain consciousness. He drills and blasts
for gold in South Africa in a gallery dank with the steam of hot
springs, and in steel mills he handles metal which is so much

liquid fire. He huddles in cities of stone and steel, there to fall prey to germs of which he knew nothing in his primitive hunting life of a few thousand years ago. Upon his eyes and his ears sights and sounds impinge that wear down his nerves. He creates an artificial environment for himself and in it lives an artificial life. Clothes, lights, rooms, plumbing, steam-heat, cooked food, dishes, knives and forks, even the atmosphere in an air-conditioned theatre, hotel, or ship — everything is artificial. He is as much a forced product as a hothouse grape. Can this primitive savage, who only ten thousand years ago kept body and soul together by trapping and stoning forest animals and spearing fish, stand the nervous strain of the machine world that he has fashioned for himself? Ever since Darwin's day physiologists and anatomists have had their doubts. Latterly the doubts are more audible than ever.

At a recent congress of the American College of Surgeons, Dr. R. C. Buerki, past president of the American Hospital Association, presented a picture of this modern man, a victim of high blood pressure, enlarged heart, failing circulation, jangled nerves — afflictions brought about by inventions that make it possible to do several things at the same time, such as gulping down more food in five minutes than a Zulu can gather in a day and listening to broadcast jazz or reading a newspaper. And in the course of the Terry lectures delivered at Yale the Nobel prize-winner, Sir Joseph Barcroft, showed how delicate is the balance between mind and body and how quickly the mind succumbs when the conditions under which the body naturally thrives are only slightly changed. At the 1936 meeting of the British Association for the Advancement of Science the distinguished paleontologist Prof. H. L. Hawkins dubbed man "the only irrational creature". And at the Harvard Tercentenary the specialists in nervous disorders made it plain that the pace set by our machines is too fast for the harassed organism.

The glory and the curse of man are his brain. It raises him above the beasts of the field and the forest, but it also dooms him as a species. For that brain of his is overdeveloped, overspecialized. It endows him with a mind that conceives new machines to take the place of muscles, new instruments to supplement inadequate senses, new and more complex ways of living in communities. The poor body cannot adapt itself rapidly enough to the social and technical changes conceived by the mind. Heart and muscles belong to the jungle; the modern mind to an environment of its own creation. The verdict seems to be that man must crack under the strain.

First we consider the story told by the fossil bones of creatures that once possessed the earth and then vanished. They scream Cassandra prophecies.

"We developed now this organ and now that to secure an advantage over our enemies in the struggle for existence," they warn. "See how some of us increased our speed, others waxed stronger and larger, and still others practised the art of mimicry in adapting ourselves to our environment. All in vain. One by one we perished."

They ask ominous questions – these bones. "Where are the first things that crawled out of the sea? Where are the ptero-dactyls – hugest creatures that ever flew? Where are the dinosaurs that once shook the earth? Where are the common ancestors of apes and men? Where, for that matter, are the first, crude men of Java, China, Rhodesia, and England, the half-apes that ruled the forest a million years ago? Where are the Neander-thalers and Cro-Magnons of only fifty thousand years ago?"

The bones preach sermons on the virtues of simplicity. On the whole it is the simple organisms that endure – the one-celled organisms best of all. These are not brilliant, clever specialists but biological jacks-of-all-trades. Not that complexity and specializa-tion are necessarily fatal. They are merely highly dangerous. The lowly things are harmonious wholes. Introduce specialization – a more efficient way of gathering and devouring food, a surer hold on a rock or tree, a nervous system more responsive to the dangers of the environment – and the old harmony is impaired, the road to extinction cleared. When man learned how to use his mind, more was involved than the mere development of reasoning power. Stories have been written by Wells and others of superintellectual ants that defeated man and assumed ascendancy. Good fiction, but bad biology. Man had to pass through a creepy, slimy, slithery, finny, furry past before he could acquire his complex central nervous system and his brain. He came out of the oyster and the starfish, the shark and the tiger, the cow and something from which he and the ape sprang.

Each upward step was marked by an important physical change – a better co-ordination of mind and body. The foot and the hand of the chimpanzee, man's nearest lower relative, are different in structure and even in function from our feet and hands. Jaws, brow, teeth are different in structure, too. Adapting himself to an upright position, acquiring the art of walking on two feet instead of four, making a clutching and holding tool of the hand – all this was accompanied by the evolution of the brain, the most complicated single piece of apparatus in the world.

Apparently this rise from the oyster is not yet ended. Moreover, it has not been a uniform process. Sometimes it was this organ that shot ahead, sometimes that. The central nervous system, of which the brain is the vertex, has outstripped all else. Man is an overspecialized animal by reason of his brain. And it is overspecialization that dooms him to ultimate extinction.

Surveying man with a critical eye, the late Professor Elie Metchnikoff of the Pasteur Institute found him anything but the piece of work that Hamlet held up for admiration. What is the good of hair? asked the Russian derogator. It catches germs; it is a vestige of the ape within us. Look at the caecum (blind gut, in yeoman's English) and the large intestine. Utterly useless. Mere cesspools. Cut them out, was Metchnikoff's advice – surgical operations actually performed with success. Then there is the eye. We might overlook the optical mistakes made in its design and construction if only it would maintain its efficiency. At forty-five, the lens is already old. Walking on two feet has brought with it fallen arches, varicose veins; a now illogical distribution of valves in the circulatory system, congested livers and a hundred other lapses from physical perfection. Man as a social animal needs correction and improvement. The surgeon is helpless. Speed up evolution, was the conclusion reached by the great Russian rebel against nature. Unless that is done man must fall a victim to his own brain and works.

The strain upon the nervous system is as nothing compared with that to come if the engineers and inventors maintain the present pace. Utopians like Professor H. J. Muller predict that each of us will some day be in potentially immediate communication with everyone on earth. Can the race stand it? Even the prospect of more speed terrifies a physiologist such as Barcroft. "What of the accidents that befall aeronauts in pursuit of records?" he asks. "It is the human element which gives way, and it is not the body of man but his mind."

Metchnikoff is not alone. Anatomists, physiologists, paleontologists agree with him on the whole. Listen to Sir Arthur Keith:

Beyond a doubt civilization is submitting the human body to a vast and critical experiment. Civilization has laid bare some of the weak points in the human body, but the conditions which have provoked them are not of nature's ordaining but of man's choosing.

And next to Dr. Charles B. Davenport, geneticist of the Carnegie Institution of Washington:

Apparently man is to be compared with the great horny and armored dinosaurs, the great elk, and many fossil nautili in which an exaggeration of a part was followed by extinction....

Inherent laws of mutation and evolutionary change will work themselves out and man will in time go the way of all other species.

And lastly, Professor H. L. Hawkins, speaking in 1936 before the British Association for the Advancement of Science:

... the high cerebral specialization that makes possible all these developments and the extraordinary rate at which success has been attained both point to the conclusion that this is a species destined to a spectacular rise and an equally spectacular fall, more complete and rapid than the world has yet seen.

Consider now the story told by the physiologist about a body attuned to the wilderness. For a moment limit yourself to the blood alone and see what happens to the mind when its physical and chemical balance is disturbed ever so slightly.

Overheat the blood, and you rave. Yet men must work nearly at the raving point in deep, steaming gold mines, in hot boiler rooms, at the mouths of blazing furnaces, to produce the things demanded in making an artificial environment.

Chill the blood, as Sir Joseph Barcroft did by lying naked in an icy room while an assistant watched. For a time the body tries to combat the cold. Barcroft's mind told him to get up, walk, keep his blood in circulation. But he refused for the sake of science. Then the mind gave up the battle. He stretched out his legs. He felt warm. "It was as if I were basking in the cold," he says. He was content to lie still, blissfully indifferent to a death from which his vigilant assistant saved him. His mind had ceased to watch over him.

Take away oxygen from the blood. The mind loses its reasoning ability. At 18,000 feet in the Andes, Barcroft and his assistants suffered from "mountain sickness" — a sign of oxygen deficiency. Not a man thought of inhaling oxygen from cylinders brought along for just such an emergency. Later in England Barcroft pedaled a stationary bicycle in a room from which oxygen was gradually withdrawn. He had planned to manipulate certain gas valves. Observers noted the mistakes that he made. Yet he was willing to swear in court that he had turned the handle correctly. His mind was beginning to crack.

So with the breathlessness that affects men who fly at great heights. They suffer not from an affection of the chest muscles, as they think, but of the nerves that control the muscles. The central nervous system has failed to perform its duty.

Decrease the calcium in the blood by half. Convulsions, coma, then death follow. Double the calcium. The blood thickens so that it can hardly flow. Heaviness, indifference, unconsciousness mark successive stages of the mind's dethronement. Again death is the end.

Reduce the amount of sugar in the blood, ever so little. There is a feeling of "goneness," at the worst a blotting out of the mind. Then death. Increase the sugar a few milligrams to the cubic centimeter and fear seizes the mind – fear of trifles. Double images form. Speech is thick. There are illusions.

Blood is slightly alkaline. Acidify it slightly. Coma follows, meaning that the mind is a blank. Make the blood a little more alkaline. Convulsions foretell the end.

Take water from the blood. We collapse from weakness. Add water. We suffer from headaches, nausea, dizziness.

Change anything about the blood – the amount of oxygen, carbon dioxide, a score of chemicals – and always the mind gives way. The point is that some of the diseases that civilization has brought upon us do affect the physical and chemical constitution of the blood. Diabetes, for example. So the chemical analysis of the blood has become an almost indispensable aid in diagnosing many afflictions. And because it is indispensable it speaks eloquently of that downfall which paleontologists predict.

It may be urged that we do not deliberately interfere with the organism as Barcroft did. But we do. Divers and tunnelers, for example, must work under high air pressure. More gas is driven into the blood stream. It cannot be without its physiological effect. "No doubt," says Barcroft, "the thoughts of the human mind, its power to solve differential equations or to appreciate exquisite music involves some sort of physical or chemical pattern, which would be blurred in a milieu itself undergoing violent changes." This means in plain English that a change in the environment – the kind of change that invention dictates – may be too much for body and hence for mind.

Professor Harlow Shapley, a zoologist who became the distinguished director of Harvard's astronomical observatory, once tellingly compared the ant with man. Both are social creatures. But the ant adapted itself to its environment 360,000,000 years ago. Volcanoes have spewed lava, continents have split and floated apart, ice ages have come and gone, climates have changed, but the ant has emerged from each cataclysm unruffled and serene.

Today it is much the same ant that it was geological epochs ago. It is a highly specialized creature, this ant. But it subdivides its specialties – such matters as reproduction, working, fighting – among castes. And so it manages to strike a nice balance between its environment and its social self. It is all but stagnant in an evolutionary sense. But it seems to be permanent.

But man? An unstable thing. A dozen species of him have been evolved and destroyed in the last million years. He is an upstart compared with any social insect. He has changed his mode of community living time and time again in the last 25,000 years, but the ant's social organization has come down intact much as it was when the earth was younger. If survival is the test of fitness in the Darwinian sense, we ought not only go to the ant and consider her ways but prostrate ourselves before her. Some day, as Shapley imagines, an ant will crawl out of the eye socket of an extinct man and soliloquize: "A marvelous experiment of nature's. What a brain! Alas, the poor creature did not understand the business of survival."

There may be compensation in this rise and decline of man. If mere survival as a species is the *summmum bonum*, the ant is indeed the ideal social animal. To annihilate distance and time with airplanes and radio, to convert night into day with lamps that are miniature suns, to clothe oneself in fabrics woven from fibers that nature never knew, to see on the screen players who enact the events of purely imaginary lives — all this is beyond the unshakable ant. In us a mind that yearns is at work, but the reward of successful yearning is extinction.

Suppose that man does go the way of the dodo, the brontosaurus, and the saber-toothed tiger. Is that the end of spirituality? Must the world relapse to mere savagery, just as magnificent cities of ancient Yucatan and India relapsed to the primeval jungle? Biologists as a class dislike the notion of purpose and direction in evolution. Yet it is hard to believe that life is "but a disease of matter in its old age," as Sir James Jeans once hazarded in tracing the evolution of worlds.

Measured in terms of the brain, the trend of evolution has been up and on. Nature is willing to experiment with countless species, to toss them aside, as it did thousands of birds, fishes, and four-footed creatures, but in the end she sees to it that something better evolves. From her pitiless destruction of primordial half-apes and of such fine specimens of true humanity as the Cro-

Magnons, it may be inferred that modern man is a poor thing in her eyes, ready even now for the scrap heap. But something else will take his place if the past is any guide.

Perhaps we are only preliminary sketches, a preparation for some grander creature, a significant experiment in developing a spirituality higher than the tiger and the ape within us permit us to achieve. Perhaps extinction, the price of evolution, is not too high.

CRITIQUE AND QUESTIONS

In the final paragraph of *The Origin of Species* Charles Darwin, commenting on his theory of evolution, wrote: "There is grandeur in this view of life ... that, whilst this planet has gone cycling on according to the fixed laws of gravity, from so simple a beginning endless forms most beautiful and most wonderful have been, and are being evolved."

Kaempffert in this essay reflects on man's active part in his own evolution. While accepting Darwin's principle of slow biological development over vast periods of time, Kaempffert produces contemporary evidence that suggests thoughts considerably less optimistic than those stimulated by Darwin's closing words. The exposition of his ideas is so skilful as to be worth studying closely.

His opening catches our interest immediately. The first paragraph creates a vivid impression of modern man in his civilized frenzy, rushing to make his environment more and more unnatural. Even on your first reading you may have noticed the rhythmic surge of the first few sentences, all dominated by strong verbs of action. Another reading will reveal that this rhythm does not remain completely regular. It changes suddenly in the fifth sentence, recovers the original beat in the sixth, and in the seventh breaks into a rapid series of short, sharp words. The tempo of the style suggests the swift, nervously unpredictable pace of modern life.

In the second paragraph he begins his technique of quoting modern scientists. We cannot find refuge in the hope that the sombre views expressed in "Man and His World" proceed from a morbidly disordered mind; Kaempffert's method of exposition makes it clear that they represent a rational judgment reached after wide and intelligent reading. He is like a master lawyer calling his witnesses to the stand. The first three to give testimony, Buerki, Barcroft, and Hawkins, announce that twentieth-century man is in a biologically untenable position. We ordinary readers may not find the message agreeable, but how can we refute such authorities — men whose judgment is backed by the most expert knowledge? Kaempffert is employing with great skill a cardinal rule of expository writing: always build a generalization on evidence that is solid and definite. In the third paragraph when he states the thesis that is to be developed by the rest of the essay, his case seems already half proved.

Having set forth his basic opinion, backed by impeccable scientific authority, Kaempffert now moves on to adduce further evidence. Note that he changes his method somewhat. Instead of quoting living men, he personifies the long dead relics of vanished creatures and has them "scream Cassandra prophecies". What advantage might there be in this shift of technique? And why does he have these prophetic bones ask questions as well as make pronouncements?

After using these "voices" to make a case for "the virtues of simplicity", Kaempffert briefly summarizes the process of evolution from the relatively simple to the increasingly complex, and comes to the conclusion that for man "it is over-specialization that dooms him to extinction" — really a reiteration of his thesis stated in the third paragraph. He began his essay with a formidable combination of rhetoric and specific evidence. What has he added in the way of proof? Has he carried you along to complete agreement with him in the conclusion quoted above? Perhaps he has gone a little too far, too fast. His next tactic is to underpin his conclusion with more evidence from research scientists. Man is, as everyone acknowledges, an amazingly complicated creature. It is a characteristic upon which he compliments himself. Kaempffert introduces an eminent biologist, Elie Metchnikoff, to shock us with the inefficiency of this human complexity. But one expert does not make a gospel, so Kaempffert quotes again from Sir Joseph Barcroft and from three other scientists, Keith, Davenport, and Hawkins. You will notice that these authorities each make a comment which powerfully reinforces Kaempffert's main argument, and that they speak in a planned sequence. Why does he have his impressive witnesses give evidence in this particular order? Take a close look at what the last two men have to say. What relationship can you see between their statements and those of the oracular bones that Kaempffert has made speak earlier?

All these quotations may be persuasive, but perhaps they still generalize too inclusively and too rashly. Generalizations are suspect, even when made by a scientist of the stature of Sir Joseph Barcroft. Kaempffert now turns to one specific element in the body — the blood. His choice is worth pondering a moment. Why does he select this aspect of human physiology rather than another? When you re-examine this part of the essay, you will find that he mentions ten changes in the condition of human blood, some of them illustrated by specific experiments. As you read, consider the advantages of mentioning definite experiments that have been printed in scientific journals. And look for the sentence which drives home the point that he is making in citing all these examples.

Kaempffert terminates his alarming array of evidence with a vivid contrast between man and the ant, a contrast drawn originally by a famous zoologist, and then he concludes with a thought that is reminiscent of Darwin's closing words. Darwin had been struck by the beauty of the many creatures that had been and *"are being evolved"*. In his final paragraph Kaempffert looks beyond the cosmic veils of time and foresees a possible evolutionary replacement for man. Most of us, however, will draw but cold comfort from that distant consolation.

Although Faulkner's address (see page 1) is much shorter, and was written to be heard rather than read, it is interesting to compare it with "Man and His World", if only because it is so different in opinion and method of argument. Kaempffert painstakingly amasses evidence from his reading, much as Darwin himself collected fossil skeletons and barnacles during his historic voyage on the *Beagle*. Faulkner, however, does not prove; he is the poet, the seer; he merely declares what he knows is true.

Kaempffert's expository method we might compare to the method of science in which conclusions rest upon experimental evidence, whereas Faulkner's is the intuitive method of the mystic. Just as the scientist states his conclusions tentatively, no matter how confident he is of his observations, so does Kaempffert have some reticence about his conclusions. For all his apparent confidence, he is not really sure. He says, "It may be inferred that man is doomed", and "Perhaps we are only preliminary sketches . . ." But Faulkner's knowledge is immediate and certain. It has come to him as a personal insight "in the agony and sweat of the human spirit". If we compare the last sentence in each of the two essays, we find that the key word in Kaempffert's is "extinction", and in Faulkner's, "prevail". Which sentence shall we accept?

QUESTIONS (FAULKNER)

1. Faulkner sees modern man as existing in a tragic situation. What has caused this tragedy?

2. What does he consider a major failing of some modern writers?

3. To what group does Faulkner address his remarks? Why does he speak to these people in particular?

4. In Faulkner's view what is the writer's mission?

5. Examining the prose of a great writer can bring us closer to the creative working of his mind. Using your knowledge of how writers can obtain certain effects through sentence structure and imagery, write a comment on Faulkner's style in this essay.

QUESTIONS (KAEMPFFERT)

1. From your own observation of human environment, what other sources of nervous strain could you add to the author's list?

2. Offer some possible techniques that human beings might develop to reduce the nervous strain imposed by human inventions.

3. From the facts and theories presented in this essay, can you draw any conclusions which differ from those of the author?

*Hugh*
*MacLennan*

# Remembrance day, 2010 A.D.

*Hugh MacLennan (b. 1907) was born in Cape Breton and educated at Dalhousie, Oxford, and Princeton. A scholar and a teacher (he taught between 1935 and 1945 at Lower Canada College, Montreal, and is now Associate Professor of English at McGill University), MacLennan published his first novel,* Barometer Rising, *in 1941 and has won the Governor-General's Award for Fiction for his novels,* Two Solitudes *(1945),* The Precipice *(1948), and* The Watch That Ends the Night *(1959). In 1949, he won the Governor-General's Award for Creative Non-Fiction with his volume of essays,* Cross-Country. *His essays appear in leading magazines here and abroad, and his fiction has a wide audience in both Britain and the United States. "Remembrance Day, 2010 A.D." is reprinted from* Scotchman's Return and Other Essays *by Hugh MacLennan, by permission of The Macmillan Company of Canada, Ltd.*

THE TIME HAS COME, the President feels, when it is essential to pay the homage of a day of remembrance, and what we are required to remember is the period of our history, and especially the men who lived in it, which made possible the world we inhabit now.

Those men are so remote that in our eyes they seem almost like primitives, yet it must be understood that they had few of our advantages. In their time education by conditioned reflex was confined only to the elementary schools and to the outer selling fringes of commerce; they were burdened by a great weight of superstition from the pre-scientific past which made thinking such a dangerous activity that their most successful men found it impractical to think about anything above the level of a technical problem; wherever they looked they were surrounded by reactionaries who sapped their vitality by telling them that if they continued on the path they had chosen, they would destroy all human life on the planet Earth.

But they did continue; they defeated reaction by refusing to be reactionary; they did not call a halt. The President therefore feels that a tribute to these men of the sixth decade of the twentieth century is long overdue, and he has given me the assignment of telling their story.

As in most truly creative periods of history, events in the sixth decade of the twentieth century followed so fast on one another that the leaders had no understanding of what they were doing. They, too, were handicapped by superstitions inherited from the past: they went to church and they mouthed the old platitudes. Yet somehow they contrived in one part of their brain to live in the past and in another to live in the present. But whatever they may have said to the contrary, there can be no doubt that they acted according to the two great principles of psychology on which our present civilization rests and draws its power.

The first principle they accepted and made operative – one which today every conditioned child regards as self-evident – was simply this: *Man would sooner die than be bored.* The President feels that the acceptance of this principle at that particular time was the most remarkable leap the human mind had made since it accepted the earlier principle that the world is round and not flat.

Recall how people talked in those days. The reactionaries still babbled about the delights of peace, and insisted that true happiness comes only to the man who lives free of fear and anxiety. They even talked in hushed voices of the peace of God which passeth understanding, and failed to recognize that what passed their own understanding was that for men who lived as they did, and as we do, this so-called peace of God would far better have been named Hell. For how can a man whose nervous system has been conditioned by progress to repeated shocks, dislocations, surprises, terrors and wonders be happy if these stimuli are taken away from him? It is incredible, but the reactionaries of that time pretended that peace was what progressive man truly desires!

It was the manner of our grandfathers' acceptance of this dynamic principle, the President feels, which sheds a peculiar glory on them. On the other side of the world the Russians were behaving in their chronically efficient way: they had liquidated their reactionaries and closed those fonts of superstition, the churches. They had banned or rewritten the moral teachings of the pre-scientific past, and had compelled their satellites by brute force to live as they did themselves. It was easier for the Russians then, just as it is easier for them now. For our grandfathers, like ourselves, were compelled by their morality to obtain their results by the processes of democracy. They could not tolerate the idea of a satellite country; the countries in their orbit had to be their friends. They closed no churches, on the contrary they proclaimed it their duty to defend the principles on which these institutions rested. They jailed no reactionaries; instead they so honoured them that in a popularity poll two religious teachers called the Pope and Albert Schweitzer ranked close in esteem to the President himself. They listened with respectful attention to every negative argument advanced by men like these, they made available to them all the usual channels of publicity, and yet, without ever departing from the principles of democracy, they achieved the necessary results. With a rapidity which seems astonishing even to us, they advanced to the acceptance of the second great psychological principle which our children take for granted, the one we now call *The Love-Hate Syndrome.*

We have proof (so obvious that every child recognizes it) that the two most mighty forces in the world are love and hate: not love by itself or hate by itself, but love and hate working together like a pair of legs underneath the body. On the leg of love a nation can stand almost indefinitely, but it stands still; on the leg of hate a nation twitches so violently that it falls flat on its face, as happened to a country called Germany, now extinct, in the reign of a leader called Hitler, now forgotten. But if one leg is love and the other is hate, the nation advances on the run, and it accomplishes miracles under the spur of the chain reaction this syndrome sets in motion — pride and contempt, hope and despair, terror and relief. Under the Love-Hate Syndrome these psychic hormones are daily pumped into the national blood-stream, and progress not only becomes possible, it becomes irresistible.

To us the truth and value of this syndrome are self-evident, but not to the men of the sixth decade of the twentieth century, and that is one more reason why the President feels that it is essential to give you some more information about them.

The chief of their many superstitions was the one they called Christianity. Democracy in those days was so committed to defend the Christian religion that its leaders never dared to make a public speech without mentioning God, never went to war without claiming they did so to preserve the spirit of brotherly love and never did anything without being quick to inform the people they would have been unable to do it without God's guidance. They still honoured a book — though few of them seem to have read it — called the Bible, and at the President's suggestion I myself obtained a copy from the inner vault where it is kept side by side with the Constitution and the old Declaration of Independence. Let me tell you a little about this book.

To begin with, it is the most dangerous book ever compiled. If it were widely read and supported today, and if people believed even a fraction of what it contains, civilization as we know it would not endure as long as a single year. The chief author of the official superstition was a man who possessed astonishing powers of language — far greater, I freely admit, than those of our present Minister of Education. This man, who was liquidated by some ancient government so long ago it does not matter when, declared that it is impossible for a human being to serve two masters, his theory being that he will love the one and despise the other. He said that nobody can serve both God and Mammon, or gain the world and save his soul, or be happy and miserable at the same time. Repeatedly he talked about the beauties of peace and brotherly love, even carrying his argument to the point that we should love our enemies. So pervasive was this man's propaganda in the sixth decade of the twentieth century that even the Russians — this is almost incredible but it is true — paid constant lip service to it. Whenever the Russians of that time made a war, their leaders never failed to say they were establishing peace. Whenever they butchered a satellite, they announced they were coming to the aid of the peace-loving citizens within the satellite.

The Russians, we may believe, were cynical in these statements as they are in the statements they make today. But our grandfathers were not cynical. They really believed that they desired peace and they really believed that they were acting according to Christian principles when they made those great decisions which resulted in the Love-Hate Syndrome becoming operative once and for all in our democratic society.

The President feels, and so do I, that if we are to pay our grandfathers the proper meed of respect we must fully appreciate the appalling technical problem they faced. For consider some of the facts.

Then, as now, the world was divided into the two systems. Our grandfathers loved their system as no system had ever been loved before, and they hated the Russian system as no system had ever been hated. The Russian attitude was ours in reverse. And when the Love-Hate Syndrome became operative, the tension it set up, the creative tension, drove both systems to achievements greater than its citizens could comprehend.

Our system built a bomb which annihilated a single city in a minute; the Russians matched it a few years later. The Russians then built a bomb which would obliterate a whole province; we matched it in a matter of months. We built a submarine which could fire a rocket from the floor of the ocean and hit a target hundreds of miles away; the Russians countered with an earth-satellite useless in itself, but terrifying in its implication that they possessed stronger rockets than we. We fired off a fusillade of rockets into space, some of them so far we lost track of them, and then set frantically to work catching up with the Russians in this important department of technological culture. Within a matter of a year and a half, progress on both sides was so rapid that thousands of rockets were zero-ed in on every important city, air base and military target in the world.

Think what a technical problem this situation created! For a time of several years not only the life of every human being, but technical progress itself, hung on the balance of a hair-trigger! Imagine if you can the nerve the people of our grandfathers' day possessed to live like this and act like this!

It was of course easier for the Russians than for us, for the Russian leaders were not democratic and had silenced all their reactionaries. But our reactionaries were not silent, far from it. "Call it off!" they howled. "Call it off before we're all dead!" In their response to this final challenge, the President feels, our grandfathers saved civilization. For to the cry, "Call it off before we're all dead!" they answered, in effect, "We'd sooner be dead than call it off!"

Without their being able to understand it, the Love-Hate Syndrome was saving them. By making it impossible to yield to the Russians in any particular, it was already transforming their entire society in such a way as to eradicate all traces of the reactionary superstitions which hitherto had held it back. Under the spur of love of country and hate of the enemy, of fear and competition, of hope and despair, of all these emotions which are now our common spiritual food, our grandfathers reformed their whole educational system. They scrapped every element which did not directly pertain to science, engineering and propaganda. They let their old so-called humanists and religious teachers wither on the vine. They bred a generation – us – so progressively-minded that nothing has been able to hold us back.

At the last moment, in the very nick of time, their faith was justified. For at the very instant when their nerves, and the Russians' nerves, were at the snapping point, the progress which had been set in motion by the Love-Hate Syndrome crossed a new frontier. The moon was occupied by human beings.

The President feels no shame in having me admit that it was

the Russians, and not ourselves, who established the first actual base on the moon with flesh and blood humans in it, for the establishment of this base was important only in so far as it proved that it was now possible for both systems to continue doing what they liked doing and survive. It outmoded the old technical problem of how the Love-Hate Syndrome, plus progress, could continue to operate full blast without annihilating all life on the planet. It made it not only possible, it made it inevitable, that we could now engage in the all-out war for which we had planned and prepared ourselves for years.

Within three days of the establishment of the Russian base on the moon, we established one of our own about five hundred miles distant. A meeting of international lawyers, quickly convened in Calcutta to argue points of ownership and establish a treaty whereby our system could share the moon with Russia, broke up with mutual abuse, and before the lawyers were halfway home the rockets were moving moon-wards and our base and the Russian base were simultaneously obliterated. In the political sense the First Battle of the Moon ended in a draw, but in the technical sense it did not. After computations had been made, our scientists were able to prove that the force of our explosions exceeded those of the Russians by some half a million megatons.

The first space war was now on, and try to imagine what a feeling of release, what a sense of joy swept through the minds of men when they realized that the wonderful devices they had been stock-piling for years could actually be used! Instead of outmoding them before they were employed, now each new model could be sent instantly into action. More than this was proved by the First Battle of the Moon. It was proved that our way of life could now go on indefinitely and that progress would never cease.

The decade following the First Battle of the Moon was the most spectacular in the history of the universe up to the present time. In less than a year and a half, working on two separate crash programs, our electronic engineers and lense-makers beat the Russians in producing telescopic television which relayed from space platforms the planetary expeditions from the moment of their setting out to their final obliteration when the rockets found them. Our democratic ingenuity enabled us to overcome what had hitherto seemed an insuperable obstacle, that of transmitting sound through space itself. But we beat the Russians to it, and by the first decade of the present century we had in operation twelve different channels which enabled our citizens to follow the planetary wars and even to hear faint echoes of the explosions. We beat the Russians in sound by two and a half months, and our programmes were always better than theirs because they were more democratic, while the Russians stultified theirs by interrupting them constantly with mechanical voices which repeated propaganda from empty space.

Now I must change the key of this message; I must tell you the real reason why the President feels it necessary for us to observe a day of remembrance in honour of the men who made possible the world we now inhabit. It is because he thinks the time is at hand when we, too, will require all the nerve and courage at our disposal if we are not to fail. He feels, and I agree with him, that now is the time to remember that if our ancestors could keep their nerve, so also can we.

The government of Russia — the possibility had long been foreseen, despite the election propaganda of the President's opponent — is now in the hands of a lunatic. How he got there cannot be explained beyond mentioning that in Russian history there has always been a high frequency of insanity in the higher echelons of government. This creature now threatens to blow up the world unless he gets his own way. And the President, who has always been frank with the people, feels that it is right and proper that the situation be laid fairly before them, in order that the people may decide for themselves on the course of action they will follow. He has full confidence that the people will decide rightly.

As you know, the Russians have been established on Venus for a year, a move which was inevitable after we decided it was necessary to blow up the moon in order to provide ourselves with a sufficient number of adequate space platforms for further scientific experiments, and also for an improved television

service. The Russian advance to Venus made it inevitable that
we should advance to Mars, where we have been established
for five months. Both of these outer bases have been inactive up
to the present pending completion of television stations on the
fragments of the moon which will enable us to follow the operations farther out. Military operations are scheduled to begin,
however, the moment our super-television service is ready, and
they will begin on schedule about nine months from now unless
the Russians beat us to it, which hardly seems probable.

But now, owing to the state of mind of the Russian leader, we
are faced with the gravest crisis in a quarter of a century. He
has stated that unless we withdraw from Mars, he will attack us in
our own heartland. When the President first learned of this
threat, he of course made the routine answer that if the Russians
annihilated us, we would also annihilate them. But intelligence
has since confirmed that the Russian leader is a genuine psycho-
tic, and not merely the emotionally unstable brute we assume all
Russian leaders to be. His answer to the President's message must
be taken with extreme seriousness, and his actual words must
be reported. What he transmitted to the President was the
briefest, crudest, and most uncivilized note in the history of
diplomacy. It was this: "I don't care whether you get me so
long as I get you. Get off Mars."

I don't think it necessary to say that the President does not
contemplate for an instant yielding to a threat of this nature.
But he feels, and surely he is right, that the public should understand that the threat is real. This lunatic really means what he says.
He has literally put the rocket to our heads.

That is why the President believes that we should observe a
day of remembrance in honour of our grandfathers who outfaced
a danger equally great, and a future equally uncertain, and did
not fail their destiny. At that time, ignorant though they were,
they knew if they showed a moment's weakness they would
merely encourage the worst elements in the Russian government.
The situation is precisely the same now. If we withdraw from
Mars, it will mean only one thing to Russia: that our nerve is
failing. But if we stand firm, even knowing that this lunatic

means literally what he says, who knows what may happen? Our grandfathers stood firm, and just at the moment when their obliteration seemed inevitable, they were saved by the Russian action in occupying the moon. There are a variety of ways in which we can be saved now, provided we stand firm. This Russian will not lose his nerve, because lunatics never do. But is it unreasonable to suppose that he will be liquidated by his own cabinet? Horrible though the Russian cabinet members are, they are not lunatics. And they are — we might as well admit it — as progressively-minded as ourselves.

Here, then, is the political reason for our day of remembrance. If, at the height of our present crisis, we take out a day to honour the men who made our civilization possible, we will give to the Russians the clearest possible proof that our nerves are staunch and that we will never yield. And the very stars in their courses will fight on our side, for they are up there, billions of them, waiting to be visited, exploited or blown up by us. Our technology is more lovable than the Russian technology, and in the end it is bound to prevail. We are only beginning. We have just reached the outer fringes of the Solar System. Can any sane man possibly argue that we should stop there?

QUESTIONS

Verbal irony is a method of stating or presenting a fact, a truth, or a value, by way of its opposite. In an ironic statement, the real meaning is in contradiction to the apparent meaning. Sarcasm is a broad form of irony. We say, "What a lovely disposition she has!" about the young lady who has just thrown another tantrum. But irony can be subtle, and the reader must be on the alert in the presence of a skilled ironist. For in irony, guilt may be presented *as though* it were innocence, love *as though* it were hate, the here and now *as though* it were eternity, and the present *as though* it were the future or the past.

Irony is sometimes (although not always) an instrument of satire. Satire might be defined as the art of ridicule aimed at the correction of vices and follies. For instance, by pretending ironically that guilt is innocence, one might be able to ridicule an evil social situation and thus try to effect an improvement in that situation. Gulliver's naïve praise of European civilization to the King of the Brobdingnags is ironic because it only serves to expose the evils of the very civilization he is praising. And the episode is satirical because the author, Jonathan Swift, uses the ironic contrast as a means of ridiculing the prejudices and follies of European man (with some hope of improving him thereby).

1. At what points in the essay does the author's description of the year 2010 suggest that he is thinking of the present rather than the future?

2. Are we to understand the author literally when he talks of "superstitions" such as church-going and Christianity?

3. What is the function in the essay of the words, "reactionary" and "progressive"?

4. Is the author ironic in his use of the term, "The Love-Hate Syndrome"? Does the term apply to attitudes and strategies current in our society now?

5. How — and why — was the Love-Hate Syndrome equated with Christian principles?

6. Why does the President declare a day of remembrance for the men of the 1950's?

7. Why does the author pound away at phrases like "stand firm" and "loss of nerve"?

8. What are the author's real beliefs and attitudes beneath the ironic surface of the essay? What is he making the future say to the present?

*Sir Arthur*
*Quiller-Couch*

# On jargon

*Sir Arthur Quiller-Couch (1863-1944) is known for his work*
*as novelist:* The Splendid Spur *(1889), and* The Ships of Stars
*(1899); as writer of short stories:* I Saw Three Ships *(1892); as*
*editor:* The Oxford Book of English Verse *(1920), and* The
Oxford Book of English Prose *(1925); and as Shakespearean*
*critic:* Shakespeare's Workmanship *(1918). He was also an*
*excellent teacher. In 1912 he was appointed Professor of English*
*Literature at Cambridge University. Some of the lectures that*
*he gave at Cambridge were later collected and published under*
*the title,* On the Art of Writing *(1916). "On Jargon" was one*
*of these Cambridge lectures. The style of this essay exemplifies*
*his respect for clear, honest writing. It is reprinted here by*
*permission of the Cambridge University Press.*

WE PARTED, Gentlemen, upon a promise to discuss the capital
difficulty of Prose, as we have discussed the capital difficulty of
Verse. But, although we shall come to it, on second thoughts I
ask leave to break the order of my argument and to interpose
some words upon a kind of writing which, from a superficial
likeness, commonly passes for prose in these days, and by lazy
folk is commonly written for prose, yet actually is not prose at
all; my excuse being the simple practical one that, by first clearing
this sham prose out of the way, we shall the better deal with

honest prose when we come to it. The proper difficulties of prose will remain: but we shall be agreed in understanding what it is, or at any rate what it is not, that we talk about. I remember to have heard somewhere of a religious body in United States of America which had reason to suspect one of its churches of accepting Spiritual consolation from a coloured preacher – an offence against the laws of the Synod – and despatched a Disciplinary Committee with power to act; and of the Committee's returning to report itself unable to take any action under its terms of reference, for that while a person undoubtedly coloured had undoubtedly occupied the pulpit and had audibly spoken from it in the Committee's presence, the performance could be brought within no definition of preaching known or discoverable. So it is with that infirmity of speech – that flux, that determination of words to the mouth, or to the pen – which, though it be familiar to you in parliamentary debates, in newspapers, and as the staple language of Blue Books, Committees, Official Reports, I take leave to introduce to you as prose which is not prose and under its real name of Jargon.

You must not confuse this Jargon with what is called Journalese. The two overlap, indeed, and have a knack of assimilating each other's vices. But Jargon finds, maybe, the most of its votaries among good douce people who have never written to or for a newspaper in their life, who would never talk of "adverse climatic conditions" when they mean "bad weather"; who have never trifled with verbs such as "obsess", "recrudesce", "envisage", "adumbrate", or with phrases such as "the psychological moment", "the true inwardness", "it gives furiously to think". It dallies with Latinity – "sub silentio", "de die in diem", "cui bono?" (always in the sense, unsuspected by Cicero, of "What is the profit?") – but not for the sake of style. Your journalist at the worst is an artist in his way: he daubs paint of this kind upon the lily with a professional zeal; the more flagrant (or, to use his own word, arresting) the pigment, the happier is his soul. Like the Babu he is trying all the while to embellish our poor language, to make it more floriferous, more poetical – like the Babu for example who, reporting his mother's death, wrote "Regret to inform you, the hand that rocked the cradle has kicked the bucket."

*There* is metaphor: *there* is ornament: *there* is a sense of poetry, though as yet groping in a world unrealized. No such gusto marks – no such zeal, artistic or professional, animates – the practitioners of Jargon, who are, most of them (I repeat), douce respectable persons. Caution is its father; the instinct to save everything and especially trouble: its mother, Indolence. It looks precise, but is not. It is in these times, *safe*: a thousand men have said it before and not one to your knowledge had been prosecuted for it. And so, like respectability in Chicago, Jargon stalks unchecked in our midst. It is becoming the language of Parliament; it has become the medium through which Boards of Government, County Councils, Syndicates, Committees, Commercial Firms, express the processes as well as the conclusions of their thought and so voice the reason of their being.

Has a Minister to say "No" in the House of Commons? Some men are constitutionally incapable of saying no: but the Minister conveys it thus – "The answer to the question is in the negative." That means "no". Can you discover it to mean anything less, or anything more except that the speaker is a pompous person? – which was no part of the information demanded.

That is Jargon, and it happens to be accurate. But as a rule Jargon is by no means accurate, its method being to walk circumspectly around its target; and its faith, that having done so it has either hit the bull's-eye or at least achieved something equivalent, and safer.

Thus the Clerk of a Board of Guardians will minute that –

> In the case of John Jenkins deceased, the coffin provided was of the usual character.

Now this is not accurate. "In the case of John Jenkins deceased", for whom a coffin was supplied, it is wholly superfluous to tell us that he is deceased. But actually John Jenkins never had more than one case, and that was the coffin. The Clerk says he had two, – a coffin in a case: but I suspect the Clerk to be mistaken, and I am sure he errs in telling us that the coffin was of the usual character: for coffins have no character, usual or unusual.

For another example (I shall not tell you whence derived) —

> In the case of every candidate who is placed in the first class (So you see the lucky fellow gets a case as well as a first class. He might be a stuffed animal: perhaps he is) the class-list will show by some convenient mark (1) the Section or Sections for proficiency in which he is placed in the first class and (2) the Section or Sections (if any) in which he has passed with special distinction.

"The Section or Sections (if any)" — But, how if they are not any, could they be indicated by a mark however convenient?

> The Examiners will have regard to the style and method of the candidate's answers, and will give credit for excellence *in these respects.*

Have you begun to detect the two main vices of Jargon? The first is that it uses circumlocution rather than short straight speech. It says "In the case of John Jenkins deceased, the coffin" when it means "John Jenkins's coffin": and its yea is not yea, neither is its nay nay: but its answer is in the affirmative or in the negative, as the foolish and superfluous "case" may be. The second vice is that it habitually chooses vague woolly abstract nouns rather than concrete ones. I shall have something to say by-and-by about the concrete noun, and how you should ever be struggling for it whether in prose or in verse. For the moment I content myself with advising you, if you would write masculine English, never to forget the old tag of your Latin Grammar —

> Masculine will only be
> Things that you can touch and see.

But since these lectures are meant to be a course in First Aid to Writing, I will content myself with one or two extremely rough rules: yet I shall be disappointed if you do not find them serviceable.

The first is: — Whenever in your reading you come across one of these words, case, instance, character, nature, condition, persuasion, degree – whenever in writing your pen betrays you to one or another of them – pull yourself up and take thought. If it be "case" (I choose it as Jargon's dearest child – "in Heaven yclept Metonymy") turn to the dictionary, if you will, and seek out what meaning can be derived from *casus*, its Latin ancestor; then try how, with a little trouble, you can extricate yourself from that case. The odds are, you will feel like a butterfly who has discarded his chrysalis.

Here are some specimens to try your hand on –

(1) All those tears which inundated Lord Hugh Cecil's head were dry in the case of Mr. Harold Cox.

Poor Mr. Cox: left gasping in his aquarium!

(2) (From a cigar-merchant) In any case, let us send you a case on approval.
(3) It is contended that Consols have fallen in consequence: but such is by no means the case.

"Such", by the way, is another spoilt child of Jargon, especially in Committee's Rules – "Co-opted members may be eligible as such; such members to continue to serve for such time as" – and so on.

(4) Even in the purely Celtic areas, only in two or three cases do the Bishops bear Celtic names.

For "cases" read "dioceses".

*Instance.* In most instances the players were below their form. But what were they playing at? Instances?
*Character – Nature.* There can be no doubt that the accident was caused through the dangerous nature of the spot, the hidden character of the by-road, and the utter absence of any warning or danger signal.

Mark the foggy wording of it all. And yet the man hit something and broke his neck. Contrast that explanation with the verdict of a coroner's jury in the West of England on a drowned postman – "We find that deceased met his death by an act of

God, caused by sudden overflowing of the river Walkham and helped out by the scandalous neglect of the way-wardens."

The Aintree course is notoriously of a trying nature.

On account of its light character, purity and age, Usher's whiskey is a whiskey that will agree with you.

*Order.* The mesalliance was of a pronounced order.

*Condition.* He was conveyed to his place of residence in an intoxicated condition.

"He was carried home drunk."

*Quality and Section.* Mr. ———, exhibiting no less than five works, all of a superior quality, figures prominently in the oil section.

— This was written of an exhibition of pictures.

*Degree.* A singular degree of rarity prevails in the earlier editions of this romance.

That is Jargon. In prose it runs simply "The earlier editions of this romance are rare" — or "are very rare" — or even (if you believe what I take leave to doubt), "are singularly rare"; which should mean that they are rarer than the editions of any other work in the world.

Now what I ask you to consider about these quotations is that in each the writer was using Jargon to shirk prose, palming off periphrases upon us when with a little trouble he could have gone straight to the point. "A singular degree of rarity prevails", "the accident was caused through the dangerous nature of the spot", "but such is by no means the case". We may not be capable of much; but we can all write better than that, if we take a little trouble. In place of, "the Aintree course is of a trying nature" we can surely say, "Aintree is a trying course", or "the Aintree course is a trying one" — just that and nothing more.

Next, having trained yourself to keep a look-out for these worst offenders (and you will be surprised to find how quickly you get into the way of it), proceed to push your suspicions out among the whole cloudy host of abstract terms. "How excellent a thing is sleep", sighed Sancho Panza, "it wraps a man round like a cloak" — an excellent example, by the way, of how to say a thing concretely; a Jargoneer would have said that "among the beneficent qualities of sleep its capacity for withdrawing the human consciousness from the contemplation of immediate circumstances may perhaps be accounted not the least remarkable." How vile a thing — shall we say? — is the abstract noun. It wraps a man's thoughts round like cotton wool.

For another rule — just as rough and ready, but just as useful: Train your suspicions to bristle up whenever you come upon "as regards", "with regard to", "in respect of", "in connection with", "according as to whether", and the like. They are all dodges of Jargon, circumlocutions for evading this or that simple statement: and I say that it is not enough to avoid them nine times out of ten, or nine-and-ninety times out of a hundred. You should never use them. That is positive enough, I hope? Though I cannot admire his style, I admire the man who wrote to me, "Re Tennyson — your remarks anent his *In Memoriam* make me sick": for though re is not a preposition of the first water, and "anent" has enjoyed its day, the finish crowned the work.

Perpend this, Gentlemen, and maybe you will not hereafter set it down to my reproach that I wasted one hour of a May morning in a denunciation of Jargon, and in exhorting you upon a technical matter at first sight so trivial as the choice between abstract and definite words.

A lesson about writing your own language may go deeper than language; for language (as in a former lecture I tried to preach you) is your reason, your λόγος. So long as you prefer abstract words, which express other men's summarised concepts of things, to concrete ones which lie as near as can be reached to things themselves and are the first-hand material for your thoughts, you will remain, at the best, writers at second-hand. If your language is Jargon, your intellect, if not your whole character, will almost certainly correspond. Where your mind should go straight, it will dodge: the difficulties it should approach with a fair front and grip with a firm hand it will be seeking to evade or circumvent. For the Style is the Man, and where a man's treasure is there his heart, and his brain, and his writing, will be also.

QUESTIONS

1. When Sir Arthur Quiller-Couch gave this lecture at Cambridge University, the students listened with close attention. Judging from this published version of it, what qualities in the address might account for their interest?

2. The author calls jargon "sham prose". Why does he refuse to admit it as real prose?

3. (a) What distinction does he make between journalese and jargon?
   (b) What technique of argument does he use to convince his audience that journalese is an unworthy off-shoot of true prose?

4. (a) What are the reasons given by the author why many people, "douce respectable persons," prefer jargon to plain prose?
   (b) In explaining the motives of these jargoneers, he uses personification and metaphor. Explain why these figures of speech are particularly effective here.

5. Quiller-Couch quotes many examples of jargon — from official pamphlets, advertising, business letters, reports, and so on. Refer to three of his quoted examples and show what method he uses to make each one seem ridiculous.

6. On pp. 31-32 Quiller-Couch uses contrast to point up the fuzziness of jargon. Pick out this contrast and explain why it is effective.

7. Examine the paragraph on p. 32 beginning, "Next, having trained yourself . . ."
   (a) What main idea does this paragraph develop?
   (b) Show how Quiller-Couch has used example and contrast to develop this idea.

8. (a) Quiller-Couch advocates a "masculine style". What does he mean by this term?

(b) Pick out several passages in this essay which you think demonstrate that he practises what he preaches.

9. Tonight pay close attention to the newspaper, or radio or television broadcasts, and try to pick out an example of jargon to quote in class tomorrow. Be ready to explain why you consider it jargon.

*Charles*

*Lamb*

# Juke Judkins

---

*Charles Lamb ( 1775-1834), the son of a barrister's clerk, attended school at Christ's Hospital in London from 1782 to 1789, his only period of formal education. In 1792, he became a clerk in the accountant's office of the East India Company, in whose employ he remained until he retired in 1825. In spite of great domestic troubles – he cared for a beloved sister who was tormented by occasional seizures of murderous violence – he maintained a cheerful and witty manner both in his personal life and in his writing. Here is a partial list of his works:* A Tale of Rosamund Gray and Old Blind Margaret *( 1748),* Tales From Shakespeare *( 1807), and* Specimens of English Dramatic Poets *( 1808). He is best known for his engaging personal essays which began to appear in 1820 in* The London Magazine *and were later collected in two volumes,* The Essays of Elia *( 1823) and* Last Essays of Elia *( 1833).*

---

I AM THE ONLY SON of a considerable brazier in Birmingham, who, dying in 1803, left me successor to the business, with no other encumbrance than a sort of rent-charge, which I am enjoined to pay out of it, of ninety-three pounds sterling *per annum*, to his widow, my mother: and which the improving state of the concern, I bless God, has hitherto enabled me to discharge with punctuality. (I say, I am enjoined to pay the said sum, but not strictly obligated: that is to say, as the will is worded. I believe the law would relieve me from the payment of it; but the wishes of a dying parent should in some sort have the effect of law.) So that, though the annual profits of my business, on an average of the last three or four years, would appear to an indifferent observer, who should inspect my shop-books, to amount to the sum of one thousand three hundred and three pounds, odd shillings, the real proceeds in that time have fallen short of that sum to the amount of the aforesaid payment of ninety-three pounds sterling annually.

I was always my father's favourite. He took a delight, to the very last, in recounting the little sagacious tricks and innocent artifices of my childhood. One manifestation thereof I never heard him repeat without tears of joy trickling down his cheeks. It seems that when I quitted the parental roof (Aug. 27, 1788), being then six years and not quite a month old, to proceed to the Free School at Warwick, where my father was a sort of trustee, my mother — as mothers are usually provident on these occasions — had stuffed the pockets of the coach, which was to convey me and six more children of my own growth that were going to be entered along with me at the same seminary, with a prodigious quantity of gingerbread, which I remember my father said was more than was needed: and so indeed it was; for, if I had been to eat it all myself, it would have got stale and mouldy before it had been half spent. The consideration whereof set me upon my contrivances how I might secure to myself as much of the ginger-bread as would keep good for the next two or three days, yet none of the rest in manner be wasted. I had a little pair of pocket compasses, which I usually carried about me for the purpose of making draughts and measurements, at which I was always very ingenious, of the various engines and mechanical inventions in which such a town as Birmingham abounded. By means of these, and a small penknife which my father had given me, I cut out the one-half of the cake, calculating that the remainder would reasonably serve my turn; and subdividing it into many little slices, which were curious to see for the neatness and niceness of their proportion, I sold it out in so many pennyworths to my young companions as served us all the way to Warwick, which is a distance of some twenty miles from this town: and very merry, I assure you, we made ourselves with it, feasting all the way. By this honest stratagem I put double the prime cost of the gingerbread into my purse, and secured as much as I thought would keep good and moist for my next two or three days' eating. When I told this to my parents on their first visit to me at Warwick, my father (good man) patted me on the cheek, and stroked my head, and seemed as if he could never make enough of me; but my mother unaccountably burst into tears, and said, "it was a very niggardly action", or some such expression, and that "she would rather it would please God to take me" — meaning (God help me!) that I should die — "than that she should live to see me grow up a *mean man*": which shows the difference of parent from parent, and how some mothers are more harsh and intolerant to their children than some fathers; when we might expect quite the contrary. My father, however, loaded me with presents from that time, which made me the envy of my school-fellows. As I felt this growing disposition in them, I naturally sought to avert it by all the means in my power: and from that time I used to eat my little packages of fruit, and other nice things, in a corner, so privately that I was never found out. Once, I remember, I had a huge apple sent me, of that sort which they call *cats'-heads*. I concealed this all day under my pillow; and at night, but not before I had ascertained that my bed-fellow was sound asleep — which I did by pinching him rather smartly two or three times, which he seemed to perceive no more than a dead person, though once or twice he made a motion as if he would turn, which frightened me — I say, when I had made all sure, I fell to work upon my apple; and, though it was as big as an ordinary man's two fists, I made shift to get through it before it was time to get up. And a more delicious feast I never made; thinking all night what a good parent I had (I mean my father) to send me so many nice things, when the poor lad that lay by me had no parent or friend in the world to send him anything nice; and thinking of his desolate condition. I munched and munched as silently as I could, that I might not set him a-longing if he overheard me. And yet, for all this considerateness and attention to other people's feelings, I was never much of a favourite with my school-fellows; which I have often wondered at, seeing that I never defrauded any one of them of the value of a half-penny, or told stories of them to their master, as some little lying boys would do, but was ready to do any of them all the services in my power, that were consistent with my own well-doing. I think nobody can be expected to go farther than that. But I am detaining my reader too long in recording my juvenile days. It is time I should go forward to a season when it became natural that I should have some thoughts of marrying, and, as they say, settling in the world. Nevertheless, my reflections on what I may call the boyish period of my life may have their use to some readers. It is pleasant to trace the man in the boy; to observe shoots of generosity in those young years; and to watch the progress of liberal sentiments, and what I may call a genteel way of thinking, which is discernible in some children at a very early age, and usually lays the foundation of all that is praiseworthy in the manly character afterwards.

With the warmest inclinations towards that way of life, and a serious conviction of its superior advantages over a single one, it has been the strange infelicity of my lot never to have entered into the respectable estate of matrimony. Yet I was once very near it. I courted a young woman in my twenty-seventh year; for so early I began to feel symptoms of the tender passion! She was well to do in the world, as they call it; but yet not such a fortune, as, all things considered, perhaps I might have pretended to. It was not my own choice altogether; but my mother very strongly pressed me to it. She was always putting it to me, that I had "comings-in sufficient" — that I "need not stand upon a portion"; though the young woman, to do her justice, had considerable expectations, which yet did not quite come up to my mark, as I told you before. My mother had this saying always in her mouth, that I had "money enough"; that it was time I enlarged my housekeeping, and to show a spirit befitting my circumstances. In short, what with her importunities, and my own desires *in part* co-operating — for, as I said, I was not yet quite twenty-seven, —

a time when the youthful feelings may be pardoned if they
show a little impetuosity — I resolved, I say, upon all these
considerations, to set about the business of courting in right
earnest. I was a young man then; and having a spice of romance in
my character (as the reader has doubtless observed long ago),
such as that sex is apt to be taken with, I had reason in no long
time to think my addresses were anything but disagreeable.
Certainly the happiest part of a young man's life is the time when
he is going a-courting. All the generous impulses are then awake,
and he feels a double existence in participating his hopes and
wishes with another being. Return yet again for a brief moment,
ye visionary views — transient enchantments! ye moonlight
rambles with Cleora in the Silent Walk at Vauxhall, (N.B. —
About a mile from Birmingham, and resembling the gardens of
that name near London, only that the price of admission is lower),
when the nightingale has suspended her notes in June to listen to
our loving discourses, while the moon was overhead! (for we
generally used to take our tea at Cleora's mother's before we set
out, not so much to save expenses as to avoid the publicity of a
repast in the gardens — coming in much about the time of half-
price, as they call it), — ye soft inter-communions of soul, when
exchanging mutual vows, we prattled of coming felicities! The
loving disputes we have had under those trees, when this house
(planning our future settlement) was rejected, because, though
cheap, it was dull; and the other house was given up, because,
though agreeably situated, it was too high-rented! — one was
too much in the heart of the town, another was too far from
business. These minutiae will seem impertinent to the aged and
the prudent. I write them only to the young. Young lovers, and
passionate as being young (such were Cleora and I then), alone
can understand me. After some weeks wasted, as I may now call
it, in this sort of amorous colloquy, we at length fixed upon the
house in the High Street, No. 203, just vacated by the death of
Mr. Hutton of this town, for our future residence. I had all the
time lived in lodgings (only renting a shop for business), to be
near my mother — near, I say: not in the same house; for that
would have been to introduce confusion in our housekeeping,

which it was desirable to keep separate. Oh the loving wrangles, the endearing differences, I had with Cleora, before we could quite make up our minds to the house that was to receive us! — I pretending, for argument's sake, the rent was too high, and she insisting that the taxes were moderate in proportion; and love at last reconciling us in the same choice. I think at that time, moderately speaking, she might have had anything out of me for asking. I do not, nor shall ever, regret that my character at that time was marked with a tinge of prodigality. Age comes fast enough upon us, and, in its good time, will prune away all that is inconvenient in these excesses. Perhaps it is right that it should do so. Matters, as I said, were ripening to a conclusion between us, only the house was yet not absolutely taken — some necessary arrangements, which the ardour of my youthful impetuosity could hardly brook at that time (love and youth will be precipitate) — some preliminary arrangements, I say, with the landlord, respecting fixtures, very necessary things to be considered in a young man about to settle in the world, though not very accordant with the impatient state of my then passions — had hitherto precluded (and I shall always think providentially) my final closes with his offer; when one of those accidents which, unimportant in themselves, often rise to give a turn of the most serious intentions of our life, intervened, and put an end at once to my projects of wiving and of housekeeping.

I was never much given to theatrical entertainments; that is, at no time of my life was I ever what they call a regular playgoer; but on some occasion of a benefit-night, which was expected to be very productive, and indeed turned out so, Cleora expressing a desire to be present, I could do no less than offer, as I did very willingly, to squire her and her mother to the pit. At that time it was not customary in our town for tradesfolk, except some of the very topping ones, to sit, as they now do, in the boxes. At the time appointed I waited upon the ladies, who had brought with them a young man, a distant relation, whom it seems they had invited to be of the party. This a little disconcerted me, as I had about me barely silver enough to pay for our three selves at the door, and did not at first know that their relation had

proposed paying for himself. However, to do the young man
justice, he not only paid for himself, but for the old lady besides;
leaving me only to pay for two, as it were. In our passage to the
theatre the notice of Cleora was attracted to some orange wenches
that stood about the doors vending their commodities. She was
leaning on my arm; and I could feel her every now and then
giving me a nudge, as it is called, which I afterwards discovered
were hints that I should buy some oranges. It seems it is a custom
in Birmingham, and perhaps in other places, when a gentleman
treats ladies to the play — especially when a full night is expected,
and that the house will be inconveniently warm — to provide
them with this kind of fruit, oranges being esteemed for their
cooling property. But how could I guess at that, never having
treated ladies to a play before, and being, as I said, quite a novice
at entertainments of this kind? At last she spoke plain out, and
begged that I would buy some of "those oranges," pointing to a
particular barrow. But when I came to examine the fruit, I did
not think the quality of it was answerable to the price. In this way
I handled several baskets of them; but something in them all
displeased me. Some had thin rinds, and some were plainly over-
ripe, which is as great a fault as not being ripe enough; and I
could not (what they call) make a bargain. While I stood haggling
with the women, secretly determining to put off my purchase
till I should get within the theatre, where I expected we should
have better choice, the young man, the cousin (who, it seems,
had left us without my missing him), came running to us with his
pockets stuffed out with oranges, inside and out, as they say. It
seems, not liking the look of the barrow-fruit any more than myself, he had slipped away to an eminent fruiterer's, about three
doors distant, which I never had the sense to think of, and had
laid out a matter of two shillings in some of the best St. Michael's,
I think, I ever tasted. What a little hinge, as I said before, the
most important affairs in life may turn upon! The mere in-
advertence to the fact that there was an eminent fruiterer's
within three doors of us, though we had just passed it without
the thought once occurring to me, which he had taken advantage
of, lost me the affection of my Cleora. From that time she visibly

cooled towards me; and her partiality was as visibly transferred to this cousin. I was long unable to account for this change in her behaviour; when one day, accidentally discoursing of oranges to my mother, alone, she let drop a sort of reproach to me as if I had offended Cleora by my *nearness*, as she called it, that evening. Even now, when Cleora has been wedded some years to that same officious relation, as I may call him, I can hardly be persuaded that such a trifle could have been the motive to her inconstancy; for could she suppose that I would sacrifice my dearest hopes in her to the paltry sum of two shillings, when I was going to treat her to the play, and her mother too (an expense of more than four times that amount), if the young man had not interfered to pay for the latter, as I mentioned? But the caprices of the sex are past finding out: and I begin to think my mother was in the right; for doubtless women know women better than we can pretend to know them.

QUESTIONS

1. What do you understand by the term, "dramatic irony"?

(a) In what way does Lamb's method in this character sketch resemble dramatic irony?

(b) What advantages has this method of characterizing Juke, over the method in which the author describes and comments on his subject?

2. Although a lover of books, of plays, and of leisure, Lamb had to spend his days "in the irksome confinement of an office". Never in all his thirty-five years as a clerk did he make half as much per year as the average annual income that Mr. Judkins admits to.

(a) What defects of character in the nineteenth century business man does Lamb appear to be satirizing in this essay?

(b) In the very first paragraph, Lamb gives us indications of at least two of Juke Judkins' dominant character traits. Name the traits, and explain how you deduced them from Juke's opening remarks.

3. As Juke plods on in his account, there are frequent clashes between

his interpretation of an act and the reader's interpretation. Give three
examples in which this clash is particularly striking. For each example,
explain what interpretation the reader is likely to make.

4. The parenthetic remarks with which Juke sprinkles his autobiog-
raphy are important sources of humour. Note, for instance, the
passage in which he addresses the vanished delights of love: "Return
yet again for a brief moment, ye visionary views — transient enchantments!" What effect is produced by the parenthetic comment on
Vauxhall that immediately follows this rhapsody? Give two more
examples of parenthetic comments and explain the likely effect of
each on the reader.

5. (a) In the background, through the transparent scrim of Juke's
   words, appear his mother and father. What impressions of their
   characters do you receive? How does Lamb give you these impressions?
   (b) What other characters are there? State what kind of person
   each appears to be, and why you formed these judgments of them.

6. Although "Juke Judkins" appears among the essays in this book,
arguments could be advanced for calling it a story. Let us assume for
the sake of argument that we may define a short story as a short prose
composition in which some kind of conflict is developed through a
sequence of related incidents that culminate in a climax of victory
or defeat for the main character — the incidents being so composed
by the writer as to produce a calculated effect on the reader. Can
"Juke Judkins," according to this definition, be called a story?
Express and defend an opinion, using either the proposed definition
or one of your own.

*Phyllis*
*McGinley*

# Some of my best friends . . .

*Phyllis McGinley (b. 1905), American poetess and writer of
children's books, was born in Oregon. When she was still a child,
the family moved to Colorado and later to Utah, where she
attended the University of Utah. After a year as a teacher, she
moved to New York and held various jobs, ranging from writing
advertising copy to teaching school. While in New York, she
published a volume of light verse,* On the Contrary *(1934). This
was followed by* One More Manhattan *(1937), and* A Pocketful
of Wry *(1940). In 1944, her first children's book appeared,*
The Horse Who Lived Upstairs. *Other volumes of her poetry
are* A Short Walk From the Station *(1951) and* The Love
Letters of Phyllis McGinley *(1954). She wrote her first essay,
"Suburbia, of Thee I Sing", as a protest against the picture of
suburbia as "a dreary stronghold of mediocrity". This essay was
so well received that she wrote more. They were published in
1959 under the title,* The Province of the Heart *(copyright 1956
by Phyllis McGinley), from which "Some of My Best Friends"
is reprinted by permission of The Viking Press, Inc.*

ALTHOUGH THE STORY goes that woman was contrived from
Adam's rib, I have a different theory. In her public sense, she
sprang full-panoplied out of his imagination. For centuries woman battened on male illusion, finding she was cherished in

direct proportion to how well she lived up to her myth. Even today, with medicine and sociology chipping away at our legend so that we are in danger of losing much of our armour and a good deal of allure, certain misconceptions linger. We find it useful to foster them. So I hope I won't be read out of the party if I smash one more masculine belief — the belief that women dislike other women.

For quite the contrary is true. Women like other women fine. The more feminine she is, the more comfortable a woman feels with her own sex. It is only the occasional and therefore noticeable adventuress who refuses to make friends with us. (I speak now of genuine friendship. Our love we reserve for its proper object, man.)

What has been misconstrued, perhaps, is woman's behaviour during what I must bluntly call the hunting season. We are immensely practical. If the race is to continue, we like to provide a second parent. So we go about the serious business of finding husbands in a serious manner which allows no time for small luxuries like mercy toward competitors. Nature turns red in tooth and claw, every method is fair, and rivals get no quarter.

Once triumphant, however, with a man for our hearth, a fresh generation on its way, we sheathe our swords. We lay aside, as it were, certain secret weapons, and reaccept the company of our own kind. We choose each other for neighbours. We dress for one another's approval. We borrow loaves of bread, exchange recipes and sympathy, talk over our problems together. Watch women at cocktail parties. All eyes and smiles for the gentlemen at first, the safe (by which I mean the satisfactorily married) ladies begin gradually to drift away from the bantering males. They do it tactfully. The fiction must be maintained that men are their sole concern. But by almost imperceptible degrees women edge toward some sofa where another woman is ensconced. There, while the talk seethes and bubbles around them, they whisper cozily together of truly important things like baby-sitters and little dressmakers.

Do I imply by this that women are as frivolous and unintellectual as they have been accused of being in other eras? Or that the larger issues do not concern them? Far from it. I am simply trying to convey the natural attraction that binds us together. Those two women on the sofa might well go on from household problems to the lesser topics of literature, space rockets, or politics. I know. For I am frequently one of the ladies on the sofa. In other words, I like women.

My reasons are many and sufficient. I like them for their all-around, all-weather dependability. I like them because they are generally so steady, realistic, and careful about tidying up after a hot shower. I admire them for their prudence, thrift, gallantry, common sense, and knobless knees, and because they are neither so vain nor so given to emotion as their opposite numbers. I like the way they answer letters promptly, put shoe trees in their shoes at night, and are so durable physically. Their natures may not be so fine or their hearts so readily touched as man's, but they are not so easily imposed on either. I respect them, too, because they are so good at handling automobiles.

Don't misunderstand me. Some of my best friends are male drivers. And they seldom go to sleep at the wheel or drive 90 on a 45-mile-an-hour highway or commit any other of the sins of which statistics accuse them. But insurance companies have been busy as bees proving that I don't get around among the right people.

In New York State, where I live, they have even made it expensive to have sons. Car insurance costs twice as much if there are men in the family under twenty-five as if there are only women. Obviously the female of the species makes the best chauffeur. And well she ought. Women get the most practice. Aside from truck- and taxi-drivers, it is they who most consistently handle the cars of the nation. For five days of the week they are in command, — slipping cleverly through the traffic on their thousand errands, parking neatly in front of chain stores, ferrying their husbands to and from commuting trains, driving the young to schools and dentists and dancing classes and Scout meetings. It is only on Saturdays and Sundays that men get their innings, not to speak of their outings, and it is over week ends that most of the catastrophes occur.

Not that I *blame* men. It is in their natures to dream greatly, even amid traffic. The young ones cannot help showing off to their dates, and the older ones must not be held culpable for a tendency to compete with the red Jaguar in front. It's just that I feel safer with a woman at the wheel. For one thing, she is apt to get where she is going with a minimum of fuss and temper. She is not too proud to inquire directions, and when they are given to her she listens. Men would rather pore endlessly over maps, however inadequate, or else make out by intuition.

Now I have nothing against intuition. It is one of men's inborn and most endearing qualities. But their trust in it baffles the ordinary straight-thinking woman. In every field from horse racing to national politics we prefer to marshal facts, estimate them calmly, and then make our choices, rather than rely on some sixth sense. Something is always telling a man — some peculiar inner voice — that Senator Humphrey Grough is really going to solve the farm problem, or that the storm windows don't need to go up this week end because we're certain to have a mild November, or that tonight is his lucky night and he's bound to fill that inside straight.

There are, I admit, areas where intuition pays off. If Columbus hadn't had a hunch that he could sail to India by way of the Atlantic Ocean, he'd never have bumped into San Salvador. Wellington felt in his bones that he could stop Napoleon at Waterloo, just as those prospectors in California felt there was gold lying around the vicinity; and their bones were speaking true. Moreover, few businesses could burgeon or stock markets flourish or plays get produced without the impulsiveness of Adam's heir.

Just the same, women choose to proceed less rashly. They know that if their hunches go astray they will have to pick up the pieces. Even in small things a woman likes to be guided by fact. Let her loose in a delicatessen and she comes out with the loaf of rye bread and the half-pint of cream which she had put down on her list instead of the olives stuffed with anchovies, the assorted cheeses, pumpernickels, pickles, herring, potato salad, breast of turkey, pastes, spreads, and relishes which her husband dreamed the larder might need over the week end. And if she has a sore throat she does not ignore it completely on the theory that rude germs go away if one doesn't speak to them, or else take, groaning, to her bed because she has an intuition she will die before nightfall. She consults her doctor or a thermometer.

Of course women can keep calm about illnesses because, as a sex, we are so much less fragile than men — a point which scarcely needs belabouring. Again, statistics prove it. Wives consistently outlive their husbands. If one of a pair of twins succumbs in infancy, it is nearly always the delicate boy rather than the sturdy girl. Despite the severer tensions of a woman's life (and what hard-driven executive would exchange his routine for the soul-lacerating vexations of a housewife's day?) we are not so prone to ulcers, alcoholism, or gout. We survive shipwreck, bankruptcy, and childbirth with notorious aplomb.

Even the small ordeals find us less vulnerable. We are brave at the dentist's, self-possessed in the doctor's office, and disinclined to faint while being vaccinated. Again, we deserve no credit. Providence simply has provided us with that extra bit of stamina.

Providence has, indeed, almost made men expendable — or is trying to. I read with apprehension last spring that scientists had found they could raise turkeys from unfertilized eggs without benefit of a male turkey. They called it parthenogenesis. The scientists when last heard from were dubiously experimenting with some of the higher vertebrates such as rabbits. It gives one to think.

Extra stamina accounts for much. It explains why, no matter how they may clamour for equality, men can never hope to compete with women in certain sports and occupations. Men may do well enough in less demanding fields. They can throw a ball overhand, hurl a discus about, climb an unimportant mountain. But put them down in a crowded department store at holiday time for some jolly scrimmage and they collapse at the first counter. A woman in three-inch heels, with a tote bag weighing forty pounds on her arm as handicap, can outwalk a man on a shopping expedition any day — and outdance him again at night. In one morning she can wash, iron, turn mattresses, wrestle with the sweeper, paper the ceiling of the dinette, and do it on black coffee and a slice of toast.

Which brings me to another admirable female trait: the ability to get along on a restricted diet. A husband before breakfast is more terrible than an army with banners. Deprive him of his lunch and he wilts like a plucked dandelion. And the dinnerless male is something too dismal to contemplate. So, when undertaking a vital mission, women like to have women for companions. They are not always having to be stoked with food. If they *must* stop along the line of march for sustenance, they are willing to settle for a teashop instead of the most expensive café in town, and to divide the bill fairly afterward. This I find consoling. One of man's most exasperating qualities is his insistence on lavish gestures when he is settling a restaurant charge.

Notice what happens when two couples are dining out. Mr. and Mrs. Whitehouse, an unextravagant pair, have taken the $3.50 blue-plate special with a martini apiece. Mr. and Mrs. Blair have each downed two or three cocktails and gone on to beef tenderloin, asparagus hollandaise, and for dessert something flaming in a silver dish. But when the bill is brought, Mr. Whitehouse says expansively, "We'll just split it," and pays his unequal share without a murmur.

You won't catch us ladies behaving so. When we lunch or dine together we tot up every item ("Marge, you had the chicken sandwich on nut-and-raisin bread, and Evelyn, did you order two cups of coffee with that lemon sponge?"), figure how the cost should fall, and even divide the tip in proper ratio.

It's this no-nonsense side of women that is pleasant to deal with. They are the real sportsmen. They don't constantly have to be building up frail egos by large public performances like overtipping the hat-check girl, speaking fluent French to the Hungarian waiter, and sending back the wine to be recooled. They are neither too proud to carry packages nor too timid to ask a dilatory clerk for service.

What I enjoy, too, about my feminine friends is their downright honesty. Ask a woman if she likes your hairdo and she *tells* you. Make a small bet with her and she expects to be paid. And when she passes on a bit of scandal, she doesn't call it "shop talk," thus lending it a spurious moral air. Of course we women gossip on occasion. But our appetite for it is not as avid as a man's. It is in the boys' gyms, the college fraternity houses, the club locker rooms, the paneled offices of business that gossip reaches its luxuriant flower. More tidbits float around the corridors of one major advertising firm in an afternoon than Louella Parsons ever matched in a year's output. Commuting trains buzz with it. The professions grow fat on it. The fluffiest blonde of a private secretary locks more secrets in her chic head than the granite-jawed tycoon who employs her. Women, in fact, are the secret-keepers. Forced by biological circumstance to live a subtler life than their brothers, they have learned to hold their tongues. "Kiss and tell" is a male and not a female slogan. There is something about man's naïve character, something less than flintlike in his soul, which makes him a poor risk for a confidence.

That additional flint in a woman helps her, moreover, to keep her head. She is not always out on some rash adventure — leading a lost cause, buying shares in El Dorado, or lending money to a brave little widow with nine famishing and nonexistent children. If we have not man's compassion, we also lack his gullibility.

And then from the purely technical point of view, I do like women's mechanical handiness. They are so reassuringly clever about mending things — about fixing locks on doors and putting in new fuses and repairing leaky faucets and stopping windows from rattling.

Now and then a gifted man sets out to be his own plumber or carpenter or electrician. But did you ever watch him at his work? To begin with, he must first invest in an elaborate set of tools, expensive as Russian sable. These he brings out lovingly, one by one, fondling them as a hunter does his rifles. Then he commandeers as helpers anyone unfortunate enough to be within earshot. People must hold things. Someone must hand him things. The ladder has to be supported. He has to have fetched to him, intermittently, sharpeners for his chisels, cloths for wiping his hands, hot water from the sink, and cups of coffee or cold drinks at frequent intervals. Papers must be laid down around him and the entire household listen to his exhortations, arguments, and complaints. Particularly, there must be some obliging menial to look on, admire, and deposit the laurel wreath on his brow when the job, as it sometimes does, gets finished. But I've seen women merely give a sharp slap to a reluctant washing machine or a dig in the ribs to a sulky toaster, and off it goes.

Mechanically deft as they are, not to speak of honest, clean, courteous, brave, reverent, and loyal, women are the proper objects of woman's admiration. Oh, why, I often wonder, in defiance of Henry Higgins, can't men be more like us!

But I always hear myself answering, "How splendid that they aren't!" Expendable they may be. But into our hard, practical lives they bring tenderness and sentiment. They give existence its meaning, its essential *élan*. They encourage our better natures. And they are esthetically so appealing too! Who better graces a drawing room? What prettier sight can one see at evening under the soft glow of the lamp than a man dressed in his old tweed jacket and lounging slippers?

No, without men we should be the poorer. Brightness would fall from the air, life would lose most of its colour and all of its romance. And there would be no one to help us lift our monotonous daily burdens. Besides having to go to the office every morning, we would also have to write all the novels, paint all the pictures, start all the wars; and we have better business than that already. Women are the fulfilled sex. Through our children we are able to produce our own immortality, so we lack that divine restlessness which sends men charging off in pursuit of fortune or fame or an imagined Utopia. That is why we number so few geniuses among us. The wholesome oyster wears no pearl, the healthy whale no ambergris, and as long as we can keep on adding to the race, we harbour a sort of health within ourselves.

Sometimes I have a notion that what might improve the situation is to have women take over the occupations of government and trade and to give men their freedom. Let them do what they are best at. While we scrawl interoffice memos and direct national or extranational affairs, men could spend *all* their time inventing wheels, peering at stars, composing poems, carving statues, exploring continents – discovering, reforming, or crying out in a sacramental wilderness. Efficiency would probably increase, and no one would have to worry so much about the Gaza Strip or an election.

On the other hand, though, I like our status too much to make the suggestion seriously. For everybody knows it's a man's world and they have not managed it very well, but at least it's theirs. If women took over, we might find ourselves thrashing around in the very masculine morasses we have so far managed to avoid.

QUESTIONS

1. The title of this essay consists of the first five words of a cliché.
   (a) What are some of the common ways of concluding this cliché?
   (b) What topic might you expect the writer to develop in an essay with such a title?
   (c) Why is the title deceptive here?

2. What main opinion, or thesis, does Phyllis McGinley advance?

3. In the body of the essay, how does she conclude the sentence begun in the title?

4. She begins by defending her male friends who drive, but ends in a criticism of male drivers in general. How does she effect this transition?

5. Note the anti-climax in the ironic sentence, "It is in their natures to dream greatly, even in traffic." This sentence introduces one of her main contrasts between men and women. What is this contrast? What method does she use to develop it?

6. One humorous technique that Phyllis McGinley employs is to take what she considers to be a popular male fallacy regarding women and show that this fallacious belief is actually true when it is applied to men. Give an example of this technique. Explain why this technique is or is not convincing.

7. We are all interested in seeing a common human weakness dramatized comically. When she presents the two little scenes in the

restaurant — one involving the two couples and the one involving a group of women — what point is she making? Is this a fair technique of argument? Justify your answer.

8. In ironically reversing what men usually like to think of as male virtues and female frailties, Phyllis McGinley works up to a climax of comedy. What is the climactic picture that she presents?

9. According to her, why do women permit men the illusion of mastery?

*Max*

*Beerbohm*

# The fire

_____

*Max Beerbohm (1872-1959) was born in London and educated
at Oxford. Drama critic, caricaturist, essayist, and wit, he is best
known for his satirical portraits and his parodies of well-known
writers. Characteristically, his first publication was entitled,*
The Works of Max Beerbohm *(1896). His only novel,* Zuleika
Dobson, *was published in 1911. Beerbohm was knighted in 1939.
His works include* The Poet's Corner *(1904),* A Christmas
Garland *(1912),* Rossetti and His Circle *(1922),* Variety of
Things *(1928), and* Mainly in the Air *(1947). "The Fire", from
a collection of Mr. Beerbohm's essays entitled* Yet Again, *is re-
printed by permission of the publisher, William Heinemann, Ltd.*

_____

IF I WERE "seeing over" a house, and found in every room an iron
cage let into the wall, and were told by the caretaker that these
cages were for me to keep lions in, I think I should open my eyes
rather wide. Yet nothing seems to me more natural than a fire in
the grate.

Doubtless, when I began to walk, one of my first excursions
was to the fender, that I might gaze more nearly at the live thing
roaring and raging behind it; and I dare say I dimly wondered by
what blessed dispensation this creature was allowed in a domain
so peaceful as my nursery. I do not think I ever needed to be
warned against scaling the fender. I knew by instinct that the

creature within it was dangerous — fiercer still than the cat which had once strayed into the room and scratched me for my advances. As I grew older, I ceased to wonder at the creature's presence and learned to call it "the fire", quite lightly. There are so many queer things in the world that we have no time to go on wondering at the queerness of the things we see habitually. We are lucky when by some chance we see again, for a fleeting moment, this thing or that as we saw it when it first came within our ken. We are in the habit of saying that "first impressions are best", and that we must approach every question "with an open mind"; but we shirk the logical conclusion that we were wiser in our infancy than we are now. "Make yourself even as a little child," we often say, but recommending the process on moral rather than on intellectual grounds, and inwardly preening ourselves all the while on having "put away childish things", as though clarity of vision were not one of them.

I look around the room I am writing in — a pleasant room, and my own, yet how irresponsive, how smug and lifeless! The pattern of the wallpaper blamelessly repeats itself from wainscot to cornice; and the pictures are immobile and changeless within their glazed frames — faint, flat mimicries of life. The chairs and tables are just as their carpenter fashioned them, and stand with stiff obedience just where they have been posted. On one side of the room, encased in coverings of cloth and leather, are myriads of words, which to some people, but not to me, are a fair substitute for human company. All around me, in fact, are the products of modern civilisation. But in the whole room there are but three things living: myself, my dog, and the fire in my grate. And of these lives the third is very much the most intensely vivid. My dog is descended, doubtless, from prehistoric wolves; but you could hardly decipher his pedigree on his mild, domesticated face. My dog is as tame as his master (in whose veins flows the blood of the old cavemen). But time has not tamed fire. Fire is as wild a thing as when Prometheus snatched it from the empyrean. Fire in my grate is as fierce and terrible a thing as when it was lit by my ancestors, night after night, at the mouths of their caves, to scare away the ancestors of my dog. And my dog regards it with the old wonder and misgiving. Even in his sleep he opens ever and again one eye to see that we are in no danger. And the fire glowers and roars through its bars at him with the scorn that a wild beast must needs have for a tame one. "You are free," it rages, "and yet you do not spring at that man's throat and tear him limb from limb and make a meal of him!" and gazing at me, it licks its red lips; and I, laughing good-humouredly, rise and give the monster a shovelful of its proper food, which it leaps at and noisily devours.

Fire is the only one of the elements that inspires awe. We breathe air, tread earth, bathe in water. Fire alone we approach with deference. And it is the only one of the elements that is always alert, always good to watch. We do not see the air we breathe — except sometimes in London and who shall say that the sight is pleasant? We do not see the earth revolving; and the trees and other vegetables that are put forth by it come up so slowly that there is no fun in watching them. One is apt to lose patience with the good earth, and to hanker for a sight of those multitudinous fires whereover it is, after all, but a thin and comparatively recent crust. Water, when we get it in the form of a river, is pleasant to watch for a minute or so, after which period the regularity of its movement becomes as tedious as stagnation. It is only a whole seaful of water that can rival fire in variety and in loveliness. But even the spectacle of sea at its very best — say in an Atlantic storm — is less thrilling than the spectacle of one building ablaze. And for the rest, the sea has its hours of dullness and monotony, even when it is not wholly calm. Whereas in the grate even a quite little fire never ceases to be amusing and inspiring until you let it out. As much fire as would correspond with a handful of earth or a tumblerful of water is yet a joy to the eyes, and a lively suggestion of grandeur. The other elements, even as presented in huge samples, impress us as less august than fire. Fire alone, according to the legend, was brought down from heaven: the rest were here from the dim outset. When we call a thing earthy we impute cloddishness; by "watery" we imply insipidness; "airy" is for something trivial. "Fiery" has always a noble significance. It denotes such things as faith, courage, genius. Earth lies heavy, and air is void, and water flows down; but flames aspire, flying back towards the heaven they came from. They typify for us the spirit of man, as apart from aught that is gross in him. They are the symbol of purity, of triumph over corruption. Water, air, earth, can all harbour corruption; but where the flames are, or have been, there is innocence. Our love of fire comes partly, doubtless, from our natural love of destruction for destruction's sake. Fire is savage, and so, even after all these centuries, are we, at heart. Our civilisation is but as the aforesaid crust that encloses the old planetary flames. To destroy is still the strongest instinct of our nature. Nature is still "red in tooth and claw", though she has begun to make fine flourishes with tooth-brush and nail-scissors. Even the mild dog on my hearth-rug has been known to behave like a wolf to his own species. Scratch his master and you will find the caveman. But the scratch must be a sharp one: I am thickly veneered. Outwardly, I am as gentle as you, gentle reader. And one reason for our delight in fire is that there is no humbug about flames: they are frankly, primevally savage. But this is not, I am glad to say, the sole reason. We have a sense of good and evil. I do not pretend that it carries us very far. It is by the tooth-brush and nail-scissors that we flourish. Our innate instincts, not this acquired sense, are what the world really hinges on. But this acquired sense is an integral part of our minds. And we revere fire because we have come to regard it as especially the foe of evil — as a means for destroying weeds, not flowers; a destroyer of wicked cities, not of good ones.

The idea of hell, as inculcated in the books given to me when I was a child, never really frightened me at all. I conceived the possibility of a hell in which were eternal flames to destroy every one who had not been good. But a hell whose flames were eternally impotent to destroy these people, a hell where evil was to go on writhing yet thriving for ever and ever, seemed to me, even at that age, too patently absurd to be appalling. Nor indeed do I think that to the more credulous children in England can the idea of eternal burning have ever been quite so forbidding as their nurses meant it to be. Credulity is but a form of incaution.

I, as I have said, never had any wish to play with fire; but most English children are strongly attracted, and are much less afraid of fire than of the dark. Eternal darkness, with a biting east-wind, were to the English fancy a far more fearful prospect than eternal flames. The notion of these flames arose in Italy, where heat is no luxury, and shadows are lurked in, and breezes prayed for. In England the sun, even at its strongest, is a weak vessel. True, we grumble whenever its radiance is a trifle less watery than usual. But that is precisely because we are a people whose nature the sun has not mellowed — a dour people, like all north-erners, ever ready to make the worst of things. Inwardly, we love the sun, and long for it to come nearer to us, and to come more often. And it is partly because this craving is unsatisfied that we cower so fondly over our open hearths. Our fires are make-shifts for sunshine. Autumn after autumn, "we see the swallows gathering in the sky, and in the osier-isle we hear their noise," and our hearts sink. Happy, selfish little birds, gathering so lightly to fly whither we cannot follow you, will you not, this once, forgo the lands of your desire? "Shall not the grief of the old time follow?" Do winter with us, this once! We will strew all England, every morning, with breadcrumbs for you, will you but stay and help us to play at summer! But the delicate cruel rogues pay no heed to us, skimming sharplyer than ever in pur-suit of gnats as the hour draws near for their long flight over gnatless seas.

Only one swallow have I ever known to relent. It had built its nest under the eaves of a cottage that belonged to a friend of mine, a man who loved birds. He had a power of making birds trust him. They would come at his call, circling round him, perch-ing on his shoulders, eating from his hand. One of the swallows would come too, from his nest under the eaves. As the summer wore on, he grew quite tame. And when summer waned and the other swallows flew away, this one lingered, day after day, flut-tering dubiously over the threshold of the cottage. Presently, as the air grew chilly, he built a new nest for himself, under the mantelpiece in my friend's study. And every morning, so soon as the fire burned brightly, he would flutter down to perch on the fender and bask in the light and warmth of the coals. But after a few weeks he began to ail; possibly because the study was a small one, and he could not get in it the exercise that he needed; more probably because of the draughts. My friend's wife, who was very clever with her needle, made for the swallow a little jacket of red flannel, and sought to divert his mind by teaching him to perform a few simple tricks. For a while he seemed to regain his spirits. But presently he moped more than ever, crouching nearer than ever to the fire, and, sidelong, blinking dim weak reproaches at his disappointed master and mistress. One swallow, as the adage truly says, does not make a summer. So this one's mistress hurriedly made for him a little overcoat of sealskin, wearing which, in a muffled cage, he was personally conducted by his master straight through to Sicily. There he was nursed back to health, and liberated on a sunny plain. He never returned to his English home; but the nest he built under the mantelpiece is still preserved, in case he should come at last.

When the sun's rays slant down upon your grate, then the fire blanches and blenches, cowers, crumbles, and collapses. It cannot compete with its archetype. It cannot suffice a sun-steeped swallow, or ripen a plum, or parch the carpet. Yet, in its modest way, it is to your room what the sun is to the world; and where, during the greater part of the year, would you be without it? I do not wonder that the poor, when they have to choose between fuel and food, choose fuel. Food nourishes the body; but fuel, warming the body, warms the soul too. I do not wonder that the hearth has been regarded from time immemorial as the centre, and used as the symbol, of the home. I like the social tradition that we must not poke a fire in a friend's drawing-room unless our friendship dates back full seven years. It rests evidently, this tradition, on the sentiment that a fire is a thing sacred to the members of the household in which it burns. I daresay the fender has a meaning, as well as a use, and is as the rail round an altar. In *The New Utopia* these hearths will all have been rased, of course, as demoralising relics of an age when people went in for privacy and were not always thinking exclusively about the State. Such heat as may be needed to prevent us from catching colds (whereby our vitality would be lowered, and our usefulness to the State impaired) will be supplied through hot-water pipes (white-enameled), the supply being strictly regulated from the municipal water-works. Or has Mr. Wells arranged that the sun shall always be shining on us? I have mislaid my copy of the book. Anyhow, fires and hearths will have to go. Let us make the most of them while we may.

Personally, though I appreciate the radiance of a family fire, I give preference to a fire that burns for myself alone. And dearest of all to me is a fire that burns thus in the house of another. I find an inalienable magic in my bedroom fire when I am staying with friends; and it is at bedtime that the spell is strongest. "*Good* night," says my host, shaking my hand warmly on the threshold; "you've everything you want?" "Everything," I assure him; "good *night.*" "Good *night.*" "*Good* night," and I close my door, close my eyes, heave a long sigh, open my eyes, draw the armchair close to the fire (*my* fire), sink down, and am at peace, with nothing to mar my happiness except the feeling that it is too good to be true.

At such moments I never see in my fire any likeness to a wild beast. It roars me as gently as a sucking dove, and is as kind and cordial as my host and hostess and the other people in the house. And yet I do not have to say anything to it, I do not have to make myself agreeable to it. It lavishes its warmth on me, asking nothing in return. For fifteen mortal hours or so, with few and brief intervals, I have been making myself agreeable, saying the right thing, asking the apt question, exhibiting the proper shade of mild or acute surprise, smiling the appropriate smile or laughing just so long and just so loud as the occasion seemed to demand. If I were naturally a brilliant and copious talker, I suppose that to stay in another's house would be no strain on me. I should be able to impose myself on my host and hostess and their guests without any effort, and at the end of the day retire quite unfatigued, pleasantly flushed with the effect of my own magnetism. Alas, there is no question of my imposing myself. I can repay hospitality only by strict attention to the humble, arduous process of making myself agreeable. When I go up to dress for dinner, I have always a strong impulse to go to bed and sleep off my fatigue; and it is only by exerting all my will-power that I can array myself for the final labours: to wit, making myself agreeable to some man or woman for a minute or two before dinner, to two women during dinner, to men after dinner, then again to women in the drawing-room, and then once again to men in the smoking-room. It is a dog's life. But one has to have suffered before one gets the full savour out of joy. And I do not grumble at the price I have to pay for the sensation of basking, at length, in solitude and the glow of my own fireside.

Too tired to undress, too tired to think, I am more than content to watch the noble and ever-changing pageant of the fire. The finest part of this spectacle is surely when the flames sink, and gradually the red-gold caverns are revealed, gorgeous, mysterious, with inmost recesses of white heat. It is often thus that my fire welcomes me when the long day's task is done. After I have gazed long into its depths, I close my eyes to rest them, opening them again, with a start, whenever a coal shifts its place, or some belated little tongue of flame spurts forth with a hiss.... Vaguely I liken myself to the watchman one sees by night in London, wherever a road is up, huddled half-awake in his tiny cabin of wood, with a cresset of live coal before him.... I have come down in the world, and am a night-watchman, and I find the life as pleasant as I had always thought it must be, except when I let the fire out, and awake shivering.... Shivering I awake, in the twilight of dawn. Ashes, white and grey, some rusty cinders, a crag or so of coal, are all that is left over from last night's splendour. Grey is the lawn beneath my window, and little ghosts of rabbits are nibbling and hobbling there. But anon the east will be red, and, ere I awake, the sky will be blue, and the grass quite green again, and my fire will have arisen from its ashes, a cackling and comfortable phoenix.

QUESTIONS

The "familiar essay" has the air of a gentleman's game. Never strenuous or anxious in movement, seemingly casual in form, easy and intimate in tone and gesture, the essay of this kind (the essay as practised by Lamb, Hazlitt, Chesterton, and Beerbohm), can sometimes be a subtle athletic discipline. Under the affectation of careless ease, the muscles of the mind may be slyly and persistently at work. What has seemed to be a procession of after-thoughts and almost accidental asides and detours, may suddenly (just at the goal-line) be seen to be a carefully executed passing play, a clever strategy to put you off your guard. The "familiar" essayist (despite his relaxed "gentlemanliness") may be just as eager to score his points as any of his angry journalistic descendents. But he will never betray this eagerness. And you will never be *quite* sure of his intentions.

There is always, in these essays, a real "amateurism", play for play's sake, a delight in making the ordinary seem wonderful and the wonderful seem ordinary. The game *is* played for fun. But watch your goal-line!

1. Why does the author begin with the child's sense of what fire is? Why, at the very beginning, does he suggest that the child is wiser than the man? Is it possible that the whole essay is an attempt to see reality "even as a little child" would see it?

2. What is the connection between the talk of the child's vision and the discussion of the "elements" and of ancient, even primitive beliefs about the nature of things?

3. By what process of logic does the author relate the fire in the grate to a sense of the meaning of civilization, to tooth-brushes and nail-scissors, to ideas of good and evil?

4. What is the significance of the episode of the swallow?

5. Why does the author detest central heating?

6. How does he relate, at the end, the image of the sun to the image of the fire, and both to the vision of the child?

*Conrad*
*Aiken*

# Mr. Arcularis

*Conrad Aiken (b. 1889) was born in Savannah, Georgia, and
educated at Harvard. As poet, novelist, and short-story writer,
he occupies an important place in modern American letters.
As editor and critic, he has had a wide influence on the taste of
our times. His volumes of poetry include* Earth Triumphant
*(1914);* Turns and Movies *(1916); and* The House of Dust
*(1920). Perhaps his best novels are* Blue Voyage *(1927) and*
Great Circle *(1933). Aiken's best known short stories are
contained in the two volumes,* Bring! Bring! and Other Stories
*(1925) and* Costumes by Eros *(1928); and his anthologies,*
Modern American Poets *(1923) and* American Poetry: A Com-
prehensive Anthology *(1929), are in wide use. "Mr. Arcularis"
(copyright 1931 by Conrad Aiken) is reprinted from* The Short
Stories of Conrad Aiken *by permission of The World Publishing
Company*

MR. ARCULARIS stood at the window of his room in the hospital
and looked down at the street. There had been a light shower,
which had patterned the sidewalks with large drops, but now
again the sun was out, blue sky was showing here and there
between the swift white clouds, a cold wind was blowing the
poplar trees. An itinerant band had stopped before the building
and was playing, with violin, harp, and flute, the finale of *Caval-*

*leria Rusticana*. Leaning against the windowsill—for he felt extraordinarily weak after his operation—Mr. Arcularis suddenly, listening to the wretched music, felt like crying. He rested the palm of one hand against a cold window pane and stared down at the old man who was blowing the flute, and blinked his eyes. It seemed absurd that he should be so weak, so emotional, so like a child—and especially now that everything was over at last. In spite of all their predictions, in spite, too, of his own dreadful certainty that he was going to die, here he was, as fit as a fiddle—but what a fiddle it was, so out of tune!—with a long life before him. And to begin with, a voyage to England ordered by the doctor. What could be more delightful? Why should he feel sad about it and want to cry like a baby? In a few minutes Harry would arrive with his car to take him to the wharf; in an hour he would be on the sea, in two hours he would see the sunset behind him, where Boston had been, and his new life would be opening before him. It was many years since he had been abroad. June, the best of the year to come—England, France, the Rhine—how ridiculous that he should already be homesick!

There was a light footstep outside the door, a knock, the door opened, and Harry came in.

"Well, old man, I've come to get you. The old bus actually got here. Are you ready? Here, let me take your arm. You're tottering like an octogenarian!"

Mr. Arcularis submitted gratefully, laughing, and they made the journey slowly along the bleak corridor and down the stairs to the entrance hall. Miss Hoyle, his nurse, was there, and the Matron, and the charming little assistant with freckles who had helped to prepare him for the operation. Miss Hoyle put out her hand.

"Good-by, Mr. Arcularis," she said, "and *bon voyage*."

"Good-by, Miss Hoyle, and thank you for everything. You were very kind to me. And I fear I was a nuisance."

The girl with the freckles, too, gave him her hand, smiling. She was very pretty, and it would have been easy to fall in love with her. She reminded him of someone. Who was it? He tried in vain to remember while he said good-by to her and turned to the Matron.

"And not too many latitudes with the young ladies, Mr. Arcularis!" she was saying.

Mr. Arcularis was pleased, flattered, by all this attention to a middle-aged invalid, and felt a joke taking shape in his mind, and no sooner in his mind than on his tongue.

"Oh, no latitudes," he said, laughing. "I'll leave the latitudes to the ship!"

"Oh, come now," said the Matron, "we don't seem to have hurt him much, do we?"

"I think we'll have to operate on him again and *really* cure him," said Miss Hoyle.

He was going down the front steps, between the potted palmettoes, and they all laughed and waved. The wind was cold, very cold for June, and he was glad he had put on his coat. He shivered.

"Damned cold for June!" he said. "Why should it be so cold?"

"East wind," Harry said, arranging the rug over his knees. "Sorry it's an open car, but I believe in fresh air and all that sort of thing. I'll drive slowly. We've got plenty of time."

They coasted gently down the long hill towards Beacon Street, but the road was badly surfaced, and despite Harry's care Mr. Arcularis felt his pain again. He found that he could alleviate it a little by leaning to the right, against the arm-rest, and not breathing too deeply. But how glorious to be out again! How strange and vivid the world looked! The trees had innumerable green fresh leaves — they were all blowing and shifting and turning and flashing in the wind; drops of rainwater fell downward sparkling; the robins were singing their absurd, delicious little four-noted songs; even the street cars looked unusually bright and beautiful, just as they used to look when he was a child and had wanted above all things to be a motorman. He found himself smiling foolishly at everything, foolishly and weakly, and wanted to say something about it to Harry. It was no use, though — he had no strength, and the mere finding of words would be almost more than he could manage. And even if he should succeed in saying it, he would then most likely burst into tears. He shook his head slowly from side to side.

"Ain't it grand?" he said.

"I'll bet it looks good," said Harry.

"Words fail me."

"You wait till you get out to sea. You'll have a swell time."

"Oh, swell! ... I hope not. I hope it'll be calm."

"Tut tut."

When they passed the Harvard Club Mr. Arcularis made a slow and somewhat painful effort to turn in his seat and look at it. It might be the last chance to see it for a long time. Why this sentimental longing to stare at it, though? There it was, with the great flag blowing in the wind, the Harvard seal now concealed by the swift folds and now revealed, and there were the windows in the library, where he had spent so many delightful hours reading — Plato, and Kipling, and the Lord knows what — and the balconies from which for so many years he had watched the finish of the Marathon. Old Talbot might be in there now, sleeping with a book on his knee, hoping forlornly to be interrupted by anyone, for anything.

"Good-by to the old club," he said.

"The bar will miss you," said Harry, smiling with friendly irony and looking straight ahead.

"But let there be no moaning," said Mr. Arcularis.

"What's *that* a quotation from?"

"*The Odyssey.*"

In spite of the cold, he was glad of the wind on his face, for it helped to dissipate the feeling of vagueness and dizziness that came over him in a sickening wave from time to time. All of a sudden everything would begin to swim and dissolve, the houses would lean their heads together, he had to close his eyes, and there would be a curious and dreadful humming noise, which at regular intervals rose to a crescendo and then drawlingly subsided again. It was disconcerting. Perhaps he still had a trace of fever. When he got on the ship he would have a glass of whisky. ... From one of these spells he opened his eyes and found that they were on the ferry, crossing to East Boston. It must have been the ferry's engines that he had heard. From another spell he woke to find himself on the wharf, the car at a standstill beside a pile of yellow packing-cases.

"We're here because we're here because we're here," said Harry.

"Because we're here," added Mr. Arcularis.

He dozed in the car while Harry — and what a good friend Harry was! — attended to all the details. He went and came with tickets and passports and baggage checks and porters. And at last he unwrapped Mr. Arcularis from the rugs and led him up the steep gangplank to the deck, and thence by devious windings to a small cold stateroom with a solitary porthole like the eye of a cyclops.

"Here you are," he said, "and now I've got to go. Did you hear the whistle?"

"No."

"Well, you're half asleep. It's sounded the all-ashore. Good-by old fellow, and take care of yourself. Bring me back a spray of edelweiss. And send me a picture post card from the Absolute."

"Will you have it finite or infinite?"

"Oh, infinite. But with your signature on it. Now you'd better turn in for a while and have a nap. Cheerio!"

Mr. Arcularis took his hand and pressed it hard, and once more felt like crying. Absurd! Had he become a child again?

"Good-by," he said.

He sat down in the little wicker chair, with his overcoat still on, closed his eyes, and listened to the humming of the air in the ventilator. Hurried footsteps ran up and down the corridor. The chair was too comfortable, and his pain began to bother him again, so he moved, with his coat still on, to the narrow berth and fell asleep. When he woke up, it was dark, and the porthole had been partly opened. He groped for the switch and turned on the light. Then he rang for the steward.

"It's cold in here," he said. "Would you mind closing the port?"

The girl who sat opposite him at dinner was charming. Who

was it she reminded him of? Why, of course, the girl at the hospital, the girl with the freckles. Her hair was beautiful, not quite red, not quite gold, nor had it been bobbed; arranged with a sort of graceful untidiness, it made him think of a Melozzo da Forli angel. Her face was freckled, she had a mouth which was both humorous and voluptuous. And she seemed to be alone.

He frowned at the bill of fare and ordered the thick soup.

"No hors d'oeuvres?" asked the steward.

"I think not," said Mr. Arcularis. "They might kill me."

The steward permitted himself to be amused and deposited the menu card on the table against the water-bottle. His eyebrows were lifted. As he moved away, the girl followed him with her eyes and smiled.

"I'm afraid you shocked him," she said.

"Impossible," said Mr. Arcularis. "These stewards, they're dead souls. How could they be stewards otherwise? And they think they've seen and known everything. They suffer terribly from the *déjà vu*. Personally, I don't blame them."

"It must be a dreadful sort of life."

"It's because they're dead that they accept it."

"Do you think so?"

"I'm sure of it. I'm enough of a dead soul myself to know the signs!"

"Well, I don't know what you mean by that!"

"But nothing mysterious! I'm just out of hospital, after an operation. I was given up for dead. For six months I had given *myself* up for dead. If you've ever been seriously ill you know the feeling. You have a posthumous feeling — a mild, cynical tolerance for everything and everyone. What is there you haven't seen or done or understood? Nothing."

Mr. Arcularis waved his hands and smiled.

"I wish I could understand you," said the girl, "but I've never been ill in my life."

"Never?"

"Never."

"Good God!"

The torrent of the unexpressed and inexpressible paralyzed

him and rendered him speechless. He stared at the girl, wondering who she was and then, realizing that he had perhaps stared too fixedly, averted his gaze, gave a little laugh, rolled a pill of bread between his fingers. After a second or two he allowed himself to look at her again and found her smiling.

"Never pay any attention to invalids," he said, "or they'll drag you to the hospital."

She examined him critically, with her head tilted a little to one side, but with friendliness.

"You don't *look* like an invalid," she said.

Mr. Arcularis thought her charming. His pain ceased to bother him, the disagreeable humming disappeared, or rather, it was dissociated from himself and became merely, as it should be, the sound of the ship's engines, and he began to think the voyage was going to be really delightful. The parson on his right passed him the salt.

"I fear you will need this in your soup," he said.

"Thank you. Is it as bad as that?"

The steward, overhearing, was immediately apologetic and solicitous. He explained that on the first day everything was at sixes and sevens. The girl looked up at him and asked him a question.

"Do you think we'll have a good voyage?" she said.

He was passing the hot rolls to the parson, removing the napkins from them with a deprecatory finger.

"Well, madam, I don't like to be a Jeremiah, but —"

"Oh, come," said the parson, "I hope we have no Jeremiahs."

"What do you mean?" said the girl.

Mr. Arcularis ate his soup with gusto — it was nice and hot.

"Well, maybe I shouldn't say it, but there's a corpse on board, going to Ireland; and I never yet knew a voyage with a corpse on board that we didn't have bad weather."

"Why, steward, you're just superstitious! What nonsense."

"That's a very ancient superstition," said Mr. Arcularis. "I've heard it many times. Maybe it's true. Maybe we'll be wrecked. And what does it matter, after all?" He was very bland.

"Then let's be wrecked," said the parson coldly.

Nevertheless, Mr. Arcularis felt a shudder go through him on hearing the steward's remark. A corpse in the hold — a coffin? Perhaps it was true. Perhaps some disaster would befall them. There might be fogs. There might be icebergs. He thought of all the wrecks of which he had read. There was the *Titanic*, which he had read about in the warm newspaper room at the Harvard Club — it had seemed dreadfully real, even there. That band, playing *Nearer My God to Thee* on the after-deck while the ship sank! It was one of the darkest of his memories. And the *Empress of Ireland* — all those poor people trapped in the smoking-room, with only one door between them and life, and that door locked for the night by the deck-steward, and the deck-steward nowhere to be found! He shivered, feeling a draft, and turned to the parson.

"How do these strange delusions arise?" he said.

The parson looked at him searchingly, appraisingly — from chin to forehead, from forehead to chin — and Mr. Arcularis, feeling uncomfortable, straightened his tie.

"From nothing but fear," said the parson. "Nothing on earth but fear."

"How strange!" said the girl.

Mr. Arcularis again looked at her — she had lowered her face — and again tried to think of whom she reminded him. It wasn't only the freckle-faced girl at the hospital — both of them had reminded him of someone else. Someone far back in his life: remote, beautiful, lovely. But he couldn't think. The meal came to an end, they all rose, the ship's orchestra played a feeble fox-trot, and Mr. Arcularis, once more alone, went to the bar to have his whisky. The room was stuffy, and the ship's engines were both audible and palpable. The humming and throbbing oppressed him, the rhythm seemed to be the rhythm of his own pain, and after a short time he found his way, with slow steps, holding on to the walls in his moments of weakness and dizziness, to his forlorn and white little room. The port had been — thank God! — closed for the night: it was cold enough anyway. The white and blue ribbons fluttered from the ventilator, the bottle and glasses clicked and clucked as the ship swayed gently to the

long, slow motion of the sea. It was all very popular – it was all
like something he had experienced somewhere before. What was
it? Where was it? . . . He untied his tie, looking at his face in the
glass, and wondered, and from time to time put his hand to his
side to hold in the pain. It wasn't at Portsmouth, in his childhood,
nor at Salem, nor in the rose-garden at his Aunt Julia's, nor in
the schoolroom at Cambridge. It was something very queer, very
intimate, very precious. The jackstones, the Sunday School cards
which he had loved when he was a child . . . He fell asleep.

The sense of time was already hopelessly confused. One hour
was like another, the sea looked always the same, morning was
indistinguishable from afternoon – and was it Tuesday or Wed-
nesday? Mr. Arcularis was sitting in the smoking-room, in his
favorite corner, watching the parson teach Miss Dean to play
chess. On the deck outside he could see the people passing and
repassing in their restless round of the ship. The red jacket went
by, then the black hat with the white feather, then the purple
scarf, the brown tweed coat, the Bulgarian mustache, the monocle, the Scotch cap with fluttering ribbons, and in no time at
all the red jacket again, dipping past the windows with its own
peculiar rhythm, followed once more by the black hat and the
purple scarf. How odd to reflect on the fixed little orbits of these
things – as definite and profound, perhaps, as the orbits of the
stars, and as important to God or the Absolute. There was a kind
of tyranny in this fixedness, too – to think of it too much made
one uncomfortable. He closed his eyes for a moment, to avoid
seeing for the fortieth time the Bulgarian mustache and the pursuing monocle. The parson was explaining the movements of
knights. Two forward and one to the side: Miss Dean repeated
the words several times with reflective emphasis. Here, too, was
the terrifying fixed curve of the infinite, the creeping curve of
logic which at last must become the final signpost at the edge of
nothing. After that – the deluge. The great white light of annihilation. The bright flash of death . . . Was it merely the sea
which made these abstractions so insistent, so intrusive? The
mere notion of *orbit* had somehow become extraordinarily naked;
and to rid himself of the discomfort and also to forget a little the

pain which bothered his side whenever he sat down, he walked slowly and carefully into the writing-room, and examined a pile of superannuated magazines and catalogues of travel. The bright colors amused him, the photographs of remote islands and mountains, savages in sampans or sarongs or both — it was all very far off and delightful, like something in a dream or a fever. But he found that he was too tired to read and was incapable of concentration. Dreams! Yes, that reminded him. That rather alarming business — sleep-walking!

Later in the evening — at what hour he didn't know — he was telling Miss Dean about it, as he had intended to do. They were sitting in deck-chairs on the sheltered side. The sea was black, and there was a cold wind. He wished they had chosen to sit in the lounge.

Miss Dean was extremely pretty — no, beautiful. She looked at him, too, in a very strange and lovely way, with something of inquiry, something of sympathy, something of affection. It seemed as if, between the question and the answer, they had sat thus for a very long time, exchanging an unspoken secret, simply looking at each other quietly and kindly. Had an hour or two passed? And was it at all necessary to speak?

"No," she said, "I never have."

She breathed into the low words a note of interrogation and gave him a slow smile.

"That's the funny part of it. I never had either until last night. Never in my life. I hardly ever even dream. And it really rather frightens me."

"Tell me about it, Mr. Arcularis."

"I dreamed at first that I was walking, alone, in a wide plain covered with snow. It was growing dark, I was very cold, my feet were frozen and numb, and I was lost. I came then to a signpost — at first it seemed to me there was nothing on it. Nothing but ice. Just before it grew finally dark, however, I made out on it the one word 'Polaris'."

"The Polar Star."

"Yes — and you see, I didn't myself know that. I looked it up only this morning. I suppose I must have seen it somewhere? And of course it rhymes with my name."

"Why, so it does!"

"Anyway, it gave me — in the dream — an awful feeling of despair, and the dream changed. This time, I dreamed I was standing *outside* my stateroom in the little dark corridor, or *cul-de-sac*, and trying to find the door-handle to let myself in. I was in my pajamas, and again I was very cold. And at this point I woke up. ... The extraordinary thing is that's exactly where I was!"

"Good Heavens. How strange!"

"Yes. And now the question is, *where had I been?* I was frightened, when I came to — not unnaturally. For among other things I *did* have, quite definitely, the feeling that I *had been* somewhere. Somewhere where it was very cold. It doesn't sound very proper. Suppose I had been seen!"

"That might have been awkward," said Miss Dean.

"Awkward! It might indeed. It's very singular. I've never done such a thing before. It's this sort of thing that reminds one — rather wholesomely perhaps, don't you think?" — and Mr. Arcularis gave a nervous little laugh — "how extraordinarily little we know about the workings of our own minds or souls. After all, what *do* we know?"

"Nothing — nothing — nothing — nothing," said Miss Dean slowly.

"*Absolutely* nothing."

Their voices had dropped, and again they were silent; and again they looked at each other gently and sympathetically, as if for the exchange of something unspoken and perhaps unspeakable. Time ceased. The orbit — so it seemed to Mr. Arcularis — once more became pure, became absolute. And once more he found himself wondering who it was that Miss Dean — Clarice Dean — reminded him of. Long ago and far away. Like those pictures of the islands and mountains. The little freckle-faced girl at the hospital was merely, as it were, the stepping-stone, the signpost, or, as in algebra, the "equals" sign. But what was it they both "equalled"? The jackstones came again into his mind and his Aunt Julia's rose-garden — at sunset; but this was ridiculous.

It couldn't be simply that they reminded him of his childhood! And yet why not?

They went into the lounge. The ship's orchestra, in the oval-shaped balcony among faded palms, was playing the finale of *Cavalleria Rusticana*, playing it badly.

"Good God!" said Mr. Arcularis, "can't I ever escape from that damned sentimental tune? It's the last thing I heard in America, and the last thing I *want* to hear."

"But don't you like it?"

"As music? No! It moves me too much, but in the wrong way."

"What, exactly, do you mean?"

"Exactly? Nothing. When I heard it at the hospital — when was it? — it made me feel like crying. Three old Italians tootling it in the rain. I suppose, like most people, I'm afraid of my feelings."

"Are they so dangerous?"

"Now then, young woman! Are you pulling my leg?"

The stewards had rolled away the carpets, and the passengers were beginning to dance. Miss Dean accepted the invitation of a young officer, and Mr. Arcularis watched them with envy. Odd, that last exchange of remarks — very odd; in fact, everything was odd. Was it possible that they were falling in love? Was that what it was all about — all these concealed references and recollections? He had read of such things. But at his age! And with a girl of twenty-two!

After an amused look at his old friend Polaris from the open door on the sheltered side, he went to bed.

The rhythm of the ship's engines was positively a persecution. It gave one no rest, it followed one like the Hound of Heaven, it drove one out into space and across the Milky Way and then back home by way of Betelgeuse. It was cold there, too. Mr. Arcularis, making the round trip by way of Betelgeuse and Polaris, sparkled with frost. He felt like a Christmas tree. Icicles on his fingers and icicles on his toes. He tinkled and spangled in the void, halloed to the waste echoes, rounded the buoy on the verge of the Unknown, and tacked glitteringly homeward. The wind whistled. He was barefooted. Snowflakes and tinsel blew past him. Next time, by George, he would go farther still – for altogether it was rather a lark. Forward into the untrodden! as somebody said. Some intrepid explorer of his own backyard, probably, some middle-aged professor with an umbrella: those were the fellows for courage! But give us time, thought Mr. Arcularis, give us time, and we will bring back with us the night-rime of the Obsolute. Or was it Absolete? If only there weren't this perpetual throbbing, this iteration of sound, like a pain, these circles and repetitions of light – the feeling as of everything coiling inward to a center of misery . . .

Suddenly, it was dark, and he was lost. He was groping, he touched the cold, white, slippery woodwork with his fingernails, looking for an electric switch. The throbbing of course, was the throbbing of the ship. But he was almost home – almost home. Another corner to round, a door to be opened, and there he would be. Safe and sound. Safe in his father's house.

It was at this point that he woke up: in the corridor that led to the dining saloon. Such pure terror, such horror, seized him as he had never known. His heart felt as if it would stop beating. His back was towards the dining saloon; apparently he had just come from it. He was in his pajamas. The corridor was dim, all but two lights having been turned out for the night, and – thank God! – deserted. Not a soul, not a sound. He was perhaps fifty yards from his room. With luck he could get to it unseen. Holding tremulously to the rail that ran along the wall, a brown, greasy rail, he began to creep his way forward. He felt very weak, very dizzy, and his thoughts refused to concentrate. Vaguely he remembered Miss Dean – Clarice – and the freckled girl, as if they were one and the same person. But he wasn't in the hospital, he was on the ship. Of course. How absurd. The Great Circle. Here we are, old fellow . . . steady round the corner . . . hold hard to your umbrella . . .

In his room, with the door safely shut behind him, Mr. Arcularis broke into a cold sweat. He had no sooner got into his bunk, shivering, than he heard the night watchman pass.

"But where — " he thought, closing his eyes in agony — "have I been? ..."

A dreadful idea had occurred to him.

"It's nothing serious — how could it be anything serious? Of course it's nothing serious," said Mr. Arcularis.

"No, it's nothing serious," said the ship's doctor urbanely.

"I knew you'd think so. But just the same —"

"Such a condition is the result of worry," said the doctor. "Are you worried — do you mind telling me — about something? Just try to think."

"Worried?"

Mr. Arcularis knitted his brows. *Was* there something? Some little mosquito of a cloud disappearing into the southwest, the northeast? Some little gnat-song of despair? But no, that was all over. All over.

"Nothing," he said, "nothing whatever."

"It's very strange," said the doctor.

"Strange! I should say so. I've come to sea for a rest, not for a nightmare! What about a bromide?"

"Well, I can give you a bromide, Mr. Arcularis —"

"Then, please, if you don't mind, give me a bromide."

He carried the little phial hopefully to his stateroom, and took a dose at once. He could see the sun through his porthole. It looked northern and pale and small, like a little peppermint, which was only natural enough, for the latitude was changing with every hour. But why was it that doctors were all alike? and all, for that matter, like his father, or that fellow at the hospital? Smythe, his name was. Doctor Smythe. A nice, dry little fellow, and they said he was a writer. Wrote poetry, or something like that. Poor fellow — disappointed. Like everybody else. Crouched in there, in his cabin, night after night, writing blank verse or something — all about the stars and flowers and love and death; ice and the sea and the infinite; time and tide — well, every man to his own taste.

"But it's nothing serious," said Mr. Arcularis, later, to the parson. "How could it be?"

"Why, of course not, my dear fellow," said the parson, patting his back. "How could it be?"

"I know it isn't and yet I worry about it."

"It would be ridiculous to think it serious," said the parson.

Mr. Arcularis shivered: it was colder than ever. It was said that they were near icebergs. For a few hours in the morning there had been a fog, and the siren had blown — devastatingly — at three-minute intervals. Icebergs caused fog — he knew that.

"These things always come," said the parson, "from a sense of guilt. You feel guilty about something. I won't be so rude as to inquire what it is. But if you could rid yourself of the sense of guilt —"

And later still, when the sky was pink.

"But is it anything to worry about?" said Miss Dean. "Really?"

"No, I suppose not."

"Then don't worry. We aren't children any longer!"

"Aren't we? I wonder!"

They leaned, shoulders touching, on the deck-rail, and looked at the sea, which was multitudinously incarnadined. Mr. Arcularis scanned the horizon in vain for an iceberg.

"Anyway," he said, "the colder we are the less we feel!"

"I hope that's no reflection on you," said Miss Dean.

"Here . . . feel my hand," said Mr. Arcularis.

"Heaven knows it's cold!"

"It's been to Polaris and back! No wonder."

"Poor thing, poor thing!"

"Warm it."

"May I?"

"You can."

"I'll try."

Laughing, she took his hand between both of hers, one palm under and one palm over, and began rubbing it briskly. The decks were deserted, no one was near them, everyone was dressing for dinner. The sea grew darker, the wind blew colder.

"I wish I could remember who you are," he said.

"And you — who are you?"

"Myself."

"Then perhaps *I* am yourself."

"Don't be metaphysical!"

"But I *am* metaphysical!"

She laughed, withdrew, pulled the light coat about her shoulders.

The bugle blew the summons for dinner — *The Roast Beef of Old England* — and they walked together along the darkening deck toward the door, from which a shaft of soft light fell across the deck-rail. As they stepped over the brass door-sill Mr. Arcularis felt the throb of the engines again; he put his hand quickly to his side.

"*Auf wiedersehen,*" he said. "*Tomorrow and tomorrow and tomorrow.*"

Mr. Arcularis was finding it impossible, absolutely impossible, to keep warm. A cold fog surrounded the ship, had done so, it seemed, for days. The sun had all but disappeared, the transition from day to night was almost unnoticeable. The ship, too, seemed scarcely to be moving — it was as if anchored among walls of ice and rime. Monstrous, that merely because it was June, and supposed, therefore, to be warm, the ship's authorities should consider it unnecessary to turn on the heat! By day, he wore his heavy coat and sat shivering in the corner of the smoking-room. His teeth chattered, his hands were blue. By night, he heaped blankets on his bed, closed the porthole's black eye against the sea, and drew the yellow curtains across it, but in vain. Somehow, despite everything, the fog crept in, and the icy fingers touched his throat. The steward, questioned about it, merely said, "Icebergs." Of course — any fool knew that. But how long, in God's name, was it going to last? They surely ought to be past the Grand Banks by this time! And surely it wasn't necessary to sail to England by way of Greenland and Iceland!

Miss Dean — Clarice — was sympathetic.

"It's simply because," she said, "your vitality has been lowered by your illness. You can't expect to be your normal self so soon after an operation! When was your operation, by the way?"

Mr. Arcularis considered. Strange — he couldn't be quite sure. It was all a little vague — his sense of time had disappeared.

"Heaven knows!" he said. "Centuries ago. When I was a tad-pole and you were a fish. I should think it must have been about the time of the Battle of Teutoburg Forest. Or perhaps when I was a Neanderthal man with a club!"

"Are you sure it wasn't farther back still?"

What did she mean by that?

"Not at all. Obviously, we've been on this damned ship for ages — for eras — for aeons. And even on this ship, you must re-member, I've had plenty of time, in my nocturnal wanderings, to go several times to Orion and back. I'm thinking, by the way, of going farther still. There's a nice little star off to the left, as you round Betelgeuse, which looks as if it might be right at the edge. The last outpost of the finite. I think I'll have a look at it and bring you back a frozen rime-feather."

"It would melt when you got it back."

"Oh, no, it wouldn't — not on *this* ship!"

Clarice laughed.

"I wish I could go with you," she said.

"If only you would! If only — "

He broke on his sentence and looked hard at her —.how lovely she was, and how desirable! No such woman had ever before come into his life; there had been no one with whom he had at once felt so profound a sympathy and understanding. It was a miracle, simply — a miracle. No need to put his arm around her or to kiss her — delightful as such small vulgarities would be. He had only to look at her, and to feel, gazing into those extraordin-ary eyes, that she knew him, had always known him. It was as if, indeed, she might be his own soul.

But as he looked thus at her, reflecting, he noticed that she was frowning.

"What is it?" he said.

She shook her head, slowly.

"I don't know."

"Tell me."

"Nothing. It just occurred to me that perhaps you weren't looking quite so well."

Mr. Arcularis was startled. He straightened himself up.

"What nonsense! Of course this pain bothers me — and I feel astonishingly weak — "

"It's more than that — much more than that. Something is worrying you horribly." She paused, and then with an air of challenging him, added, "Tell me, did you?"

Her eyes were suddenly asking him blazingly the question he had been afraid of. He flinched, caught his breath, looked away. But it was no use, as he knew: he would have to tell her. He had known all along that he would have to tell her.

"Clarice," he said — and his voice broke in spite of his effort to control it — "it's killing me, it's ghastly! Yes, I did."

His eyes filled with tears, he saw that her own had done so also. She put her hand on his arm.

"I knew," she said. "I knew. But tell me."

"It's happened twice again — *twice* — and each time I was farther away. The same dream of going round a star, the same terrible coldness and helplessness. That awful whistling curve. . . . He shuddered.

"And when you woke up — " she spoke quietly — "where were you when you woke up? Don't be afraid!"

"The first time I was at the farther end of the dining saloon. I had my hand on the door that leads into the pantry."

"I see. Yes. And the next time?"

Mr. Arcularis wanted to close his eyes in terror — he felt as if he were going mad. His lips moved before he could speak, and when at last he did speak it was in a voice so low as to be almost a whisper.

"I was at the bottom of the stairway that leads down from the pantry to the hold, past the refrigerating-plant. It was dark, and I was crawling on my hands and knees . . . *Crawling on my hands and knees!* . . .

"Oh!" she said, and again, "Oh!"

He began to tremble violently; he felt the hand on his arm trembling also. And then he watched a look of unmistakable horror come slowly into Clarice's eyes, and a look of understanding, as if she saw . . . She tightened her hold on his arm.

"Do you think . . ." she whispered.

They stared at each other.

"I know," he said. "And so do you ... Twice more — three times — and I'll be looking down into an empty ..."

It was then that they first embraced — then, at the edge of the infinite, at the last signpost of the finite. They clung together desperately, forlornly, weeping as they kissed each other, staring hard one moment and closing their eyes the next. Passionately, passionately, she kissed him, as if she were indeed trying to give him her warmth, her life.

"But what nonsense!" she cried, leaning back and holding his face between her hands, her hands which were wet with his tears. "What nonsense! It can't be!"

"It is," said Mr. Arcularis slowly.

"But how do you know? ... How do you know where the —"

For the first time Mr. Arcularis smiled.

"Don't be afraid, darling — you mean the coffin?"

"How could you know where it is?"

"I don't need to," said Mr. Arcularis ... "I'm already almost there."


Before they separated for the night, in the smoking-room, they had several whisky cocktails.

"We must make it gay!" Mr. Arcularis said. "Above all, we must make it gay. Perhaps even now it will turn out to be nothing but a nightmare from which both of us will wake! And even at the worst, at my present rate of travel, I ought to need two or more nights! It's a long way, still, to that little star."

The parson passed them at the door.

"What! turning in so soon?" he said. "I was hoping for a game of chess."

"Yes, both turning in. But tomorrow?"

"Tomorrow, then, Miss Dean! And good-night!"

"Good-night."

They walked once round the deck, then leaned on the railing and stared into the fog. It was thicker and whiter than ever. The ship was moving barely perceptibly, the rhythm of the engines was slower, more subdued and remote, and at regular intervals, mournfully, came the long reverberating cry of the fog-horn. The sea was calm, and lapped only very tenderly against the side of the ship, the sound coming up to them clearly, however, because of the profound stillness.

" 'On such a night as this —' " quoted Mr. Arcularis grimly.

" 'On such a night as this —' "

Their voices hung suspended in the night, time ceased for them, for an eternal instant they were happy. When at last they parted it was by tacit agreement on a note of the ridiculous.

"Be a good boy and take your bromide!" she said.

"Yes, mother, I'll take my medicine!"

In his stateroom, he mixed himself a strong potion of bromide, a very strong one, and got into bed. He would have no trouble in falling asleep: he felt more tired, more supremely exhausted, than he had ever been in his life; nor had bed ever seemed so delicious. And that long, magnificent, delirious swoop of dizziness . . . the Great Circle . . . the swift pathway to Arcturus . . .

It was all as before, but infinitely more rapid. Never had Mr. Arcularis achieved such phenomenal, such supernatural, speed. In no time at all he was beyond the moon, shot past the North Star as if it were standing still (which perhaps it was?), swooped in a long, bright curve round the Pleiades, shouted his frosty greetings to Betelgeuse, and was off to the little blue star which pointed the way to the unknown. Forward into the untrodden! Courage, old man, and hold on to your umbrella! Have you got your garters on? Mind your hat! In no time at all we'll be back to Clarice with the frozen time-feather, the rime-feather, the snowflake of the Absolute, the Obsolete. If only we don't wake . . . if only we needn't wake . . . if only we don't wake in that — in that — time and space . . . somewhere or nowhere . . . cold and dark . . . *Cavalleria Rusticana* sobbing among the palms; if a lonely . . . if only . . . the coffers of the poor — not coffers, not coffers, not coffers. Oh, God not coffers, but light, delight, supreme white and brightness, and above all whirling lightness, whirling lightness above all — and freezing — freezing — freezing . . .

At this point in the void the surgeon's last effort to save Mr. Arcularis's life had failed. He stood back from the operating table and made a tired gesture with a rubber-gloved hand.

"It's all over," he said. "As I expected."

He looked at Miss Hoyle, whose gaze was downward, at the basin she held. There was a moment's stillness, a pause, a brief flight of unexchanged comment, and then the ordered life of the hospital was resumed.

## CRITIQUE AND QUESTIONS

This is a story with a "surprise" ending which, at second glance, is not really a surprise at all. It is the kind of story which must be "rerun" as soon as you have finished it. You think back to the beginning, and in recollection you stand off and observe your own impressions, your own guesses, your own suspicions as they took form at the *first* reading. When did you first begin to wonder about Mr. Arcularis? What are the hints, laid down at intervals as though in a paper-chase, which lead you forward in imagination to the coffin in the hold of the ship, and to a wild surmise of the truth?

There is, of course, the hospital, the operation and, in the first paragraph, the strangely ambiguous phrase, "everything was over at last". The tune from *Cavalleria Rusticana* seems innocent enough as it trickles through the hospital window. But are you not puzzled when the same tune is played by the ship's band? You are all the more puzzled, surely, when faces appear on shipboard which remind Mr. Arcularis of faces in the hospital. Then, too, from the very beginning, there is the repeated emphasis on cold. "The wind was cold, very cold for June." Despite the chill in his marrow, Mr. Arcularis suspects that he is still feverish and sick. There are sickening waves of dizziness, a throbbing hum in the air which "became" the sound of the ship's engines. Yet "the rhythm seemed to be the rhythm of his own pain". The cold grows more intense. There is talk of the Absolute and the infinite. And the steward, whom Mr. Arcularis describes as a "dead soul", mentions the corpse which the ship carries in its hold. Mr. Arcularis shivers and the reader feels the equation of death and cold.

The life on shipboard seems real enough — the promenades on deck, the games, the oddly assorted people. But is there not a disquieting hint in the phrase, "it was all like something he had experienced somewhere before"? Do you not begin to feel, also, that there is an almost *desperate* realism about life on shipboard, as though bits and pieces dredged up from distant memories (from "something experienced before") are forced into the foreground of the mind and made to revolve and revolve before the mind's eye — made to repeat themselves so that Mr. Arcularis can reassure himself they are really there. Note, at a moment when "the sense of time" is "hopelessly confused" —

> The red jacket went by, then the black Bulgarian
> mustache, the monocle, the Scotch cap with fluttering
> ribbons, and in no time the red jacket again, dipping
> past the window with its own peculiar rhythm, followed
> once more by the black hat and the purple scarf.

And Mr. Arcularis thinks at once of "the fixed orbit of the stars", "the great white light of annihilation", "the bright flash of death". Even the repetition of the real is no firm reassurance. Nothing can conceal the close presence of death.

The story comes to its centre in the sequence of dreams and sleep-walks. In the dreams Mr. Arcularis fares forward, spangled with cold, towards the outer bounds of space. He sees a signpost pointing to "Polaris", the Polar Star ("it rhymes with my name"). We may well wonder now about this strange name of his and why it "rhymes" with the name of the cold Polar star. *Arcula* is a stone coffin or casket. "Arcularis" would seem to mean a man who has to do with these coffins or caskets. And then we notice that after each dream flight to the edge of the cold Absolute, Mr. Arcularis awakens one step nearer the coffin, nearer the *casket* — in the ship's hold. The star and the casket rhyme, indeed. The dreams spiral toward death.

Awake, Mr. Arcularis fares, not forward, but backward into lost memories — the jackstones, the rose-garden. It is as though he craves to be possessed again by his own youth. The girl mysteriously becomes his own soul — as though he saw his soul separate from his body and must embrace it and cling to it. In this plunge backwards from death, time reels and fades out. Mr. Arcularis fumbles, desperately, beyond and beneath his own birth to the birth of the species, to the cradle of life itself ("when I was a tadpole and you were a fish").

We know, without being told, that it is the dream which is real and the "real" which is dreamed. And we become aware, not quite clearly at first, of a terrible struggle, of a clutching backwards at the roots of time and place and life which will no longer hold. Images of the hospital reappear. (Miss Dean is identified suddenly as "the freckled face girl".) The bars of *Cavalleria Rusticana* sound again. The cold deepens and is Absolute. Mr. Arcularis has found his casket in the ship's hold. And he is whirled beyond the far, shivering rim of Polaris.

The imaginative effect of the story rests on the subtle reversal of dream and fact. Appearance and reality are made to change places. And one is carried along by hints and guesses to a "surprise" ending that is no mere trick because it serves to confirm all our guesses and all our fears. We leave the story with the sense that we have been caught up in (and held by) a dramatic and universal battle between life and death.

1. Has the author cheated? Is the ship, and are the people, too "real"?

2. To what extent does this imaginative method of telling of a death struggle control or even overcome the implicit sadness or morbidity of the subject-matter?

3. Why does the author use a sea-voyage as the setting for the story?

4. Does the story have a "moral"?

5. Does the author suggest his own view of the meaning of death — and life?

6. What is the purpose — and effect — of the last paragraph of the story?

*James*

*Thurber*

# The secret life of Walter Mitty

*James Thurber (1894-1961), American humourist and illustrator,
was born in Columbus, Ohio, to an eccentric family whose*
penchant *for ludicrous situations early formed his comic view of
humanity. Graduating from Ohio State University in 1919, he
worked in Paris as a newspaperman until 1926, when he returned
to America as a member of the* New Yorker *staff. He resigned
in 1933 to become a free-lance writer and cartoonist. Among his
writings are* Is Sex Necessary? *in collaboration with E. B. White
(1929),* My Life and Hard Times *(1933),* Let Your Mind
Alone *(1937),* The Male Animal, *a play written in collaboration
with Elliott Nugent (1940), and* Thurber Country *(1952).
The prototype of the domineering Mrs. Mitty has appeared
frequently in Thurber's cartoons. She is at once frightening and
funny. Nature, Thurber seems to say, has decreed war in union
in condemning man and woman to each other. In 1940, this story
was made into a very successful movie, and it is reprinted here
by permission; copyright, 1939, The New Yorker Magazine, Inc.*

"WE'RE GOING THROUGH!" The Commander's voice was like thin
ice breaking. He wore his full-dress uniform, with the heavily
braided white cap pulled down rakishly over one cold gray eye.
"We can't make it, sir. It's spoiling for a hurricane, if you ask

me." "I'm not asking you, Lieutenant Berg," said the Commander. "Throw on the power lights! Rev her up to 8,500! We're going through!" The pounding of the cylinders increased: ta-pocketa-pocketa-pocketa-*pocketa-pocketa*. The Commander stared at the ice forming on the pilot window. He walked over and twisted a row of complicated dials. "Switch on No. 8 auxiliary!" he shouted. "Switch on No. 8 auxiliary!" repeated Lieutenant Berg. "Full strength in No. 3 turret!" shouted the Commander. "Full strength in No. 3 turret!" The crew, bending to their various tasks in the huge, hurtling, eight-engined Navy hydroplane, looked at each other and grinned. "The Old Man'll get us through," they said to one another. "The Old Man ain't afraid of Hell!" . . .

"Not so fast! You're driving too fast!" said Mrs. Mitty. "What are you driving so fast for?"

"Hum?" said Walter Mitty. He looked at his wife, in the seat beside him, with shocked astonishment. She seemed grossly unfamiliar, like a strange woman who had yelled at him in a crowd. "You were up to fifty-five," she said. "You know I don't like to go more than forty. You were up to fifty-five." Walter Mitty drove on toward Waterbury in silence, the roaring of the SN202 through the worst storm in twenty years of Navy flying fading in the remote, intimate airways of his mind. "You're tensed up again," said Mrs. Mitty. "It's one of your days. I wish you'd let Dr. Renshaw look you over."

Walter Mitty stopped the car in front of the building where his wife went to have her hair done. "Remember to get those overshoes while I'm having my hair done," she said. "I don't need overshoes," said Mitty. She put her mirror back into her bag. "We've been all through that," she said, getting out of the car. "You're not a young man any longer." He raced the engine a little. "Why don't you wear your gloves? Have you lost your gloves?" Walter Mitty reached in a pocket and brought out the gloves. He put them on, but after she had turned and gone into the building and he had driven on to a red light, he took them off again. "Pick it up, brother!" snapped a cop as the light changed, and Mitty hastily pulled on his gloves and lurched

ahead. He drove around the streets aimlessly for a time, and then
he drove past the hospital on his way to the parking lot.

. . . "It's the millionaire banker, Wellington McMillan," said
the pretty nurse. "Yes?" said Walter Mitty, removing his gloves
slowly. "Who has the case?" "Dr. Renshaw and Dr. Benbow, but
there are two specialists here, Dr. Remington from New York
and Dr. Pritchard-Mitford from London. He flew over." A door
opened down a long, cool corridor and Dr. Renshaw came out.
He looked distraught and haggard. "Hello, Mitty," he said.
"We're having the devil's own time with McMillan, the millionaire banker and close personal friend of Roosevelt. Obstreosis of
the ductal tract. Tertiary. Wish you'd take a look at him." "Glad
to," said Mitty.

In the operating room there were whispered introductions:
"Dr. Remington, Dr. Mitty. Dr. Pritchard-Mitford, Dr. Mitty."
"I've read your book on streptothricosis," said Pritchard-Mitford, shaking hands. "A brilliant performance, sir." "Thank
you," said Walter Mitty. "Didn't know you were in the States,
Mitty," grumbled Remington. "Coals to Newcastle, bringing
Mitford and me up here for a tertiary." "You are very kind,"
said Mitty. A huge, complicated machine, connected to the operating table, with many tubes and wires, began at this moment
to go pocketa-pocketa-pocketa. "The new anaesthetizer is giving
away!" shouted an interne. "There is no one in the East who
knows how to fix it!" "Quiet, man!" said Mitty, in a low, cool
voice. He sprang to the machine, which was now going pocketa-
pocketa-queep-pocketa-queep. He began fingering delicately a
row of glistening dials. "Give me a fountain pen!" he snapped.
Someone handed him a fountain pen. He pulled a faulty piston
out of the machine and inserted the pen in its place. "That will
hold for ten minutes," he said. "Get on with the operation."
A nurse hurried over and whispered to Renshaw, and Mitty
saw the man turn pale. "Coreopsis has set in," said Renshaw
nervously. "If you would take over, Mitty?" Mitty looked at
him and at the craven figure of Benbow, who drank, and at the
grave, uncertain faces of the two great specialists. "If you wish,"

he said. They slipped a white gown on him; he adjusted a mask and drew on thin gloves; nurses handed him shining ...

"Back it up, Mac! Look out for that Buick!" Walter Mitty jammed on the brakes. "Wrong lane, Mac," said the parking-lot attendant, looking at Mitty closely. "Gee. Yeh," muttered Mitty. He began cautiously to back out of the lane marked "Exit Only." "Leave her sit there," said the attendant. "I'll put her away." Mitty got out of the car. "Hey, better leave the key." "Oh," said Mitty, handing the man the ignition key. The attendant vaulted into the car, backed it up with insolent skill, and put it where it belonged.

They're so damn cocky, thought Walter Mitty, walking along Main Street; they think they know everything. Once he had tried to take his chains off, outside New Milford, and he had got them wound around the axles. A man had to come out in a wrecking car and unwind them, a young, grinning garageman. Since then Mrs. Mitty always made him drive to a garage to have the chains taken off. The next time, he thought, I'll wear my right arm in a sling; they won't grin at me then. I'll have my right arm in a sling and they'll see I couldn't possibly take the chains off myself. He kicked at the slush on the sidewalk. "Overshoes," he said to himself, and he began looking for a shoe store.

When he came out into the street again, with the overshoes in a box under his arm, Walter Mitty began to wonder what the other thing was his wife had told him to get. She had told him, twice before they set out from their house for Waterbury. In a way he hated these weekly trips to town — he was always getting something wrong. Kleenex, he thought, Squibb's, razor blades? No. Toothpaste, toothbrush, bicarbonate, carborundum, initiative and referendum? He gave it up. But she would remember it. "Where's the what's-its-name?" she would ask. "Don't tell me you forgot the what's-its-name." A newsboy went by shouting something about the Waterbury trial.

... "Perhaps this will refresh your memory." The District Attorney suddenly thrust a heavy automatic at the quiet figure on the witness stand. "Have you ever seen this before?" Walter Mitty took the gun and examined it expertly. "This is my Webley-Vickers 50.80," he said calmly. An excited buzz ran around the courtroom. The Judge rapped for order. "You are a crack shot with any sort of firearms, I believe?" said the District Attorney, insinuatingly. "Objection!" shouted Mitty's attorney. "We have shown that the defendant could not have fired the shot. We have shown that he wore his right arm in a sling on the night of the fourteenth of July." Walter Mitty raised his hand briefly and the bickering attorneys were stilled. "With any known make of gun," he said evenly, "I could have killed Gregory Fitzhurst at three hundred feet *with my left hand*." Pandemonium broke loose in the courtroom. A woman's scream rose above the bedlam and suddenly a lovely, dark-haired girl was in Walter Mitty's arms. The District Attorney struck at her savagely. Without rising from his chair, Mitty let the man have it on the point of the chin. "You miserable cur!" ...

"Puppy biscuit," said Walter Mitty. He stopped walking and the buildings of Waterbury rose up out of the misty courtroom and surrounded him again. A woman who was passing laughed. "He said 'Puppy biscuit,'" she said to her companion. "That man said 'Puppy biscuit' to himself." Walter Mitty hurried on. He went into an A. & P., not the first one he came to but a smaller one farther up the street. "I want some biscuit for small, young dogs," he said to the clerk. "Any special brand, sir?" The greatest pistol shot in the world thought a moment. "It says 'Puppies Bark for It' on the box," said Walter Mitty.

His wife would be through at the hairdresser's in fifteen minutes, Mitty saw in looking at his watch, unless they had trouble drying it; sometimes they had trouble drying it. She didn't like to get to the hotel first; she would want him to be there waiting for her as usual. He found a big leather chair in the lobby, facing a window, and he put the overshoes and the puppy biscuit on the floor beside it. He picked up an old copy of *Liberty* and sank down into the chair. "Can Germany Conquer the World Through the Air?" Walter Mitty looked at the pictures of bombing planes and of ruined streets.

... "The cannonading has got the wind up in young Raleigh, sir," said the sergeant. Captain Mitty looked up at him through tousled hair. "Get him to bed," he said wearily, "with the others. I'll fly alone." "But you can't, sir," said the sergeant anxiously. "It takes two men to handle that bomber and the Archies are pounding hell out of the air. Von Richtman's circus is between here and Saulier." "Somebody's got to get that ammunition dump," said Mitty. "I'm going over. Spot of brandy?" He poured a drink for the sergeant and one for himself. War thundered and whined around the dugout and battered at the door. There was a rending of wood, and splinters flew through the room. "A bit of a near thing," said Captain Mitty carelessly. "The box barrage is closing in," said the sergeant. "We only live once, Sergeant," said Mitty, with his faint, fleeting smile. "Or do we?" He poured another brandy and tossed it off. "I never see a man could hold his brandy like you, sir," said the sergeant. "Begging your pardon, sir." Captain Mitty stood up and strapped on his huge Webley-Vickers automatic. "It's forty kilometres through hell, sir," said the sergeant. Mitty finished one last brandy. "After all," he said softly, "what isn't?" The pounding of the cannon increased; there was the rat-tat-tatting of machine guns, and from somewhere came the menacing pocketa-pocketa-pocketa of the new flame-throwers. Walter Mitty walked to the door of the dugout humming *Auprès de Ma Blonde*. He turned and waved to the sergeant. "Cheerio!" he said. . . .

Something struck his shoulder. "I've been looking all over this hotel for you," said Mrs. Mitty. "Why do you have to hide in this old chair? How did you expect me to find you?" "Things close in," said Walter Mitty vaguely. "What?" Mrs. Mitty said. "Did you get the what's-its-name? The puppy biscuit? What's in that box?" "Overshoes," said Mitty. "Couldn't you have put them on in the store?" "I was thinking," said Walter Mitty. "Does it ever occur to you that I am sometimes thinking?" She looked at him. "I'm going to take your temperature when I get you home," she said.

They went out through the revolving doors that made a faintly derisive whistling sound when you pushed them. It was two blocks to the parking lot. At the drugstore on the corner she said, "Wait here for me. I forgot something. I won't be a minute." She was more than a minute. Walter Mitty lighted a cigarette. It began to rain, rain with sleet in it. He stood up against the wall of the drugstore, smoking. . . . He put his shoulders back and his heels together. "To hell with the handkerchief," said Walter Mitty scornfully. He took one last drag on his cigarette and snapped it away. Then, with that faint, fleeting smile playing about his lips, he faced the firing squad; erect and motionless, proud and disdainful, Walter Mitty the Undefeated, inscrutable to the last.

QUESTIONS

1. Since this story first appeared in the *New Yorker* in 1939, it has been reprinted in dozens of anthologies. Suggest some reasons for its widespread popularity.

2. At first, Walter Mitty's opening dream seems like a standard adventure story situation. A more careful reading reveals some ludicrous details. What are they?

3. The incidents of the story alternate between dream and reality, the reality forming a comic contrast to the dream. Re-read the incident that follows the first dream. Describe Thurber's method of characterizing Walter Mitty in this incident. In your analysis, mention the qualities of character you see in Mitty.

4. Notice that Thurber gives us almost no indication of the actual appearance of either Mitty or his wife. Does the story suffer from this omission? What hints does he supply so that we may imagine what they look like?

5. There are five dream incidents and four anti-climactic drops from dreams to reality, all of which are plausibly linked together. Trace the development of these incidents and show that each of Walter's dreams results from a definite stimulus in the real world.

6. The dream-world Mitty is a man of spectacular courage. What other qualities does he possess which contrast with those of the real-world Mitty? Do the two personalities share any quality in common?

7. This story follows the drab outward routine of a day's shopping in town. In the real events, there is no climax to end the story in victory or defeat. What incident comes closest to showing Mitty rebelling against his wife?

8. (a) Explain why Thurber ended with a dream instead of reality.
   (b) What details make this conclusion particularly effective?

*Herbert George*
*Wells*

# The door in the wall

*Herbert George Wells (1866-1946), scientist, novelist and*
*historian, was born at Bromley, Kent, of a lower middle-class*
*family. After periods of apprenticeship to a draper and a*
*chemist, he won a scholarship which enabled him to study science*
*at London University, from which he graduated in 1888.*
*Tuberculosis interrupted a subsequent teaching career, and upon*
*recovery he wrote his first novel,* The Time Machine *(1895).*
*His early stories and novels were science fiction tinged with*
*socialist political philosophy. Belonging to this period are*
The Island of Dr. Moreau *(1897),* The War of the Worlds
*(1898) and* Tales of Space and Time *(1899). Later novels like*
Kipps *(1905) and* The History of Mr. Polly *(1910), were*
*novels of social comment. In 1920 he published* The Outline of
History *and in 1929,* The Science of Life, *written with Julian*
*Huxley and G. P. Wells. His later books were increasingly*
*political, as typified by* The Shape of Things to Come *(1933),*
*and, after the Second World War, increasingly gloomy, as can be*
*seen in* Mind at the End of Its Tether *(1945). "The Door in*
*the Wall" is reprinted from* The Time Machine and Other
Stories *by permission of the executors of Mr. Wells' Estate and*
*A. P. Watt and Son.*

ONE CONFIDENTIAL EVENING, not three months ago, Lionel Wallace told me this story of the Door in the Wall. And at the time
I thought that so far as he was concerned it was a true story.

He told it me with such direct simplicity of conviction that I could not do otherwise than believe in him. But in the morning, in my own flat, I woke to a different atmosphere; and as I lay in bed and recalled the things he had told me, stripped of the glamour of his earnest slow voice, denuded of the focused, shaded table light, the shadowy atmosphere that wrapped about him and me, and the pleasant bright things, the dessert and glasses and napery of the dinner we had shared, making them for the time a bright little world quite cut off from everyday realities, I saw it all as frankly incredible. "He was mystifying!" I said, and then: "How well he did it! . . . It isn't quite the thing I should have expected of him, of all people, to do well."

Afterwards as I sat up in bed and sipped my morning tea, I found myself trying to account for the flavour of reality that perplexed me in his impossible reminiscences, by supposing they did in some way suggest, present, convey — I hardly know which word to use — experiences it was otherwise impossible to tell.

Well, I don't resort to that explanation now. I have got over my intervening doubts. I believe now, as I believed at the moment of telling, that Wallace did to the very best of his ability strip the truth of his secret for me. But whether he himself saw, or only thought he saw, whether he himself was the possessor of an inestimable privilege or the victim of a fantastic dream, I cannot pretend to guess. Even the facts of his death, which ended my doubts for ever, throw no light on that.

That much the reader must judge for himself.

I forget now what chance comment or criticism of mine moved so reticent a man to confide in me. He was, I think, defending himself against an imputation of slackness and unreliability I had made in relation to a great public movement, in which he had disappointed me. But he plunged suddenly. "I have," he said, "a preoccupation —"

"I know," he went on, after a pause, "I have been negligent. The fact is — it isn't a case of ghosts or apparitions — but — it's an odd thing to tell of, Redmond — I am haunted. I am haunted by something — that rather takes the light out of things, that fills me with longings . . ."

He paused, checked by that English shyness that so often over-comes us when we speak of moving or grave or beautiful things. "You were at Saint Athelstan's all through," he said, and for a moment that seemed to me quite irrelevant. "Well" — and he paused. Then very haltingly at first, but afterwards more easily, he began to tell of the thing that was hidden in his life, the haunt-ing memory of a beauty and happiness that filled his heart with insatiable longings, that made all the interests and spectacle of wordly life seem dull and tedious and vain to him.

Now that I have the clue to it, the thing seems written visibly in his face. I have a photograph in which that look of detachment has been caught and intensified. It reminds me of what a woman once said of him — a woman who had loved him greatly. "Sud-denly," she said, "the interest goes out of him. He forgets you. He doesn't care a rap for you — under his very nose . . ."

Yet the interest was not always out of him, and when he was holding his attention to a thing Wallace could contrive to be an extremely successful man. His career, indeed, is set with suc-cesses. He left me behind him long ago; he soared up over my head, and cut a figure in the world that I couldn't cut — anyhow. He was still a year short of forty, and they say now that he would have been in office and very probably in the new Cabinet if he had lived. At school he always beat me without effort — as it were by nature. We were at school together at Saint Athelstan's College in West Kensington for almost all our school-time. He came into the school as my co-equal, but he left far above me, in a blaze of scholarships and brilliant performance. Yet I think I made a fair average running. And it was at school I heard first of the "Door in the Wall" — that I was to hear of a second time only a month before his death.

To him at least the Door in the Wall was a real door, leading through a real wall to immortal realities. Of that I am now quite assured.

And it came into his life quite early, when he was a little fellow between five and six. I remember how, as he sat making his con-fession to me with a slow gravity, he reasoned and reckoned the date of it. "There was," he said, "a crimson Virginia creeper in it – all one bright uniform crimson, in a clear amber sunshine against a white wall. That came into the impression somehow, though I don't clearly remember how, and there were horse-chestnut leaves upon the clean pavement outside the green door. They were blotched yellow and green, you know, not brown nor dirty, so that they must have been new fallen. I take it that means October. I look out for horse-chestnut leaves every year and I ought to know.

"If I'm right in that, I was about five years and four months old."

He was, he said, rather a precocious little boy – he learned to talk at an abnormally early age, and he was so sane and "old-fashioned", as people say, that he was permitted an amount of initiative that most children scarcely attain by seven or eight. His mother died when he was two, and he was under the less vigilant and authoritative care of a nursery governess. His father was a stern, preoccupied lawyer, who gave him little attention and expected great things of him. For all his brightness he found life grey and dull, I think. And one day he wandered.

He could not recall the particular neglect that enabled him to get away, nor the course he took among the West Kensington roads. All that had faded among the incurable blurs of memory. But the white wall and the green door stood out quite distinctly.

As his memory of that childish experience ran, he did at the very first sight of that door experience a peculiar emotion, an attraction, a desire to get to the door and open it and walk in. And at the same time he had the clearest conviction that either it was unwise or it was wrong of him – he could not tell which – to yield to this attraction. He insisted upon it as a curious thing that he knew from the very beginning – unless memory has played him the queerest trick – that the door was unfastened, and that he could go in as he chose.

I seem to see the figure of that little boy, drawn and repelled. And it was very clear in his mind, too, though why it should be so was never explained, that his father would be very angry if he went in through that door.

Wallace described all these moments of hesitation to me with the utmost particularity. He went right past the door, and then, with his hands in his pockets and making an infantile attempt to whistle, strolled right along beyond the end of the wall. There he recalls a number of mean dirty shops, and particularly that of a plumber and decorator with a dusty disorder of earthenware pipes, sheet lead, ball taps, pattern books of wallpaper, and tins of enamel. He stood pretending to examine these things, and *coveting*, passionately desiring, the green door.

Then, he said, he had a gust of emotion. He made a run for it, lest hesitation should grip him again; he went plumb with outstretched hand through the green door and let it slam behind him. And so, in a trice, he came into the garden that has haunted all his life.

It was very difficult for Wallace to give me his full sense of that garden into which he came.

There was something in the very air of it that exhilarated, that gave one a sense of lightness and good happening and well-being; there was something in the sight of it that made all its colour clean and perfect and subtly luminous. In the instant of coming into it one was exquisitely glad — as only in rare moments, and when one is young and joyful one can be glad in this world. And everything was beautiful there. . . .

Wallace mused before he went on telling me. "You see," he said, with the doubtful inflection of a man who pauses at incredible things, "there were two great panthers there. . . . Yes, spotted panthers. And I was not afraid. There was a long wide path with marble-edged flower borders on either side, and these two huge velvety beasts were playing there with a ball. One looked up and came towards me, a little curious as it seemed. It came right up to me, rubbed its soft round ear very gently against the small hand I held out, and purred. It was, I tell you, an enchanted garden. I know. And the size? Oh! it stretched far and wide, this way and that. I believe there were hills far away. Heaven knows where West Kensington had suddenly got to. And somehow it was just like coming home.

"You know, in the very moment the door swung to behind me, I forgot the road with its fallen chestnut leaves, its cabs and tradesmen's carts, I forgot the sort of gravitational pull back to the discipline and obedience of home, I forgot all hesitations and fear, forgot discretion, forgot all the intimate realities of this life. I became in a moment a very glad and wonder-happy little boy — in another world. It was a world with a different quality, a warmer, more penetrating, and mellower light, with a faint clear gladness in its air, and wisps of sun-touched cloud in the blueness of its sky. And before me ran this long wide path, invitingly, with weedless beds on either side, rich with untended flowers, and these two great panthers. I put my little hands fearlessly on their soft fur, and caressed their round ears and the sensitive corners under their ears, and played with them, and it was as though they welcomed me home. There was a keen sense of homecoming in my mind, and when presently a tall, fair girl appeared in the pathway and came to meet me, smiling, and said, 'Well?' to me, and lifted me and kissed me, and put me down and led me by the hand, there was no amazement, but only an impression of delightful rightness, of being reminded of happy things that had in some strange way been overlooked. There were broad red steps, I remember, that came into view between spikes of delphinium, and up these we went to a great avenue between very old and shady dark trees. All down this avenue, you know, between the red chapped stems, were marble seats of honour and statuary, and very tame and friendly white doves.

"Along this cool avenue my girl-friend led me, looking down — I recall the pleasant lines, the finely-modelled chin of her sweet kind face — asking me questions in a soft, agreeable voice, and telling me things, pleasant things, I know, though what they were I was never able to recall. . . . Presently a Capuchin monkey, very clean, with a fur of ruddy brown and kindly hazel eyes, came down a tree to us and ran beside me, looking up at me and grinning, and presently leaped to my shoulder. So we two went on our way in great happiness."

He paused.

"Go on," I said.

"I remember little things. We passed an old man musing among laurels, I remember, and a place gay with parakeets, and came through a broad shaded colonnade to a spacious cool palace, full of pleasant fountains, full of beautiful things, full of the quality and promise of heart's desire. And there many things and many people, some that still seem to stand out clearly and some that are vaguer; but all these people were beautiful and kind. In some way – I don't know how – it was conveyed to me that they all were kind to me, glad to have me there, and filling me with gladness by their gestures, by the touch of their hands, by the welcome and love in their eyes. Yes –"

He mused for a while. "Playmates I found there. That was much to me, because I was a lonely little boy. They played delightful games in a grass-covered court where there was a sundial set about with flowers. And as one played one loved. . . .

"But – it's odd – there's a gap in my memory. I don't remember the games we played. I never remembered. Afterwards, as a child, I spent long hours trying, even with tears, to recall the form of that happiness. I wanted to play it all over again – in my nursery – by myself. No! All I remember is the happiness and two dear playfellows who were most with me. . . . Then presently came a sombre dark woman, with a grave, pale face and dreamy eyes, a sombre woman, wearing a soft long robe of pale purple, who carried a book, and beckoned and took me aside with her into a gallery above a hall – though my playmates were loth to have me go, and ceased their game and stood watching as I was carried away. 'Come back to us!' they cried. 'Come back to us soon!' I looked up at her face, but she heeded them not at all. Her face was very gentle and grave. She took me to a seat in the gallery, and I stood beside her, ready to look at her book as she opened it upon her knee. The pages fell open. She pointed, and I looked, marvelling, for in the living pages of that book I saw myself; it was a story about myself, and in it were all the things that had happened to me since ever I was born. . . .

"It was wonderful to me, because the pages of that book were not pictures, you understand, but realities."

Wallace paused gravely – looked at me doubtfully.

"Go on," I said. "I understand."

"They were realities – yes, they must have been; people moved and things came and went in them; my dear mother, whom I had near forgotten; then my father, stern and upright, the servants, the nursery, all the familiar things of home. Then the front door and the busy streets, with traffic to and fro. I looked and marvelled, and looked half doubtfully again into the woman's face and turned the pages over, skipping this and that, to see more of this book and more, and so at last I came to myself hovering and hesitating outside the green door in the long white wall, and felt again the conflict and the fear.

" 'And next?' I cried, and would have turned on, but the cool hand of the grave woman delayed me.

" 'Next?' I insisted, and struggled gently with her hand, pulling up her fingers with all my childish strength, and as she yielded and the page came over she bent down upon me like a shadow and kissed my brow.

"But the page did not show the enchanted garden, nor the panthers, nor the girl who had led me by the hand, nor the playfellows who had been so loth to let me go. It showed a long grey street in West Kensington, in that chill hour of afternoon before the lamps are lit; and I was there, a wretched little figure, weeping aloud, for all that I could do to restrain myself, and I was weeping because I could not return to my dear playfellows who had called after me, 'Come back to us! Come back to us soon!' I was there. This was no page in a book, but harsh reality; that enchanted place and the restraining hand of the grave mother at whose knee I stood had gone — whither had they gone?"

He halted again, and remained for a time staring into the fire.

"Oh! the woefulness of that return!" he murmured.

"Well?" I said, after a minute or so.

"Poor little wretch I was! — brought back to this grey world again! As I realized the fullness of what had happened to me, I gave way to quite ungovernable grief. And the shame and humiliation of that public weeping and my disgraceful home-coming remain with me still. I see again the benevolent-looking old gentleman in gold spectacles who stopped and spoke to me — prodding me first with his umbrella. 'Poor little chap,' said he; 'and are you lost then?' — and me a London boy of five and more!

And he must needs bring in a kindly young policeman and make a crowd of me, and so march me home. Sobbing, conspicuous, and frightened, I came back from the enchanted garden to the steps of my father's house.

"That is as well as I can remember my vision of that garden — the garden that haunts me still. Of course, I can convey nothing of that indescribable quality of translucent unreality, that difference from the common things of experience that hung about it all; but that — that is what happened. If it was a dream, I am sure it was a day-time and altogether extraordinary dream. . . . H'm! — naturally there followed a terrible questioning, by my aunt, my father, the nurse, the governess — everyone. . . .

"I tried to tell them, and my father gave me my first thrashing for telling lies. When afterwards I tried to tell my aunt, she punished me again for my wicked persistence. Then, as I said, everyone was forbidden to listen to me, to hear a word about it. Even my fairy-tale books were taken away from me for a time — because I was too 'imaginative'. Eh! Yes, they did that! My father belonged to the old school. . . . And my story was driven back upon myself. I whispered it to my pillow — my pillow that was often damp and salt to my whispering lips with childish tears. And I added always to my official and less fervent prayers this one heartfelt request: 'Please God I may dream of the garden. O! take me back to my garden.' Take me back to my garden! I dreamt often of the garden. I may have added to it, I may have changed it; I do not know. . . . All this, you understand, is an attempt to reconstruct from fragmentary memories a very early experience. Between that and the other consecutive memories of my boyhood there is a gulf. A time came when it seemed impossible I should ever speak of that wonder glimpse again."

I asked an obvious question.

"No," he said. "I don't remember that I ever attempted to find my way back to the garden in those early years. This seems odd to me now, but I think that very probably a closer watch was kept on my movements after this misadventure to prevent my going astray. No, it wasn't till you knew me that I tried for the garden again. And I believe there was a period — incredible as it seems now — when I forgot the garden altogether — when I was about eight or nine it may have been. Do you remember me as a kid at Saint Athelstan's?"

"Rather!"

"I didn't show any signs, did I, in those days of having a secret dream?"

He looked up with a sudden smile.

"Did you ever play North-West Passage with me? ... No, of course you didn't come my way!

"It was the sort of game," he went on, "that every imaginative child plays all day. The idea was the discovery of a North-West Passage to school. The way to school was plain enough; the game consisted of finding some way that wasn't plain, starting off ten minutes early in some almost hopeless direction, and working my way round through unaccustomed streets to my goal. And one day I got entangled among some rather low-class streets on the other side of Campden Hill, and I began to think that for once the game would be against me and that I should get to school late. I tried rather desperately a street that seemed a cul-de-sac, and found a passage at the end. I hurried through that with renewed hope. 'I shall do it yet,' I said, and passed a row of frowsy little shops that were inexplicably familiar to me, and behold! there was my long white wall and the green door that led to the enchanted garden!

"The thing whacked upon me suddenly. Then, after all, that garden, that wonderful garden, wasn't a dream!"

He paused.

"I suppose my second experience with the green door marks the world of difference there is between the busy life of a schoolboy and the infinite leisure of a child. Anyhow, this second time I didn't for a moment think of going in straight away. You see —. For one thing, my mind was full of the idea of getting to school in time — set on not breaking my record for punctuality. I must surely have felt *some* little desire at least to try the door — yes. I must have felt that.... But I seem to remember the attraction of the door mainly as another obstacle to my overmastering determination to get to school. I was immensely interested by this discovery I had made, of course — I went on with my mind full of it — but I went on. It didn't check me. I ran past, tugging out my watch, found I had ten minutes still to spare, and then I was going downhill into familiar surroundings. I got to school, breathless, it is true, and wet with perspiration, but in time. I can remember hanging up my coat and hat.... Went right by it and left it behind me. Odd, eh?"

He looked at me thoughtfully. "Of course I didn't know then that it wouldn't always be there. Schoolboys have limited imaginations. I suppose I thought it was an awfully jolly thing to have it there, to know my way back to it; but there was the school tugging at me. I expect I was a good deal distraught and inattentive that morning, recalling what I could of the beautiful strange people I should presently see again. Oddly enough I had no doubt in my mind that they would be glad to see me.... Yes, I must have thought of the garden that morning just as a jolly sort of place to which one might resort in the interludes of a strenuous scholastic career.

"I didn't go that day at all. The next day was a half-holiday, and that may have weighed with me. Perhaps, too, my state of inattention brought down impositions upon me, and docked the margin of time necessary for the *détour*. I don't know. What I do know is that in the meantime the enchanted garden was so much upon my mind that I could not keep it to myself.

"I told — what was his name? — a ferrety-looking youngster we used to call Squiff."

"Young Hopkins," said I.

"Hopkins it was. I did not like telling him. I had a feeling that in some way it was against the rules to tell him, but I did. He was walking part of the way home with me; he was talkative, and if we had not talked about the enchanted garden we should have talked of something else, and it was intolerable to me to think about any other subject. So I blabbed.

"Well, he told my secret. The next day in the play interval I found myself surrounded by half a dozen bigger boys, half teasing, and wholly curious to hear more of the enchanted garden.

There was that big Fawcett — you remember him? — and Carnaby and Morley Reynolds. You weren't there by any chance? No, I think I should have remembered if you were. . . .

"A boy is a creature of odd feelings. I was, I really believe, in spite of my secret self-disgust, a little flattered to have the attention of these big fellows. I remember particularly a moment of pleasure caused by the praise of Crawshaw — you remember Crawshaw major, the son of Crawshaw the composer? — who said it was the best lie he had ever heard. But at the same time there was a really painful undertow of shame at telling what I felt was indeed a sacred secret. That beast Fawcett made a joke about the girl in green —"

Wallace's voice sank with the keen memory of that shame. "I pretended not to hear," he said. "Well, then Carnaby suddenly called me a young liar, and disputed with me when I said the thing was true. I said I knew where to find the green door, could lead them all there in ten minutes. Carnaby became outrageously virtuous, and said I'd have to — and bear out my words or suffer. Did you ever have Carnaby twist your arm? Then perhaps you'll understand how it went with me. I swore my story was true. There was nobody in the school then to save a chap from Carnaby, though Crawshaw put in a word or so. Carnaby had got his game. I grew excited and red-eared, and a little frightened. I behaved altogether like a silly little chap, and the outcome of it all was that instead of starting alone for my enchanted garden, I led the way presently — cheeks flushed, ears hot, eyes smarting, and my soul one burning misery and shame — for a party of six mocking, curious, and threatening schoolfellows.

"We never found the white wall and the green door. . . ."

"You mean —"

"I mean I couldn't find it. I would have found it if I could.

"And afterwards when I could go alone I couldn't find it. I never found it. I seem now to have been always looking for it through my schoolboy days, but I never came upon it — never."

"Did the fellows — make it disagreeable?"

"Beastly. . . . Carnaby held a council over me for wanton lying. I remember how I sneaked home and upstairs to hide the marks of my blubbering. But when I cried myself to sleep at last it wasn't for Carnaby, but for the garden, for the beautiful afternoon I had hoped for, for the sweet friendly women and the waiting playfellows, and the game I had hoped to learn again, that beautiful forgotten game. . . .

"I believed firmly that if I had not told — . . . . I had bad times after that — crying at night and wool-gathering by day. For two terms I slacked and had bad reports. Do you remember? Of course you would! It was *you* — your beating me in mathematics that brought me back to the grind again."

For a time my friend stared silently into the red heart of the fire. Then he said: "I never saw it again until I was seventeen.

"It leaped upon me for the third time — as I was driving to Paddington on my way to Oxford and a scholarship. I had just one momentary glimpse. I was leaning over the apron of my hansom smoking a cigarette, and no doubt thinking myself no end of a man of the world, and suddenly there was the door, the wall, the dear sense of unforgettable and still attainable things.

"We clattered by — I too taken by surprise to stop my cab until we were well past and round a corner. Then I had a queer moment, a double and divergent movement of my will: I tapped the little door in the roof of the cab, and brought my arm down to pull out my watch. 'Yes, sir!' said the cabman smartly. 'Er — well — it's nothing,' I cried. '*My* mistake! We haven't much time! Go on!' And he went on. . . .

"I got my scholarship. And the night after I was told of that I sat over my fire in my little upper room, my study, in my father's house, with his praise — his rare praise — and his sound counsels ringing in my ears, and I smoked my favourite pipe — the formidable bulldog of adolescence — and thought of that door in the long white wall. 'If I had stopped,' I thought, 'I should have missed my scholarship, I should have missed Oxford — muddled all the fine career before me! I begin to see things better!' I fell to musing deeply, but I did not doubt then this career of mine was a thing that merited sacrifice.

"Those dear friends and that clear atmosphere seemed very

sweet to me, very fine but remote. My grip was fixing now upon the world. I saw another door opening – the door of my career."

He stared again into the fire. Its red light picked out a stubborn strength in his face for just one flickering moment, and then it vanished again.

"Well," he said and sighed. "I have served that career. I have done – much work, much hard work. But I have dreamt of the enchanted garden a thousand dreams, and seen its door, or at least glimpsed its door, four times since then. Yes – four times. For a while this world was so bright and interesting, seemed so full of meaning and opportunity, that the half-effaced charm of the garden was by comparison gentle and remote. Who wants to pat panthers on the way to dinner with pretty women and distinguished men? I came down to London from Oxford, a man of bold promise that I have done something to redeem. Something – and yet there have been disappointments. . . .

"Twice I have been in love – I will not dwell on that – but once, as I went to some one who, I knew, doubted whether I dared to come, I took a short cut at a venture through an unfrequented road near Earl's Court, and so happened on a white wall and a familiar green door. 'Odd!' said I to myself, 'but I thought this place was on Campden Hill. It's the place I never could find somehow – like counting Stonehenge – the place of that queer daydream of mine.' And I went by it intent upon my purpose. It had no appeal to me that afternoon.

"I had just a moment's impulse to try the door, three steps aside were needed at the most – though I was sure enough in my heart that it would open to me – and then I thought that doing so might delay me on the way to that appointment in which my honour was involved. Afterwards I was sorry for my punctuality – I might at least have peeped in and waved a hand to those panthers, but I knew enough by this time not to seek again belatedly that which is not found by seeking. Yes, that time made me very sorry. . . .

"Years of hard work after that, and never a sight of the door. It's only recently it has come back to me. With it there has come a sense as though some thin tarnish had spread itself over my

world. I began to think of it as a sorrowful and bitter thing that
I should never see that door again. Perhaps I was suffering a little
from overwork — perhaps it was what I've heard spoken of as
the feeling of forty. I don't know. But certainly the keen brightness that makes effort easy has gone out of things recently, and
that just at a time — with all these new political developments —
when I ought to be working. Odd, isn't it? But I do begin to find
life toilsome, its rewards, as I come near them, cheap. I began a
little while ago to want the garden quite badly. Yes — and I've
seen it three times."

"The garden?"

"No — the door! And I haven't gone in!"

He leaned over the table to me, with an enormous sorrow in
his voice as he spoke. "Thrice I have had my chance — *thrice!*
If ever that door offers itself to me again, I swore, I will go in,
out of this dust and heat, out of this dry glitter of vanity, out of
these toilsome futilities. I will go and never return. This time I
will stay. . . . I swore it, and when the time came — I *didn't* go.

"Three times in one year I have passed that door and failed to
enter. Three times in the last year.

"The first time was on the night of the snatch division on the
Tenants' Redemption Bill, on which the Government was saved
by a majority of three. You remember? No one on our side —
perhaps very few on the opposite side — expected the end that
night. Then the debate collapsed like egg-shells. I and Hotchkiss
were dining with his cousin at Brentford; we were both unpaired,
and we were called up by telephone, and set off at once in his
cousin's motor. We got in barely in time, and on the way we
passed my wall and the door — livid in the moonlight, blotched
with hot yellow as the glare of our lamps lit it, but unmistakable.
'My God!' cried I. 'What?' said Hotchkiss. 'Nothing!' I answered, and the moment passed.

" 'I've made a great sacrifice,' I told the whip as I got in. 'They
all have,' he said, and hurried by.

"I do not see how I could have done otherwise then. And the
next occasion was as I rushed to my father's bedside to bid that
stern old man farewell. Then, too, the claims of life were

imperative. But the third time was different; it happened a week ago. It fills me with hot remorse to recall it. I was with Gurker and Ralphs — it's no secret now, you know, that I've had my talk with Gurker. We had been dining at Frobisher's, and the talk had become intimate between us. The question of my place in the reconstructed Ministry lay always just over the boundary of the discussion. Yes — yes. That's all settled. It needn't be talked about yet, but there's no reason to keep a secret from you ... Yes — thanks! thanks! But let me tell you my story.

"Then, on that night things were very much in the air. My position was a very delicate one. I was keenly anxious to get some definite word from Gurker, but was hampered by Ralphs' presence. I was using the best power of my brain to keep that light and careless talk not too obviously directed to the point that concerned me. I had to. Ralphs' behaviour since has more than justified my caution. . . . Ralphs, I knew, would leave us beyond the Kensington High Street, and then I could surprise Gurker by a sudden frankness. One has sometimes to resort to these little devices. . . . And then it was that in the margin of my field of vision I became aware once more of the white wall, the green door before us down the road.

"We passed it talking. I passed it. I can still see the shadow of Gurker's marked profile, his opera hat tilted forward over his prominent nose, the many folds of his neck wrap going before my shadow and Ralphs' as we sauntered past.

"I passed within twenty inches of the door. 'If I say good night to them, and go in,' I asked myself, 'what will happen?' And I was all a-tingle for that word with Gurker.

"I could not answer that question in the tangle of my other problems. 'They will think me mad,' I thought. 'And suppose I vanish now? — Amazing disappearance of a prominent politician!' That weighed with me. A thousand inconceivable petty worldlinesses weighed with me in that crisis."

Then he turned on me with a sorrowful smile, and, speaking slowly, "Here I am!" he said.

"Here I am!" he repeated, "and my chance has gone from me. Three times in one year the door has been offered me — that door that goes into peace, into delight, into a beauty beyond dreaming, a kindness no man on earth can know. And I have rejected it, Redmond, and it has gone —"

"How do you know?"

"I know. I know. I am left now to work it out, to stick to the tasks that held me so strongly when my moments came. You say I have success — this vulgar, tawdry, irksome, envied thing. I have it." He had a walnut in his big hand. "If that was my success," he said, and crushed it, and held it out for me to see.

"Let me tell you something, Redmond. This loss is destroying me. For two months, for ten weeks nearly now, I have done no work at all, except the most necessary and urgent duties. My soul is full of inappeasable regrets. At nights — when it is less likely I shall be recognized — I go out. I wander. Yes. I wonder what people would think of that if they knew. A Cabinet Minister, the responsible head of that most vital of all departments, wandering alone — grieving — sometimes near audibly lamenting — for a door, for a garden!"

I can see now his rather pallid face, and the unfamiliar sombre fire that had come into his eyes. I see him very vividly tonight. I sit recalling his words, his tones, and last evening's *Westminster Gazette* still lies on my sofa, containing the notice of his death. At lunch today the club was busy with his death. We talked of nothing else.

They found his body very early yesterday morning in a deep excavation near East Kensington Station. It is one of two shafts that have been made in connexion with an extension of the railway southward. It is protected from the intrusion of the public by a hoarding upon the high road, in which a small doorway has been cut for the convenience of some of the workmen who live in that direction. The doorway was left unfastened through a misunderstanding between two gangers, and through it he made his way.

My mind is darkened with questions and riddles.

It would seem he walked all the way from the House that night — he has frequently walked home during the past Session —

and so it is I figure his dark form coming along the late and empty streets, wrapped up, intent. And then did the pale electric lights near the station cheat the rough planking into a semblance of white? Did that fatal unfastened door awaken some memory?

Was there, after all, ever any green door in the wall at all?

I do not know. I have told his story as he told it to me. There are times when I believe that Wallace was no more than the victim of the coincidence between a rare but not unprecedented type of hallucination and a careless trap, but that indeed is not my profoundest belief. You may think me superstitious, if you will, and foolish; but, indeed, I am more than half convinced that he had, in truth, an abnormal gift, and a sense, something — I know not what — that in the guise of a wall and door offered him an outlet, a secret and peculiar passage of escape into another and altogether more beautiful world. At any rate, you will say, it betrayed him in the end. But did it betray him? There you touch the inmost mystery of these dreamers, these men of vision and the imagination. We see our world fair and common, the hoarding and the pit. By our daylight standard he walked out of security into darkness, danger, and death.

But did he see like that?

QUESTIONS

1. Like many stories by H. G. Wells, "The Door in the Wall" blends fantasy with a rather sad comment on the painful realities of human existence. Through the medium of this story, what do you think the author is saying about man and his search for truth?

2. (a) What method does Wells use in the first four paragraphs to build up an atmosphere of mystery surrounding Wallace?
(b) In the next six paragraphs, he establishes some important character traits of Wallace. Tell what these are, and explain the author's methods of revealing them.
(c) In what way does our knowledge of these traits prepare us for Wallace's story?

3. In describing his first mystical experience, Wallace includes a

wealth of detail — his precise age, the time of year, the whereabouts of the door, and the appearance of the garden and its occupants. What might be the author's purposes in having him recount his early experience in such detail?

4. Briefly describe the circumstances of Wallace's second and third discoveries of the door. In your account of the two occasions, compare his motives for decision each time.

5. Years pass by, and Wallace does not catch sight of the door at all. What suggestions does the author put into the story to account for this gap?

6. As Wallace's narrative to Redmond draws to a close, how does Wells indicate to us that the life of the former is moving rapidly towards some kind of climax?

7. At the end of the third part of the story, the author carefully inserts the last detail necessary to make plausible the manner of Wallace's death. What is this detail?

8. Readers are apt to hold strong views about conclusions like the one in this story. Explain your opinion regarding the appropriateness of the ending to "The Door in the Wall".

*Colin Malcolm*
*McDougall*

# The firing squad

*Colin Malcolm McDougall (b. 1917) was born in Montreal and educated at Lower Canada College. After graduation from McGill University in 1940, he joined the Canadian Army in which he served with distinction, being mentioned in dispatches, and being awarded the Distinguished Service Order. After the war, he had his short stories published in various magazines. McDougall is at present the registrar at McGill University. In 1953, "The Firing Squad" won first prize in Maclean's' fiction-contest and the President's Medal (University of Western Ontario) as the best story of the year by a Canadian. His novel, Execution, was developed from this story and received the Governor General's Award for Fiction in 1959. "The Firing Squad" appears here by permission of the author.*

HE WAS THE FIRST Canadian soldier sentenced to death, and rear headquarters in Italy seethed with the prospect of carrying it out. At his marble-topped desk in Rome Major-General Paul Vincent read the instructions from London with distaste. The findings of the court martial had been confirmed by Ottawa — that meant by a special session of the cabinet, the General supposed — and it was now the direct responsibility of the Area Commander that the execution of Private Sydney Jones should be proceeded with "as expeditiously as possible."

The hum of voices and the quick beat of teletypes in the outer office marked the measure of Rome's agitation. No one had expected this confirmation of sentence. Not even the officers who had sentenced Private Jones to death. For them, indeed, there had been little choice; Jones had even wanted to plead guilty, but the court had automatically changed his plea, and gone on to record its inevitable finding and sentence.

The salient facts of the case filed quickly through the neat corridors of General Vincent's mind. This Jones, a young soldier of twenty-two, had deserted his unit, had joined with a group of deserter-gangsters who operated in Rome and Naples, and had been present when his companions shot and killed a U.S. military policeman. All this Jones admitted, and the court could pass no other sentence. The execution of a Canadian soldier, however, was more than a military matter: it touched on public policy; and higher authorities had never before confirmed a sentence of death. But now the confirming order was in his hands and the train of events must be set in motion.

General Vincent sighed. He preferred to think of himself as the business executive he happened to be rather than a general officer whose duty it was to order a man's death. An execution was something alien and infinitely distasteful. Well, if this thing had to be done under his command at least it need not take place under his personal orders. From the beginning he had known just the man for the job. Already the teletype had clicked off its command to Volpone, the reinforcement base where Private Jones was imprisoned, and a staff car would now be rushing the commander of that base, Brigadier Benny Hatfield, to Rome. The General sighed again and turned to some more congenial correspondence on his desk.

A dirt track spiraled out of Volpone and mounted in white gashes upon the forested mountain side. Fifty infantry reinforcements, fresh from Canada, were spaced along the first two miles of zigzag road. They carried all the paraphernalia of their fledgling trade: rifles, machine guns, and light mortars. Some were trying to run, lurching ahead with painful steps; others stopped to stand panting in their own small lakes of sweat. One or two lay at the roadside, faces turned from the sun, awaiting the stabbing scorn of their sergeant with spent indifference. But they all spat out the clogging dust, and cursed the officer who led them.

Farther up the hillside this man ran with the gait of an athlete pushing himself to the limit of endurance. Head down he ran doggedly through the dust and the heat; he ran as though trying to outdistance some merciless pursuer. His eyes were shut tight and he was inhaling from an almost empty reservoir of breath. Captain John Adam was going to run up that mountainside until he could run no more. He was running from last night, and all the nights which still lay ahead. He was running from his own sick self.

Then, almost at the halfway mark, he aimed himself at a patch of bush underneath the cliff and smashed into it headlong. He lay quite still; he had achieved exhaustion: the closest condition to forgetfulness he could ever find.

For Captain John Adam found it unbearable to live with himself and with his future. He had lost his manhood. As an infantry company commander he had drawn daily strength and sustenance from the respect of his fellow fighting men. They knew him as a brave leader, a compassionate man. He had been granted the trust and friendship of men when it is all they have left to give, and this he knew to be the ultimate gift, the highest good. And then, one sun-filled morning, he had forfeited these things for ever. He had cracked wide open; he had cried his fear and panic to the world; he had run screaming from the battle, through the ranks of his white-faced men. He had been sent back here to Volpone in unexpressed disgrace while the authorities decided what to do with him.

Now Captain John Adam rolled over. There was always some supremely unimportant next matter which had to be decided. He lighted a cigarette and gave his whole attention to the small column of climbing smoke. Well, he would sit here until Sergeant Konzuk whipped this miserable, straggling pack up to him, and then he would reveal their next phase of training.

He stood up, a tall young man, looking brisk and competent. His sun-browned face, his blue eyes, the power of his easy movements, even the cigarette dangling negligently from his lips, all seemed to proclaim that here was the ideal young infantry officer.

"Sergeant Konzuk," Captain Adam called now. "Get these men the hell back to barracks, and leave me alone here!"

The sergeant did not look surprised. He was used to such things by now, and this was no officer to argue with. Sure, he'd take them back to barracks, and let Adam do his own explaining. "All right, you guys — on your feet!" said Konzuk. It was no skin to him.

It was late afternoon by the time he had smoked the last of his cigarettes and Adam came down from the mountain. Striding through the camp he frowned with displeasure when he saw the hulking form of Padre Dixon planted squarely in his path. Normally, he knew, he would have liked this big chaplain. There was a sense of inner calm, of repose and reliability about Padre Dixon. Although in his early fifties he had served with devoted competence as chaplain to an infantry battalion. But Adam considered himself to be an outcast, no longer holding any claims upon the men who did the fighting: the men who still owned their self-respect. He made a point of refusing the friendliness which this big man was trying to offer.

"Mind if I walk along with you, son?" Adam was forced to stop while the Padre knocked his pipe against his boot.

The two men walked on together through the dusk, picking their way between the huts and the barrack blocks. As they neared the officers' mess the Padre stopped and his fingers gripped Adam's arm. He pointed to a small grey hut just within the barbed wire of the camp entrance. "That's where poor Jones is waiting out his time," the Padre said.

"Well?"

The Padre shrugged and seemed busy with his pipe. "No matter what he's done he's a brave boy, and he's in a dreadful position now."

"He won't be shot." Adam repeated the general feeling of the camp without real interest. "They'll never confirm the sentence."

The Padre looked him directly in the face. "Adam," he said. "It *has* been confirmed. He is going to be executed!"

"No!" Adam breathed his disbelief aloud. He was truly shocked, and for this instant his own sick plight was forgotten. This other thing seemed so — improper. That a group of Canadians could come together in this alien land for the purpose of destroying one of their own kind ... And every day, up at the battle, every effort was being made to *save* life; there were so few of them in Italy, and so pitifully many were being killed every day. This thing was simply — not right.

His eyes sought for the Padre's. "But why?" he asked, with a kind of hurt in his voice. "Tell me — why?"

"The boy's guilty, after all."

"Technically — he was only a witness. And even if he is guilty, do you think this thing is right?"

The Padre could not ignore the urgency in Adam's voice. He spoke at last with unaccustomed sharpness. "No," he said. "It may be something that has to be done — but it will never be right."

The two men looked at one another in the gathering Italian night. For a moment their thoughts seemed to merge and flow together down the same pulsing stream. But then a new idea came to Adam. "Padre," he said. "Why are you telling *me* about this?"

Then they both saw the figure running toward them from the officers' mess. It was Ramsay, the ever-flurried, ever-flustered Camp Adjutant. He panted to a stop in front of them. "Adam," he gasped out. "The Brigadier wants you at once!"

Brigadier Benny Hatfield waited patiently in his office. He liked to feed any new or disturbing thoughts through the mill of his mind until the gloss of familiarity made them less troublesome. Early in his career he had discovered that the calibre of his mind was not sufficiently large for the rank he aspired to, and so deliberately he had cultivated other qualities which would achieve the same end. He emphasized an air of outspoken bluntness, his physical toughness, a presumed knowledge of the way the "troops" thought, and his ability to work like a horse. Indeed the impression he sometimes conveyed was that of a grizzled war horse, fanatic about good soldiering, but with it all intensely loyal, and a very good fellow. His appearance served to support this role: there was something horselike in the wide grin that lifted his straggling mustache, a grin that proved how affable and immensely approachable he really was.

Now he sat and considered his interview with General Vincent. He understood his superior's unexpressed motives perfectly well: it was a straight question of passing the buck and he intended staying up all night looking after his own interests. This execution was a simple matter of military discipline, after all, and he would ensure that it was carried out in such a way that no possible discredit could reflect on himself. The General, he believed, had made an intelligent choice, and he had an equally good selection of his own in mind. The file of Captain John Adam lay open on his desk.

The Brigadier sat up straight. Ramsay was ushering Captain Adam into his presence.

This was the interview Adam had dreaded since his arrival at the reinforcement base. But he showed no sign now of the sickness and fear that gnawed inside him. He stood at attention while the Brigadier leafed through the file before him.

The Brigadier looked up at last. "Well," he stated. "Captain John Adam." His eyes bored steadily at Adam's face and he waited in silence. He knew that in a moment his unwavering stare would force some betrayal of guilt or inferiority. He waited and at last he was rewarded: the sweat swelled on Adam's forehead, and the man before him felt it essential to break the intolerable silence. "Yes, sir," Adam had to say.

The Brigadier stood up then. "Well," he said again. "It can't be as bad as all that, can it, boy?" His mouth lifted the straggling mustache in a grimace of affability, and despite himself Adam felt a small rush of gratitude.

But then the smile died. "It does not please me," the Brigadier said coldly, "to receive the worst possible reports about you." He consulted the notes on his desk. "You have been AWL twice; there is some question of a jeep you took without permission; and my officers say that you act with no sense of responsibility."

The Brigadier was frowning, his lips pursed. His glance

bored steadily at Adam. But then there was a sudden transforma-
tion. His smile was reborn in new and fuller glory. "Sit down,
boy," he urged. He clapped Adam on the shoulder and guided
him into the chair beside his desk.

The Brigadier hitched forward in his seat. Now there was a
warmth of friendly concern in his voice. "Adam, boy," he said.
"*We* know none of that piddling stuff matters. However – you
have read this report from Colonel Dodd?"

It was a needless question. Adam knew the report by memory.
It was an "adverse" report: it was the reason why he was back
here at Volpone. That piece of paper was his doom. "Not fit to
command men in action," it read; "not suitable material for the
field." And Colonel Dodd had phrased it as gently as possible; in
his own presence he had written it down with pity on his face.

With ungoverned ease his mind slipped back to that sun-filled
morning on the Hitler Line. They were walking through a
meadow – slowly, for there were Schu mines in the grass – and
they moved toward a hidden place of horror: a line of dug-in
tank turrets, and mine-strewn belts of wire. And then the earth
suddenly erupted with shell and mortar bursts; they floundered
in a beaten zone of observed machine-gun fire. A few men got as
far as the wire, but none of them lived. There was a regrouping
close to the start line, and Adam was ordered to attack again.

The first symptom he noticed was that his body responded to
his mind's orders several seconds too late. He became worried at
this time lag, the fact that his mind and body seemed about to
divide, to assume their own separate identities. Then the air
bursts shook the world; no hole in the ground was shelter from
the rain of deafening black explosions in the sky above them.
Then he remembered the terrible instant that the separation became complete, that he got up and shouted his shame to the
world. He got up from his ditch, and he ran blubbering like a
baby through his white-faced men. And some of his men followed him, back into the arms of Colonel Dodd.

"Yes," Adam said now, his face white. "I've read the report."

Brigadier Hatfield spoke softly. "If that report goes forward
from here you'll be in a bad way – at least returned to Canada

for Adjutant General's disposal, some second-rate kind of discharge, the reputation always clinging to you ..." The Brigadier shook his head. "That would be a pity."

*If* the report goes forward ... A pulse of excitement beat in Adam's throat. What did he mean — was there any possibility that the report could be stopped here, that in the eyes of the world he could retain some shreds of self-respect? Adam's breath came faster; he sat up straight.

"Adam!" The Brigadier pounded a fist upon his desk. "*I* have confidence in you. Of all the officers under my command I have selected *you* for a mission of the highest importance."

Adam blinked his disbelief, but the hope swelled strong inside him.

"Yes," the Brigadier said steadily. "*You* are to command the firing squad for the execution of Private Jones!"

Adam blinked again and he turned his head away. For a moment he was weak with nausea the flood of shame was so sour inside him. "No," he heard his voice saying. "I can't do it."

The Brigadier's smile grew broader, and he spoke with soft assurance. "But you can, my boy. But you can." And the Brigadier told him how.

It was all very neatly contrived. Adam had his choice, of course. On the one hand he could choose routine disposal of his case by higher authorities. Colonel Dodd's report, together with Brigadier Hatfield's own statement, would ensure an outcome which, as the Brigadier described it, would cause "deep shame to his family and friends," and Adam was sure of that. On the other hand if he performed this necessary act of duty, this simple military function, then Colonel Dodd's report would be destroyed. He could return to Canada as soon as he desired, bearing Brigadier Hatfield's highest recommendations.

The Brigadier went on to say that the man Jones was a convicted murderer — that Adam should have no scruples on that score; that he relied on his known ability to handle men under difficult circumstances ...

Adam listened and each soft word seemed to add to his

degradation. This was where the Hitler Line had brought him; this was the inevitable consequence of his lost manhood.

The Brigadier's voice was kindly; his words flowed endlessly like a soft stream of liquid. Then the voice paused. "Of course," the Brigadier said, "it is a task for a determined and courageous man." His glance darted over Adam's bent head and flickered around the room.

Adam broke the silence at last. He spoke without looking up. "All right," he said. "I'll do it."

The Brigadier's response was quick and warm. "Good," he said. "Good *fellow!*" His smile was almost caressing. But to Adam that smile seemed to spread across the horselike face like a stain. The small office and the space between the two men was suddenly close and unbearably warm.

"One more thing, Adam." The Brigadier spoke with soft emphasis. "The members of the firing squad can be detailed later, but your sergeant must be a first-rate man, and — it is most desirable that he be a volunteer. Do you understand?"

Adam forced himself to nod.

The Brigadier stared directly in Adam's face. His voice now rang with the steel of command. "All right," he said. "Bring me the sergeant's name and a draft of your parade orders by 1100 hours tomorrow. Any questions?"

"No, sir." Adam stood up.

"Good boy. Get to it, and remember — I'm relying on you."

"Yes, sir."

The Brigadier leaned back and allowed the smile to possess his face. He had selected exactly the right man for this delicate job: a man of competence who was *bound* to carry the thing through to its final conclusion.

By next morning the news had raced to every Canadian in Italy. At the battle up north men heard about this execution with a dull kind of wonder. Advancing into the attack it was brought to them like bad news in a letter from home; they looked at each other uneasily, or they laughed and turned away. It was not the death of one man back in a place called Volpone that mattered. It was simply that up here they measured and counted their own existence so dear that an unnecessary death, a *planned* death of one of their own fellows seemed somehow shameful. It made them sour and restless as they checked their weapon and ammunition loads.

In the camp at Volpone it was the sole topic of conversation. All officers had been instructed by Brigadier Hatfield to explain to the men that the prisoner, Jones, had been convicted of murder, and therefore had to pay the penalty that the law demanded. But the law was not clear to these men: from their own close knowledge of sudden death they did not understand how a man could commit a murder without lifting a weapon. And those who had seen Private Sydney Jones could not picture that harmless boy as a murderer. Still, the officers went to great pains to explain the legal point involved.

It was soon known that the news had reached the prisoner also, although, to be sure, it did not seem to have changed his routine in the least. All his waking hours were busied with an intense disdisplay of military activity. The guard sergeant reported that he made and remade his bed several times a day, working earnestly to achieve the neatest possible tuck of his blanket. The floor was swept five times a day and scrubbed at least once. His battle-dress was ironed to knife-edge exactitude, and his regimental flashes resewn to his tunic as though the smartest possible fit at the shoulder was always just eluding him. At times he would glance at the stack of magazines the Padre brought him, but these were thrown aside as soon as a visitor entered his room. Private Jones would spring to a quiveringly erect position of attention; he would respond to questions with a quick, cheerful smile. He was the embodiment of the keen, alert, and well turned-out private soldier.

The truth was, of course, that Private Jones was a somewhat pliable young man who was desperately anxious to please. He was intent on proving himself such a good soldier that the generals would take note and approve, and never do anything very bad to him. The idea that some of his fellow soldiers might take him out and shoot him was a terrible abstraction, quite beyond his imagination. Consequently Private Jones did not believe in the possibility of his own execution. Even when the Padre came and tried to prepare him Private Jones simply jumped eagerly to attention, polished boots glittering, and rattled off, head high: "Yes, sir. Very good, sir."

A surprising amount of administrative detail is required to arrange an execution. The Brigadier was drawing up an elaborate operation order, with each phase to be checked and double-checked. There were the official witness, the medical officers, the chaplain, the guards, the firing squad, of course; and the conveyance and placing of all these to the proper spot at the right time.

But Captain Adam's first problem was more serious than any of this: his first attempts to recruit the sergeant for his firing squad met with utter failure. After conferring with the Brigadier he decided upon a new approach, and he went in search of Sergeant Konzuk.

The sergeant was lying at ease on his bed reading a magazine. When Adam came in Konzuk scowled. He swung his boots over the side of the bed and he crossed his thick arms over his chest.

Adam wasted no time. "Konzuk," he said. "I want you as sergeant of the firing squad."

The sergeant laughed rudely.

"Never mind that," Adam said. "Wait till you hear about this deal."

"Look," Sergeant Konzuk said. He stood up and his eyes were angry on Adam's face. "I done my share of killing. Those that like it can do this job."

Adam's tone did not change. "You're married, Konzuk. You've a wife and two kids. Well, you can be back in Winnipeg within the month."

Konzuk's mouth opened; his eyes were wide. His face showed all the wild thoughts thronging through his mind. The sergeant had left Canada in 1940; his wife wrote him one laborious letter a month. But his frown returned and his fists were clenched.

"Look," Konzuk said, fumbling with his words. "This kid's one of us — see. It ain't right!"

"Winnipeg — within the month."

Konzuk's eyes shifted and at last his glance settled on the floor. "All right," he said, after a moment. "All right, I'll do it."

"Good." Adam sought for and held the sergeant's eyes. "And remember this, Konzuk — that 'kid' is a murderer!"

"Yes, sir."

Then they sat down together. Adam found no satisfaction in his victory, in the full obedience he now commanded. Sitting on the iron bed in Konzuk's room they spoke in lowered voices, and Adam felt as though they were conspiring together to commit some obscene act.

The ten members of the firing squad were detailed the same day. Adam and Konzuk prepared the list of names and brought the group to be interviewed by Brigadier Hatfield in his office. And after that Sergeant Konzuk had a quiet talk with each man. Adam did not ask what the sergeant said; he was satisfied that none of the men came to him to protest.

Adam found his time fully occupied. He had installed his ten men in a separate hut of their own; there were some drill movements to be practised; and Sergeant Konzuk was drawing new uniforms from the quartermaster's stores. Ten new rifles had also been issued.

Crossing the parade square that night he encountered Padre Dixon, and he realized that this man had been avoiding him during the past two days. "Padre," he called out. "I want to talk to you."

The Padre waited. His big face showed no expression.

"Padre — will you give me your advice?"

The Padre's glance was cold. "Why?" he asked. "It won't change anything."

And looking into that set face Adam saw that the Padre was regarding him with a dislike he made no attempt to conceal. He flushed. He had not expected this. Only days ago this man had been trying to help him.

His anger slipped forward. "What's the matter, Padre — you feeling sorry for the boy-murderer?"

Adam regretted his words at once; indeed he was shocked that he could have said them. The Padre turned his back and started away.

Adam caught at his arm. "Ah, no," he said. "I didn't mean that. Padre — is what I'm doing so awful, after all?"

"You've made your choice. Let it go at that."

"But — my duty . . ." Adam felt shame as he used the word.

The Padre stood with folded arms. "Listen," he said. "I told you before: no matter how necessary this thing is it will never be right!"

Adam was silent. Then he reached out his hand again. "Padre," he said in a low voice. "Is there no way it can be stopped?"

The Padre sighed. "The train has been set in motion," he said. "Once it could have been stopped — in Ottawa — but now . . ." He shrugged. He looked at Adam searchingly and he seemed to reflect. "There *might* be one way — ." After a moment he blinked and looked away. "But no — that will never come to pass. I suppose I should wish you good luck," he said. "Good night, Adam."

That meeting made Adam wonder how his fellow officers regarded him. In the officers' mess that night he looked about him and found out. Silence descended when he approached a group and slowly its members would drift away; there was a cleared circle around whichever chair he sat in. Even the barman seemed to avoid his glance.

All right, Adam decided then, and from the bar he looked murderously around the room. All right, *he* would stick by Benny Hatfield — the two of them, at least, knew what duty and soldiering was! Why, what was he doing that was so awful? He was simply commanding a firing squad to execute a soldier who had committed a murder. That's all — he was commanding a firing squad; he was, he was — an executioner!

His glass crashed to the floor. Through all the soft words exchanged with Brigadier Hatfield, all the concealing echelons of military speech, the pitiless truth now leaped out at him. He was an executioner. Captain John Adam made a noise in his throat, and the faces of the other men in the room went white.

When he left the mess some instinct led him toward the small grey hut standing at the camp entrance. Through the board walls of that hut he could see his victim, Jones, living out his allotted time, while he, Adam the executioner, walked implacably close by. The new concept of victim and executioner seized and threatened to suffocate him.

His eyes strained at the Italian stars in their dark-blue heaven. How had it happened? Only days ago he had regarded the possibility of this execution with horror, as something vile. But now he stood in the front rank of those who were pushing it forward with all vigour. For an instant his mind flamed with the thought of asking Brigadier Hatfield to release him, but at once the fire flickered out, hopelessly. That night John Adam stayed in his room with the light burning. He tried to pray.

Brigadier Hatfield had the most brilliant inspiration of his career: The place of execution would be changed to Rome! There was ample justification, of course, since the effect on the troops' morale at Volpone would be bad to say the least. No one could dispute this, and all the while the Brigadier relished in imagination the face of General Vincent when he found the affair brought back to his own doorstep. It only showed that a regular soldier could still teach these civilian generals a thing or two!

The Brigadier was in high good humor as he presided at the conference to discuss this change. All the participants were present, including one newcomer, an officer from the Provost Corps, introduced as Colonel McGuire. This colonel said nothing, but nodded his head in agreement with the Brigadier's points. His eyes roamed restlessly from face to face and his cold glance seemed to strip bare the abilities of every person in the room.

Colonel McGuire, the Brigadier announced, had been instrumental in finding the ideal place for the affair. It was a former Fascist barracks on the outskirts of Rome, and all the — ah, facilities — were readily available. Everyone taking part, and he trusted that each officer was now thoroughly familiar with his duties, would move by convoy to Rome that very afternoon. The execution — here he paused for a solemn moment — the execution would take place at 0800 hours tomorrow morning. Any questions? No? Thank you, gentlemen.

Adam was moving away when the Brigadier stopped him. "John," he called. He had slipped into the habit of using his first name now. "I want you to meet Colonel McGuire."

They shook hands and Adam flushed under the chill exposure of those probing eyes. After a moment the Colonel's glance dropped; he had seen sufficient. As Adam moved off to warn his men for the move he felt those cold eyes following him to the door, and beyond.

Adam kept his eyes closed while Sergeant Konzuk drove. In the back of the jeep Padre Dixon had not spoken since the convoy was marshaled; it was clear that these were not the traveling companions of his choice.

Although Adam would not look all his awareness was centred on a closed three-ton truck which lumbered along in the middle of the convoy. The condemned man and his guards rode inside that vehicle.

The concept of victim and executioner filled Adam's mind to the exclusion of all else. He had tried throwing the blame back to the comfortable politicians sitting at their polished table in Ottawa, but it was no use. He knew that it was *his* voice that would issue the last command. *He* was the executioner ... Then another thought came to torment him without mercy: How did his victim, Jones, *feel* now?

They stopped for ten minutes outside a hilltop town, where pink villas glinted among the green of olive trees. Adam followed Padre Dixon to the place where he sat in an orchard. The Padre looked up at him wearily.

"How is he taking it?" Adam demanded at once.

The Padre scrambled to his feet. His eyes flashed with anger. "Who? The boy-murderer?"

"Please, Padre — I've *got* to know!"

The Padre stared at Adam's drawn face. Then he passed a hand across his eyes. "Adam — forgive me. I know it's a terrible thing for you. If it makes it any easier ... well, Jones is brave; he's smiling and polite, and that's all. But Adam — the boy still doesn't understand. He doesn't believe that it's really going to happen!" The Padre's voice shook with his agitation.

Adam nodded his head. "That other time, Padre — you said there might be a way of stopping it —."

"No, forget that — it's too late." The spluttering cough of motorcycles roared between them. "Come. It is time to go." And the Padre laid his hand on Adam's arm.

Adam and Konzuk stood on the hard tarmac and surveyed the site gloomily. The place they had come to inspect was a U-shaped space cut out of the forest. The base of the U was a red-brick wall, and down each side marched a precise green line of cypresses. The wall was bullet-pocked because this place had been used as a firing range, although imagination balked at what some of the targets must have been. On the right wing of the U a small wooden grandstand was set in front of the cypresses. Adam looked around at all this, and then his gaze moved over the trees and up to the pitilessly blue sky above. "All right, Konzuk," he said. "You check things over." And he went away to be alone.

Adam was lying on his bed in the darkness. His eyes were wide open but he made no move when he saw the Padre's big form stumble into his room. Then the Padre stood over his bed, eyes groping for him. He was breathing loudly.

"Adam — he wants to see you!"

"No!"

"You must!"

"I couldn't!" Now Adam sat up in bed. His battle-dress tunic was crumpled. His face was protected by the dark, but his voice was naked.

"No, Padre," he pleaded. "I couldn't."

"Look, son — it's your job. You've no choice. Do you understand?"

There was silence. Adam made a noise in the darkness which seemed to take all the breath from his body.

"Yes, I understand." He was fumbling for his belt and cap in the dark.

"Padre — what time is it?"

"Twelve o'clock."

"Eight hours."

"Yes."

"Well. Good-by, Padre."

"Good-by, son."

The Provost Sergeant came to attention and saluted. His face was stiff but he could not keep the flicker of curiosity from his eyes. Adam saw that this was a real prison: concrete flooring, steel doors, and iron bars. They stood in what seemed to be a large brightly lit guardroom. A card game had been taking place, and there were coffee mugs, but the guards stood now at respectful attention.

"Where is he?" Adam turned to the Sergeant.

A dark-haired young man stepped from among the group of guards. A smartly dressed soldier, clean and good-looking in his freshly pressed battle-dress. "Here I am, sir," the young man said.

Adam took a step back; he flashed a glance at the door.

The Sergeant spoke then, apologetically. "He wanted company, sir. I thought it would be all right."

"It was good of you to come, sir." This was Private Jones speaking for his attention.

Adam forced himself to return the glance. "Yes," he said. "I mean — it's no trouble. I — I was glad to."

The two men looked one another in the face, perhaps surprised to find how close they were in years. Jones' smile was friendly. He was like a host easing the embarrassment of his guest. "Would you like to sit down, sir?"

"Yes. Oh, yes."

They sat in Jones' cell, on opposite sides of a small table. Because he had to Adam held his eyes on the prisoner's face and now he could see the thin lines of tension spreading from the eyes and at the mouth. It was certain that Jones *now* believed in the truth of his own death, and he carried this fact with quiet dignity. Adam was gripped by a passion of adoration for this boy; he would have done anything for him — he who was his executioner.

"It was good of you to come," Private Jones said again. "I have a request."

Surely, Adam thought, it took more courage to act as Jones did now than to advance through that meadow to the Hitler Line ...

"Well, sir," Jones went on, his face set. "I'm ready to take — tomorrow morning. But one thing worries me: I don't want you and the other boys to feel bad about this. I thought it might help if I shook hands with all the boys before — before it happens."

Adam looked down at the concrete floor. This was worse than a thousand Hitler Lines; *he knew now he would be able to go back there anytime.* A dim electric-light bulb hung from the ceiling and swayed hypnotically between them. Well, he had to say something. The thing was impossible, of course: he'd never get his men to fire if they shook hands first.

But Jones read the working of his face. "Never mind, sir — maybe you'd just give them that message for me — ."

"I will, Jones. I *will!*"

He stood up; he could not stay here another moment.

Jones said, "Maybe — *you* would shake hands with me?"

Adam stood utterly still. His voice came out as a whisper in that small space. "Jones," he said, "I was going to ask you if I could."

When he came back to the guardroom Adam looked ill. The Provost Sergeant took his arm and walked him back to his quarters.

It was a softly fragrant Italian morning. The dew was still fresh on the grass and a light ground mist rolled away before the heat of the climbing sun. In the forest clearing the neat groups of soldiers looked clean and compact in their khaki battle-dress with the bright regimental flashes gleaming at their shoulders.

The firing squad stood "at ease," but with not the least stir or motion. Sergeant Konzuk was on their right; Captain Adam stood several paces apart at the left, aligned at right angles to his ten-man rank. The grandstand was filled with a small group of official witnesses. A cordon of military policemen stayed at rigid attention along the top and down each side of the U.

In front of the grandstand stood Brigadier Benny Hatfield, an erect military figure, his stern eye ranging with satisfaction around the precise groupings and arrangements he had ordered. A step behind the Brigadier was Ramsay, his adjutant; then Padre

Dixon, and the chief medical officer. The assembly was complete — except for one man.

Somewhere in the background a steel door clanged, a noise which no one affected to hear. Then there came the sound of rapid marching. Three military figures came into view and halted smartly in front of Brigadier Hatfield. Private Jones, hatless, stood in the centre, a provost sergeant on each side. The boy's lips were white, his cheeks lacked color, but he held his head high, his hands were pressed tight against the seams of his battle-dress trousers. It was impossible not to notice the brilliant shine of his polished boots as they glittered in the morning sun.

Brigadier Hatfield took a paper from Ramsay's extended hand. He read some words from it but his voice came as an indistinct mumble in the morning air. The Brigadier was in a hurry. Everyone was in a hurry; every person there suffered an agony of haste. Each body strained and each mind willed: Go! Go! Have this thing over and done with!

The Brigadier handed the paper back to Ramsay with a little gesture of finality. But the three men remained standing in front of him as though locked in their attitudes of attention. Seconds of silence ticked by. The Brigadier's hand sped up to his collar and he cleared his throat with violence. "*Well*, sergeant?" his voice rasped. "Carry on, man!"

"Yessir. Left turn — quick march!"

The three men held the same brisk pace, marching in perfect step. The only sound was the thud of their heavy boots upon the tarmac. They passed the firing squad and halted at the red-brick wall. Then the escorting NCOs seemed to disappear and Private Jones stood alone against his wall. A nervous little smile was fixed at the corners of his mouth.

Again there was silence. Adam had not looked at the marching men, nor did he now look at the wall. Head lowered, he frowned as he seemed to study the alignment of his ten men in a row. More seconds ticked by.

"Captain Adam!"

It was a bellow from Brigadier Hatfield and it brought Adam's head up. Then his lips moved soundlessly, as though rehearsing what he had to say. "Squad," Captain Adam ordered, "Load!" Ten left feet banged forward on the tarmac, ten rifles hit in the left hand, ten bolts smashed open and shut in unison. Ten rounds were positioned in their chambers.

There were just two remaining orders: "Aim!" and "Fire!" and these should be issued immediately, almost as one. But at that moment a late rooster crowed somewhere and the call came clear and sweet through the morning air, full of rich promise for the summer's day which lay ahead.

Adam took his first glance at the condemned man. Jones' mouth still held hard to its smile, but his knees looked loose. His position of attention was faltering.

"Squad!" Adam ordered in a ringing voice, "Unload! Rest!" Ten rifles obeyed in perfect unison.

Adam turned half right so that he faced Brigadier Hatfield. "Sir," he called clearly. "I refuse to carry out this order!"

Every voice in that place joined in the sound which muttered across the tarmac.

The Brigadier's face was deathly white. He peered at Private Jones, still in position against the wall, knees getting looser. He had a split second to carry the thing through. "Colonel Mc-Guire!" he shouted.

"Yes, sir!" McGuire came running toward the firing squad. He knew what had to be done, and quickly. The Brigadier's face had turned purple now; he appeared to be choking with the force of his rage. "Colonel McGuire," he shouted. "Place that officer under close arrest!"

"Sir?" McGuire stopped where he was and his mouth dropped open. Private Jones began to fall slowly against the wall. Then a rifle clattered loudly on the tarmac. Sergeant Konzuk was racing toward the wall and in an instant he had his big arms tight around Jones' body.

"McGuire!" The Brigadier's voice was a hoarse shriek now. "March the prisoner away!"

Padre Dixon stood rooted to the ground. His lips were moving and he stared blindly at Adam's stiffly erect figure. "He found the way!" he cried then in a ringing voice, and he moved about in triumph, although no one paid him attention. At his side Ramsay was spluttering out his own ecstasy of excitement: "Jones will get a reprieve after this! It will have to be referred to London, and then to Ottawa. And they'll never dare to put him through this again —."

Ramsay looked up as he felt the Padre's fingers bite into his shoulder.

He laughed nervously. "Yes," he chattered on. "Jones may get a reprieve, but Adam's the one for sentencing now." He peered across the tarmac where Adam still stood alone, his face slightly lifted to the warmth of the morning sun. He looked at Adam's lone figure with fear and admiration. "Yes," he said, suddenly sobered. "God help Adam now."

"Don't worry about that, son," said the Padre, starting to stride across the tarmac. "He already has."

QUESTIONS

In this story we see two men, Captain John Adam and Private Jones, each of whom has committed a wrong which he must atone for through suffering. The plot is based on their respective ordeals.

Note that although their lives are intertwined, events are given mainly from Adam's point of view.

1. (a) Explain how McDougall uses description of physical traits, description of actions, flashbacks, and the thoughts of Sergeant Konzuk, to give you definite first impressions of John Adam.

    (b) Jones appears directly only in the latter part of the story. Describe the author's methods of characterizing him (1) *before* he actually appears in a detailed incident, and (2) *during* his appearance in such an incident.

    (c) What effect does the author gain by delaying Jones' appearance until just before the climax?

2. (a) Express in a sentence or two the main conflict in the plot of "Firing Squad".

    (b) What incident starts this conflict?

    (c) Analyze this inciting incident to show how McDougall has succeeded in winning your sympathies for Adam and making you dislike Brigadier Benny Hatfield.

3. Using a sentence or two for each, briefly outline the incidents which develop Adam's conflict within himself and with other characters in the story.

4. (a) What incident is the climax of this conflict?
(b) A climax fails unless the writer has prepared you to accept it as plausible. What details earlier in the story have prepared you for Adam's decision?
(c) Examine the climactic incident carefully. By referring to details of setting and action, show how the author has managed to make this a very poignant scene.
(d) Many other incidents are narrated so that you can see into Adam's thoughts and emotions. Why does McDougall present the "execution scene" so that you cannot read Adam's thoughts?

5. Explain the function of the final comments of Ramsay and Padre Dixon.

*Sir Charles*

*G. D. Roberts*

# "The young ravens that call upon him"

*Sir Charles G. D. Roberts (1860-1943) was born near Fredericton, New Brunswick, and educated in his native university. After a brief career as professor at King's College, Nova Scotia, he turned to the profession of letters; and as editor, poet, and fiction writer, he had a decisive influence on the development of writing in this country. After prolonged sojourns in London and New York, he returned to Canada in 1925 and took up residence in Toronto. His major works include* In Divers Tones *(1886),* Earth's Enigmas *(1895),* The Book of the Native *(1896),* The Kindred of the Wild *(1902), and* The Vagrant of Time *(1927). Representative selections of his poems and stories have been made available in paperback editions. Roberts was knighted in 1935 in recognition of his great service to writing — and writers — in Canada. The following story is reprinted from* The Last Barrier *by permission of McClelland and Stewart, Ltd.*

IT WAS JUST BEFORE DAWN, and a grayness was beginning to trouble the dark about the top of the mountain.

Even at that cold height there was no wind. The veil of cloud that hid the stars hung but a hand-breadth above the naked summit. To eastward the peak broke away sheer, beetling in a perpetual menace to the valleys and the lower hills. Just under the brow, on a splintered and creviced ledge, was the nest of the eagles.

As the thick dark shrank down the steep like a receding tide, and the grayness reached the ragged heap of branches forming the nest, the young eagles stirred uneasily under the loose droop of the mother's wings. She raised her head and peered about her, slightly lifting her wings as she did so; and the nestlings, complaining at the chill air that came in upon their unfledged bodies, thrust themselves up amid the warm feathers of her thighs. The male bird, perched on a jutting fragment beside the nest, did not move. But he was awake. His white, narrow, flat-crowned head was turned to one side, and his yellow eye, under its straight, fierce lid, watched the pale streak that was growing along the distant eastern sea-line.

The great birds were racked with hunger. Even the nestlings, to meet the petitions of whose gaping beaks they stinted themselves without mercy, felt meagre and uncomforted. Day after day the parent birds had fished almost in vain; day after day their wide and tireless hunting had brought them scant reward. The schools of alewives, mackerel, and herring seemed to shun their shores that spring. The rabbits seemed to have fled from all the coverts about their mountain.

The mother eagle, larger and of mightier wing than her mate, looked as if she had met with misadventure. Her plumage was disordered. Her eyes, fiercely and restlessly anxious, at moments grew dull as if with exhaustion. On the day before, while circling at her viewless height above a lake far inland, she had marked a huge lake-trout, basking near the surface of the water. Dropping upon it with half-closed, hissing wings, she had fixed her talons in its back. But the fish had proved too powerful for her. Again and again it had dragged her under water, and she had been almost drowned before she could unloose the terrible grip of her claws. Hardly, and late, had she beaten her way back to the mountain-top.

And now the pale streak in the east grew ruddy. Rust-red stains and purple, crawling fissures began to show on the rocky face of the peak. A piece of scarlet cloth, woven among the fagots of the nest, glowed like new blood in the increasing light. And presently a wave of rose appeared to break and wash down over the summit, as the rim of the sun came above the horizon.

The male eagle stretched his head far out over the depth, lifted his wings and screamed harshly, as if in greeting of the day. He paused a moment in that position, rolling his eye upon the nest. Then his head went lower, his wings spread wider, and he launched himself smoothly and swiftly into the abyss of air as a swimmer glides into the sea. The female watched him, a faint wraith of a bird darting through the gloom, till presently, completing his mighty arc, he rose again into the full light of the morning. Then on level, all but moveless wing, he sailed away toward the horizon.

As the sun rose higher and higher, the darkness began to melt on the tops of the lower hills and to diminish on the slopes of the upland pastures, lingering in the valleys as the snow delays there in spring. As point by point the landscape uncovered itself to his view, the eagle shaped his flight into a vast circle, or rather into a series of stupendous loops. His neck was stretched toward the earth, in the intensity of his search for something to ease the bitter hunger of his nestlings and his mate.

Not far from the sea, and still in darkness, stood a low, round hill, or swelling upland. Bleak and shelterless, whipped by every wind that the heavens could let loose, it bore no bush but an occasional juniper scrub. It was covered with mossy hillocks, and with a short grass, meagre but sweet. There in the chilly gloom, straining her ears to catch the lightest footfall of approaching peril, but hearing only the hushed thunder of the surf, stood a lonely ewe over the lamb to which she had given birth in the night.

Having lost the flock when the pangs of travail came upon her, the unwonted solitude filled her with apprehension. But as soon as the first feeble bleating of the lamb fell upon her ear, everything was changed. Her terrors all at once increased tenfold — but they were for her young, not for herself; and with them came a strange boldness such as her heart had never known before. As the little weakling shivered against her side, she uttered low, short bleats and murmurs of tenderness. When an owl hooted in the woods across the valley, she raised her head angrily and faced the sound, suspecting a menace to her young. When a mouse scurried past her, with a small, rustling noise amid the withered mosses of the hillock, she stamped fiercely, and would have charged had the intruder been a lion.

When the first gray of dawn descended over the pasture, the ewe feasted her eyes with the sight of the trembling little creature, as it lay on the wet grass. With gentle nose she coaxed it and caressed it, till presently it struggled to its feet, and, with its pathetically awkward legs spread wide apart to preserve its balance, it began to nurse. Turning her head as far around as she could, the ewe watched its every motion with soft murmurings of delight.

And now that wave of rose, which had long ago washed the mountain and waked the eagles, spread tenderly across the open pasture. The lamb stopped nursing; and the ewe, moving forward two or three steps, tried to persuade it to follow her. She was anxious that it should as soon as possible learn to walk freely, so they might together rejoin the flock. She felt that the open pasture was full of dangers.

The lamb seemed afraid to take so many steps. It shook its ears and bleated piteously. The mother returned to its side, caressed it anew, pushed it with her nose, and again moved away a few feet, urging it to go with her. Again the feeble little creature refused, bleating loudly. At this moment there came a terrible hissing rush out of the sky, and a great form fell upon the lamb. The ewe wheeled and charged madly; but at the same instant the eagle, with two mighty buffetings of his wings, rose beyond her reach and soared away toward the mountain. The lamb hung limp from his talons; and with piteous cries the ewe ran beneath, gazing upward, and stumbling over the hillocks and juniper bushes.

In the nest of the eagles there was content. The pain of their hunger appeased, the nestlings lay dozing in the sun, the neck of one resting across the back of the other. The triumphant male sat erect upon his perch, staring out over the splendid world that displayed itself beneath him. Now and again he half lifted his wings and screamed joyously at the sun. The mother bird, perched upon a limb on the edge of the nest, busily rearranged her plumage. At times she stooped her head into the nest to utter over her sleeping eaglets a soft chuckling noise, which seemed to come from the bottom of her throat.

But hither and thither over the round bleak hill wandered the ewe, calling for her lamb, unmindful of the flock, which had been moved to other pastures.

QUESTIONS

In his animal stories, Sir Charles G. D. Roberts is often concerned with evidences of the blind struggle for existence that goes on ceaselessly in the world of nature. The evolutionary theory of Darwin had more than confirmed Tennyson's vision of nature as "red in tooth and claw." Roberts pursues the vision in the backwoods of New Brunswick.

1. In this story, representative of his best work, what is his attitude toward the struggle for survival?

2. Are your sympathies meant to be with the eagle, the lamb, both, or neither?

3. The force that strikes at the innocent young is usually "the villain". By what different means does the author make the eagle less than a villain, with a real claim on our sympathies?

4. Note that both the eagle and the lamb first appear through the darkness, just before dawn. What is the value for the story — and for your sympathies — of the descriptive references to the changes in light and colour from the beginning of the story to the end?

5. Note particularly the scarlet cloth in the eagle's nest which "glowed like new blood in the increasing light". Is this an image of the destroyer (the villain), of the provider, or of both?

6. What does the title tell you about the meaning of the story and the intention of the author? [See *The Book of Job*, xxxviii. 41 and *Psalms*, cxlvii. 9]

*Willa*
*Cather*

# Paul's case

*Willa Cather (1873-1947), at the age of eight, moved from Winchester, Virginia, her birthplace, to Nebraska, at that time still a pioneer area. She grew up in the town of Red Cloud. After graduating from the University of Nebraska in 1895, she went to Pittsburgh, Pennsylvania, earning her living there first as drama critic for the* Daily Leader *and later as an English teacher in the Allegheny High School. Her experience as a teacher no doubt contributed to her psychological insight in "Paul's Case". In 1905 she moved to New York city as an editor of* McClure's Magazine. *Except for periods of travel in Europe and America, she lived in New York for the rest of her life. Willa Cather has written verse and short stories, but her reputation rests mainly on her novels, of which the best known are* O Pioneers! *(1913),* The Song of the Lark *(1915),* My Antonia *(1918),* A Lost Lady *(1923),* Death Comes to the Archbishop *(1927), and* Shadows on the Rock *(1931). "Paul's Case" presents a theme common in her work: a sensitive personality attempts to cope with an alien and uncongenial environment. This story is reprinted here from* Youth and the Bright Medusa *by Willa Cather, by permission of Alfred A. Knopf, Inc.*

IT WAS PAUL'S AFTERNOON to appear before the faculty of the Pittsburgh High School to account for his various misdemeanors. He had been suspended a week ago, and his father had called at the Principal's office and confessed his perplexity about his son. Paul entered the faculty room suave and smiling. His clothes were a trifle outgrown, and the tan velvet on the collar of his open overcoat was frayed and worn; but for all that there was something of the dandy about him, and he wore an opal pin in his neatly knotted black four-in-hand, and a red carnation in his buttonhole. This latter adornment the faculty somehow felt was not properly significant of the contrite spirit befitting a boy under the ban of suspension.

Paul was tall for his age and very thin, with high, cramped shoulders and a narrow chest. His eyes were remarkable for a certain hysterical brilliancy, and he continually used them in a conscious, theatrical sort of way, peculiarly offensive in a boy. The pupils were abnormally large, as though he were addicted to belladonna, but there was a glassy glitter about them which that drug does not produce.

When questioned by the Principal as to why he was there, Paul stated, politely enough, that he wanted to come back to school. This was a lie, but Paul was quite accustomed to lying; found it, indeed, indispensable for overcoming friction. His teachers were asked to state their respective charges against him, which they did with such a rancour and aggrievedness as evinced that this was not a usual case. Disorder and impertinence were among the offenses named, yet each of his instructors felt that it was scarcely possible to put into words the real cause of the trouble, which lay in a sort of hysterically defiant manner of the boy's; in the contempt which they all knew he felt for them, and which he seemingly made not the least effort to conceal. Once, when he had been making a synopsis of a paragraph at the black-board, his English teacher had stepped to his side and attempted to guide his hand. Paul had started back with a shudder and thrust his hands violently behind him. The astonished woman could scarcely have been more hurt and embarrassed had he struck at her. The insult was so involuntary and definitely personal as to be unforgettable. In one way and another, he had made all his teachers, men and women alike, conscious of the same feeling of physical aversion. In one class he habitually sat with his hand shading his eyes; in another he always looked out of the window during the recitation; in another he made a running commentary on the lecture, with humorous intent.

His teachers felt this afternoon that his whole attitude was symbolized by his shrug and his flippantly red carnation flower, and they fell upon him without mercy, his English teacher leading the pack. He stood through it smiling, his pale lips parted over his white teeth. (His lips were continually twitching, and he had a habit of raising his eyebrows that was contemptuous and irritating to the last degree.) Older boys than Paul had broken down and shed tears under that ordeal, but his set smile did not once desert him, and his only sign of discomfort was the nervous trembling of the fingers that toyed with the buttons of his overcoat, and an occasional jerking of the other hand which held his hat. Paul was always smiling, always glancing about him, seeming to feel that people might be watching him and trying to detect something. This conscious expression, since it was as far as possible from boyish mirthfulness, was usually attributed to insolence or "smartness."

As the inquisition proceeded, one of his instructors repeated an impertinent remark of the boy's, and the Principal asked him whether he thought that a courteous speech to make to a woman. Paul shrugged his shoulders slightly and his eyebrows twitched.

"I don't know," he replied. "I didn't mean to be polite or impolite, either. I guess it's a sort of way I have, of saying things regardless."

The Principal asked him whether he didn't think that a way it would be well to get rid of. Paul grinned and said he guessed so. When he was told that he could go, he bowed gracefully and went out. His bow was like a repetition of the scandalous red carnation.

His teachers were in despair, and his drawing master voiced the feeling of them all when he declared there was something about the boy which none of them understood. He added: "I don't really believe that smile of his comes altogether from insolence; there's something sort of haunted about it. The boy is

not strong, for one thing. There is something wrong about the
fellow."

The drawing master had come to realize that, in looking at
Paul, one saw only his white teeth and the forced animation of
his eyes. One warm afternoon the boy had gone to sleep at his
drawing board, and his master had noted with amazement what a
white, blue-veined face it was; drawn and wrinkled like an old
man's about the eyes, the lips twitching even in his sleep.

His teachers left the building dissatisfied and unhappy; humil-
iated to have felt so vindictive toward a mere boy, to have
uttered this feeling in cutting terms, and to have set each other
on, as it were, in the gruesome game of intemperate reproach.
One of them remembered having seen a miserable street cat set
at bay by a ring of tormentors.

As for Paul, he ran down the hill whistling the Soldiers' Chorus
from *Faust*, looking wildly behind him now and then to see
whether some of his teachers were not there to witness his light-
heartedness. As it was now late in the afternoon and Paul was on
duty that evening as usher at Carnegie Hall, he decided that he
would not go home to supper.

When he reached the concert hall the doors were not yet open.
It was chilly outside, and he decided to go up into the picture
gallery — always deserted at this hour — where there were some
of Raffelli's gay studies of Paris streets and an airy blue Venetian
scene or two that always exhilarated him. He was delighted to
find no one in the gallery but the old guard, who sat in the corner,
a newspaper on his knee, a black patch over one eye and the
other closed. Paul possessed himself of the place and walked
confidently up and down, whistling under his breath. After a
while he sat down before a blue Rico and lost himself. When he
bethought him to look at his watch, it was after seven o'clock,
and he rose with a start and ran downstairs, making a face at
Augustus Caesar, peering out from the cast-room, and an evil
gesture at the Venus of Milo as he passed her on the stairway.

When Paul reached the ushers' dressing-room half a dozen
boys were there already, and he began excitedly to tumble into his
uniform. It was one of the few that at all approached fitting, and

Paul thought it very becoming – though he knew the tight, straight coat accentuated his narrow chest, about which he was exceedingly sensitive. He was always excited while he dressed, twanging all over to the tuning of the strings and the preliminary flourishes of the horns in the music-room; but tonight he seemed quite beside himself, and he teased and plagued the boys until, telling him that he was crazy, they put him down on the floor and sat on him.

Somewhat calmed by his suppression, Paul dashed out to the front of the house to seat the early comers. He was a model usher. Gracious and smiling he ran up and down the aisles. Nothing was too much trouble for him; he carried messages and brought pro-grammes as though it were his greatest pleasure in life, and all the people in his section thought him a charming boy, feeling that he remembered and admired them. As the house filled, he grew more and more vivacious and animated, and the color came to his cheeks and lips. It was very much as though this were a great reception and Paul were the host. Just as the musicians came out to take their places, his English teacher arrived with checks for the seats which a prominent manufacturer had taken for the season. She betrayed some embarrassment when she handed Paul the tickets, and a *hauteur* which subsequently made her feel very foolish. Paul was startled for a moment, and had the feeling of wanting to put her out; what business had she here among all these fine people and gay colors? He looked her over and de-cided that she was not appropriately dressed and must be a fool to sit downstairs in such togs. The tickets had probably been sent her out of kindness, he reflected, as he put down a seat for her, and she had about as much right to sit there as he had.

When the symphony began Paul sank into one of the rear seats with a long sigh of relief, and lost himself as he had done before the Rico. It was not that symphonies, as such, meant any-thing in particular to Paul, but the first sigh of the instruments seemed to free some hilarious spirit within him; something that struggled there like the Genius in the bottle found by the Arab fisherman. He felt a sudden zest of life; the lights danced before his eyes and the concert hall blazed into unimaginable splendour.

When the soprano soloist came on, Paul forgot even the nastiness of his teacher's being there, and gave himself up to the peculiar intoxication such personages always had for him. The soloist chanced to be a German woman, by no means in her first youth, and the mother of many children; but she wore a satin gown and a tiara, and she had that indefinable air of achievement, that world-shine upon her, which always blinded Paul to any possible defects.

After a concert was over, Paul was often irritable and wretched until he got to sleep, — and tonight he was even more than usually restless. He had the feeling of not being able to let down; of its being impossible to give up this delicious excitement which was the only thing that could be called living at all. During the last number he withdrew and, after hastily changing his clothes in the dressing-room, slipped out to the side door where the singer's carriage stood. Here he began pacing rapidly up and down the walk, waiting to see her come out.

Over yonder the Schenley, in its vacant stretch, loomed big and square through the fine rain, the windows of its twelve stories glowing like those of a lighted cardboard house under a Christmas tree. All the actors and singers of any importance stayed there when they were in the city, and a number of the big manufacturers of the place lived there in the winter. Paul had often hung about the hotel, watching the people go in and out, longing to enter and leave schoolmasters and dull care behind him forever.

At last the singer came out, accompanied by the conductor, who helped her into her carriage and closed the door with a cordial *auf wiedersehen*, — which set Paul to wondering whether she were not an old sweetheart of his. Paul followed the carriage over to the hotel, walking so rapidly as not to be far from the entrance when the singer alighted and disappeared behind the swinging glass doors which were opened by a Negro in a tall hat and a long coat. In the moment that the door was ajar, it seemed to Paul that he, too, entered. He seemed to feel himself go after her up the steps, into the warm, lighted building, into an exotic, a tropical world of shiny, glistening surfaces and basking ease. He reflected upon the mysterious dishes that were brought into the dining-room, the green bottles in buckets of ice, as he had seen them in the supper party pictures of the Sunday supplement. A quick gust of wind brought the rain down with sudden vehemence, and Paul was startled to find that he was still outside in the slush of the gravel driveway; that his boots were letting in the water and his scanty overcoat was clinging wet about him; that the lights in front of the concert hall were out, and that the rain was driving in sheets between him and the orange glow of the windows above him. There it was, what he wanted – tangibly before him, like the fairy world of a Christmas pantomime; as the rain beat his face, Paul wondered whether he were destined always to shiver in the black night outside, looking up at it.

He turned and walked reluctantly toward the car tracks. The end had to come some time; his father in his night-clothes at the top of the stairs, explanations that did not explain, hastily improvised fictions that were forever tripping him up, his upstairs room and its horrible yellow wall paper, the creaking bureau with the greasy plush collar-box, and over his painted wooden bed the pictures of George Washington and John Calvin, and the framed motto, "Feed my Lambs," which had been worked in red worsted by his mother, whom Paul could not remember.

Half an hour later, Paul alighted from the Negley Avenue car and went slowly down one of the side streets off the main thoroughfare. It was a highly respectable street, where all the houses were exactly alike, and where business men of moderate means begot and reared large families of children, all of whom went to Sabbath-school and learned the shorter catechism, and were interested in arithmetic; all of whom were as exactly alike as their homes, and of a piece with the monotony in which they lived. Paul never went up Cordelia Street without a shudder of loathing. His home was next to the house of the Cumberland minister. He approached it tonight with the nerveless sense of defeat, the hopeless feeling of sinking back forever into ugliness and commonness that he had always had when he came home. The moment he turned into Cordelia Street he felt the waters close above his head. After each of these orgies of living, he experienced all the physical depression which follows a debauch; the loathing of respectable beds, of common food, of a house permeated by kitchen odors; a shuddering repulsion for the flavorless, colorless mass of everyday existence; a morbid desire for cool things and soft lights and fresh flowers.

The nearer he approached the house, the more absolutely unequal Paul felt to the sight of it all; his ugly sleeping chamber; the cold bathroom with the grimy zinc tub, the cracked mirror, the dripping spiggots; his father, at the top of the stairs, his hairy legs sticking out from his nightshirt, his feet thrust into carpet slippers. He was so much later than usual that there would certainly be inquiries and reproaches. Paul stopped short before the door. He felt that he could not be accosted by his father tonight; that he could not toss again on that miserable bed. He would not go in. He would tell his father that he had no car fare, and it was raining so hard he had gone home with one of the boys and stayed all night.

Meanwhile, he was wet and cold. He went around to the back of the house and tried one of the basement windows, found it open, raised it cautiously, and scrambled down the cellar wall to the floor. There he stood, holding his breath, terrified by the noise he had made; but the floor above him was silent, and there was no creak on the stairs. He found a soap-box, and carried it over to the soft ring of light that streamed from the furnace door, and sat down. He was horribly afraid of rats, so he did not try to sleep, but sat looking distrustfully at the dark, still terrified lest he might have awakened his father. In such reactions, after one of the experiences which made days and nights out of the dreary blanks of the calendar, when his senses were deadened, Paul's head was always singularly clear. Suppose his father had heard him getting in at the window and had come down and shot him for a burglar? Then, again, suppose his father had come down, pistol in hand, and he had cried out in time to save himself, and his father had been horrified to think how nearly he had killed him? Then, again, suppose a day should come when his father would remember that night, and wish there had been no warning cry to stay his hand? With this last supposition Paul entertained himself until daybreak.

The following Sunday was fine; the sodden November chill

was broken by the last flash of autumnal summer. In the morning Paul had to go to church and Sabbath-school, as always. On seasonable Sunday afternoons the burghers of Cordelia Street usually sat out on their front "stoops", and talked to their neighbours on the next stoop, or called to those across the street in neighbourly fashion. The men sat placidly on gay cushions placed upon the steps that led down to the sidewalk, while the women, in their Sunday "waists", sat in rockers on the cramped porches, pretending to be greatly at their ease. The children played in the streets; there were so many of them that the place resembled the recreation grounds of a kindergarten. The men on the steps – all in their shirt sleeves, their vests unbuttoned – sat with their legs well apart, their stomachs comfortably protruding, and talked of the prices of things, or told anecdotes of the sagacity of their various chiefs and overlords. They occasionally looked over the multitude of squabbling children, listened affectionately to their high-pitched, nasal voices, smiling to see their own proclivities reproduced in their offspring, and interspersed their legends of the iron kings with remarks about their sons' progress at school, their grades in arithmetic, and the amounts they had saved in their toy banks. On this last Sunday of November, Paul sat all the afternoon on the lowest step of his stoop, staring into the street, while his sisters, in their rockers, were talking to the minister's daughters next door about how many shirtwaists they had made in the last week, and how many waffles someone had eaten at the last church supper. When the weather was warm, and his father was in a particularly jovial frame of mind, the girls made lemonade, which was always brought out in a red-glass pitcher, ornamented with forget-me-nots in blue enamel. This the girls thought very fine, and the neighbours joked about the suspicious color of the pitcher.

Today Paul's father, on the top step, was talking to a young man who shifted a restless baby from knee to knee. He happened to be the young man who was daily held up to Paul as a model, and after whom it was his father's dearest hope that he would pattern. This young man was of a ruddy complexion, with a compressed, red mouth, and faded, near-sighted eyes, over which he wore thick spectacles, with gold bows that curved about his ears. He was clerk to one of the magnates of a great steel corporation, and was looked upon in Cordelia Street as a young man with a future. There was a story that, some five years ago — he was now barely twenty-six — he had been a trifle "dissipated", but in order to curb his appetites and save the loss of time and strength that a sowing of wild oats might have entailed, he had taken his chief's advice, oft reiterated to his employees, and at twenty-one had married the first woman whom he could persuade to share his fortunes. She happened to be an angular school mistress, much older than he, who also wore thick glasses, and who had now borne him four children, all near-sighted, like herself.

The young man was relating how his chief, now cruising in the Mediterranean, kept in touch with all the details of the business, arranging his office hours on his yacht just as though he were at home, and "knocking off work enough to keep two stenographers busy." His father told, in turn, the plan his corporation was considering, of putting in an electric railway plant at Cairo. Paul snapped his teeth; he had an awful apprehension that they might spoil it all before he got there. Yet he rather liked to hear these legends of the iron kings, that were told and retold on Sundays and holidays; these stories of palaces in Venice, yachts on the Mediterranean, and high play at Monte Carlo appealed to his fancy, and he was interested in the triumphs of cash boys who had become famous, though he had no mind for the cash-boy stage.

After supper was over, and he had helped to dry the dishes, Paul nervously asked his father whether he could go to George's to get some help in his geometry, and still more nervously asked for car fare. This latter request he had to repeat, as his father, on principle, did not like to hear requests for money, whether much or little. He asked Paul whether he could not go to some boy who lived nearer, and told him that he ought not to leave his school work until Sunday; but he gave him the dime. He was not a poor man, but he had a worthy ambition to come up in the world. His only reason for allowing Paul to usher was that he thought a boy ought to be earning a little.

Paul bounded upstairs, scrubbed the greasy odor of the dish-water from his hands with the ill-smelling soap he hated, and then shook over his fingers a few drops of violet water from the bottle he kept hidden in his drawer. He left the house with his geometry conspicuously under his arm, and the moment he got out of Cordelia Street and boarded a downtown car, he shook off the lethargy of two deadening days, and began to live again.

The leading juvenile of the permanent stock company which played at one of the downtown theaters was an acquaintance of Paul's, and the boy had been invited to drop in at the Sunday night rehearsal whenever he could. For more than a year Paul had spent every available moment loitering about Charley Edwards's dressing-room. He had won a place among Edwards's following not only because the young actor, who could not afford to employ a dresser, often found him useful, but because he recognized in Paul something akin to what churchmen term "vocation."

It was at the theatre and at Carnegie Hall that Paul really lived; the rest was but a sleep and a forgetting. This was Paul's fairy tale, and it had for him all the allurement of a secret love. The moment he inhaled the gassy, painty, dusty odor behind the scenes, he breathed like a prisoner set free, and felt within him the possibility of doing or saying splendid, brilliant things. The moment the cracked orchestra beat out the overture from *Martha*, or jerked at the serenade from *Rigoletto*, all stupid and ugly things slid from him, and his senses were deliciously, yet delicately fired.

Perhaps it was because, in Paul's world, the natural nearly always wore the guise of ugliness, that a certain element of artificiality seemed to him necessary in beauty. Perhaps it was because his experience of life elsewhere was so full of Sabbath-school picnics, petty economies, wholesome advice as to how to succeed in life, and the unescapable odors of cooking that he found this existence so alluring, these smartly-clad men and women so attractive, that he was so moved by these starry apple orchards that bloomed perennially under the limelight.

It would be difficult to put it strongly enough how convincingly the stage entrance of that theatre was for Paul the actual portal of Romance. Certainly none of the company ever suspected it, least of all Charley Edwards. It was very like the old stories that used to float about London of fabulously rich Jews, who had subterranean halls, with palms, and fountains, and soft lamps and richly apparelled women who never saw the disenchanting light of London day. So, in the midst of that smoke-palled city, enamoured of figures and grimy toil, Paul had his secret temple, his wishing-carpet, his bit of blue-and-white Mediterranean shore bathed in perpetual sunshine.

Several of Paul's teachers had a theory that his imagination had been perverted by garish fiction; but the truth was, he scarcely ever read at all. The books at home were not such as would either tempt or corrupt a youthful mind, and as for reading the novels that some of his friends urged upon him — well, he got what he wanted much more quickly from music; any sort of music, from an orchestra to a barrel organ. He needed only the spark, the indescribable thrill that made his imagination master of his senses, and he could make plots and pictures enough of his own. It was equally true that he was not stage-struck — not, at any rate, in the usual acceptance of that expression. He had no desire to become an actor, any more than he had to become a musician. He felt no necessity to do any of these things; what he wanted was to see, to be in the atmosphere, float on the wave of it, to be carried out, blue league after blue league, away from everything.

After a night behind the scenes, Paul found the school-room more than ever repulsive; the bare floors and naked walls; the prosy men who never wore frock coats, or violets in their button-holes; the women with their dull gowns, shrill voices, and pitiful seriousness about prepositions that govern the dative. He could not bear to have the other pupils think, for a moment, that he took these people seriously; he must convey to them that he considered it all trivial, and was there only by way of a joke, anyway. He had autograph pictures of all the members of the stock company which he showed his classmates, telling them the most incredible stories of his familiarity with these people, of his acquaintance with the soloists who came to Carnegie Hall, his suppers with them and the flowers he sent them. When these stories lost their effect, and his audience grew listless, he would bid all the boys good-by, announcing that he was going to travel for a while; going to Naples, to California, to Egypt. Then, next Monday, he would slip back, conscious and nervously smiling; his sister was ill, and he would have to defer his voyage until spring.

Matters went steadily worse with Paul at school. In the itch to let his instructors know how heartily he despised them, and how thoroughly he was appreciated elsewhere, he mentioned once or twice that he had no time to fool with theorems; adding — with a twitch of the eyebrows and a touch of that nervous bravado which so perplexed them — that he was helping the people down at the stock company; they were old friends of his.

The upshot of the matter was, that the Principal went to Paul's father, and Paul was taken out of school and put to work. The manager at Carnegie Hall was told to get another usher in his stead; the doorkeeper at the theatre was warned not to admit him to the house; and Charley Edwards remorsefully promised the boy's father not to see him again.

The members of the stock company were vastly amused when some of Paul's stories reached them — especially the women. They were hard-working women, most of them supporting indolent husbands or brothers, and they laughed rather bitterly at having stirred the boy to such fervid and florid inventions. They agreed with the faculty and with his father, that Paul's was a bad case.

The east-bound train was plowing through a January snowstorm; the dull dawn was beginning to show gray when the engine whistled a mile out of Newark. Paul started up from the seat where he had lain curled in uneasy slumber, rubbed the breath-misted window glass with his hand, and peered out. The snow was whirling in curling eddies above the white bottom lands, and the drifts lay already deep in the fields and along the fences, while here and there the long dead grass and dried weed stalks protruded black above it. Lights shone from the scattered houses, and a gang of laborers who stood beside the track waved their lanterns.

Paul had slept very little, and he felt grimy and uncomfortable. He had made the all-night journey in a day coach because he was afraid if he took a Pullman he might be seen by some Pittsburgh business man who had noticed him in Denny & Carson's office. When the whistle woke him, he clutched quickly at his breast pocket, glancing about him with an uncertain smile. But the little, clay-bespattered Italians were still sleeping, the slatternly women across the aisle were in open-mouthed oblivion, and even the crumby, crying babies were for the nonce stilled. Paul settled back to struggle with his impatience as best he could.

When he arrived at Jersey City station, he hurried through his breakfast, manifestly ill at ease and keeping a sharp eye about him. After he reached the Twenty-third Street station, he consulted a cabman, and had himself driven to a men's furnishing establishment which was just opening for the day. He spent upward of two hours there, buying with endless reconsidering and great care. His new street suit he put on in the fitting-room; the frock coat and dress clothes he had bundled into the cab with his new shirts. Then he drove to a hatter's and a shoe house. His next errand was at Tiffany's, where he selected silver-mounted brushes and a scarf-pin. He would not wait to have his silver marked, he said. Lastly, he stopped at a trunk shop on Broadway, and had his purchases packed into various travelling bags.

It was a little after one o'clock when he drove up to the Waldorf, and, after settling with the cabman, went into the office. He registered from Washington; said his mother and father had been abroad, and that he had come down to await the arrival of their steamer. He told his story plausibly and had no trouble, since he offered to pay for them in advance, in engaging his rooms; a sleeping-room, sitting room, and bath.

Not once, but a hundred times Paul had planned this entry into New York. He had gone over every detail of it with Charley

Edwards, and in his scrap book at home there were pages of description about New York hotels, cut from the Sunday papers.

When he was shown to his sitting room on the eighth floor, he saw at a glance that everything was as it should be; there was but one detail in his mental picture that the place did not realize, so he rang for the bell boy and sent him down for flowers. He moved about nervously until the boy returned, putting away his new linen and fingering it delightedly as he did so. When the flowers came, he put them hastily into water, and then tumbled into a hot bath. Presently he came out of his white bathroom, resplendent in his new silk underwear, and playing with the tassels of his red robe. The snow was whirling so fiercely outside his windows that he could scarcely see across the street; but within, the air was deliciously soft and fragrant. He put the violets and jonquils on the tabouret beside the couch, and threw himself down with a long sigh, covering himself with a Roman blanket. He was thoroughly tired; he had been in such haste, he had stood up to such a strain, covered so much ground in the last twenty-four hours, that he wanted to think how it had all come about. Lulled by the sound of the wind, the warm air, and the cool fragrance of the flowers, he sank into deep, drowsy retrospection.

It had been wonderfully simple; when they had shut him out of the theatre and concert hall, when they had taken away his bone, the whole thing was virtually determined. The rest was a mere matter of opportunity. The only thing that at all surprised him was his own courage — for he realized well enough that he had always been tormented by fear, a sort of apprehensive dread that, of late years, as the meshes of the lies he had told closed about him, had been pulling the muscles of his body tighter and tighter. Until now, he could not remember a time when he had not been dreading something. Even when he was a little boy, it was always there — behind him, or before, or on either side. There had always been the shadowed corner, the dark place into which he dared not look, but from which something seemed always to be watching him — and Paul had done things that were not pretty to watch, he knew.

But now he had a curious sense of relief, as though he had at last thrown down the gauntlet to the thing in the corner.

Yet it was but a day since he had been sulking in the traces; but yesterday afternoon that he had been sent to the bank with Denny & Carson's deposit, as usual — but this time he was instructed to leave the book to be balanced. There was above two thousand dollars in checks, and nearly a thousand in the bank notes which he had taken from the book and quietly transferred to his pocket. At the bank he had made out a new deposit slip. His nerves had been steady enough to permit of his returning to the office, where he had finished his work and asked for a full day's holiday tomorrow, Saturday, giving a perfectly reasonable pretext. The bank book, he knew, would not be returned before Monday or Tuesday, and his father would be out of town for the next week. From the time he slipped the bank notes into his pocket until he boarded the night train for New York, he had not known a moment's hesitation.

How astonishingly easy it had all been; here he was, the thing done; and this time there would be no awakening, no figure at the top of the stairs. He watched the snowflakes whirling by his window until he fell asleep.

When he awoke, it was four o'clock in the afternoon. He bounded up with a start; one of his precious days gone already! He spent nearly an hour in dressing, watching every stage of his toilet carefully in the mirror. Everything was quite perfect; he was exactly the kind of boy he had always wanted to be.

When he went downstairs, Paul took a carriage and drove up Fifth Avenue toward the Park. The snow had somewhat abated; carriages and tradesmen's wagons were hurrying soundlessly to and fro in the winter twilight; boys in woolen mufflers were shoveling off the doorsteps; the avenue stages made fine spots of colour against the white street. Here and there on the corners whole flower gardens blooming behind glass windows, against which the snow flakes stuck and melted; violets, roses, carnations, lilies of the valley — somehow vastly more lovely and alluring that they blossomed thus unnaturally in the snow. The Park itself was a wonderful state winter-piece.

When he returned, the pause of the twilight had ceased, and the tune of the streets had changed. The snow was falling faster, lights streamed from the hotels that reared their many stories fearlessly up into the storm, defying the raging Atlantic winds. A long, black stream of carriages poured down the avenue, inter-sected here and there by other streams, tending horizontally. There were a score of cabs about the entrance of his hotel, and his driver had to wait. Boys in livery were running in and out of the awning stretched across the sidewalk, up and down the red velvet carpet laid from the door to the street. Above, about, within it all, was the rumble and roar, the hurry and toss of thousands of human beings as hot for pleasure as himself, and on every side of him towered the glaring affirmation of the omni-potence of wealth.

The boy set his teeth and drew his shoulders together in a spasm of realization; the plot of all dramas, the text of all ro-mances, the nerve-stuff of all sensations was whirling about him like the snowflakes. He burnt like a faggot in a tempest.

When Paul came down to dinner, the music of the orchestra floated up the elevator shaft to greet him. As he stepped into the thronged corridor, he sank back into one of the chairs against the wall to get his breath. The lights, the chatter, the perfumes, the bewildering medley of colour — he had, for a moment, the feeling of not being able to stand it. But only for a moment; these were his own people he told himself. He went slowly about the corridors, through the writing-rooms, smoking-rooms, recep-tion-rooms, as though he were exploring the chambers of an enchanted palace, built and peopled for him alone.

When he reached the dining room he sat down at a table near a window. The flowers, the white linen, the many-coloured wine glasses, the gay toilettes of the women, the low popping of corks, the undulating repetitions of the *Blue Danube* from the orchestra, all flooded Paul's dream with bewildering radiance. When the roseate tinge of his champagne was added — that cold, precious, bubbling stuff that creamed and foamed in his glass — Paul won-dered that there were honest men in the world at all. This was what all the world was fighting for, he reflected; this was what all the struggle was about. He doubted the reality of his past. Had he ever known a place called Cordelia Street, a place where fagged-looking business men boarded the early car? Mere rivets in a machine they seemed to Paul, — sickening men, with combings of children's hair always hanging to their coats, and the smell of cooking in their clothes. Cordelia Street — Ah, that belonged to another time and country! Had he not always been thus, had he not sat here night after night, from as far back as he could remember, looking pensively over just such shimmering textures, and slowly twirling the stem of a glass like this one between his thumb and middle finger? He rather thought he had.

He was not in the least abashed or lonely. He had no especial desire to meet or to know any of these people; all he demanded was the right to look on and conjecture, to watch the pageant. The mere stage properties were all he contended for. Nor was he lonely later in the evening, in his loge at the Opera. He was entirely rid of his nervous misgivings, of his forced aggressiveness, of the imperative desire to show himself different from his surroundings. He felt now that his surroundings explained him. Nobody questioned the purple; he had only to wear it passively. He had only to glance down at his dress coat to reassure himself that here it would be impossible for anyone to humiliate him.

He found it hard to leave his beautiful sitting room to go to bed that night, and sat long watching the raging storm from his turret window. When he went to sleep, it was with the lights turned on in his bedroom; partly because of his old timidity, and partly so that, if he should wake in the night, there would be no wretched moment of doubt, no horrible suspicion of yellow wall paper, or of Washington and Calvin above his bed.

On Sunday morning the city was practically snow-bound. Paul breakfasted late, and in the afternoon he fell in with a wild San Francisco boy, a freshman at Yale, who said he had run down for a "little flyer" over Sunday. The young man offered to show Paul the night side of the town, and the two boys went off together after dinner, not returning to the hotel until seven o'clock the next morning. They had started out in the confiding warmth of a champagne friendship, but their parting in the elevator was singularly cool. The freshman pulled himself together to make his train, and Paul went to bed. He awoke at two o'clock in the afternoon, very thirsty and dizzy, and rang for ice water, coffee, and the Pittsburgh papers.

On the part of the hotel management, Paul excited no suspicion. There was this to be said for him, that he wore his spoils with dignity and in no way made himself conspicuous. His chief greediness lay in his ears and eyes, and his excesses were not offensive ones. His dearest pleasures were the gray winter twilights in his sitting room; his quiet enjoyment of his flowers, his clothes, his wide divan, his cigarette and his sense of power. He could not remember a time when he had felt so at peace with himself. The mere release from the necessity of petty lying, lying every day and every day, restored his self-respect. He had never lied for pleasure, even at school; but to make himself noticed and admired, to assert his difference from other Cordelia Street boys; and he felt a good deal more manly, more honest, even, now that he had no need for boastful pretensions, now that he could, as his actor friends used to say, "dress the part." It was characteristic that remorse did not occur to him. His golden days went by without a shadow, and he made each as perfect as he could.

On the eighth day after his arrival in New York, he found the whole affair exploited in the Pittsburgh papers, exploited with a wealth of detail which indicated that local news of a sensational nature was at a low ebb. The firm of Denny & Carson announced that the boy's father had refunded the full amount of his theft, and that they had no intention of prosecuting. The Cumberland minister had been interviewed, and expressed his hope of yet reclaiming the motherless lad, and Paul's Sabbath-school teacher declared that she would spare no effort to that end. The rumour had reached Pittsburgh that the boy had been seen in a New York hotel, and his father had gone East to find him and bring him home.

Paul had just come in to dress for dinner; he sank into a chair, weak in the knees, and clasped his head in his hands. It was to be worse than jail, even; the tepid waters of Cordelia Street were to close over him finally and forever. The gray monotony stretched before him in hopeless, unrelieved years; Sabbath-school, Young People's Meeting, the yellow-papered room, the damp dish-towels; it all rushed back upon him with sickening vividness. He had the old feeling that the orchestra had suddenly stopped, the sinking sensation that the play was over. The sweat broke out on his face, and he sprang to his feet, looked about him with his white, conscious smile, and winked at himself in the mirror. With something of the childish belief in miracles with which he had so often gone to class, all his lessons unlearned, Paul dressed and dashed whistling down the corridor to the elevator.

He had no sooner entered the dining room and caught the measure of the music, than his remembrance was lightened by his old elastic power of claiming the moment, mounting with it, and finding it all sufficient. The glare and glitter about him, the mere scenic accessories had again, and for the last time, their old potency. He would show himself that he was game, he would finish the thing splendidly. He doubted, more than ever, the ex- istence of Cordelia Street, and for the first time he drank his wine recklessly. Was he not, after all, one of these fortunate beings? Was he not still himself, and in his own place? He drummed a nervous accompaniment to the music and looked about him, tell- ing himself over and over that it had paid.

He reflected drowsily, to the swell of the violin and the chill sweetness of his wine, that he might have done it more wisely. He might have caught an outbound steamer and been well out of their clutches before now. But the other side of the world had seemed too far away and too uncertain then; he could not have waited for it; his need had been too sharp. If he had to choose over again, he would do the same thing tomorrow. He looked affectionately about the dining room, now gilded with a soft mist. Ah, it had paid indeed!

Paul was awakened next morning by a painful throbbing in his head and feet. He had thrown himself across the bed without undressing, and had slept with his shoes on. His limbs and hands were lead heavy, and his tongue and throat were parched. There came upon him one of those fateful attacks of clear-headedness that never occurred except when he was physically exhausted and his nerves hung loose. He lay still and closed his eyes and let the tide of realities wash over him.

His father was in New York; "stopping at some joint or other," he told himself. The memory of successive summers on the front stoop fell upon him like a weight of black water. He had not a hundred dollars left; and he knew now, more than ever, that money was everything, the wall that stood between all he loathed and all he wanted. The thing was winding itself up; he had thought of that on his first glorious day in New York, and had even provided a way to snap the thread. It lay on his dressing-table now; he had got it out last night when he came blindly up from dinner, — but the shiny metal hurt his eyes, and he disliked the look of it, anyway.

He rose and moved about with a painful effort, succumbing now and again to attacks of nausea. It was the old depression exaggerated; all the world had become Cordelia Street. Yet somehow he was not afraid of anything, was absolutely calm; perhaps because he had looked into the dark corner at last, and knew. It was bad enough, what he saw there; but somehow not so bad as his long fear of it had been. He saw everything clearly now. He had a feeling that he had made the best of it, that he had lived the sort of life he was meant to live, and for half an hour he sat staring at the revolver. But he told himself that was not the way, so he went downstairs and took a cab to the ferry.

When Paul arrived at Newark, he got off the train and took another cab, directing the driver to follow the Pennsylvania tracks out of the town. The snow lay heavy on the roadways and had drifted deep in the open fields. Only here and there the dead grass or dried weed stalks projected, singularly black, above it. Once well into the country, Paul dismissed the carriage and walked, floundering along the tracks, his mind a medley of irrelevant things. He seemed to hold in his brain an actual picture of everything he had seen that morning. He remembered every feature of both his drivers, the toothless old woman from whom he had bought the red flowers in his coat, the agent from whom he had got his ticket, and all of his fellow-passengers on the ferry. His mind, unable to cope with vital matters near at hand, worked feverishly and deftly at sorting and grouping these images. They made for him a part of the ugliness of the world, of the ache in his head, and the bitter burning on his tongue. He stooped and put a handful of snow into his mouth as he walked, but that, too, seemed hot. When he reached a little hillside, where the tracks ran through a cut some twenty feet below him, he stopped and sat down.

The carnations in his coat were drooping with the cold, he noticed; all their red glory over. It occurred to him that all the flowers he had seen in the show windows that first night must have gone the same way, long before this. It was only one splendid breath they had, in spite of their brave mockery at the winter outside the glass. It was a losing game in the end, it seemed, this revolt against the homilies by which the world is run. Paul took one of the blossoms carefully from his coat and scooped a little hole in the snow, where he covered it up. Then he dozed a while, from his weak condition, seeming insensible to the cold.

The sound of an approaching train woke him, and he started to his feet, remembering only his resolution, and afraid lest he should be too late. He stood watching the approaching locomotive, his teeth chattering, his lips drawn away from them in a frightened smile; once or twice he glanced nervously sidewise, as though he were being watched. When the right moment came, he jumped. As he fell, the folly of his haste occurred to him with merciless clearness, the vastness of what he had left undone. There flashed through his brain, clearer than ever before, the blue of Adriatic water, the yellow of Algerian sands.

He felt something strike his chest, — his body was being thrown swiftly through the air, on and on, immeasurably far and fast, while his limbs gently relaxed. Then, because the picture-making mechanism was crushed, the disturbing visions flashed into black, and Paul dropped back into the immense design of things.

QUESTIONS

1. This sad and beautiful story presents the case of an outsider, a misfit, who stole his hour in the artificial sunlight and could not bear to pay the penalty. Willa Cather shows us Paul's defiance and fastidiousness early in the story. Describe her methods of making these characteristics clear to us.

2. What touches of characterization in the early part of the story prepare us for Paul's eventual suicide?

3. In describing Paul's relationships with his teachers, Willa Cather shows some remarkable insights into human nature. Mention some of these.

4. One day the drawing master observes Paul asleep at his drawing board. What is the purpose of this incident in the story?

5. (a) Although not creatively artistic himself, Paul derives great satisfaction from being close to the world of art. Briefly describe the incidents which show this aspect of his character.
   (b) What is it about the life of the concert hall and the theatre that he enjoys so much?
   (c) What point is Willa Cather making clear in the concert hall meeting of Paul and his English teacher?

6. (a) What connection is there between Paul's vigil outside the hotel in which the German soprano was staying and his theft some days later?
   (b) Explain how contrast is used in the narration of this vigil.

7. Cordelia Street is described at length from Paul's point of view.
   (a) Name the dominant impression created by this description.
   (b) List some of the descriptive details used to achieve this impression.
   (c) Why is this description important to the plot of the story?

8. (a) What reasons might the author have had for narrating Paul's arrival in New York before revealing his theft?
   (b) She makes the flashback which outlines the theft fit smoothly into the story. How does she do it?

9. From the very beginning of the New York adventure, Willa Cather repeatedly reminds us of the cold and the snow that surround Paul's new world of luxury. Why does she do this?

10. There are several references to flowers in "Paul's Case". Explain the symbolic meaning of Paul's last action with the red carnation, and relate this final gesture to his first appearance in the story.

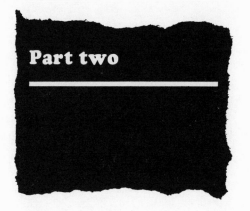

# Part two

*Stephen*

*Leacock*

# My remarkable uncle

---

*Stephen Leacock (1869-1944), at the age of six, accompanied his family from England to York County, Ontario, where they settled on a farm a few miles south of Lake Simcoe. He attended Upper Canada College and the University of Toronto. After receiving his degree, he taught at Upper Canada College, and then, following graduate study in economics and political science at the University of Chicago, received an appointment to teach at McGill University in Montreal. From 1908 to 1936, he was head of the Department of Economics and Political Science at McGill. Although the author of learned works related to his profession, Leacock is most famous for his humorous writings, of which the most popular are* Literary Lapses *(1910),* Nonsense Novels *(1911), and* Sunshine Sketches of a Little Town *(1912). "My Remarkable Uncle" is a good example of Leacock's belief that true humour is based upon "the strange incongruity between our aspiration and our achievement". This essay is reprinted here by permission of McClelland and Stewart, Ltd.*

---

*A Personal Document*

THE MOST REMARKABLE MAN I have ever known in my life was my uncle Edward Philip Leacock — known to ever so many people in Winnipeg fifty or sixty years ago as E.P. His character was so exceptional that it needs nothing but plain narration. It was so exaggerated already that you couldn't exaggerate it.

When I was a boy of six, my father brought us, a family flock, to settle on an Ontario farm. We lived in an isolation unknown, in these days of radio, anywhere in the world. We were thirty-five miles from a railway. There were no newspapers. Nobody came and went. There was nowhere to come and go. In the solitude of the dark winter nights the stillness was that of eternity.

Into this isolation there broke, two years later, my dynamic Uncle Edward, my father's younger brother. He had just come from a year's travel around the Mediterranean. He must have been about twenty-eight, but seemed a more than adult man, bronzed and self-confident, with a square beard like a Plantagenet King. His talk was of Algiers, of the African slave market; of the Golden Horn and the Pyramids. To us it sounded like the *Arabian Nights*. When we asked, "Uncle Edward, do you know the Prince of Wales?" he answered, "Quite intimately" – with no further explanation. It was an impressive trick he had.

In that year, 1878, there was a general election in Canada. E.P. was in it up to the neck in less than no time. He picked up the history and politics of Upper Canada in a day, and in a week knew everybody in the countryside. He spoke at every meeting, but his strong point was the personal contact of electioneering, of bar-room treats. This gave full scope for his marvellous talent for flattery and make-believe.

"Why, let me see" – he would say to some tattered country specimen beside him glass in hand – "surely, if your name is Framley, you must be a relation of my dear old friend General Sir Charles Framley of the Horse Artillery?" "Mebbe," the flattered specimen would answer. "I guess, mebbe; I ain't kept track very good of my folks in the old country." "Dear me! I must tell Sir Charles that I've seen you. He'll be so pleased." ... In this way in a fortnight E.P. had conferred honours and distinctions on half the township of Georgina. They lived in a recaptured atmosphere of generals, admirals and earls. Vote? How else could they vote than conservative, men of family like them?

It goes without saying that in politics, then and always E.P. was on the conservative, the aristocratic side, but along with that was hail-fellow-well-met with the humblest. This was instinct. A democrat can't condescend. He's down already. But when a conservative stoops, he conquers.

The election, of course, was a walk-over. E.P. might have stayed to reap the fruits. But he knew better. Ontario at that day was too small a horizon. For these were the days of the hard times of Ontario farming, when mortgages fell like snowflakes, and farmers were sold up, or sold out, or went "to the States", or faded humbly underground.

But all the talk was of Manitoba now opening up. Nothing would do E.P. but that he and my father must go west. So we had a sale of our farm, with refreshments, old-time fashion, for the buyers. The poor, lean cattle and the broken machines fetched less than the price of the whiskey. But E.P. laughed it all off, quoted that the star of the Empire glittered in the west, and off to the West they went, leaving us children behind at school.

They hit Winnipeg just on the rise of the boom, and E.P. came at once into his own and rode on the crest of the wave. There is something of magic appeal in the rush and movement of a "boom" town — a Winnipeg of the 80's, a Carson City of the 60's. . . . Life comes to a focus; it is all here and now, all *present*, no past and no outside — just a clatter of hammers and saws, rounds of drinks and rolls of money. In such an atmosphere every man seems a remarkable fellow, a man of exception; individuality separates out and character blossoms like a rose.

E.P. came into his own. In less than no time he was in everything and knew everybody, conferring titles and honours up and down Portage Avenue. In six months he had a great fortune, on paper; took a trip east and brought back a charming wife from Toronto; built a large house beside the river; filled it with pictures that he said were his ancestors, and carried on in it a roaring hospitality that never stopped.

His activities were wide. He was president of a bank (that never opened), head of a brewery (for brewing the Red River) and, above all, secretary-treasurer of the Winnipeg Hudson Bay and Arctic Ocean Railway that had a charter authorizing it to build a road to the Arctic Ocean, when it got ready. They had no track, but they printed stationery and passes, and in return E.P. received passes over all North America.

But naturally his main hold was politics. He was elected right away into the Manitoba Legislature. They would have made him Prime Minister but for the existence of the grand old man of the Province, John Norquay. But even at that in a very short time Norquay ate out of E.P.'s hand, and E.P. led him on a string. I remember how they came down to Toronto, when I was a schoolboy, with an adherent group of "Westerners", all in heavy buffalo coats and bearded like Assyrians. E.P. paraded them on King Street like a returned explorer with savages.

Naturally E.P.'s politics remained conservative. But he pitched the note higher. Even the ancestors weren't good enough. He invented a Portuguese Dukedom (some one of our family once worked in Portugal) — and he conferred it, by some kind of reversion, on my elder brother Jim who had gone to Winnipeg to work in E.P.'s office. This enabled him to say to visitors in his big house, after looking at the ancestors — to say in a half-whisper behind his hand, "Strange to think that two deaths would make that boy a Portuguese Duke." But Jim never knew which two Portuguese to kill.

To aristocracy E.P. also added a touch of peculiar prestige by always being apparently just about to be called away — imperially. If some one said, "Will you be in Winnipeg all winter, Mr. Leacock?" he answered, "It will depend a good deal on what happens in West Africa." Just that; West Africa beat them.

Then came the crash of the Manitoba boom. Simple people, like my father, were wiped out in a day. Not so E.P. The crash just gave him a lift as the smash of a big wave lifts a strong swimmer. He just went right on. I believe that in reality he was left utterly bankrupt. But it made no difference. He used credit instead of cash. He still had his imaginary bank, and his railway to the Arctic Ocean. Hospitality still roared and the tradesmen still paid for it. Any one who called about a bill was told that E.P.'s movements were uncertain and would depend a good deal on what happened in Johannesburg. That held them another six months.

It was during this period that I used to see him when he made his periodic trips "east", to impress his creditors in the West. He floated, at first very easily, on hotel credit, borrowed loans and unpaid bills. A banker, especially a country town banker, was his natural mark and victim. He would tremble as E.P. came in, like a stock-dove that sees a hawk. E.P.'s method was so simple; it was like showing a farmer peas under thimbles. As he entered the banker's side-office he would say: "I say. Do you fish? Surely that's a greenhart casting-rod on the wall?" (E.P. knew the names of everything). In a few minutes the banker, flushed and pleased, was exhibiting the rod, and showing flies in a box out of a drawer. When E.P. went out he carried a hundred dollars with him. There was no security. The transaction was all over.

He dealt similarly with credit, with hotels, livery stables and bills in shops. They all fell for his method. He bought with lavish generosity, never asking a price. He never suggested pay till just as an afterthought, just as he was going out. And then: "By the way, please let me have the account promptly. I may be going away," and, in an aside to me, as if not meant for the shop, "Sir Henry Loch has cabled again from West Africa." And so out; they had never seen him before, nor since.

The proceeding with a hotel was different. A country hotel was, of course, easy, in fact too easy. E.P. would sometimes pay such a bill in cash, just as a sportsman won't shoot a sitting partridge. But a large hotel was another thing. E.P., on leaving — that is, when all ready to leave, coat, bag and all — would call for his bill at the desk. At the sight of it he would break out into enthusiasm at the reasonableness of it. "Just think!" he would say in his "aside" to me, "compare that with the Hotel Crillon in Paris!" The hotel proprietor had no way of doing this; he just felt that he ran a cheap hotel. Then another "aside," "Do remind me to mention to Sir John how admirably we've been treated; he's coming here next week." "Sir John" was our Prime Minister and the hotel keeper hadn't known he was coming — and he wasn't.... Then came the final touch — "Now, let me see ...

seventy-six dollars ... seventy-six ... You give me" — and E.P.
fixed his eye firmly on the hotel man — "give me twenty-four
dollars, and then I can remember to send an even hundred." The
man's hand trembled. But he gave it.

This does not mean that E.P. was in any sense a crook, in any
degree dishonest. His bills to him were just "deferred pay", like
the British debts to the United States. He never did, never contemplated, a crooked deal in his life. All his grand schemes were
as open as sunlight — and as empty.

In all his interviews E.P. could fashion his talk to his audience.
On one of his appearances, I introduced him to a group of college
friends, young men near to degrees, to whom degrees mean
everything. In casual conversation E.P. turned to me and said,
"Oh, by the way, you'll be glad to know that I've just received
my honorary degree from the Vatican — at last!" The "at last"
was a knock-out — a degree from the Pope, and overdue at that!

Of course it could not last. Gradually credit crumbles. Faith
weakens. Creditors grow hard, and friends turn their faces away.
Gradually E.P. sank down. The death of his wife had left him
a widower, a shuffling, half-shabby figure, familiar on the street,
that would have been pathetic but for his indomitable self-belief,
the illumination of his mind. Even at that, times grew hard with
him. At length even the simple credit of the barrooms broke
under him. I have been told by my brother Jim — the Portuguese
Duke — of E.P. being put out of a Winnipeg bar, by an angry
bartender who at last broke the mesmerism. E.P. had brought in
a little group, spread up the fingers of one hand and said, "Mr.
Leacock, five!" ... The bartender broke into oaths. E.P. hooked
a friend by the arm. "Come away," he said. "I'm afraid the poor
fellow's crazy! But I hate to report him."

Presently even his power to travel came to an end. The rail-
ways found out at last that there wasn't any Arctic Ocean, and
anyway the printer wouldn't print.

Just once again he managed to "come east." It was in June of
1891. I met him forging along King Street in Toronto — a trifle
shabby but with a plug hat with a big band of crepe round it.
"Poor Sir John," he said. "I felt I simply must come down for

his funeral." Then I remembered that the Prime Minister was dead, and realized that kindly sentiment had meant free transportation.

That was the last I ever saw of E.P. A little after that some one paid his fare back to England. He received, from some family trust, a little income of perhaps two pounds a week. On that he lived, with such dignity as might be, in a lost village of Worcestershire. He told the people of the village — so I learned later — that his stay was uncertain; it would depend a good deal on what happened in China. But nothing happened in China; there he stayed, years and years. There he might have finished out, but for a strange chance of fortune, a sort of poetic justice, that gave to E.P. an evening in the sunset.

It happened that in the part of England where our family belonged there was an ancient religious brotherhood, with a monastery and dilapidated estates that went back for centuries. E.P. descended on them, the brothers seeming to him an easy mark, as brothers indeed are. In the course of his pious "retreat", E.P. took a look into the brothers' finances, and his quick intelligence discovered an old claim against the British Government, large in amount and valid beyond a doubt.

In less than no time E.P. was at Westminster, representing the brothers. He knew exactly how to handle British officials; they were easier even than Ontario hotel keepers. All that is needed is hints of marvellous investment overseas. They never go there but they remember how they just missed Johannesburg or were just late on Persian oil. All E.P. needed was his Arctic Railway. "When you come out, I must take you over our railway. I really think that as soon as we reach the Coppermine River we must put the shares on here; it's too big for New York . . ."

So E.P. got what he wanted. The British Government are so used to old claims that it would as soon pay as not. There are plenty left.

The brothers got a whole lot of money. In gratitude they invited E.P. to be their permanent manager; so there he was, lifted into ease and affluence. The years went easily by, among gardens, orchards and fishponds old as the Crusades.

When I was lecturing in London in 1921 he wrote to me: "Do come down; I am too old now to travel; but any day you like I will send a chauffeur with a car and two lay-brothers to bring you down." I thought the "lay-brothers" a fine touch — just like E.P.

I couldn't go. I never saw him again. He ended out his days at the monastery, no cable calling him to West Africa. Years ago I used to think of E.P. as a sort of humbug, a source of humour. Looking back now I realize better the unbeatable quality of his spirit, the mark, we like to think just now, of the British race.

If there is a paradise, I am sure he will get in. He will say at the gate — "Peter? Then surely you must be a relation of Lord Peter of Tichfield?"

But if he fails, then, as the Spaniards say so fittingly, "May the earth lie light upon him."


CRITIQUE AND QUESTIONS

On a first reading, "My Remarkable Uncle" might appear to be a story, since it has the short story elements of character, incidents, and conflict. It is, however, really an essay, a character sketch. A short story requires that some kind of conflict be developed through a series of incidents that are closely related by cause and effect, a related sequence, which "My Remarkable Uncle" lacks. In spite of our general awareness of E. P.'s career, his meteoric westward and eastward soarings, what Leacock gives us is not a connected development, but only isolated samplings of E.P.'s riotous life. If we were to represent by a graph what the author tells us of his uncle, we would have to make a series of disconnected dots, not a continuous line.

However, to say that it is not a short story is not to diminish its worth. It appears to have been the author's favourite piece. In 1942, Whit Burnett, editor of the prose anthology, *This is My Best,* invited him to contribute the one unit from all his humorous output which he thought represented him at his best creative moment. He chose this sketch, saying in a foreword to it:

> I have suggested the selection of this example of my
> writing because, with all becoming modesty, I am proud of
> it. It is only after long practice and much interest in the
> work that one can set down plain truth, without over-
> embellishment or wandering from the point. When this is
> done the writing takes on an inevitable aspect, as if there
> were no other way to say what is said. . . . When this is
> done even the truth itself sounds a little better than true,
> which is the basis of what is called literature.

As we begin reading, we see at once that the author distinguishes
between "plain truth" and "bald fact," for clearly the hand of the
artist is fashioning uncle Edward for us. The author makes him leap
into vivid life with one regal simile and one bit of dialogue. To
young Stephen Leacock, he "seemed a more than adult man, bronzed
and self-confident, with a square beard like a Plantagenet King. . . .
When we asked, 'Uncle Edward, do you know the Prince of
Wales?' he answered, 'Quite intimately' — with no further explanation." E.P. never loses this wonderful aplomb in calmly affirming
the outrageously untrue.

Most humour depends on some incongruity, some inappropriate-
ness of action or appearance that stirs in us the ancient urge to
mock. What could be more incongruous, what could offer a sharper
comic contrast than the scene in which uncle Edward persuades
an Ontario farmer that he is conservative by aristocratic ties of blood?
Says E.P., " 'Surely if your name is Framley, you must be a relation
of my dear old friend General Sir Charles Framley of the Horse
Artillery?' 'Mebbe', the flattered specimen would answer. 'I guess,
mebbe. I ain't kept track very good of my folks in the old country.' "
Listen to the incongruity between that ringing though fictitious
title and the flat Ontario diction of the "tattered country specimen".

But if incongruity is at the basis of humour, it is also a cause of
pathos. The contrast between what is and what ought to be is the
source of tears. "Ontario at that day was too small a horizon" for
uncle Edward; and because he is so unselfish, so entirely self-deceived
in his fraudulence, so gallant an optimist, we cannot help wanting
him to triumph. But the time comes in his Canadian adventure when
the highest reach of his art can bring him only a free trip on the
C.P.R. to attend Sir John A. Macdonald's funeral. And though,

earlier in the sketch, we smile when we read that under E.P.'s influence, the Leacock family has auctioned the farm, and that "the poor lean cattle and the broken machines fetched less than the price of the whiskey", we can see that there is pathos here, too. The father has acted out of desperation, "For these were the days of the hard times of Ontario farming when mortgages fell like snowflakes and farmers were sold up, or sold out, or went to the States, or faded humbly underground." Like all great comedians, Stephen Leacock knew that laughter and tears have a common well-spring.

Exaggeration, too, plays an important part in this sketch, as it does in all of Leacock's humour. "It was so exaggerated already that you couldn't exaggerate it," he tells us of his uncle's character. Still, the comedy of this essay rests on exaggeration, with or without a little help from the author; and what makes this exaggeration so successful is that just when we think that we have reached the comic climax of an incident, the climax is capped with still further exaggeration. An example is E. P.'s invention of the Portuguese Dukedom to satisfy his insatiable appetite for aristocratic honours. The incident concludes with E.P.'s pungent whisper, "Strange to think that two deaths would make that boy a Portuguese Duke", which is fairly funny in itself, but then the narrator caps the climax with the comment, "But Jim never knew which two Portuguese to kill." E.P. himself demonstrates what seems a family trait — the Leacock ability to climb a summit of exaggeration and then go a foot beyond it. In the hearing of young Stephen's college friends he says, "Oh, by the way, you'll be glad to know that I've just received my honorary degree from the Vatican — at last!" The author comments, "The 'at last' was a knock-out — a degree from the Pope, and overdue at that!" The reader can find other examples of the same technique, the best of which, perhaps, is E.P.'s last letter to his nephew.

Laughter is as much bounded by tears as our life is "rounded with a sleep", and this cleverly comical sketch ends with a sentence that reminds us that even certain death is itself uncertain. The narrow door of the grave is sure, but not the gates of Heaven. Perhaps even uncle Edward's splendid passwords **may** not serve him there: "But if he fails then, as the Spaniards say so fittingly, 'May the earth lie light upon him.' "

1. In his opening paragraph, Stephen Leacock states of his uncle's character, "It was so exaggerated already that you couldn't exaggerate it." Discuss the element of exaggeration in this essay.

2. Although the incidents in this sketch are widely separated in time and not closely linked by cause and effect, uncle Edward's adventures do move towards a type of climax. Identify this incident and explain why you consider it the climax.

3. Besides working an incident up to a climax of exaggeration, the author will occasionally bring an exaggerated statement toppling by means of a comment that forms an anti-climax. Give an example of his use of this technique, and try to explain why the example is comical.

4. Uncle Edward is a fraud and a cheat, and yet the author somehow contrives to make us like and even admire him. How does he achieve this effect?

5. Exaggeration is effective only when controlled by artistic restraint. Write a sketch of about 500 words characterizing some colourful person whom you know or can imagine, and using the techniques employed by Stephen Leacock in "My Remarkable Uncle".

*Sir Charles P.*

*Snow*

# Man in society

━━━━━━━━━━━━━━━━

*Sir Charles P. Snow (b. 1905) was born in Leicester and educated at University College, Leicester, and at Cambridge. He was trained as a physicist and was awarded the Ph.D. by Cambridge in 1930. An experienced editor and college teacher, he published his first novel,* The Search, *in 1935. In 1948,* The Light and the Dark *appeared — the first of a series of novels under the general title,* The New Men. *Others in the series have been* The Time of Hope *(1949),* The Masters *(1951),* The New Men *(1954),* The Search *(1958), and* The Affair *(1960). C. P. Snow has been deeply interested in the effect of modern science on our civilization. His views are brilliantly stated in* The Two Cultures and the Scientific Revolution *(1959). The following essay is reprinted by permission of the author.*

━━━━━━━━━━━━━━━━

AUSCHWITZ AND HIROSHIMA. We have seen all that; in some of it we have acquiesced or helped. No wonder we are morally guilty. Men like ourselves have done such things — and at the same time men like ourselves, sometimes the same men who have taken a hand in the horrors, have been showing more concern for the unlucky round them than has ever been shown by a large society in human history. That is the moral paradox in which we have to live.

It is wrong to try to domesticate the horrors. The mass slaughter of the concentration camps was both the most awful and the most degrading set of actions that men have done so far. This set of actions was ordered and controlled by abnormally wicked men, if you like, but down the line the orders were carried out by thousands of people like the rest of us, civil servants, soldiers, engineers, all brought up in an advanced Western and Christian society. While it was people not like the rest of us but a great deal better, people who for imagination and morality, not to speak of intellect, stand among the finest of our race, people like Einstein, Niels Bohr, and Franck, who got caught up in the tangle of events which led to Hiroshima and Nagasaki. The dropping of those bombs was of a lesser order of wickedness from what was done at Auschwitz. But Western man ought not to forget that he did it; Eastern man certainly won't.

At the same time we ought not to forget what there is to our credit. Some kinds of optimism about man's nature are dangerous — but so are some kinds of pessimism. Think of the care the Swedes and the Danes are taking of their old and poor, or of prisoners, or of social misfits. Nothing like that has been done at any period or in any place until our lifetime. We can congratulate ourselves in this country, too. The Scandinavians have not made anything like a perfect society. In some ways we have not got as near to it as they have. But they and we have made a better shot at it than anyone before us.

This country is a much fairer and a much kinder society than the one I was born into in 1905. It may seem sentimental to have consciences troubled about capital punishment, about removing one life when Western man has recently eliminated twenty million: yet it is a sign of moral sensitivity. So is the attempt, however grudging, to treat women as though they were equal human beings. So is the feeling behind the Wolfenden Report. So is the conviction — so urgent in the United States — that children have a special right to happiness.

Some of these feelings may lead to practical follies (I believe that the American one is making a mess of their education), but that is not the point. They are signs of a development of something very rare in the world up to now, which one might call moral kindness. I have no doubt that in Scandinavia, this country, some, though not all, of the United States, and perhaps three or four other countries in the West, the amount of fairness, tolerance, and effective kindness within the society would seem astonishing to any nineteenth-century man.

It would also seem astonishing to any nineteenth-century man how much we know. There is probably no one now alive as clever as Clerk Maxwell or Gauss; but thousands of people know more than Clerk Maxwell or Gauss, and understand more of those parts of the world that they spent their lives trying to understand. Put those two down, or even greater men, such as Newton and Archimedes, in front of what is now understood — and they would think it wonderful. So it is, and we can take pride and joy in it. It will go on; the search to understand is one of the most human things about us. Compared with our ancestors, there are some trivial physical differences. We are a good deal taller and heavier, we live much longer. But above all, we know more.

All this it would be reasonable to call progress, so long as we don't expect of progress more than it can give. In each of our individual lives there is, of course, something beyond human help. Each of us has to live part of his life alone: and he has to die alone. That part of our experience is right outside of time and history, and progress has no meaning there. In this sense, the individual condition is tragic. But that is no excuse for not doing our best with the social condition.

To think otherwise, to take refuge in facile despair, has been the characteristic intellectual treachery of our day. It is shoddy. We have to face the individual condition: for good and evil, for pettiness and the occasional dash of grandeur, we have to know what men are capable of: and then we can't contract out. For we are part, not only of the privileged North European-British-American *enclave* of progress, but of another progress which is altering the whole world.

I mean something brutally simple. Most people in Asia still haven't enough to eat: but they have a bit more than before. Most people in Asia are still dying before their time (on the average, Indians live less than half as long as Englishmen): but they are living longer than before. Is *that* progress? This is not a subject to be superior or refined or ingenious about, and the answer is: *of course it is.*

It is because Western man has grown too far away from that elemental progress that we can't get on terms with most of the human race. Through luck we got in first with the scientific-industrial revolution; as a result, our lives became, on the average, healthier, longer, more comfortable to an extent that had never been imagined; it doesn't become us to tell our Chinese and Indian friends that that kind of progress is not worth having.

We know what it is like to live among the shops, the cars, the radios, of Leicester, and Orebro, and Des Moines. We know what it is like to ask the point of it all, and to feel the Swedish sadness or the American disappointment or the English Welfare State discontent. But the Chinese and Indians would like the chance of being well-fed enough to ask what is the point of it all. They are in search of what Leicester, Orebro, and Des Moines take for granted, food, extra years of life, modest comforts. When they have got these things, they are willing to put up with a dash of the Swedish sadness or American disappointment. And their de-termination to get these things is likely in the next thirty years to prove the strongest social force on earth.

Will they get them? Will the social condition everywhere reach within foreseeable time something like the standard of the privileged Western enclave? There is no technical reason why not. If it does, the level of moral kindness will go up in parallel. These ought to be realistic hopes. There seems only one fatality that might destroy them. That is, it goes without saying, an H-bomb war. That is the only method of committing the final disloyalty to the species, of stopping the hope of progress dead.

No one can pretend that it is not possible. For myself, I think that it won't happen — even though we have seen how good and conscientious men have become responsible for horrors, even though two atomic bombs have been dropped already, and by Western man. But I still think, partly as a guess, partly as a calcu-lation, that we shall escape the H-bomb war — just as I think we shall escape the longer-term danger of Malthusian over-population.

It may easily be that I am letting hope run away with me about the H-bomb war. Some of the wisest disagree with me. Let us imagine that they are right and that the H-bombs go off. Is that going to be the end? I find it difficult to believe. In this country a lot of us would be dead, our children with us. A lot of Americans and Russians would also be killed outright. No one knows how many would die afterwards through effects of radiation. But I don't believe that men have at present the resources to destroy the race.

If that is so, and if after an H-bomb war a viable fraction of the world population were left untouched (my own guess is that it would be a very large fraction, at least two-thirds and probably much bigger), then we should all be amazed how soon hope of progress took possession again. The human species is biologically a very tough one, and tough in a sense no animal species can be, through its intelligence, its organisation of knowledge, the capacity of its members not to be totally bound within the rapacious self. After the most hideous H-bomb war, the inhabitants of Africa and India and South America would have the strength of those qualities to build on. The material and scientific gap, left through the devastation of the West and Russia, would be filled up at a speed not flattering to Western or Russian self-esteem. What would the moral scar be?

I think we can already answer that question, for we too have, as I said at the beginning, witnessed horrors and assisted at them. Most of us don't live constantly in the presence of Hiroshima and Auschwitz: the memory doesn't prevent us getting morally concerned about the fate of one murderer or cross because a lonely and impoverished old man doesn't have enough calls from the District Visitor.

It would be just the same if the Northern hemisphere became more or less destroyed. Men elsewhere would not live under that shadow; they would be busy with their own societies. If those societies were less fair and morally sensitive than ours is now, they would soon catch up. Within a bizarrely short interval, after hundreds of millions of people had been incinerated by H-bombs, men in countries unaffected would be passionately debating capital punishment. It sounds mad: but it is the kind of madness which makes human beings as tough as they are, and as capable of behaving better than they have so far behaved.

So there remains a sort of difficult hope. So long as men continue to be men, individual man will perceive the same darkness about his solitary condition as any of us does now. But he will also feel occasional intimations that his own life is not the only one. In the midst of his egotisms, pettinesses, power-seekings, and perhaps the horrors these may cause, he will intermittently stretch a little beyond himself. That little, added to the intelligence and growing knowledge of the species, will be enough to make his societies more decent, to use the social forces for what, in the long sight of history, are good ends.

None of it will be easy. As individuals, each of us is almost untouched by this progress. It is no comfort to remember how short human history is. As individuals, that seems just an irony. But as a race, we have scarcely begun to live.

QUESTIONS

Sir Charles Snow, a scientist as well as an eminent novelist, believes, as the novelist William Faulkner believes, that modern man will somehow survive the destructive powers recently made available by the genius of modern science. It would be instructive to compare not only the ideas of these two writers (see Section One for Faulkner's essay) but also the tone and the intensity of the two essays. Snow has the cool head of the scientist. He guesses — but even his guesses are calculated. Faulkner proclaims a faith. He writes with religious passion and conviction. His is the tone of the poet-priest. He does not calculate — he asserts; he does not guess — he knows.

1. Which of the two essayists is more convincing? More reassuring? Why?

2. Faulkner rests his case for survival on the intrinsic creativeness

of man. What evidences does Snow advance from recent history to prove man's intrinsic destructiveness?

3. Discuss Snow's distinction between guilty men and guilty societies? Were all Germans as guilty as Hitler?

4. Are creative men like Einstein guilty of the destruction of Hiroshima? Can we rely on creative men to save man from destruction?

5. What evidence is there, in Snow's view, that man has made and is making moral as well as intellectual progress?

6. Does Snow think we can feel secure because of this progress?

7. What, in Snow's view, would be the effects on civilization of an H-bomb war?

8. Is he justified in his "difficult hope" for the future?

9. Does Snow rely too much, in his hope, on man as intelligent animal and not enough on Faulkner's vision of man as creative spirit?

10. What would Faulkner think of Snow's argument; and *vice versa?*

11. What would each of them think of Hugh MacLennan's satirical piece, "Remembrance Day, 2010" (Section One)?

*Bruce*

*Hutchison*

# The Canadian personality

---

*Bruce Hutchison (b. 1901) was born in Prescott, Ontario, but is strongly identified with Western Canada. He was Associate Editor of the* Winnipeg Free Press *from 1949 to 1950, and has been Editor of the* Victoria Daily Times *since 1950. A journalist with a wide knowledge of political and economic affairs, Mr. Hutchison is also a romantic with a deep love for the places and the peoples of Canada. His panoramic book about Canada,* The Unknown Country, *won him the Governor General's Award for Creative Non-Fiction in 1943. The Incredible* Canadian *(1952), his biography of Mackenzie King, was a "best-seller". Other works include a novel,* The Hollow Men *(1944),* The Fraser *(1950),* The Struggle for the Border *(1955), and* Canada: To-morrow's Giant *(1957). The following essay is reprinted by permission of Longmans, Green and Company.*

---

SOMEWHERE ACROSS this broad land of Canada tonight there is a lost and desperate man trying to find the smallest needle in the largest haystack in the world. He is one of the best American journalists in the business, he has covered important stories in countless countries, but his assignment in Canada has stumped him. His assignment is to discover, analyze and spread on paper for the American public, the inner meaning of Canadian life.

Well, I did the best I could for the poor fellow. I talked to him all last night but when I had finished he was still pacing my room, aflame with the mystery of his mission and certain other stimulating refreshments I had provided — he was pacing the room at dawn and complaining that I had really told him nothing of Canada. "What I have to find," he cried out in his agony, "is the Canadian character, the Canadian personality, the Canadian dream."

When I last saw him, staggering into the sunrise, he hadn't found what he was looking for. And it suddenly occurred to me that I hadn't found it either, after half a century, that I probably wouldn't find it, that it may be forever undiscoverable. I am not surprised, therefore, when my American friend concludes that there actually is no Canadian character, personality or dream.

Nevertheless, he was wrong. But he set me thinking. And the more I thought about this thing the more confused I became, as I shall demonstrate to you in the next fifteen minutes. Yet he was wrong.

Now, it's true that you can't define the Canadian character, or at least I can't, nor can any of our statesmen, writers or artists, so far as I have seen. But nothing of importance in life is definable. Once anything yields to definition you can be sure it isn't very important.

So we needn't go on making excuses, as we always do before strangers, because we cannot spell out the life of Canada like a chemical formula. And we shouldn't apologize either because the character of Canada is so divided and complex, holding within itself at least six sub-characters — the proud, grim and inflexible character of the Maritimes; the gay but hard and practical character of Quebec; the bustling, able and rather provincial character of Ontario; the character of Toronto, a growth so rare and baffling that I shall not venture, as an outsider, to give it even an adjective; the spacious, generous and almost naïve character of the prairies; the boyish, ravenous and self-centred character of British Columbia.

Our national personality is split many ways. So is the personality of every great nation and every great man in history. Britain is commonly supposed to have the most settled and clear-cut character of any country, but set the Scotsman or the Welshman against the Englishman, set the cockney against the north-countryman, and you will observe the startling diversity and contrast of British life.

We Canadians worry too much about our diversity. For it is an illusion, very common with us, to imagine that a nation grows strong by uniformity. Why, in the basic and most essential unit of mankind, in the family itself, diversity is the surest sign of strength and talent, the best guarantee of unity. No man in his senses would try to make his children all alike, and would mercifully extinguish them at birth if he thought they would resemble him when they grew up. What folly it is, what a will-o'-the-wisp, what a national obsession, to imagine that we shall only achieve a true national character when we have at last turned out a generation as uniform as a package of chewing gum and about as durable.

Nevertheless, as my bewildered American friend told me, it won't do to say that Canadians have strong and varied local characteristics in different parts of the country. That won't prove the existence of a national character. You must be able to prove that throughout the country there are certain dominant, widely shared and fully accepted characteristics, instincts and deep feelings – certain common denominators by which the intangible thing as a whole can be measured. That is where the argument about our national character always collapses, as I have seen it collapse, over and over again, usually late at night, amid a despairing clink of glasses, from Victoria to Halifax.

It's no wonder that it's a difficult thing to clutch in your hand, the character of Canada; wonderful, rather, that there is anything to clutch. Wonderful for this reason: Whereas other nations of the past grew up in a world of watertight compartments, and hardened into individual shape before other nations could touch and dilute them, we began to build a nation here only a few years ago, in a new world, in a violent world revolution, in an age where all nations were being driven together, cheek by jowl, through the new means of transport, information and propaganda.

Our case was peculiarly difficult, much more difficult, for example, than Australia's, because we lived beside a great established nation, the most powerful magnet the world has ever known, and its ideas have washed in on us in a ceaseless tide. We were indeed, and are still today, like a youth starting out on his path, glancing over his shoulder at the ancient glories of his home in Britain or France and, when he looks ahead, dazzled by the glitter of the United States.

Despite everything, however, I think we can begin now to detect some of the special characteristics common to all Canadians, and add them up to something.

First, and most obvious, is our national humility. We are a people bounded on one side by the northern lights and on the other, by an inferiority complex just as vivid, a people distracted by the mossy grandeur of the old world from which we came and by the power, wealth and fury of our American neighbours. We are the last people to realize, and the first to deny, the material achievements of the Canadian nation which all the rest of the world has already grasped and envied. Self-depreciation is our great national habit.

This is curious, when you come to think of it, because so many of us are of British origin. A few days ago a scholar from India wrote in the London *Times* that the English consider their primary national vice to be hypocrisy, but he said, "I must insist on first things first. The root and beginning is self-admiration, and hypocrisy only its most distinguished product." Now that's an interesting epigram but its reception in England is *more* interesting. In Canada we would resent it, but the English loved it. They have had so much experience, they are so sure of themselves, that they can laugh at the impudence of outsiders. We don't laugh because we lack any self-admiration, and we're not very good at hypocrisy, either. We are hurt by the foreigner's criticism because we have a sneaking suspicion that it must be true, a suspicion that would not occur to an Englishman. Never has there been a people in all history which has accomplished so much as the Canadian people and thought so little of it. An Indian scholar won't find self-admiration here. He'll find self-apology written in big black letters across our Canadian map — no, not in big letters. We write everything small if it's Canadian.

This, perhaps, lies close to the root of another national characteristic — we are a conservative and steady people, hardly daring to believe in our own capacity in the more complex affairs of statecraft, afraid to test that capacity too far with new systems and experiments. The Canadian audience at a political meeting (a significant little test, if the glumest), the most stolid and dead-panned ever known — a collection of dull and sceptical haddock eyes to daunt the boldest politician; and our politicians truly reflect us in their stodgy competence, their unvarying pedestrianism, their high ability, their positive terror of colour and flair.

And we are a lonely people, isolated from one another, in a land where the largest city is a frail wink of lights in the darkness of the night. Lonely, and awed by the immensity of space around us, by the cold sweep of the prairies, by the stark presence of mountains leaning upon us, by the empty sea at our door, and by the fierce northern climate, which colours and toughens the weather of our spirit. And we are closer to the soil still, all of us, even in our cities, than the people of any other great industrial and urban nation.

We are more aware than others of the central physical fact of the earth, of growth, of harvest and decay. This land sense dominates all our national thinking, our politics, our economic system and our personal habits. It makes our artists instinctively rush out to paint, not the abstractions of other artists, but the hard material of rock and pine tree.

This deep instinct for the land, our constant feeling of struggle against a harsh nature — this and our concentration on the mere task of survival, must be one of the things that makes us an unimaginative people, prosaic, pitifully inarticulate and singularly lacking in humour. (We haven't even developed the great Canadian joke yet or learned to laugh at ourselves.) It may turn out that we are really filled with fire, poetry and laughter, which we have repressed, thinking it inferior to other peoples', and perhaps these things will erupt some day, with shattering violence. So far there has been hardly a rumble, nor any tinkle of a national song nor the vague shape of a national myth.

On the evidence so far you might almost say that we have constructed a national character by refusing to construct one. The great void almost becomes a solid thing, the vacuum begins to take on substance, the national silence begins to speak in a clear Canadian voice. We have taken a *nothing* — our pathological horror of expression — and erected a *something* which distinguishes us from all other people. This is not enough to make a character, I admit, but you won't find it anywhere else. And perhaps the refusal to admit achievement is an achievement in itself.

But there is something about us more important and more distinctive than any of these obvious qualities.

We are among the few peoples still in the first throes of collective growth. While older peoples have settled down and accepted certain conventions, conditions, attitudes and limitations as permanent, we accept nothing, least of all limitations. We live in a constant expectation of change, which we don't particularly relish and rather suspect, but cannot avoid. We have, every one of us, the feeling that we are involved in a process of perpetual expansion, development and revision, whose end we cannot see.

We have the feeling, not of an old and settled resident in his father's house, but of a young man building a new house for himself, without any clear plan in his head and wondering how large his future family will be.

Ours is the doubt and risk, but the unequalled satisfaction of the man who builds and makes something with his own hands, perhaps the best satisfaction that life offers; and this sense of being only at the beginning of things, this expectation of a greater structure still to be built — this, I think, is the universal and most distinctive feature of the Canadian. We are, above all, a building people, a nation of beavers.

But, my American friend says, all this does not add up to a national character, and hence he concludes there is none. All right, then. We have failed to define that character, as I told you we would. But consider this: We have built here against every obstacle of geography, economics, racial division and the magnet of our American neighbour — we have built here the greatest nation of its population in all recorded history. How did we do it? Why didn't we break up into inevitable splinters, why didn't we throw in the sponge and join the United States long ago?

No political decision, no economic planning, will explain that. Something much more than politics or economics was at work — the unshakeable will to make a nation, a home, a life of our own, for which no inconvenience was too great, from which no temptation could swerve us — a dim, impalpable and dumb thing beyond our power to express or even name.

There is the hard, silent and unyielding core of Canada, the final mystery which, like all things that matter in life, like life itself, is forever inexpressible and can only be intimated in myths and parables which, so far, we have been too busy and too reticent to invent. They will come in time, but the thing itself which they will vainly try to voice, is already here, and has been here since Champlain shivered on the rock of Quebec, in that first cruel Canadian winter, and has been carried by every Canadian boy, dumbly in his heart, to the battlefields at the ends of the earth — this dream of high mountains and deep forests and prairie skies, of summer crops and winter snow, and Canadian ways, and all the vast compact of familiar, precious things, making up together the substance of Canada which, through more than three hundred years we have refused to abandon, to sell, or even to mention.

If this is not yet a rounded and settled national character, it is, assuredly, the soil out of which a character is growing as surely as a boy grows into a man. It has grown these last few years faster than we have stopped to realize — of which the best proof, perhaps, is that, as never before, we now pause in our huge labours to ask ourselves what we are and what we hope to be. We cannot answer yet, but we know that we have within us, as our fathers had, one dominant feeling which is so general and unquestioned that we take it for granted. We quarrel about methods, political theories, economic systems, but such things do not make up a national character. Our character is not being built on them but on something much larger, a truly common denominator, the space, the beauty and the free life of Canada itself.

Well, I wonder what haystack my American friend is searching in tonight for a needle which he could not recognize even if he found it.


QUESTIONS

Poets, politicians, psychologists and sociologists have confessed, in chorus, their inability to *define* the word, "Canadian."

1. How does the author manage to suggest that the indefinable is more real than the definable?

2. How, in the author's opinion, does "our constant feeling of struggle against a harsh nature" affect and mould the national character? Do you agree with him?

3. Are we still a frontier "nation of beavers", or is Hugh MacLennan right in his recent statement that Canada now feels old and settled?

4. What is the "final mystery" of Canada which defies definition, but which we recognize as real and alive?

5. Does the author convince you that "the space, the beauty and the free life of Canada itself" marks us off as a people unique — a people unlike, for instance, the Americans?

6. It has been said that Hutchison seeks to prove his point, not by argument, but by feeling? Is there evidence of this here? Can you argue the "indefinable"?

*Henry Louis*
*Mencken*

# American slang

*Henry Louis Mencken (1880-1956), American editor, philologist,
and essayist, was born and educated in Baltimore, graduating in
1898 from the Baltimore Polytechnic Institute. Since he had
little interest in mechanics, he drifted into newspaper work,
getting a job first on the* Baltimore Morning Herald. *In 1906 he
moved to the* Baltimore Sun, *where he remained a regular staff
member until 1941. From 1914 to 1923, he was a co-editor of the*
Smart Set *with the critic George Jean Nathan, with whom he
started the* American Mercury. *Mencken was sole editor of the
latter magazine from 1924 to 1933. His greatest work was a
study of American English,* The American Language *(1919, with
supplements, 1946, 1948). Among his other books are* George
Bernard Shaw: His Plays *(1905),* In Defence of Women *(1917),*
Treatise on the Gods *(1930),* Happy Days *(1940) and* Newspaper Days *(1941). The following chapter is reprinted from*
The American Language *by H. L. Mencken, by permission of
Alfred A. Knopf, Inc., and gives some idea of how Mencken
combined enormous learning with a clear, spare style.*

SLANG IS DEFINED by the Oxford Dictionary as "language of a
highly colloquial type, considered as below the level of standard
educated speech, and consisting either of new words or of current words employed in some special sense". The origin of
the word is unknown. . . . When it first appeared in English,

about the middle of the Eighteenth Century, it was employed as
a synonym of *cant*, and so designated "the special vocabulary
used by any set of persons of a low or disreputable character";
and half a century later it began to be used interchangeably with
*argot*, which means the vocabulary special to any group, trade,
or profession. But during the past fifty years the three terms have
tended to be more or less clearly distinguished. The jargon of
criminals is both a kind of slang and a kind of argot, but it is best
described as *cant*. . . . One of the principal aims of cant is to make
what is said unintelligible to persons outside the group, a purpose
that is absent from most forms of argot and slang. . . . The essence
of slang is that it is of general dispersion, but still stands outside
the accepted canon of the language. It is, says George H. Mc-
Knight, "a form of colloquial speech created in a spirit of defiance
and aiming at freshness and novelty. . . . Its figures are con-
sciously far-fetched and are intentionally drawn from the most
ignoble of sources. Closely akin to profanity in its spirit, its aim
is to shock." Among the impulses leading to its invention, says
Henry Bradley, "the two more important seem to be the desire
to secure increased vivacity and the desire to secure increased
sense of intimacy in the use of language." "It seldom attempts,"
says the London *Times*, "to supply deficiencies in conventional
language; its object is nearly always to provide a new and different way of saying what can be perfectly well said without it".
What chiefly lies behind it is simply a kind of linguistic exuberance, an excess of word-making energy. It relates itself to the
standard language a great deal as dancing relates itself to music.
But there is something else. The best slang is not only ingenious
and amusing; it also embodies a kind of social criticism. It not
only provides new names for a series of everyday concepts, some
new and some old; it also says something about them. "Words
which produce the slang effect," observes Frank K. Sechrist,
"arouse associations which are incongruous or incompatible with
those of customary thinking."

Everyone, including even the metaphysician in his study and
the eremite in his cell, has a large vocabulary of slang, but the
vocabulary of the vulgar is likely to be larger than that of the

cultured and it is harder worked. Its content may be divided into two categories: (a) old words, whether used singly or in combination, that have been put to new uses, usually metaphorical, and (b) new words that have not yet been admitted to the standard vocabulary. Examples of the first type are *rubberneck*, for a gaping and prying person, and *iceberg*, for a cold woman; examples of the second are *hoosegow*, *flim-flam*, *blurb*, *bazoo*, and *blah*. There is a constant movement of slang terms into accepted usage. *Nice*, as an adjective of all work, signifying anything satisfactory, was once in slang use only, and the purists denounced it, but today no one would question "a *nice* day", "a *nice* time", or "a *nice* hotel". . . . The verb-phrase *to hold up* is now perfectly good American, but so recently as 1901 the late Brander Matthews was sneering at it as slang. In the same way other verb-phrases, e.g., *to cave in*, *to fill the bill*, and *to fly off the handle*, once viewed askance, have gradually worked their way to a relatively high level of the standard speech. On some indeterminate tomorrow to *stick up* and *to take for a ride* may follow them. "Even the greatest purist," says Robert Lynd, "does not object today to the inclusion of the word *bogus* in a literary vocabulary, though a hundred years ago *bogus* was an American slang word meaning an apparatus for coining false money. *Carpetbagger* and *bunkum* are other American slang words that have naturalized themselves in English speech, and *mob* is an example of English slang that was once as vulgar as *incog* or *photo*." Sometimes a word comes in below the salt, gradually wins respectability, and then drops to the level of slang, and is worked to death. An example is offered by *strenuous*. It was first used by John Marston, the dramatist, in 1599, and apparently he invented it, as he invented *puffy*, *chilblained*, *spurious*, and *clumsy*. As strange as it may seem to us today, all these words were frowned on by the purists of the time as uncouth and vulgar, and Ben Jonson attacked them with violence in his "Poetaster", written in 1601. In particular, Ben was upset by *strenuous*. But it made its way despite him, and during the next three centuries it was used by a multitude of impeccable authors, including Milton, Swift, Burke, Hazlitt, and Macaulay. And then Theodore Roosevelt invented and announced the Strenuous Life, the adjective struck the American fancy and passed into slang, and in a little while it was so horribly threadbare that all persons of careful speech sickened of it, and to this day it bears the ridiculous connotation that hangs about most slang, and is seldom used seriously.

All neologisms, of course, are not slang. At about the time the word *hoosegow*, derived from the Spanish, came into American slang use, the word *rodeo*, also Spanish, came into the standard vocabulary. The distinction between the two is not hard to make out. *Hoosegow* was really not needed. We had plenty of words to designate a jail, and they were old and good words. *Hoosegow* came in simply because there was something arresting and out-landish about it — and the users of slang have a great liking for pungent novelties. *Rodeo*, on the other hand, designated some-thing for which there was no other word in American — some-thing, indeed, of which the generality of Americans had just become aware — and so it was accepted at once. Many neologisms have been the deliberate inventions of quite serious men, e.g., *gas*, *kodak*, *vaseline*. *Scientist* was concocted in 1840 by William Whewell, professor of moral theology and casuistical divinity at Cambridge. *Ampere* was proposed solemnly by the Electric Congress which met in Paris in 1881, and was taken into all civil-ized languages instantly. *Radio* was suggested for wireless tele-grams by an international convention held in Berlin in 1906, and was extended to wireless broadcasts in the United States about 1920, though the English prefer *wireless* in the latter sense. But such words as these were never slang; they came into general and respectable use at once, along with *argon, x-ray, carburetor, stratosphere, bacillus*, and many another of the sort. These words were all sorely needed; it was impossible to convey the ideas behind them without them, save by clumsy circumlocutions. It is one of the functions of slang, also, to serve as a short cut, but it is seldom if ever really necessary. Instead, as W. D. Whitney once said, it is only a wanton product of "the exuberance of mental activity, and the natural delight of language-making". This mental activity, of course, is the function of a relatively small class. "The unconscious genius of the people," said Paul

Shorey, "no more invents slang than it invents epics. It is coined in the sweat of their brow by smart writers who, as they would say, are *out for the coin*." Or, if not out for the coin, then at least out for notice, *kudos*, admiration, or maybe simply for the satisfaction of the "natural delight of language-making". Some of the best slang emerges from the argot of college students, but everyone who has observed the process of its gestation knows that the general run of students have nothing to do with the matter, save maybe to provide an eager welcome for the novelties set before them. College slang is actually made by the campus wits, just as general slang is made by the wits of the newspapers and theaters. The idea of calling an engagement ring a *handcuff* did not occur to the young gentlemen of Harvard by mass inspiration; it occurred to a certain definite one of them, probably after long and deliberate cogitation, and he gave it to the rest and to his country. . . .

George Philip Krapp attempts to distinguish between slang and sound idiom by setting up the doctrine that the former is "more expressive than the situation demands".

"It is," he says, "a kind of hyperesthesia in the use of language. *To laugh in your sleeve* is idiom because it arises out of a natural situation; it is a metaphor derived from the picture of one raising his sleeve to his face to hide a smile, a metaphor which arose naturally enough in early periods when sleeves were long and flowing; but *to talk through your hat* is slang, not only because it is new, but also because it is a gross exaggeration of the truth." The theory, unluckily, is combated by many plain facts. *To hand it to him*, to get *away with it*, and even *to hand him a lemon* are certainly not metaphors that transcend slang. On the other hand, there is palpable exaggeration in such phrases as "*he is not worth the powder it would take to kill him*," in such adjectives as *breakbone* (fever), and in such compounds as *fire-eater*, and yet it would be absurd to dismiss them as slang. Between *blockhead* and *bonehead* there is little to choose, but the former is sound English whereas the latter is American slang. So with many familiar similes, e.g., *like greased lightning, as scarce as hens' teeth;* they are grotesque hyperboles, but hardly slang.

The true distinction, in so far as any distinction exists at all, is that indicated by Whitney, Bradley, Sechrist, and McKnight. Slang originates in the effort of ingenious individuals to make the language more pungent and picturesque — to increase the store of terse and striking words, to widen the boundaries of metaphor, and to provide a vocabulary for new shades of difference in meaning. As Dr. Otto Jespersen has pointed out, this is also the aim of poets (as, indeed, it is of prose writers), but they are restrained by consideration of taste and decorum, and also, not infrequently, by historical or logical considerations. The maker of slang is under no such limitations: he is free to confect his neologism by any process that can be grasped by his customers, and out of any materials available, whether native or foreign. He may adopt any of the traditional devices of metaphor. Making an attribute do duty for the whole gives him *stiff* for corpse, *flat-foot* for policeman, *smoke-eater* for fireman, *skirt* for woman, *lunger* for consumptive, and *yes-man* for sycophant. Hidden resemblances give him *morgue* for a newspaper's file of clippings, *bean* for head, and *sinker* for a doughnut. The substitution of far-fetched figures for literal description gives him *glad-rags* for fine clothing, *bonehead* for ignoramus, *booze-foundry* for saloon, and *cart-wheel* for dollar, and the contrary resort to a brutal literalness gives him *kill-joy*, *low-life*, and *hand-out*. He makes abbreviations with a free hand — *beaut* for beauty, *gas* for gasoline, and so on. He makes bold avail of composition, as in *attaboy* and *whatdyecallem*, and of onomatopoeia, as in *biff*, *zowie*, *honky-tonk*, and *wow*. He enriches the ancient counters of speech with picturesque synonyms, as in *guy*, *gink*, *duck*, *bird*, and *bozo* for fellow. He transfers proper names to common usage, as in *ostermoor* for mattress, and then sometimes gives them remote figurative significances, as in *ostermoors* for whiskers. Above all, he enriches the vocabulary of action with many new verbs and verb-phrases, e.g., *to burp, to neck, to gang, to frame up, to hit the pipe, to give him the works,* and so on. If, by the fortunes that condition language-making, his neologism acquires a special and limited meaning, not served by any existing locution, it enters into sound idiom and is presently wholly legitimized; if, on the contrary, it is adopted by the populace as a counterword and employed with such banal imitativeness that it soon loses any definite significance whatever, then it remains slang and is avoided by the finical. . . .

QUESTIONS

1. Many people express extreme distaste for slang. What is Mencken's attitude toward it? Since he says little by way of direct approval or disapproval, how do you become aware of his attitude?

2. (a) According to the author, what are the important differences between cant and slang?
(b) In examining the motives behind the creation of slang terms, why does he quote four other opinions as well as his own?
(c) What is common to all of these opinions?

3. (a) He divides slang into two main categories. What are they?
(b) He says: "There is a constant movement of slang terms into accepted usage." How does he illustrate this statement?
(c) What further point does he make in describing the evolutionary cycle of "strenuous"?

4. (a) What distinction is Mencken making in his comparison of "hoosegow" and "rodeo"?
(b) What similarities and what differences are there between neologisms like "radio", "ampere" and "bacillus", and the neologisms of slang?

5. The author's quoting from George Philip Krapp has a purpose quite different from that in his use of previous quotations. Explain.

6. Mencken represents the composer of slang as a kind of poetic outlaw, gaily plundering the figurative resources of poetry, but not recognizing its logical disciplines. Refer to the last paragraph to show how he supports this view.

7. Using the author's explanation of how slang expressions may become "wholly legitimized", suggest some examples of current slang which you believe may survive into standard usage. Mention some that you think may not last.

*William Makepeace*
*Thackeray*

# On being found out

---

*William Makepeace Thackeray (1811-1863) was born in India
and came to England in 1817 after the death of his father who
had been an official in the East India Company. After leaving
Cambridge in 1830 without taking a degree, he "dabbled" in
law and then in painting before turning to journalism and fiction.
His fame as a novelist was established firmly with* Vanity Fair
*(1847-8) and sustained with* The History of Pendennis
*(1848-50),* The History of Henry Esmond *(1852),* The New-
comes *(1853-55), and* The Virginians *(1857-59). One of the
shrewdest social satirists of his time, he first captured the attention
of the Victorian world with his series of sketches,* The Book of
Snobs, *which ran in the magazine,* Punch, *during 1846-47. He
continued to write sketches and essays until the end of his life,
particularly for* The Cornhill Magazine, *which he edited from
1860-62.*

---

AT THE CLOSE (let us say) of Queen Anne's reign, when I was a
boy at a private and preparatory school for young gentlemen, I
remember the wiseacre of a master ordering us all, one night, to
march into a little garden at the back of the house, and thence to
proceed one by one into a tool or hen house (I was but a tender
little thing just put into short clothes, and can't exactly say

whether the house was for tools or hens), and in that house to put our hands into a sack which stood on a bench, a candle burning beside it. I put my hand into the sack. My hand came out quite black. I went and joined the other boys in the schoolroom; and all their hands were black too.

By reason of my tender age (and there are some critics who, I hope, will be satisfied by my acknowledging that I am a hundred and fifty-six next birthday) I could not understand what was the meaning of this night excursion – this candle, this toolhouse, this bag of soot. I think we little boys were taken out of our sleep to be brought to the ordeal. We came, then, and showed our little hands to the master; washed them or not – most probably, I should say, not – and so went bewildered back to bed.

Something had been stolen in the school that day; and Mr. Wiseacre having read in a book of an ingenious method of finding out a thief by making him put his hand into a sack (which, if guilty, the rogue would shirk from doing), all we boys were subjected to the trial. Goodness knows what the lost object was, or who stole it. We all had black hands to show the master. And the thief, whoever he was, was not Found Out that time.

I wonder if the rascal is alive – an elderly scoundrel he must be by this time; and a hoary old hypocrite, to whom an old school-fellow presents his kindest regards – parenthetically remarking what a dreadful place that private school was; cold, chilblains, bad dinners, not enough victuals, and caning awful! – Are you alive still, I say, you nameless villain, who escaped discovery on that day of crime? I hope you have escaped often since, old sinner. Ah, what a lucky thing it is, for you and me, my man, that we are *not* found out in all our peccadilloes; and that our backs can slip away from the master and the cane!

Just consider what life would be, if every rogue was found out, and flogged *coram populo!* What a butchery, what an indecency, what an endless swishing of the rod! Don't cry out about my misanthropy. My good friend Mealymouth, I will trouble you to tell me, do you go to church? When there, do you say, or do you not, that you are a miserable sinner? and saying so do you believe or disbelieve it? If you are a M.S., don't you deserve correction, and aren't you grateful if you are to be let off? I say again, what a blessed thing it is that we are not all found out!

Just picture to yourself everybody who does wrong being found out, and punished accordingly. Fancy all the boys in all the schools being whipped; and then the assistants, and then the headmaster (Dr. Badford let us call him). Fancy the provost-marshal being tied up, having previously superintended the correction of the whole army. After the young gentlemen have had their turn for the faulty exercises, fancy Dr. Lincolnsinn being taken up for certain faults in *his* Essay and Review. After the clergyman has cried his peccavi, suppose we hoist up a bishop, and give him a couple of dozen! (I see my Lord Bishop of Double-Gloucester sitting in a very uneasy posture on his right reverend bench.) After we have cast off the bishop, what are we to say to the Minister who appointed him? My Lord Cinqwarden, it is painful to have to use personal correction to a boy of your age; but really — *Siste tandem, carnifex!* The butchery is too horrible. The hand drops powerless, appalled at the quantity of birch which it must cut and brandish. I am glad we are not all found out, I say again; and protest, my dear brethren, against our having our desserts.

To fancy all men found out and punished is bad enough; but imagine all women found out in the distinguished social circle in which you and I have the honor to move. Is it not a mercy that a many of these fair criminals remain unpunished and undiscovered! There is Mrs. Longbow, who is forever practising, and who shoots poisoned arrows, too; when you meet her you don't call her a liar, and charge her with the wickedness she has done and is doing. There is Mrs. Painter, who passes for a most respectable woman, and a model in society. There is no use in saying what you really know regarding her and her goings on. There is Diana Hunter — what a little haughty prude it is; and yet *we* know stories about her which are not altogether edifying. I say it is best, for the sake of the good, that the bad should not all be found out. You don't want your children to know the history of that lady in the next box, who is so handsome, and whom they admire so. Ah me, what would life be if we were all found out, and punished for all our faults? Jack Ketch would be in permanence; and then who would hang Jack Ketch?

They talk of murderers being pretty certainly found out. Psha! I have heard an authority awfully competent vow and declare that scores and hundreds of murders are committed, and nobody is the wiser. That terrible man mentioned one or two ways of committing murder, which he maintained were quite common, and were scarcely ever found out. A man, for instance, comes home to his wife, and – but I pause – I know that this Magazine* has a very large circulation. Hundreds and hundreds of thousands – why not say a million of people at once? – well, say a million, read it. And amongst these countless readers, I might be teaching some monster how to make away with his wife without being found out, some fiend of a woman how to destroy her dear husband. I will *not* then tell this easy and simple way of murder, as communicated to me by a most respectable party in the confidence of private intercourse. Suppose some gentle reader were to try this most simple and easy receipt – it seems to me almost infallible – and come to grief in consequence, and be found out and hanged? Should I ever pardon myself for having been the means of doing injury to a single one of our esteemed subscribers? The prescription whereof I speak – that is to say, whereof I *don't* speak – shall be buried in this bosom. No, I am a humane man. I am not one of your Bluebeards to go and say to my wife, "My dear! I am going away for a few days to Brighton. Here are all the keys of the house. You may open every door and closet, except the one at the end of the oak-room opposite the fireplace, with the little bronze Shakespeare on the mantel-piece (or what not)." I don't say this to a woman – unless, to be sure, I want to get rid of her – because, after such a caution, I know she'll peep into the closet. I say nothing about the closet at all. I keep the key in my pocket, and a being whom I love, but who, as I know, has many weaknesses, out of harm's way. You toss up your head, dear angel, drub on the ground with your lovely little feet, on the table with your sweet rosy fingers,

* *The Cornhill Magazine*, in which this essay first appeared.

and cry, "Oh, sneerer! You don't know the depth of woman's feeling, the lofty scorn of all deceit, the entire absence of mean curiosity in the sex, or never, never would you libel us so!" Ah, Delia! dear, dear Delia! It is because I fancy I *do* know something about you (not all, mind — no, no; no man knows that) — Ah, my bride, my ringdove, my rose, my poppet — choose, in fact, whatever name you like — bulbul of my grove, fountain of my desert, sunshine of my darkling life, and joy of my dungeoned existence, it is because I *do* know a little about you that I conclude to say nothing of that private closet, and keep my key in my pocket. You take away that closet-key then, and the house-key. You lock Delia in. You keep her out of harm's way and gadding, and so she never *can* be found out.

And yet by little strange accidents and coincidences how we are being found out every day. You remember that old story of the Abbé Kakatoes, who told the company at supper one night how the first confession he ever received was — from a murderer let us say. Presently enters to supper the Marquis de Croquemitaine. "Palsambleu, Abbé!" says the brilliant marquis, taking a pinch of snuff, "are you here? Gentlemen and ladies! I was the abbé's first penitent, and I made him a confession, which I promise you astonished him."

To be sure how queerly things are found out! Here is an instance. Only the other day I was writing in these "Roundabout Papers" about a certain man, whom I facetiously called Baggs, and who had abused me to my friends, who of course told me. Shortly after that paper was published another friend — Sacks let us call him — scowls fiercely at me as I am sitting in perfect good-humor at the club, and passes on without speaking. A cut. A quarrel. Sacks thinks it is about him that I was writing: whereas, upon my honor and conscience, I never had him once in my mind, and was pointing my moral from quite another man. But don't you see, by this wrath of the guilty-conscienced Sacks, that he had been abusing me too? He has owned himself guilty, never having been accused. He has winced when nobody thought of hitting him. I did but put the cap out, and madly butting and chafing, behold my friend rushes out to put his head into it!

Never mind, Sacks, you are found out; but I bear you no malice, my man.

And yet to be found out, I know from my own experience, must be painful and odious, and cruelly mortifying to the inward vanity. Suppose I am a poltroon, let us say. With fierce mustache, loud talk, plentiful oaths, and an immense stick, I keep up nevertheless a character for courage. I swear fearfully at cabmen and women; brandish my bludgeon, and perhaps knock down a little man or two with it: brag of the images which I break at the shooting-gallery, and pass amongst my friends for a whiskery fire-eater, afraid of neither man nor dragon. Ah me! Suppose some brisk little chap steps up and gives me a caning in St. James's Street, with all the heads of my friends looking out all the club windows. My reputation is gone, I frighten no man more. My nose is pulled by whipper-snappers, who jump up on a chair to reach it. I am found out. And in the days of my triumphs, when people were yet afraid of me, and were taken in by my swagger, I always knew that I was a lily-liver, and expected that I should be found out some day.

That certainty of being found out must haunt and depress many a bold braggadocio spirit. Let us say it is a clergyman, who can pump copious floods of tears out of his own eyes and those of his audience. He thinks to himself, "I am but a poor swindling, chattering rogue. My bills are unpaid. I have jilted several women whom I have promised to marry. I don't know whether I believe what I preach, and I know I have stolen the very sermon over which I have been snivelling. Have they found me out?" says he, as his head drops down on the cushion.

Then your writer, poet, historian, novelist, or what not? The "Beacon" says that "Jones's work is one of the first order." The "Lamp" declares that "Jones's tragedy surpasses every work since the days of Him of Avon." The "Comet" asserts that "J's 'Life of Goody Twoshoes' is a κτῆμα ἐς ἀεί, a noble and enduring monument to the fame of that admirable Englishwoman," and so forth. But then Jones knows that he has lent the critic of the "Beacon" five pounds; that his publisher has a half-share in the "Lamp;" and that the "Comet" comes repeatedly to dine with him. It is all very well. Jones is immortal until he is found out; and then down comes the extinguisher, and the immortal is dead and buried. The idea (*dies irae!*) of discovery must haunt many a man, and make him uneasy, as the trumpets are puffing in his triumph. Brown, who has a higher place than he deserves, cowers before Smith, who has found him out. What is a chorus of critics shouting "Bravo?" — a public clapping hands and flinging garlands? Brown knows that Smith has found him out. Puff, trumpets! Wave, banners! Huzza, boys, for the immortal Brown! "This is all very well," B. thinks (bowing the while, smiling, laying his hand to his heart); "but there stands Smith at the window: *he* has measured me; and some day the others will find me out too." It is a very curious sensation to sit by a man who has found you out, and who, as you know, has found you out; or *vice versâ*, to sit with a man whom *you* have found out. His talent? Bah! His virtue? We know a little story or two about his virtue, and he knows we know it. We are thinking over friend Robinson's antecedents, as we grin, bow and talk; and we are both humbugs together. Robinson a good fellow, is he? You know how he behaved to Hicks? A good-natured man, is he? Pray do you remember that little story of Mrs. Robinsons' black eye? How men have to work, to talk, to smile, to go to bed, and try and sleep, with this dread of being found out on their consciences! Bardolph, who has robbed a church, and Nym, who has taken a purse, go to their usual haunts, and smoke their pipes with their companions. Mr. Detective Bullseye appears, and says, "Oh, Bardolph! I want you about that there pyx business!" Mr. Bardolph knocks the ashes out of his pipe, puts out his hands to the little steel cuffs, and walks away quite meekly. He is found out. He must go. "Good-by, Doll Tearsheet! Good-by, Mrs. Quickly, Ma'am!" The other gentlemen and ladies *de la société* look on and exchange mute adieux with the departing friends. And an assured time will come when the other gentlemen and ladies will be found out too.

What a wonderful and beautiful provision of nature it has been that, for the most part, our womankind are not endowed with the faculty of finding us out! *They* don't doubt, and probe, and weigh, and take your measure. Lay down this paper, my benevolent friend and reader, go into your drawing-room now, and utter a joke ever so old, and I wager sixpence the ladies there will all begin to laugh. Go to Brown's house, and tell Mrs. Brown and the young ladies what you think of him, and see what a welcome you will get! In like manner, let him come to your house, and tell *your* good lady his candid opinion of you, and fancy how she will receive him! Would you have your wife and children know you exactly for what you are, and esteem you precisely at your worth? If so, my friend, you will live in a dreary house, and you will have but a chilly fireside. Do you suppose the people round it don't see your homely face as under a glamour, and, as it were, with a halo of love round it? You don't fancy you are, as you seem to them? No such thing, my man. Put away that monstrous conceit, and be thankful that *they* have not found you out.

QUESTIONS

Thackeray writes in the intimate familiar style of the nineteenth century essayist. The tone, light, half-bantering, is that of a man at his ease sharing old memories and sly little jokes with a good friend. The sound of moral indignation is nowhere to be heard. And yet Thackeray is writing with no little moral purpose. His method is therefore *ironic*; that is, he means the opposite of what he seems to say — or *almost* the opposite.

1. What is the value, for the ironic tone of the essay, of this first example of not being Found Out? Would the tone of the essay be different if the first example had been taken from adult life and high society?

2. Why does the author seem to equate the sins of the schoolboy with those of the Bishop, the Minister of State, and the haughty and respectable ladies of fashion?

3. What is the point of the "Bluebeard" passage and the "protection" of Delia?

4. Why does the author emphasize episodes in which people are Found Out only by accident or coincidence?

5. Why does the author seem to take such a *protective* interest in the braggart, the impious clergyman, and the writer with the "bought" reputation?

6. Are you meant to conclude that the undetected murderer, the dishonest cleric, and humble Mr. Brown before his fireside, are really birds of a feather?

7. Does the last paragraph tend to soften the critical intention of the essay? Are you meant to forgive all humbugs because all humans, in some degree, are humbugs? Does the recognition of yourself as a little humbug make you charitable or uncharitable towards the big humbugs?

8. If Thackeray were writing without irony and humour, what would he be saying? What *actually* is the moral attitude of this essay?

*Sir Rabindranath*

*Tagore*

# East and West

*Sir Rabindranath Tagore (1861-1941), Indian poet, playwright, and novelist, was born in Calcutta, the son of a wealthy Brahmin. Educated at private schools in India, he went to England to study at University College, London, in 1878, at which time he had already published his first book,* A Poet's Tale. *Many poems, plays, and novels followed, of which the following are in English translation:* Song Offerings *(1912),* The King of the Dark Chamber *(1914),* Lover's Gift *(1918),* The Home and the World *(1919),* The Fugitive *(1921),* Creative Unity *(1922),* Broken Ties and Other Stories *(1928),* Religion of Man *(1930), and* Collected Poems and Plays *(1938). In 1913 he received the Nobel Prize for literature, and in 1915 he was knighted. He donated all his Nobel Prize money to a school which he had founded in 1901 and which later became an international institute. Promoting international harmony was always an interest close to his heart. Most of his writing was in Bengali, but occasionally, as with the following essay, he wrote in English. This essay is reprinted from* Creative Unity *by permission of the Trustees of the Tagore Estate and Macmillan and Company, Ltd.*

IT IS NOT ALWAYS a profound interest in man that carries travellers nowadays to distant lands. More often it is the facility for rapid movement. For lack of time and for the sake of convenience we generalise and crush our human facts into the packages within the steel trunks that hold our traveller's reports.

Our knowledge of our own countrymen and our feelings about them have slowly and unconsciously grown out of innumerable facts which are full of contradictions and subject to incessant change. They have the elusive mystery and fluidity of life. We cannot define to ourselves what we are as a whole, because we know too much; because our knowledge is more than knowledge. It is an immediate consciousness of personality, any evaluation of which carries some emotion, joy or sorrow, shame or exaltation. But in a foreign land we try to find our compensation for the meagreness of our data by the compactness of the generalisation which our imperfect sympathy itself helps us to form. When a stranger from the West travels in the Eastern world he takes the facts that displease him and readily makes use of them for his rigid conclusions, fixed upon the unchallengeable authority of his personal experience. It is like a man who has his own boat for crossing his village stream, but, on being compelled to wade across some strange watercourse, draws angry comparisons as he goes from every patch of mud and every pebble which his feet encounter.

Our mind has faculties which are universal, but its habits are insular. There are men who become impatient and angry at the least discomfort when their habits are incommoded. In their idea of the next world they probably conjure up the ghosts of their slippers and dressing-gowns, and expect the latchkey that opens their lodging-house door on earth to fit their front door in the other world. As travellers they are a failure; for they have grown too accustomed to their mental easy-chairs, and in their intellectual nature love home comforts, which are of local make, more than the realities of life, which, like earth itself, are full of ups and downs, yet are one in their rounded completeness.

The modern age has brought the geography of the earth near to us, but made it difficult for us to come into touch with man. We go to strange lands and observe; we do not live there. We hardly meet men: but only specimens of knowledge. We are in haste to seek for general types and overlook individuals.

When we fall into the habit of neglecting to use the understanding that comes of sympathy in our travels, our knowledge of foreign people grows insensitive, and therefore easily becomes both unjust and cruel in its character, and also selfish and contemptuous in its application. Such has, too often, been the case with regard to the meeting of Western people in our days with others for whom they do not recognise any obligation of kinship.

It has been admitted that the dealings between different races of men are not merely between individuals; that our mutual understanding is either aided, or else obstructed, by the general emanations forming the social atmosphere. These emanations are our collective ideas and collective feelings, generated according to special historical circumstances.

For instance, the caste-idea is a collective idea in India. When we approach an Indian who is under the influence of this collective idea, he is no longer a pure individual with his conscience fully awake to the judging of the value of a human being. He is more or less a passive medium for giving expression to the sentiment of a whole community.

It is evident that the caste-idea is not creative; it is merely institutional. It adjusts human beings according to some mechanical arrangement. It emphasises the negative side of the individual — his separateness. It hurts the complete truth in man.

In the West, also, the people have a certain collective idea that obscures their humanity. Let me try to explain what I feel about it.

Lately I went to visit some battlefield of France which had been devastated by war. The awful calm of desolation, which still bore wrinkles of pain — death-struggles stiffened into ugly ridges — brought before my mind the vision of a huge demon, which had no shape, no meaning, yet had two arms that could strike and break and tear, a gaping mouth that could devour, and bulging brains that could conspire and plan. It was a purpose, which had a living body, but no complete humanity to temper it. Because it was passion — belonging to life, and yet not having the wholeness of life — it was the most terrible of life's enemies.

Something of the same sense of oppression in a different degree, the same desolation in a different aspect, is produced in my mind when I realise the effect of the West upon Eastern life – the West which, in its relation to us, is all plan and purpose incarnate, without any superfluous humanity.

I feel the contrast very strongly in Japan. In that country the old world presents itself with some ideal of perfection, in which man has his varied opportunities of self-revelation in art, in ceremonial, in religious faith, and in customs expressing the poetry of social relationship. There one feels that deep delight of hospitality which life offers to life. And side by side, in the same soil, stands the modern world, which is stupendously big and powerful, but inhospitable. It has no simple-hearted welcome for man. It is living; yet the incompleteness of life's ideal within it cannot but hurt humanity.

The wriggling tentacles of cold-blooded utilitarianism, with which the West has grasped all the easily yielding succulent portions of the East, are causing pain and indignation throughout the Eastern countries. The West comes to us, not with the imagination and sympathy that create and unite, but with a shock of passion – passion for power and wealth. This passion is a mere force, which has in it the principle of separation, of conflict.

I have been fortunate in coming into close touch with individual men and women of the Western countries, and have felt with them their sorrows and shared their aspirations. I have known that they seek the same God, who is my God – even those who deny Him. I feel certain that, if the great light of culture be extinct in Europe, our horizon in the East will mourn in darkness. It does not hurt my pride to acknowledge that, in the present age, Western humanity has received its mission to be the teacher of the world; that her science, through the mastery of laws of nature, is to liberate human souls from the dark dungeon of matter. For this very reason I have realised all the more strongly, on the other hand, that the dominant collective idea in the Western countries is not creative. It is ready to enslave or kill individuals, to drug a great people with soul-killing poison, darkening their whole future with the black mist of stupefaction, and emasculating entire races of men to the utmost degree of helplessness. It is wholly wanting in spiritual power to blend and harmonise; it lacks the sense of the great personality of man.

The most significant fact of modern days is this, that the West has met the East. Such a momentous meeting of humanity, in order to be fruitful, must have in its heart some great emotional idea, generous and creative. There can be no doubt that God's choice has fallen upon the knights-errant of the West for the service of the present age; arms and armour have been given to them; but have they yet realised in their hearts the single-minded loyalty to their cause which can resist all temptations of bribery from the devil? The world today is offered to the West. She will destroy it, if she does not use it for a great creation of man. The materials for such a creation are in the hands of science; but the creative genius is in Man's spiritual ideal.

When I was young, a stranger from Europe came to Bengal. He chose his lodging among the people of the country, shared with them their frugal diet, and freely offered them his service. He found employment in the houses of the rich, teaching them French and German, and the money thus earned he spent to help poor students in buying books. This meant for him hours of walking in the mid-day heat of a tropical summer; for, intent upon exercising the utmost economy, he refused to hire conveyances. He was pitiless in his exaction from himself of his resources, in money, time, and strength, to the point of privation; and all this for the sake of a people who were obscure, to whom he was not born, yet whom he dearly loved. He did not come to us with a professional mission of teaching sectarian creeds; he had not in his nature the least trace of that self-sufficiency of goodness, which humiliates by gifts the victims of its insolent benevolence. Though he did not know our language, he took every occasion to frequent our meetings and ceremonies; yet he was always afraid of intrusion, and tenderly anxious lest he might offend us by his ignorance of our customs. At last, under the continual strain of work in an alien climate and surroundings, his health broke down. He died, and was cremated at our burning ground, according to his express desire.

The attitude of his mind, the manner of his living, the object of his life, his modesty, his unstinted self-sacrifice for a people who had not even the power to give publicity to any benefaction bestowed upon them, were so utterly unlike anything we were accustomed to associate with the Europeans in India, that it gave rise in our mind to a feeling of love bordering upon awe.

We all have a realm, a private paradise, in our mind, where dwell deathless memories of persons who brought some divine light to our life's experience, who may not be known to others, and whose names have no place in the pages of history. Let me confess to you that this man lives as one of those immortals in the paradise of my individual life.

He came from Sweden, his name was Hammargren. What was most remarkable in the event of his coming to us in Bengal was the fact that in his own country he had chanced to read some works of my great countryman, Ram Mohan Roy, and felt an immense veneration for his genius and his character. Ram Mohan Roy lived in the beginning of the last century, and it is no exaggeration when I describe him as one of the immortal personalities of modern time. This young Swede had the unusual gift of a far-sighted intellect and sympathy, which enabled him even from his distance of space and time, and in spite of racial differences, to realise the greatness of Ram Mohan Roy. It moved him so deeply that he resolved to go to the country which produced this great man, and offer her his service. He was poor, and he had to wait some time in England before he could earn his passage money to India. There he came at last, and in reckless generosity of love utterly spent himself to the last breath of his life, away from home and kindred and all the inheritances of his motherland. His stay among us was too short to produce any outward result. He failed even to achieve during his life what he had in his mind, which was to found by the help of his scanty earnings a library as a memorial to Ram Mohan Roy, and thus to leave behind him a visible symbol of his devotion. But what I prize most in this European youth, who left no record of his life behind him, is not the memory of any service of goodwill, but the precious gift of respect which he offered to a people who are fallen upon evil times, and whom it is so easy to ignore or to humiliate. For the first time in the modern days this obscure individual from Sweden brought to our country the chivalrous courtesy of the West, a greeting of human fellowship.

The coincidence came to me with a great and delightful surprise when the Nobel prize was offered to me from Sweden. As a recognition of individual merit it was of great value to me, no doubt; but it was the acknowledgment of the East as a collaborator with the Western continents, in contributing its riches to the common stock of civilisation, which had the chief significance for the present age. It meant joining hands in comradeship by the two great hemispheres of the human world across the sea.

Today the real East remains unexplored. The blindness of contempt is more hopeless than the blindness of ignorance; for contempt kills the light which ignorance merely leaves unignited. The East is waiting to be understood by the Western races, in order not only to be able to give what is true in her, but also to be confident of her own mission.

In Indian history, the meeting of the Mussulman and the Hindu produced Akbar, the object of whose dream was the unification of hearts and ideals. It had all the glowing enthusiasm of a religion, and it produced an immediate and a vast result even in his own lifetime.

But the fact still remains that the Western mind, after centuries of contact with the East, has not evolved the enthusiasm of a chivalrous ideal which can bring this age to its fulfilment. It is everywhere raising thorny hedges of exclusion and offering human sacrifices to national self-seeking. It has intensified the mutual feelings of envy among Western races themselves, as they fight over their spoils and display a carnivorous pride in their snarling rows of teeth.

We must again guard our minds from an encroaching distrust of the individuals of a nation. The active love of humanity and the spirit of martyrdom for the cause of justice and truth which

I have met with in the Western countries have been a great lesson and inspiration to me. I have no doubt in my mind that the West owes its true greatness, not so much to its marvellous training of intellect, as to its spirit of service devoted to the welfare of man. Therefore I speak with a personal feeling of pain and sadness about the collective power which is guiding the helm of Western civilisation. It is a passion, not an ideal. The more success it has brought to Europe, the more costly it will prove to her at last, when the accounts have to be rendered. And the signs are unmistakable, that the accounts have been called for. The time has come when Europe must know that the forcible parasitism which she has been practising upon the two large Continents of the world — the two most unwieldy whales of humanity — must be causing to her moral nature a gradual atrophy and degeneration.

As an example, let me quote the following extract from the concluding chapter of *From the Cape to Cairo*, by Messrs. Grogan and Sharp, two writers who have the power to inculcate their doctrines by precept and example. In their reference to the African they are candid, as when they say, "We have stolen his land. Now we must steal his limbs." These two sentences, carefully articulated, with a smack of enjoyment, have been more clearly explained in the following statement, where some sense of that decency which is the attenuated ghost of a buried conscience, prompts the writers to use the phrase "compulsory labour" in place of the honest word "slavery"; just as the modern politician adroitly avoids the word "injunction" and uses the word "mandate". "Compulsory labour in some form," they say, "is the corollary of our occupation of the country." And they add: "It is pathetic, but it is history," implying thereby that moral sentiments have no serious effect in the history of human beings.

Elsewhere they write: "Either we must give up the country commercially, or we must make the African work. And mere abuse of those who point out the impasse cannot change the facts. We must decide, and soon. Or rather the white man of South Africa will decide." The authors also confess that they have seen too much of the world "to have any lingering belief that Western civilisation benefits native races."

The logic is simple — the logic of egoism. But the argument is simplified by lopping off the greater part of the premise. For these writers seem to hold that the only important question for the white men of South Africa is, how indefinitely to grow fat on ostrich feathers and diamond mines, and dance jazz dances over the misery and degradation of a whole race of fellow-beings of a different colour from their own. Possibly they believe that moral laws have a special domesticated breed of comfortable concessions for the service of the people in power. Possibly they ignore the fact that commercial and political cannibalism, profitably practised upon foreign races, creeps back nearer home; that the cultivation of unwholesome appetites has its final reckoning with the stomach which has been made to serve it. For, after all, man is a spiritual being, and not a mere living money-bag jumping from profit to profit, and breaking the backbone of human races in its financial leapfrog.

Such, however, has been the condition of things for more than a century; and to-day, trying to read the future by the light of the European conflagration, we are asking ourselves everywhere in the East: "Is this frightfully overgrown power really great? It can bruise us from without, but can it add to our wealth of spirit? It can sign peace treaties, but can it give peace?"

It was about two thousand years ago that all-powerful Rome in one of its eastern provinces executed on a cross a simple teacher of an obscure tribe of fishermen. On that day the Roman governor felt no falling off of his appetite or sleep. On that day there was, on the one hand, the agony, the humiliation, the death; on the other, the pomp of pride and festivity in the Governor's palace.

And today? To whom, then, shall we bow the head?

*Kasmai devaya havisha vidhema?*
(To which God shall we offer oblation?)

We know of an instance in our own history of India, when a great personality, both in his life and voice, struck the keynote of the solemn music of the soul — love for all creatures. And that music crossed seas, mountains, and deserts. Races belonging to different climates, habits, and languages were drawn together, not in the clash of arms, not in the conflict of exploitation, but in harmony of life, in amity and peace. That was creation.

When we think of it, we see at once what the confusion of thought was to which the Western poet, dwelling upon the difference between East and West, referred when he said, "Never the twain shall meet." It is true that they are not showing any real sign of meeting. But the reason is because the West has not sent out its humanity to meet the man in the East, but only its machine. Therefore the poet's line has to be changed into something like this:

Man is man, machine is machine,
And never the twain shall wed.

You must know that red tape can never be a common human bond; that official sealing-wax can never provide means of mutual attachment; that it is a painful ordeal for human beings to have to receive favours from animated pigeonholes, and condescensions from printed circulars that give notice but never speak. The presence of the Western people in the East is a human fact. If we are to gain anything from them, it must not be a mere sum-total of legal codes and systems of civil and military services. Man is a great deal more to man than that. We have our human birthright to claim direct help from the man of the West, if he has anything great to give us. It must come to us, not through mere facts in a juxtaposition, but through the spontaneous sacrifice made by those who have the gift, and therefore the responsibility.

Earnestly I ask the poet of the Western world to realise and sing to you with all the great power of music which he has, that the East and the West are ever in search of each other, and that they must meet not merely in the fulness of physical strength, but in fulness of truth; that the right hand, which wields the sword, has the need of the left, which holds the shield of safety.

The East has its seat in the vast plains watched over by the snow-peaked mountains and fertilised by rivers carrying mighty volumes of water to the sea. There, under the blaze of a tropical sun, the physical life has bedimmed the light of its vigour and lessened its claims. There man has had the repose of mind which has ever tried to set itself in harmony with the inner notes of existence. In the silence of sunrise and sunset, and on the star-crowded nights, he has sat face to face with the Infinite, waiting for the revelation that opens up the heart of all that there is. He has said, in a rapture of realisation:

"Hearken to me, ye children of the Immortal, who dwell in the Kingdom of Heaven. I have known, from beyond darkness, the Supreme Person, shining with the radiance of the sun."

The man from the East, with his faith in the eternal, who in his soul had met the touch of the Supreme Person — did he never come to you in the West and speak to you of the Kingdom of Heaven? Did he not unite the East and the West in truth, in the unity of one spiritual bond between all children of the Immortal, in the realisation of one great Personality in all human persons?

Yes, the East did once meet the West profoundly in the growth of her life. Such union became possible, because the East came to the West with the ideal that is creative, and not with the passion that destroys moral bonds. The mystic consciousness of the Infinite, which she brought with her, was greatly needed by the man of the West to give him his balance.

On the other hand, the East must find her own balance in Science — the magnificent gift that the West can bring to her. Truth has its nest as well as its sky. That nest is definite in structure, accurate in law of construction; and though it has to be changed and rebuilt over and over again, the need of it is never-ending and its laws are eternal. For some centuries the East has neglected the nest-building of truth. She has not been attentive to learn its secret. Trying to cross the trackless infinite, the East has relied solely upon her wings. She has spurned the earth, till, buffeted by storms, her wings are hurt and she is tired, sorely needing help. But has she then to be told that the messenger of the sky and the builder of the nest shall never meet?

QUESTIONS

1. Although Tagore wrote "East and West" in 1922, his message has lost none of its force in the intervening years. Sum up in your own words the core idea that he presents. Explain why this idea is of such urgency today.

2. The essay is divided into four main sections.

(a) In the introductory section he mentions some shortcomings of Westerners who visit the East. What are they?

(b) What similarity does he see between these weaknesses in Western outlook and the caste system in India?

3. What main topic does he develop in the second section?

4. In his lifetime, Tagore wrote some of India's most beautiful poetry. Thus we can expect in his writing some very striking images. Why is his use of imagery in the opening paragraph of the second section a skilful way to introduce his thoughts on the "collective idea" of the West?

5. In 1950 Bertrand Russell wrote an article (see "A Science to Save Us from Science", page 321) in which he blamed the machine age of the Western world for disrupting traditional Japanese culture and introducing "collective hysteria". Tagore in 1922 foresaw these probable effects on the Japanese.

(a) What part of his essay shows this prophetic insight?

(b) In his opinion what is the proper mission of the Western world?

6. The third section is a character study. Why does Tagore devote this section to an obscure Swede?

7. Note how the author binds together his thoughts in all four sections to form a coherent unity. For instance, how is the first sentence in the fourth section related to his introductory remarks at the beginning of the essay?

8. (a) In what way do Grogan and Smith form a sharp contrast with Hammargren?

(b) Explain what Tagore means when he refers to the reasoning of these writers as "the logic of egoism".

9. Why does he refer to the sufferings of Christ?

10. Tagore repeatedly uses the opposing terms, "ideal" and "passion". What does he mean by them?

11. The essay concludes with a beautiful image and a question. What great idea does the image illustrate? Why does Tagore end with a question?

*Graham*

*Greene*

# Across the bridge

---

*Graham Greene (b. 1904) was educated at Oxford and has been an editor of* The Times, *a film critic for* The Spectator, *and an author of popular "thrillers" and travel books. He is also one of the major novelists of our day and one who writes with a serious religious purpose. Green's "thrillers" (or, as he calls them, "entertainments") include* Stamboul Train *(1932),* This Gun for Hire *(1936), and* Confidential Agent *(1939). Most critics agree that the best of his serious novels are* Brighton Rock *(1938),* The Power and the Glory *(1940),* The Heart of the Matter *(1948), and* A Burnt-Out Case *(1961). "Across the Bridge" is reprinted from* Twenty-One Stories *by Graham Greene, by permission of Laurence Pollinger, Ltd.*

---

"THEY SAY he's worth a million," Lucia said. He sat there in the little hot damp Mexican square, a dog at his feet, with an air of immense and forlorn patience. The dog attracted your attention at once; for it was very nearly an English setter, only something had gone wrong with the tail and the feathering. Palms wilted over his head, it was all shade and stuffiness round the bandstand, radios talked loudly in Spanish from the little wooden sheds where they changed your pesos into dollars at a loss. I could tell he didn't understand a word from the way he read his newspaper — as I did myself picking out the words which were like

English ones. "He's been here a month," Lucia said. "They turned him out of Guatemala and Honduras."

You couldn't keep any secrets for five hours in this border town. Lucia had only been twenty-four hours in the place, but she knew all about Mr. Joseph Calloway. The only reason I didn't know about him (and I'd been in the place two weeks) was because I couldn't talk the language any more than Mr. Calloway could. There wasn't another soul in the place who didn't know the story – the whole story of the Halling Investment Trust and the proceedings for extradition. Any man doing dusty business in any of the wooden booths in the town is better fitted by long observation to tell Mr. Calloway's tale than I am, except that I was in – literally – at the finish. They all watched the drama proceed with immense interest, sympathy and respect. For, after all, he had a million.

Every once in a while through the long steamy day, a boy came and cleaned Mr. Calloway's shoes: he hadn't the right words to resist them – they pretended not to know his English. He must have had his shoes cleaned the day Lucia and I watched him at least half a dozen times. At midday he took a stroll across the square to the Antonio Bar and had a bottle of beer, the setter sticking to heel as if they were out for a country walk in England (he had, you may remember, one of the biggest estates in Norfolk). After his bottle of beer, he would walk down between the money changers' huts to the Rio Grande and look across the bridge into the United States: people came and went constantly in cars. Then back to the square till lunch-time. He was staying in the best hotel, but you don't get good hotels in this border town: nobody stays in them more than a night. The good hotels were on the other side of the bridge: you could see their electric signs twenty storeys high from the little square at night, like light-houses marking the United States.

You may ask what I'd been doing in so drab a spot for a fortnight. There was no interest in the place for anyone; it was just damp and dust and poverty, a kind of shabby replica of the town across the river: both had squares in the same spots; both had the same number of cinemas. One was cleaner than the other, that was all, and more expensive, much more expensive. I'd stayed across there a couple of nights waiting for a man a tourist bureau said was driving down from Detroit to Yucatan and would sell a place in his car for some fantastically small figure — twenty dollars, I think it was. I don't know if he existed or was invented by the optimistic half-caste in the agency; anyway, he never turned up and so I waited, not much caring, on the cheap side of the river. It didn't much matter; I was living. One day I meant to give up the man from Detroit and go home or go south, but it was easier not to decide anything in a hurry. Lucia was just wait- ing for a car going the other way, but she didn't have to wait so long. We waited together and watched Mr. Calloway waiting — for God knows what.

I don't know how to treat this story — it was a tragedy for Mr. Calloway, it was poetic retribution, I suppose, in the eyes of the shareholders he'd ruined with his bogus transactions, and to Lucia and me, at this stage, it was pure comedy — except when he kicked the dog. I'm not a sentimentalist about dogs, I prefer people to be cruel to animals rather than to human beings, but I couldn't help being revolted at the way he'd kick that animal — with a hint of cold-blooded venom, not in anger but as if he were getting even for some trick it had played him a long while ago. That generally happened when he returned from the bridge: it was the only sign of anything resembling emotion he showed. Otherwise he looked a small, set, gentle creature with silver hair and a silver moustache, and gold-rimmed glasses, and one gold tooth like a flaw in character.

Lucia hadn't been accurate when she said he'd been turned out of Guatemala and Honduras; he'd left voluntarily when the ex- tradition proceedings seemed likely to go through and moved north. Mexico is still not a very centralised state, and it is possible to get round governors as you can't get round cabinet ministers or judges. And so he waited there on the border for the next move. That earlier part of the story is, I suppose, dramatic, but I didn't watch it and I can't invent what I haven't seen — the long waiting in ante-rooms, the bribes taken and refused, the growing fear of arrest, and then the flight — in gold-rimmed glasses —

covering his tracks as well as he could, but this wasn't finance
and he was an amateur at escape. And so he'd washed up here,
under my eyes and Lucia's eyes, sitting all day under the bandstand, nothing to read but a Mexican paper, nothing to do but
look across the river at the United States, quite unaware, I suppose, that everyone knew everything about him, once a day kicking his dog. Perhaps in its semi-setter way it reminded him too
much of the Norfolk estate — though that, too, I suppose, was
the reason he kept it.

And the next act again was pure comedy. I hesitate to think
what this man worth a million was costing his country as they
edged him out from this land and that. Perhaps somebody was
getting tired of the business, and careless; anyway, they sent
across two detectives, with an old photograph. He'd grown his
silvery moustache since that had been taken, and he'd aged a lot,
and they couldn't catch sight of him. They hadn't been across
the bridge two hours when everybody knew that there were
two foreign detectives in town looking for Mr. Calloway —
everybody knew, that is to say, except Mr. Calloway, who
couldn't talk Spanish. There were plenty of people who could
have told him in English, but they didn't. It wasn't cruelty, it was
a sort of awe and respect: like a bull, he was on show, sitting
there mournfully in the plaza with his dog, a magnificent spectacle for which we all had ringside seats.

I ran into one of the policemen in the Bar Antonio. He was
disgusted; he had had some idea that when he crossed the bridge
life was going to be different, so much more colour and sun,
and — I suspect — love, and all he found were wide mud streets
where the nocturnal rain lay in pools, and mangy dogs, smells
and cockroaches in his bedroom, and the nearest to love, the open
door of the Academia Comercial, where pretty mestizo girls sat
all the morning learning to typewrite. Tip-tap-tip-tap-tip — perhaps they had a dream, too — jobs on the other side of the bridge,
where life was going to be so much more luxurious, refined and
amusing.

We got into conversation; he seemed surprised that I knew

who they both were and what they wanted. He said, "We've got information this man Calloway's in town."

"He's knocking around somewhere," I said.

"Could you point him out?"

"Oh, I don't know him by sight," I said.

He drank his beer and thought a while. "I'll go out and sit in the plaza. He's sure to pass sometime."

I finished my beer and went quickly off and found Lucia. I said, "Hurry, we're going to see an arrest." We didn't care a thing about Mr. Calloway, he was just an elderly man who kicked his dog and swindled the poor, and who deserved anything he got. So we made for the plaza; we knew Calloway would be there, but it had never occurred to either of us that the detectives wouldn't recognise him. There was quite a surge of people round the place; all the fruit-sellers and boot-blacks in town seemed to have arrived together; we had to force our way through, and there in the little green stuffy centre of the place, sitting on adjoining seats, were the two plain-clothes men and Mr. Calloway. I've never known the place so silent; everybody was on tiptoe, and the plain-clothes men were staring at the crowd looking for Mr. Calloway, and Mr. Calloway sat on his usual seat staring out over the money-changing booths at the United States.

"It can't go on. It just can't," Lucia said. But it did. It got more fantastic still. Somebody ought to write a play about it. We sat as close as we dared. We were afraid all the time we were going to laugh. The semi-setter scratched for fleas and Mr. Calloway watched the U.S.A. The two detectives watched the crowd, and the crowd watched the show with solemn satisfaction. Then one of the detectives got up and went over to Mr. Calloway. That's the end, I thought. But it wasn't, it was the beginning. For some reason they had eliminated him from their list of suspects. I shall never know why. The man said:

"You speak English?"

"I *am* English," Mr. Calloway said.

Even that didn't tear it. and the strangest thing of all was the way Mr. Calloway came alive. I don't think anybody had spoken

to him like that for weeks. The Mexicans were too respectful –
he was a man with a million – and it had never occurred to Lucia
and me to treat him casually like a human being; even in our eyes
he had been magnified by the colossal theft and the world-wide
pursuit.

He said, "This is rather a dreadful place, don't you think?"

"It is," the policeman said.

"I can't think what brings anybody across the bridge."

"Duty," the policeman said gloomily. "I suppose you are passing through."

"Yes," Mr. Calloway said.

"I'd have expected over here there'd have been – you know
what I mean – life. You read things about Mexico."

"Oh, life," Mr. Calloway said. He spoke firmly and precisely,
as if to a committee of shareholders. "That begins on the other
side."

"You don't appreciate your own country until you leave it."

"That's very true," Mr. Calloway said. "Very true."

At first it was difficult not to laugh, and then after a while
there didn't seem to be much to laugh at; an old man imagining
all the fine things going on beyond the international bridge. I
think he thought of the town opposite as a combination of
London and Norfolk – theatres and cocktail bars, a little shooting and a walk round the field at evening with the dog – that
miserable imitation of a setter – poking the ditches. He'd never
been across, he couldn't know that it was just the same thing
over again – even the same layout; only the streets were paved
and the hotels had ten more storeys, and life was more expensive,
and everything was a little bit cleaner. There wasn't anything
Mr. Calloway would have called living – no galleries, no book-
shops, just *Film Fun* and the local paper, and *Click* and *Focus*
and the tabloids.

"Well," said Mr. Calloway, "I think I'll take a stroll before
lunch. You need an appetite to swallow food here. I generally go
down and look at the bridge about now. Care to come, too?"

The detective shook his head. "No," he said, "I'm on duty. I'm
looking for a fellow." And that, of course, gave *him* away. As

far as Mr. Calloway could understand, there was only one "fellow" in the world anyone was looking for – his brain had eliminated friends who were seeking their friends, husbands who might be waiting for their wives, all objectives of any search but just the one. The power of elimination was what had made him a financier – he could forget the people behind the shares.

That was the last we saw of him for a while. We didn't see him going into the Botica Paris to get his aspirin, or walking back from the bridge with his dog. He simply disappeared, and when he disappeared, people began to talk, and the detectives heard the talk. They looked silly enough, and they got busy after the very man they'd been sitting next to in the garden. Then they, too, disappeared. They, as well as Mr. Calloway, had gone to the state capital to see the Governor and the Chief of Police, and it must have been an amusing sight there, too, as they bumped into Mr. Calloway and sat with him in the waiting-rooms. I suspect Mr. Calloway was generally shown in first, for everyone knew he was worth a million. Only in Europe is it possible for a man to be a criminal as well as a rich man.

Anyway, after about a week the whole pack of them returned by the same train. Mr. Calloway travelled Pullman, and the two policemen travelled in the day coach. It was evident that they hadn't got their extradition order.

Lucia had left by that time. The car came and went across the bridge. I stood in Mexico and watched her get out at the United States Customs. She wasn't anything in particular, but she looked beautiful at a distance as she gave me a wave out of the United States and got back into the car. And I suddenly felt sympathy for Mr. Calloway, as if there were something over there which you couldn't find here, and turning round I saw him back on his old beat, with the dog at his heels.

I said "Good afternoon," as if it had been all along our habit to greet each other. He looked tired and ill and dusty, and I felt sorry for him – to think of the kind of victory he'd been winning, with so much expenditure of cash and care – the prize this dirty and dreary town, the booths of the money-changers, the awful little beauty parlours with their wicker chairs and sofas looking like the reception rooms of brothels, that hot and stuffy garden by the bandstand.

He replied gloomily "Good morning," and the dog started to sniff at some ordure and he turned and kicked it with fury, with depression, with despair.

And at that moment a taxi with the two policemen in it passed us on its way to the bridge. They must have seen that kick; perhaps they were cleverer than I had given them credit for, perhaps they were just sentimental about animals, and thought they'd do a good deed, and the rest happened by accident. But the fact remains — those two pillars of the law set about the stealing of Mr. Calloway's dog.

He watched them go by. Then he said, "Why don't you go across?"

"It's cheaper here," I said.

"I mean just for an evening. Have a meal at that place we can see at night in the sky. Go to the theatre."

"There isn't a chance."

He said angrily, sucking his gold tooth, "Well, anyway, get away from here." He stared down the hill and up the other side. He couldn't see that that street climbing up from the bridge contained only the same money-changers' booths as this one.

I said, "Why don't *you* go?"

He said evasively, "Oh — business."

I said, "It's only a question of money. You don't *have* to pass by the bridge."

He said with faint interest, "I don't talk Spanish."

"There isn't a soul here," I said, "who doesn't talk English."

He looked at me with surprise. "Is that so?" he said. "Is that so?"

It's as I have said; he'd never tried to talk to anyone, and they respected him too much to talk to him — he was worth a million. I don't know whether I'm glad or sorry that I told him that. If I hadn't, he might be there now, sitting by the bandstand having his shoes cleaned — alive and suffering.

Three days later his dog disappeared. I found him looking for it, calling it softly and shamefacedly between the palms of the garden. He looked embarrassed. He said in a low angry voice, "I *hate* that dog. The beastly mongrel," and called "Rover, Rover" in a voice which didn't carry five yards. He said, "I bred setters once. I'd have shot a dog like that." It reminded him, I *was* right, of Norfolk, and he lived in the memory, and he hated it for its imperfection. He was a man without a family and without friends, and his only enemy was that dog. You couldn't call the law an enemy; you have to be intimate with an enemy.

Late that afternoon someone told him they'd seen the dog walking across the bridge. It wasn't true, of course, but we didn't know that then — they'd paid a Mexican five pesos to smuggle it across. So all that afternoon and the next Mr. Calloway sat in the garden having his shoes cleaned over and over again, and thinking how a dog could just walk across like that, and a human being, an immortal soul, was bound here in the awful routine of the little walk and the unspeakable meals and the aspirin at the botica. That dog was seeing things he couldn't see — that hateful dog. It made him mad — I think literally mad. You must remember the man had been going on for months. He had a million and he was living on two pounds a week, with nothing to spend his money on. He sat there and brooded on the hideous injustice of it. I think he'd have crossed over one day in any case, but the dog was the last straw.

Next day when he wasn't to be seen, I guessed he'd gone across and I went too. The American town is as small as the Mexican. I knew I couldn't miss him if he was there, and I was still curious. A little sorry for him, but not much.

I caught sight of him first in the only drug-store, having a coca-cola, and then once outside a cinema looking at the posters; he had dressed with extreme neatness, as if for a party, but there was no party. On my third time round, I came on the detectives — they were having coca-colas in the drug-store, and they must have missed Mr. Calloway by inches. I went in and sat down at the bar.

"Hello," I said, "you still about." I suddenly felt anxious for Mr. Calloway. I didn't want them to meet.

One of them said, "Where's Calloway?"

"Oh," I said, "he's hanging on."

"But not his dog," he said, and laughed. The other looked a little shocked, he didn't like anyone to *talk* cynically about a dog. Then they got up — they had a car outside.

"Have another?" I said.

"No thanks. We've got to keep moving."

The men bent close and confided to me, "Calloway's on this side."

"No!" I said.

"And his dog."

"He's looking for it," the other said.

"I'm damned if he is," I said, and again one of them looked a little shocked, as if I'd insulted the dog.

I don't think Mr. Calloway was looking for his dog, but his dog certainly found him. There was a sudden hilarious yapping from the car and out plunged the semi-setter and gambolled furiously down the street. One of the detectives — the sentimental one — was into the car before we got to the door and was off after the dog. Near the bottom of the long road to the bridge was Mr. Calloway — I do believe he'd come down to look at the Mexican side when he found there was nothing but the drugstore and the cinemas and the paper shops on the American. He saw the dog coming and yelled at it to go home — "home, home, home", as if they were in Norfolk — it took no notice at all, pelting towards him. Then he saw the police car coming, and ran. After that, everything happened too quickly, but I think the order of events was this — the dog started across the road right in front of the car, and Mr. Calloway yelled, at the dog or the car, I don't know which. Anyway, the detective swerved — he said later, weakly, at the enquiry, that he couldn't run over a dog, and down went Mr. Calloway, in a mess of broken glass and gold rims and silver hair, and blood. The dog was on to him before any of us could reach him, licking and whimpering and licking. I saw Mr. Calloway put up his hand, and down it went across the dog's neck and the whimper rose to a stupid bark of triumph, but Mr. Calloway was dead — shock and a weak heart.

"Poor old geezer," the detective said, "I bet he really loved that

dog," and it's true that the attitude in which he lay looked more
like a caress than a blow. I thought it was meant to be a blow, but
the detective may have been right. It all seemed to me a little too
touching to be true as the old crook lay there with his arm
over the dog's neck, dead with his million between the money-
changers' huts, but it's as well to be humble in the face of human
nature. He had come across the river for something, and it may,
after all, have been the dog he was looking for. It sat there, baying
its stupid and mongrel triumph across his body, like a piece of
sentimental statuary: the nearest he could get to the fields, the
ditches, the horizon of his home. It was comic and it was pitiable,
but it wasn't less comic because the man was dead. Death doesn't
change comedy to tragedy, and if that last gesture was one of
affection, I suppose it was only one more indication of a human
being's capacity for self-deception, our baseless optimism that is
so much more appalling than our despair.

CRITIQUE AND QUESTIONS

Graham Greene's story is written in a low key. The narrator
describes the tale as "comic". At the very end, the spectacle of the
old man lying dead with the dog baying its triumph across his body,
is said to be "comic" — "pitiable", too, but not "less comic because
the man was dead."

We seldom can give the name, "comedy", to a story or play which
ends in the death of the main character. You will notice that at
first the narrator is uncertain as to how he will tell the story, a story
which, *from the inside,* from the point of view of the main character,
must seem "tragic" indeed. Yet the narrator decides that "death
doesn't change comedy to tragedy". The story will be told *from
the outside.* Its meaning, its effect will be that of comedy, not
tragedy.

How does Mr. Greene maintain the tone of comedy in a story
which has the elements of tragedy? And *why* does he do it? In other
words, is the meaning, the purpose of the story, defined and controlled by the tone and method?

Notice, first of all, how carefully Mr. Greene keeps to his low key.

How easily the plot could have been given the excitement of a
television melodrama! A wanted man in a border town pursued
by federal agents. Splendid possibilities! The escape by night, the
frenzied pursuit, the bright stab of gun fire in the blackness. And
the setting – the exotic Mexican town with its flashing senoritas,
the half-lit cafés, the sleepless, beckoning twisted streets, the palm-
trees, the bull-fights, and the intrigue.

But there is none of this here. The town is squalid. The American
policeman has a Hollywood dream of what the Mexican town
will be like. But the town is not at all like the dream. It is nothing but
a squat, poverty-stricken replica of the American town across the
river. Nor is there a hair-raising chase and capture. The old man
crosses the bridge in search of his dog and is accidentally killed by
an automobile. This is partly what is meant by saying that the
story is written in a low key. One's expectation of something exotic
and melodramatic is deliberately disappointed. For good reason
(as we shall see) the author keeps his voice – and the reader's blood
pressure – down.

This effect is achieved in part by the device of the narrator. It is
through the eyes of the narrator that we watch the story unfold.
What is more important, it is by the casual, detached tone of the
narrator that we are kept at a distance from the old man, Mr.
Calloway, and are prevented from identifying ourselves with him.
In tragedy, we feel *with* the tragic hero, share his fear and his guilt
and his pain. In comedy, we are detached from the characters
altogether. We do not feel *with* them; we laugh *at* them – from
the outside, from a distance.

The narrator, then, is used to ensure the necessary distance between
the old man and ourselves. Notice the air of casualness which
surrounds the narrator from the beginning. It is an accident that he
is in town at all. He talks with another transient, Lucia, who tells
him the gossip about the old man and then casually leaves town
herself. The gossip is strangely impersonal. The old man never
appears as a person at first-hand. He is never a subject, but merely
the object of curiosity. He is looked upon with awe, not for himself
but for his million dollars (which he embezzled), and because he is
a marked man, wanted by the American police who seek to extradite

him. He is not only at a distance from the narrator but also from the townspeople, who pretend not to speak English. Even the American police talk to him without knowing who he is, and without his recognizing them. He is even cut off, in a sense, from his stolen money (there is no way to spend it). He is close to nothing living except the dog — the dog he hates. And it is the dog who brings him at last to his death.

The death scene *is* "pitiable", for a lonely death calls out for pity. But the *method* of the story, the detached and distant treatment of the old man's fate, is nonetheless comic, not tragic.

What, then, of the theme, the meaning of the story?

It is well to keep in mind the title, "Across the Bridge". For the purposes of Graham Greene's theme, this bridge divides rather than joins. The bridge is there to be crossed. But it is not crossed — not really. True, the American police come over it. But they cannot touch the old man; they cannot take him back. The bridge which seems to promise communication — going and coming, give and take — prevents communication. It is the opposite of what it is intended to be. It is a road-block, a barrier. To cross it means death for the old man. Not to cross it means another kind of death, a living death. This bridge which is not a bridge, represents, significantly, all the human and social and spiritual road-blocks which mark the story from beginning to end. No one person is able to communicate with another (although all the means of communication seem to be present). Thus, as we have noted, the townspeople do not talk to the old man, nor he to them; the police and the old man talk, but their talk is blind; the narrator talks to the old man and to the police, but his talk is a concealment and an evasion. The old man does talk to his dog — for the dog is a bridge to his past. Yet the past is lost; the bridge to it cannot really be crossed. Actually, the dog is at once a bridge to the past ("he lived in the memory") and a roadblock to the past ("he hated it for its imperfection" — "I'd have shot a dog like that").

The dog conjures up everything that the old man once was and now is — conjures up, too, the dark impassable river which flows between past and present. The dog is kicked methodically once a day. Is this not an act of self-hatred? Is not the old man, through the dog-image, cursing that roadblock *within himself* which stands between what he once was and what he might have been and never now can be? Is not the dog, in a sense, the old man's damnation, representing hope that is lost, representing an inner, endless torment of hopelessness?

When the dog at last crosses the bridge, it is as if part of the old man had crossed with him. The dog's crossing is a projection of the old man's desperate desire ("That dog was seeing things he couldn't see — that hateful dog"). The old man follows. But he does not cross — not really. The bridge, for him, is not a bridge. And he dies meaninglessly at the road-block, deceived within himself, unredeemed.

One remembers that the old man is a guilty man. He seeks merely to escape the consequences of his guilt — into the future by bribery and flight, into the past by the recollection of a time where he was not yet guilty. He never once faces his guilt. He never repents. He does not love. He cannot love even himself, because the self is broken by the guilt which is never faced. There can be no communication for such a man because there is no communion. Communion is an act of love and no man in flight from himself can love. No man who hates himself can love. No man who hates his failure rather than his sin can love. Nor can he hope. The bridge is a mockery because it cannot be crossed without hope, without love, without communion — without repentance.

Graham Greene has given us here, in human and temporal terms, a portrait of Hell. There is nothing "comic" about Hell. Yet Dante, the great mediaeval poet, began his *Divine Comedy* with a portrait of Hell — the loveless, faithless, hopeless place of those who have been judged and condemned. In Dante's poem, such judgement had to be placed and understood before the imagination was allowed to ascend through Purgatory to Paradise. Comedy, with its technique of detachment and distance, begins in the act of judgement and ends in the happy vision. But the judgement comes first.

"Across the Bridge" is a comedy because it is a judgement, a judgement made and expressed through the comic technique of distance and detachment. Certainly this is not the comedy of laughter, but rather, the comedy of warning and example. Tragedy would have induced us to feel *like* the old man — indeed, in our imagination, to *be* the old man. Comedy separates us from him. The comedy of warning and example says, in effect, we cannot, we *must not* be the old man.

And does not Graham Greene's comedy also say: "The bridge is not a roadblock. It *is* the bridge, the open possibility, the redemptive route. Take warning here and then take the bridge . . ."?

1. What are the various functions of the dog in the narrative and in the revelation of the old man's character?

2. Could Lucia have been dropped from the story?

3. At what point does the narrator show or feel sympathy for the old man?

4. Why does the narrator say that the old man is "pitiable", and yet insist that his fate is not "tragic"?

5. Why does the narrator say that he is uncertain just how he should tell the story?

6. Why is the American town "just the same thing over again" as the Mexican town?

7. The narrator tells the old man that the townspeople do speak English. How does this information affect the old man? Why?

8. What is implied by the fact that the old man, once he is on the American side, comes down to stare back at the Mexican side? What does this tell you about the old man? About the meaning of the bridge? About the meaning of the old man's death?

*Stephen Vincent*

*Benét*

# By the waters of Babylon

*Stephen Vincent Benét (1898-1943), American poet and story writer, was born in Bethlehem, Pennsylvania, and spent his boyhood years in various army posts to which his father, an army officer, had been assigned. Later he studied at Yale University, graduating in 1919. His early creative work,* Young Adventure *(1918),* Heavens and Earth *(1920),* Tiger Jay *(1925), and* Spanish Bayonet *(1926), won him a Guggenheim Fellowship. This grant enabled him to live and work in Paris, France, where he wrote* John Brown's Body *(1928), a narrative poem of the American Civil War for which he was awarded the Pulitzer Prize. Upon his return to the United States he continued to write poems and prose, including* Ballads and Poems *(1931),* Burning City *(1936),* Nightmare at Noon *(1938), and* Tales Before Midnight *(1939). His unfinished epic poem,* Western Star, *was published posthumously in 1943. Although the frightful destruction of the war depressed him, he continued to believe in the power of civilization to renew itself and endure, as is suggested in the following story. "By the Waters of Babylon" is reprinted from* Selected Works of Stephen Vincent Benét, *Holt, Rinehart, and Winston, Inc. (copyright 1937 by Stephen Vincent Benét), by permission of Brandt and Brandt.*

THE NORTH AND THE WEST AND THE SOUTH are good hunting ground, but it is forbidden to go east. It is forbidden to go to any of the Dead Places except to search for metal and then he who touches the metal must be a priest or the son of a priest. Afterwards, both the man and the metal must be purified. These are the rules and the laws; they are well made. It is forbidden to cross the great river and look upon the place that was the Place of the Gods — this is most strictly forbidden. We do not even say its name though we know its name. It is there that spirits live, and demons — it is there that there are the ashes of the Great Burning. These things are forbidden — they have been forbidden since the beginning of time.

My father is a priest; I am the son of a priest. I have been in the Dead Places near us, with my father — at first, I was afraid. When my father went into the house to search for the metal, I stood by the door and my heart felt small and weak. It was a dead man's house, a spirit house. It did not have the smell of man, though there were old bones in a corner. But it is not fitting that a priest's son should show fear. I looked at the bones in the shadow and kept my voice still.

Then my father came out with the metal — a good, strong piece. He looked at me with both eyes but I had not run away. He gave me the metal to hold — I took it and did not die. So he knew I was truly his son and would be a priest in my time. That was when I was very young — nevertheless my brothers would not have done it, though they are good hunters. After that, they gave me the good piece of meat and the warm corner by the fire. My father watched over me — he was glad that I should be a priest. But when I boasted or wept without a reason, he punished me more strictly than my brothers. That was right.

After a time, I myself was allowed to go into the dead houses and search for metal. So I learned the way of those houses — and if I saw bones, I was no longer afraid. The bones are light and old — sometimes they will fall into dust if you touch them. But that is a great sin.

I was taught the chants and spells — I was taught how to stop the running of blood from a wound and many secrets. A priest must know many secrets — that was what my father said. If the hunters think we do all things by chants and spells, they may believe so — it does not hurt them. I was taught how to read in the old books and how to make the old writings — that was hard and took a long time. My knowledge made me happy — it was like a fire in my heart. Most of all, I liked to hear of the Old Days and the stories of the gods. I asked myself many questions that I could not answer, but it was good to ask them. At night, I would lie awake and listen to the wind — it seemed to me that it was the voice of the gods as they flew through the air.

We are not ignorant like the Forest People — our women spin wool on the wheel, our priests wear a white robe. We do not eat grubs from the tree, we have not forgotten the old writings, although they are hard to understand. Nevertheless, my knowledge and my lack of knowledge burned in me — I wished to know more. When I was a man at last, I came to my father and said, "It is time for me to go on my journey. Give me your leave."

He looked at me for a long time, stroking his beard, then he said at last, "Yes. It is time." That night, in the house of the priesthood, I asked for and received purification. My body hurt but my spirit was a cool stone. It was my father himself who questioned me about my dreams.

He bade me look into the smoke of the fire and see — I saw and told what I saw. It was what I have always seen — a river, and, beyond it, a great Dead Place and in it the gods walking. I have always thought about that. His eyes were stern when I told him — he was no longer my father but a priest. He said, "This is a strong dream."

"It is mine," I said, while the smoke waved and my head felt light. They were singing the Star song in the outer chamber and it was like the buzzing of bees in my head.

He asked me how the gods were dressed and I told him how they were dressed. We know how they were dressed from the book, but I saw them as if they were before me. When I had finished, he threw the sticks three times and studied them as they fell.

"This is a very strong dream," he said. "It may eat you up."

"I am not afraid," I said and looked at him with both eyes. My voice sounded thin in my ears but that was because of the smoke.

He touched me on the breast and the forehead. He gave me the bow and the three arrows.

"Take them," he said. "It is forbidden to travel east. It is forbidden to cross the river. It is forbidden to go to the Place of the Gods. All these things are forbidden."

"All these things are forbidden," I said, but it was my voice that spoke and not my spirit. He looked at me again.

"My son," he said. "Once I had young dreams. If your dreams do not eat you up, you may be a great priest. If they eat you, you are still my son. Now go on your journey."

I went fasting, as is the law. My body hurt but not my heart. When the dawn came, I was out of sight of the village. I prayed and purified myself, waiting for a sign. The sign was an eagle. It flew east.

Sometimes signs are sent by bad spirits. I waited again on the flat rock, fasting, taking no food. I was very still — I could feel the sky above me and the earth beneath. I waited till the sun was beginning to sink. Then three deer passed in the valley, going east — they did not wind me or see me. There was a white fawn with them — a very great sign.

I followed them, at a distance, waiting for what should happen. My heart was troubled about going east, yet I knew that I must go. My head hummed with my fasting — I did not even see the panther spring upon the white fawn. But, before I knew it, the bow was in my hand. I shouted and the panther lifted his head from the fawn. It is not easy to kill a panther with one arrow but the arrow went through his eye and into his brain. He died as he tried to spring — he rolled over, tearing at the ground. Then I knew I was meant to go east — I knew that was my journey. When the night came, I made my fire and roasted meat.

It is eight suns' journey to the east and a man passes by many Dead Places. The Forest People are afraid of them but I am not. Once I made my fire on the edge of a Dead Place at night and, next morning, in the dead house, I found a good knife, little rusted. That was small to what came afterward but it made my heart feel big. Always when I looked for game, it was in front of my arrow, and twice I passed hunting parties of the Forest

People without their knowing. So I knew my magic was strong and my journey clean, in spite of the law.

Toward the setting of the eighth sun, I came to the banks of the great river. It was half-a-day's journey after I had left the god-road — we do not use the god-roads now for they are falling apart into great blocks of stone, and the forest is safer going. A long way off, I had seen water through trees but the trees were thick. At last, I came out upon an open place at the top of a cliff. There was a great river below, like a giant in the sun. It is very long, very wide. It could eat all the streams we know and still be thirsty. Its name is Ou-dis-sun, the Sacred, the Long. No man of my tribe had seen it, not even my father, the priest. It was magic and I prayed.

Then I raised my eyes and looked south. It was there, the Place of the Gods.

How can I tell what it was like — you do not know. It was there, in the red light, and they were too big to be houses. It was there with the red light upon it, mighty and ruined. I knew that in another moment the gods would see me. I covered my eyes with my hands and crept back into the forest.

Surely, that was enough to do, and live. Surely it was enough to spend the night upon the cliff. The Forest People themselves do not come near. Yet, all through the night, I knew that I should have to cross the river and walk in the Place of the Gods, although the gods ate me up. My magic did not help me at all and yet there was a fire in my bowels, a fire in my mind. When the sun rose, I thought, "My journey has been clean. Now I will go home from my journey." But, even as I thought so, I knew I could not. If I went to the Place of the Gods, I would surely die, but, if I did not go, I could never be at peace with my spirit again. It is better to lose one's life than one's spirit, if one is a priest and the son of a priest.

Nevertheless, as I made the raft, the tears ran out of my eyes. The Forest People could have killed me without fight, if they had come upon me then, but they did not come. When the raft was made, I said the sayings for the dead and painted myself for death. My heart was cold as a frog and my knees like water, but the burning in my mind would not let me have peace. As I pushed the raft from the shore, I began my death song — I had the right. It was a fine song.

"I am John, son of John," I sang. "My people are the Hill People. They are the men.
I go into the Dead Places but I am not slain.
I take the metal from the Dead Places but I am not blasted.
I travel upon the god-roads and am not afraid. E-yah! I have killed the panther, I have killed the fawn!
E-yah! I have come to the great river. No man has come there before.
It is forbidden to go east, but I have gone, forbidden to go on the great river, but I am there.
Open your hearts, you spirits, and hear my song.
Now I go to the Place of the Gods, I shall not return.
My body is painted for death and my limbs weak, but my heart is big as I go to the Place of the Gods!"

All the same, when I came to the Place of the Gods, I was afraid, afraid. The current of the great river is very strong — it gripped my raft with its hands. That was magic, for the river itself is wide and calm. I could feel evil spirits about me, in the bright morning; I could feel their breath on my neck as I was swept down the stream. Never have I been so much alone — I tried to think of my knowledge, but it was a squirrel's leap of winter nuts. There was no strength in my knowledge any more and I felt small and naked as a new-hatched bird — alone upon the great river, the servant of the gods.

Yet, after a while, my eyes were opened and I saw. I saw both banks of the river — I saw that once there had been god-roads across it, though now they were broken and fallen like broken vines. Very great they were and wonderful and broken — broken in the time of the Great Burning when the fire fell out of the sky. And always the current took me nearer to the Place of the Gods, and the huge ruins rose before my eyes.

I do not know the customs of rivers — we are the People of the Hills. I thought the river meant to take me past the Place of the

Gods and out into the Bitter Water of the legends. I grew angry then – my heart felt strong. I said aloud, "I am a priest and the son of a priest!" The gods heard me – they showed me how to paddle with the pole on one side of the raft. The current changed itself – I drew near to the Place of the Gods.

When I was very near, my raft struck and turned over. I can swim in our lakes – I swam to the shore. There was a great spike of rusted metal sticking out into the river – I hauled myself up upon it and sat there, panting. I had saved my bow and two arrows and the knife I found in the Dead Place but that was all. My raft went whirling downstream toward the Bitter Water. I looked after it, and thought if it had trod me under, at least I would be safely dead. Nevertheless, when I had dried my bow-string and re-strung it, I walked forward to the Place of the Gods.

It felt like ground underfoot; it did not burn me. It is not true what some of the tales say, that the ground there burns forever, for I have been there. Here and there were the marks and stains of the Great Burning, on the ruins, that is true. But they were old marks and old stains. It is not true either, what some of our priests say, that it is an island covered with frogs and enchantments. It is not. It is a great Dead Place – greater than any Dead Place we know. Everywhere in it there are god-roads, though most are cracked and broken. Everywhere there are the ruins of the high towers of the gods.

How shall I tell what I saw? I went carefully, my strung bow in my hand, my skin ready for danger. There should have been the wailings of spirits and the shrieks of demons, but there were not. It was very silent and sunny where I had landed – the wind and the rain and the birds that drop seeds had done their work – the grass grew in the cracks of the broken stone. It is a fair island – no wonder the gods built there. If I had come there, a god, I also would have built.

How shall I tell what I saw? The towers are not all broken – here and there one still stands, like a great tree in a forest, and the birds nest high. But the towers themselves look blind, for the gods are gone. I saw a fish-hawk, catching fish in the river. I saw a little dance of white butterflies over a great heap of broken stones and columns. I went there and looked about me — there was a carved stone with cut-letters, broken in half. I can read letters but I could not understand these. They said UBTREAS. There was also the shattered image of a man or a god. It had been made of white stone and he wore his hair tied back like a woman's. His name was ASHING, as I read on the cracked half of a stone. I thought it wise to pray to ASHING, though I do not know that god.

How shall I tell what I saw? There was no smell of man left, on stone or metal. Nor were there many trees in that wilderness of stone. There are many pigeons, nesting and dropping in the towers — the gods must have loved them, or, perhaps, they used them for sacrifices. There are wild cats that roam the god-roads, green-eyed, unafraid of man. At night, they wail like demons but they are not demons. The wild dogs are more dangerous, for they hunt in a pack, but them I did not meet till later. Everywhere there are the carved stones, carved with magical numbers or words.

I went North — I did not try to hide myself. When a god or a demon saw me, then I would die, but meanwhile I was no longer afraid. My hunger for knowledge burned in me — there was so much that I could not understand. After a while, I knew that my belly was hungry. I could have hunted for my meat, but I did not hunt. It is known that the gods did not hunt as we do — they got their food from enchanted boxes and jars. Sometimes these are still found in the Dead Places — once, when I was a child and foolish, I opened such a jar and tasted it and found the food sweet. But my father found out and punished me for it strictly, for, often, that food is death. Now, though, I had long gone past what was forbidden, and I entered the likeliest towers, looking for the food of the gods.

I found it at last in the ruins of a great temple in the mid-city. A mighty temple it must have been, for the roof was painted like the sky at night with its stars — that much I could see, though the colours were faint and dim. It went down into great caves and tunnels — perhaps they kept their slaves there. But when I started to climb down, I heard the squeaking of rats, so I did not go —

rats are unclean, there must have been many tribes of them, from the squeaking. But near there, I found food, in the heart of a ruin, behind a door that still opened. I ate only the fruits from the jars — they had a very sweet taste. There was drink, too, in bottles of glass — the drink of the gods was strong and made my head swim. After I had eaten and drunk, I slept on the top of a stone, my bow at my side.

When I awoke, the sun was low. Looking down from where I lay, I saw a dog sitting on his haunches. His tongue was hanging out of his mouth; he looked as if he were laughing. He was a big dog, with a grey-brown coat, as big as a wolf. I sprang up and shouted at him but he did not move — he just sat there as if he were laughing. I did not like that. When I reached for a stone to throw, he moved swiftly out of the way of the stone. He was not afraid of me; he looked at me as if I were meat. No doubt I could have killed him with an arrow, but I did not know if there were others. Moreover, night was falling.

I looked about me — not far away there was a great, broken god-road, leading North. The towers were high enough, but not so high, and while many of the Dead Houses were wrecked, there were some that stood. I went toward this god-road, keeping to the heights of the ruins, while the dog followed. When I had reached the god-road, I saw that there were others behind him. If I had slept later, they would have come upon me asleep and torn out my throat. As it was, they were sure enough of me; they did not hurry. When I went into the dead-house, they kept watch at the entrance — doubtless they thought they would have a fine hunt. But a dog cannot open a door and I knew, from the books, that the gods did not like to live on the ground but on high.

I had just found a door I could open when the dogs decided to rush. Ha! They were surprised when I shut the door in their faces — it was a good door, of strong metal. I could hear their foolish baying beyond it but I did not stop to answer them. I was in darkness — I found stairs and climbed. There were many stairs, turning around till my head was dizzy. At the top was another door — I found the knob and opened it. I was in a long small chamber — on one side of it was a bronze door that could not be opened, for it had no handle. Perhaps there was a magic word to open it but I did not have the word. I turned to the door in the opposite side of the wall. The lock of it was broken and I opened it and went in.

Within, there was a place of great riches. The god who lived there must have been a powerful god. The first room was a small ante-room — I waited there for some time, telling the spirits of the place that I came in peace and not as a robber. When it seemed to me that they had had time to hear me, I went on. Ah, what riches! Few, even, of the windows had been broken — it was all as it had been. The great windows that looked over the city had not been broken at all though they were dusty and streaked with many years. There were coverings on the floors, the colours not greatly faded, and the chairs were soft and deep. There were pictures upon the walls, very strange, very wonderful — I remember one of a bunch of flowers in a jar — if you came close to it, you could see nothing but bits of colour, but if you stood away from it, the flowers might have been picked yesterday. It made my heart feel strange to look at this picture — and to look at the figure of a bird, in some hard clay, on a table and see it so like our birds. Everywhere there were books and writings, many in tongues that I could not read. The god who lived there must have been a wise god and full of knowledge. I felt I had right there, as I sought knowledge also.

Nevertheless, it was strange. There was a washing-place but no water — perhaps the gods washed in air. There was a cooking-place but no wood and though there was a machine to cook food, there was no place to put fire in it. Nor were there candles or lamps — there were things that looked like lamps but they had neither oil nor wick. All these things were magic, but I touched them and lived — the magic had gone out of them. Let me tell one thing to show. In the washing-place, a thing said "Hot" but it was not hot to the touch — another thing said "Cold" but it was not cold. This must have been a strong magic but the magic was gone. I do not understand — they had ways — I wish that I knew.

It was close and dry and dusty in their house of the gods. I have said the magic was gone but that is not true — it had gone from the magic things but it had not gone from the place. I felt the spirits about me, weighing upon me. Nor had I ever slept in a Dead Place before — and yet, tonight, I must sleep there. When I thought of it, my tongue felt dry in my throat, in spite of my wish for knowledge. Almost I would have gone down again and faced the dogs, but I did not.

I had not gone through all the rooms when the darkness fell. When it fell, I went back to the big room looking over the city and made fire. There was a place to make fire in a box with wood in it, though I do not think they cooked there. I wrapped myself in a floor-covering and slept in front of the fire, I was very tired.

Now I tell what is very strong magic. I woke in the midst of the night. When I woke, the fire had gone out and I was cold. It seemed to me that all around me there were whisperings and voices. I closed my eyes to shut them out. Some will say that I slept again, but I do not think that I slept. I could feel the spirits drawing my spirit out of my body as a fish is drawn on a line.

Why should I lie about it? I am a priest and the son of a priest. If there are spirits, as they say, in the small Dead Places near us, what spirits must there not be in that great Place of the Gods? And would not they wish to speak? After such long years? I know that I felt myself drawn as a fish is drawn on a line. I had stepped out of my body — I could see my body asleep in front of the cold fire, but it was not I. I was drawn to look out upon the city of the gods.

It should have been dark, for it was night, but it was not dark. Everywhere there were lights — lines of light — circles and blurs of light — ten thousand torches would not have been the same. The sky itself was alight, you could barely see the stars for the glow in the sky. I thought to myself "This is strong magic" and trembled. There was a roaring in my ears like the rushing of rivers. Then my eyes grew used to the light and my ears to the sound. I knew that I was seeing the city as it had been when the gods were alive.

That was a sight indeed — yes, that was a sight: I could not have seen it in the body — my body would have died. Everywhere went the gods, on foot and in chariots — there were gods beyond number and counting and their chariots blocked the streets. They had turned night to day for their pleasure — they did not sleep with the sun. The noise of their coming and going was the noise of many waters. It was magic what they could do — it was magic what they did.

I looked out of another window — the great vines of their bridges were mended and the god-roads went East and West. Restless, restless, were the gods and always in motion! They burrowed tunnels under rivers — they flew in the air. With unbelievable tools they did giant works — no part of the earth was safe from them, for, if they wished for a thing, they summoned it from the other side of the world. And always, as they laboured and rested, as they feasted and made love, there was a drum in their ears — the pulse of the giant city, beating and beating like a man's heart.

Were they happy? What is happiness to the gods? They were great, they were mighty, they were wonderful and terrible. As I looked upon them and their magic, I felt like a child — but a little more, it seemed to me, and they would pull down the moon from the sky. I saw them with wisdom beyond wisdom and knowledge beyond knowledge. And yet not all they did was well done — even I could see that — and yet their wisdom could not but grow until all was peace.

Then I saw their fate come upon them and that was terrible past speech. It came upon them as they walked the streets of their city. I have been in the fights with the Forest People — I have seen men die. But this was not like that. When gods war with gods, they use weapons we do not know. It was fire falling out of the sky and a mist that poisoned. It was the time of the Great Burning and the Destruction. They ran about like ants in the streets of their city — poor gods, poor gods! Then the towers began to fall. A few escaped — yes, a few. The legends tell it. But, even after the city had become a Dead Place, for many years the poison was still in the ground. I saw it happen, I saw the last of them die. It was darkness over the broken city and I wept.

All this, I saw. I saw it as I have told it, though not in the body. When I woke in the morning, I was hungry, but I did not think first of my hunger for my heart was perplexed and confused. I knew the reason for the Dead Places but I did not see why it had happened, with all the magic they had. I went through the house looking for an answer. There was so much in the house I could not understand — yet I am a priest and the son of a priest. It was like being on one side of the great river, with no light to show the way.

Then I saw the dead god. He was sitting in his chair, by the window, in a room I had not entered before and, for the first moment, I thought that he was alive. Then I saw the skin on the back of his hand — it was like dry leather. The room was shut, hot and dry — no doubt that had kept him as he was. At first I was afraid to approach him — then the fear left me. He was sitting looking out over the city — he was dressed in the clothes of the gods. His age was neither young nor old — I could not tell his age. But there was wisdom in his face and great sadness. You could see that he would not have run away. He had sat at his window, watching his city die — then he himself had died. But it is better to lose one's life than one's spirit — and you could see from the face that his spirit had not been lost. I knew that, if I touched him, he would fall into dust — and yet, there was something unconquered in the face.

That is all of my story, for then I knew he was a man — I knew then that they had been men, neither gods nor demons. It is a great knowledge, hard to tell and believe. They were men — they went a dark road, but they were men. I had no fear after that — I had no fear going home, though twice I fought off the dogs and once I was hunted for two days by the Forest People. When I saw my father again, I prayed and was purified. He touched my lips and my breast, he said, "You went away a boy. You come back a man and a priest." I said, "Father, they were men! I have been in the Place of the Gods and seen it! Now slay me, if it is the law — but still I know they were men."

He looked at me out of both eyes. He said, "The law is not

always the same shape — you have done what you have done. I could not have done it in my time, but you come after me. Tell!"

I told and he listened. After that, I wished to tell all the people but he showed me otherwise. He said, "Truth is a hard deer to hunt. If you eat too much truth at once, you may die of the truth. It was not idly that our fathers forbade the Dead Places." He was right — it is better the truth should come little by little. I have learned that, being a priest. Perhaps, in the old days, they ate knowledge too fast.

Nevertheless, we make a beginning. It is not for the metal alone that we go to the Dead Places now, there are the books and the writings. They are hard to learn. And the magic tools are broken — but we can look at them and wonder. At least, we make a beginning. And, when I am chief priest we shall go beyond the great river. We shall go to the Place of the Gods — the place new-york — not one band but a company. We shall look for the images of the gods and find the god ASHING and the others — the gods Lincoln and Biltmore and Moses. But they were men who built the city, not gods or demons. They were men. I remember the dead man's face. They were men who were here before us. We must build again.

QUESTIONS

1. This is the story of a quest. Why does the author entitle it, "By the Waters of Babylon"?

2. In the very first paragraph of exposition Benét establishes the mood of the story and creates a mystery. What is this mood, and what details create mystery?

3. (a) What qualities in the boy excite our sympathy and admiration?
    (b) What methods of characterization does the author use to reveal these qualities?
    (c) How does he adapt his narrative style to make it suggest the speech of a youth from a primitive society?
    (d) Stephen Vincent Benét was primarily a poet, and some pas-

sages of this story have the lyrical quality of poetry. Pick out several of these passages. Which of those that you have selected help to emphasize some climactic moment in the boy's quest?

4. (a) Early in the story we learn of the boy-priest's visionary dreams. Which incident first indicates this clairvoyance?
   (b) Why does the author include this incident?

5. All through the story the writer plants clues, each of which suggests the identity of the civilization that dies out in "the Great Burning".
   (a) List these clues.
   (b) At what point in the story could you identify the civilization?

6. (a) The author has filled the boy's mission with mystery and suspense, but some experiences stand out as emotional peaks. What would you say are the three outstanding moments in the boy's journey?
   (b) Which one of these would you select as the climax of the story? Why?

7. Why does Benét have the boy's narrative pass so quickly over the dangers of the journey home?

8. Although the boy is the main character in the story, the two older men from whom he learns are interestingly portrayed. Identify these two men and show how the author succeeds in making them interesting to us.

9. "By the Waters of Babylon" was written in the decade before the Second World War. But it is not just a story linked to the fears of the thirties; it is a story for the twentieth century. How would you express its theme?

*Morley*
*Callaghan*

# A cap for Steve

*Morley Callaghan (b. 1903) was born in Toronto. A lawyer by
training, Callaghan never practised law, but went from reporting
(with the* Toronto Daily Star*) to free-lance writing and broad-
casting. The author of eight novels and hundreds of short stories,
Callaghan has earned an enviable international reputation and, by
many critics, is regarded as one of the finest short story writers
of this century. His novel,* The Loved and the Lost, *won the
Governor-General's Award for Fiction in 1951. Among his
major works are the novels,* Such is My Beloved *(1934),* They
Shall Inherit the Earth *(1935),* More Joy in Heaven *(1937), and*
The Many-Coloured Coat *(1960). A generous selection of his
best short stories was published in 1959 under the title,* Morley
Callaghan's Stories, *from which "A Cap for Steve" is reprinted
by permission of The Macmillan Company of Canada, Ltd.*

DAVE DIAMOND, a poor man, a carpenter's assistant, was a small,
wiry, quick-tempered individual who had learned how to make
every dollar count in his home. His wife, Anna, had been sick a
lot, and his twelve-year-old son, Steve, had to be kept in school.
Steve, a big-eyed, shy kid, ought to have known the value of
money as well as Dave did. It had been ground into him.

But the boy was crazy about baseball, and after school, when
he could have been working as a delivery boy or selling papers,

he played ball with the kids. His failure to appreciate that the family needed a few extra dollers disgusted Dave. Around the house he wouldn't let Steve talk about baseball, and he scowled when he saw him hurrying off with his glove after dinner.

When the Phillies came to town to play an exhibition game with the home team and Steve pleaded to be taken to the ball park, Dave, of course, was outraged. Steve knew they couldn't afford it. But he had got his mother on his side. Finally Dave made a bargain with them. He said that if Steve came home after school and worked hard helping to make some kitchen shelves he would take him that night to the ball park.

Steve worked hard, but Dave was still resentful. They had to coax him to put on his good suit. When they started out Steve held aloof, feeling guilty, and they walked down the street like strangers; then Dave glanced at Steve's face and, half-ashamed, took his arm more cheerfully.

As the game went on, Dave had to listen to Steve's recitation of the batting average of every Philly that stepped up to the plate; the time the boy must have wasted learning these averages began to appal him. He showed it so plainly that Steve felt guilty again and was silent.

After the game Dave let Steve drag him onto the field to keep him company while he tried to get some autographs from the Philly players, who were being hemmed in by gangs of kids blocking the way to the club-house. But Steve, who was shy, let the other kids block him off from the players. Steve would push his way in, get blocked out, and come back to stand mournfully beside Dave. And Dave grew impatient. He was wasting valuable time. He wanted to get home; Steve knew it and was worried.

Then the big, blond Philly outfielder, Eddie Condon, who had been held up by a gang of kids tugging at his arm and thrusting their score cards at him, broke loose and made a run for the club-house. He was jostled, and his blue cap with the red peak, tilted far back on his head, fell off. It fell at Steve's feet, and Steve stooped quickly and grabbed it. "Okay, Son," the outfielder called, turning back. But Steve, holding it in both hands, only stared at him.

"Give him his cap, Steve," Dave said, smiling apologetically at the big outfielder who towered over them. But Steve drew the hat closer to his chest. In an awed trance he looked up at big Eddie Condon. It was an embarrassing moment. All the other kids were watching. Some shouted, "Give him his cap."

"My cap, Son," Eddie Condon said, his hand out.

"Hey, Steve," Dave said, and he gave him a shake. But he had to jerk the cap out of Steve's hands.

"Here you are," he said.

The outfielder, noticing Steve's white, worshipping face and pleading eyes, grinned and then shrugged. "Aw, let him keep it," he said.

"No, Mister Condon, you don't need to do that," Steve protested.

"It's happened before. Forget it," Eddie Condon said, and he trotted away to the club-house.

Dave handed the cap to Steve; envious kids circled around them and Steve said, "He said I could keep it, Dad. You heard him, didn't you?"

"Yeah, I heard him," Dave admitted. The wonder in Steve's face made him smile. He took the boy by the arm and they hurried off the field.

On the way home Dave couldn't get him to talk about the game; he couldn't get him to take his eyes off the cap. Steve could hardly believe in his own happiness. "See," he said suddenly, and he showed Dave that Eddie Condon's name was printed on the sweat-band. Then he went on dreaming. Finally he put the cap on his head and turned to Dave with a slow, proud smile. The cap was away too big for him; it fell down over his ears. "Never mind," Dave said. "You can get your mother to take a tuck in the back."

When they got home Dave was tired and his wife didn't understand the cap's importance, and they couldn't get Steve to go to bed. He swaggered around wearing the cap and looking in the mirror every ten minutes. He took the cap to bed with him.

Dave and his wife had a cup of coffee in the kitchen, and Dave told her again how they had got the cap. They agreed that their boy must have an attractive quality that showed in his face, and that Eddie Condon must have been drawn to him — why else would he have singled Steve out from all the kids?

But Dave got tired of the fuss Steve made over that cap and of the way he wore it from the time he got up in the morning until the time he went to bed. Some kid was always coming in, wanting to try on the cap. It was childish, Dave said, for Steve to go around assuming that the cap made him important in the neighbourhood, and to keep telling them how he had become a leader in the park a few blocks away where he played ball in the evenings. And Dave wouldn't stand for Steve's keeping the cap on while he was eating. He was always scolding his wife for accepting Steve's explanation that he'd forgotten he had it on. Just the same, it was remarkable what a little thing like a ball cap could do for a kid, Dave admitted to his wife as he smiled to himself.

One night Steve was late coming home from the park. Dave didn't realize how late it was until he put down his newspaper and watched his wife at the window. Her restlessness got on his nerves. "See what comes from encouraging the boy to hang around with those park loafers," he said. "I don't encourage him," she protested. "You do," he insisted irritably, for he was really worried now. A gang hung around the park until midnight. It was a bad park. It was true that on one side was a good district with fine, expensive apartment houses, but the kids from that neighbourhood left the park to the kids from the poorer homes. When his wife went out and walked down to the corner it was his turn to wait and worry and watch at the open window. Each waiting moment tortured him. At last he heard his wife's voice and Steve's voice, and he relaxed and sighed; then he remembered his duty and rushed angrily to meet them.

"I'll fix you, Steve, once and for all," he said. "I'll show you you can't start coming into the house at midnight."

"Hold your horses, Dave," his wife said. "Can't you see the state he's in?" Steve looked utterly exhausted and beaten.

"What's the matter?" Dave asked quickly.

"I lost my cap," Steve whispered; he walked past his father

and threw himself on the couch in the living-room and lay with his face hidden.

"Now, don't scold him, Dave," his wife said.

"Scold him. Who's scolding him?" Dave asked, indignantly. "It's his cap, not mine. If it's not worth his while to hang on to it, why should I scold him?" But he was implying resentfully that he alone recognized the cap's value.

"So you are scolding him," his wife said. "It's his cap. Not yours. What happened, Steve?"

Steve told them he had been playing ball and he found that when he ran the bases the cap fell off; it was still too big despite the tuck his mother had taken in the band. So the next time he came to bat he tucked the cap in his pocket. Someone had lifted it; he was sure.

"And he didn't even know whether it was still in his pocket," Dave said sarcastically.

"I wasn't careless, Dad," Steve said. For the last three hours he had been wandering around to the homes of the kids who had been in the park at the time; he wanted to go on, but he was too tired. Dave knew the boy was apologizing to him, but he didn't know why it made him angry.

"If he didn't hang on to it, it's not worth worrying about now," he said, and he sounded offended.

After that night they knew that Steve didn't go to the park to play ball; he went to look for the cap. It irritated Dave to see him sit around listlessly, or walk in circles, trying to force his memory to find a particular incident which would suddenly recall to him the moment when the cap had been taken. It was no attitude for a growing, healthy boy to take, Dave complained. He told Steve firmly once and for all that he didn't want to hear any more about the cap.

One night, two weeks later, Dave was walking home with Steve from the shoemaker's. It was a hot night. When they passed the ice-cream parlour Steve slowed down. "I guess I couldn't have a soda, could I?" Steve said. "Nothing doing," Dave said firmly. "Come on now," he added as Steve hung back, looking in the window.

"Dad, look!" Steve cried suddenly, pointing at the window. "My cap! There's my cap! He's coming out!"

A well-dressed boy was leaving the ice-cream parlour; he had on a blue ball cap with a red peak, just like Steve's cap. "Hey, you!" Steve cried, and he rushed at the boy, his small face fierce and his eyes wild. Before the boy could back away Steve had snatched the cap from his head. "That's my cap!" he shouted.

"What's this?" the bigger boy said. "Hey, give me my cap or I'll give you a poke on the nose."

Dave was surprised that his own shy boy did not back away. He watched him clutch the cap in his left hand, half crying with excitement as he put his head down and drew back his right fist; he was willing to fight. And Dave was proud of him.

"Wait, now," Dave said. "Take it easy, Son," he said to the other boy, who refused to back away.

"My boy says it's his cap," Dave said.

"Well, he's crazy. It's my cap."

"I was with him when he got this cap. When the Phillies played here. It's a Philly cap."

"Eddie Condon gave it to me," Steve said. "And you stole it from me, you jerk."

"Don't you call me a jerk, you little squirt. I never saw you before in my life."

"Look," Steve said, pointing to the printing on the cap's sweat band. "It's Eddie Condon's cap. See? See, Dad?"

"Yeah. You're right, Son. Ever see this boy before, Steve?"

"No," Steve said reluctantly.

The other boy realized he might lose the cap. "I bought it from a guy," he said. "I paid him. My father knows I paid him." He said he got the cap at the ball park. He groped for some magically impressive words and suddenly found them. "You'll have to speak to my father," he said.

"Sure, I'll speak to your father," Dave said. "What's your name? Where do you live?"

"My name's Hudson. I live about ten minutes away on the other side of the park." The boy appraised Dave, who wasn't any bigger than he was and who wore a faded blue windbreaker and no tie. "My father is a lawyer," he said boldly. "He wouldn't let me keep the cap if he didn't think I should."

"Is that a fact?" Dave asked belligerently. "Well, we'll see. Come on. Let's go." And he got between the two boys and they walked along the street. They didn't talk to each other. Dave knew the Hudson boy was waiting to get to the protection of his home, and Steve knew it, too, and he looked up apprehensively at Dave. And Dave, reaching for his hand, squeezed it encouragingly and strode along, cocky and belligerent, knowing that Steve relied on him.

The Hudson boy lived in that row of fine apartment houses on the other side of the park. At the entrance to one of these houses Dave tried not to hang back and show he was impressed, because he could feel Steve hanging back. When they got into the small elevator Dave didn't know why he took off his hat. In the carpeted hall on the fourth floor the Hudson boy said, "Just a minute," and entered his own apartment. Dave and Steve were left alone in the corridor, knowing that the other boy was preparing his father for the encounter. Steve looked anxiously at his father, and Dave said, "Don't worry, Son," and he added resolutely, "No one's putting anything over on us."

A tall balding man in a brown velvet smoking-jacket suddenly opened the door. Dave had never seen a man wearing one of those jackets, although he had seen them in department-store windows. "Good evening," he said, making a deprecatory gesture at the cap Steve still clutched tightly in his left hand. "My boy didn't get your name. My name is Hudson."

"Mine's Diamond."

"Come on in," Mr. Hudson said, putting out his hand and laughing good-naturedly. He led Dave and Steve into his living-room. "What's this about that cap?" he asked. "The way kids can get excited about a cap. Well, it's understandable, isn't it?"

"So it is," Dave said, moving closer to Steve, who was awed by the broadloom rug and the fine furniture. He wanted to show Steve he was at ease himself, and he wished Mr. Hudson wouldn't be so polite. That meant Dave had to be polite and affable, too, and it was hard to manage when he was standing in the middle of the floor in his old windbreaker.

"Sit down, Mr. Diamond," Mr. Hudson said. Dave took Steve's arm and sat him down beside him on the chesterfield. The Hudson boy watched his father. And Dave looked at Steve and saw that he wouldn't face Mr. Hudson or the other boy; he kept looking up at Dave, putting all his faith in him.

"Well, Mr. Diamond, from what I gathered from my boy, you're able to prove this cap belonged to your boy."

"That's a fact," Dave said.

"Mr. Diamond, you'll have to believe my boy bought that cap from some kid in good faith."

"I don't doubt it," Dave said. "But no kid can sell something that doesn't belong to him. You know that's a fact, Mr. Hudson."

"Yes, that's a fact," Mr. Hudson agreed. "But that cap means a lot to my boy, Mr. Diamond."

"It means a lot to my boy, too, Mr. Hudson."

"Sure it does. But supposing we called in a policeman. You know what he'd say? He'd ask you if you were willing to pay my boy what he paid for the cap. That's usually the way it works out," Mr. Hudson said, friendly and smiling, as he eyed Dave shrewdly.

"But that's not right. It's not justice," Dave protested. "Not when it's my boy's cap."

"I know it isn't right. But that's what they do."

"All right. What did you say your boy paid for the cap?" Dave said reluctantly.

"Two dollars."

"Two dollars!" Dave repeated. Mr. Hudson's smile was still kindly, but his eyes were shrewd, and Dave knew that the lawyer was counting on his not having the two dollars; Mr. Hudson thought he had Dave sized up; he had looked at him and decided he was broke. Dave's pride was hurt, and he turned to Steve. What he saw in Steve's face was more powerful than the hurt to his pride: it was the memory of how difficult it had been to get an extra nickel, the talk he heard about the cost of food, the worry in his mother's face as she tried to make ends meet, and the bewildered embarrassment that he was here in a rich man's home, forcing his father to confess that he couldn't afford to spend two dollars. Then Dave grew angry and reckless. "I'll give you the two dollars," he said.

Steve looked at the Hudson boy and grinned brightly. The Hudson boy watched his father.

"I suppose that's fair enough," Mr. Hudson said. "A cap like this can be worth a lot to a kid. You know how it is. Your boy might want to sell — I mean be satisfied. Would he take five dollars for it?"

"Five dollars?" Dave repeated. "Is it worth five dollars, Steve?" he asked uncertainly.

Steve shook his head and looked frightened.

"No thanks, Mr. Hudson," Dave said firmly.

"I'll tell you what I'll do," Mr. Hudson said. "I'll give you ten dollars. The cap has a sentimental value for my boy, a Philly cap, a big-leaguer's cap. It's only worth about a buck and a half really," he added. But Dave shook his head again. Mr. Hudson frowned. He looked at his own boy with indulgent concern, but now he was embarrassed. "I'll tell you what I'll do," he said. "This cap — well, it's worth as much as a day at the circus to my boy. Your boy should be recompensed. I want to be fair. Here's twenty dollars," and he held out two ten-dollar bills to Dave.

That much money for a cap, Dave thought, and his eyes brightened. But he knew what the cap had meant to Steve; to deprive him of it now that it was within his reach would be unbearable. All the things he needed in his life gathered around him; his wife was there, saying he couldn't afford to reject the offer, he had no right to do it; and he turned to Steve to see if Steve thought it wonderful that the cap could bring them twenty dollars.

"What do you say, Steve?" he asked uneasily.

"I don't know," Steve said. He was in a trance. When Dave smiled, Steve smiled too, and Dave believed that Steve was as impressed as he was, only more bewildered, and maybe more aware that they could not possibly turn away that much money for a ball cap.

"Well, here you are," Mr. Hudson said, and he put the two

bills in Steve's hand. "It's a lot of money. But I guess you had a right to expect as much."

With a dazed, fixed smile Steve handed the money slowly to his father, and his face was white.

Laughing jovially, Mr. Hudson led them to the door. His own boy followed a few paces behind.

In the elevator Dave took the bills out of his pocket. "See, Stevie," he whispered eagerly. "That windbreaker you wanted! And ten dollars for your bank! Won't Mother be surprised?"

"Yeah," Steve whispered, the little smile still on his face. But Dave had to turn away quickly so their eyes wouldn't meet, for he saw that it was a scared smile.

Outside, Dave said, "Here, you carry the money home, Steve. You show it to your mother."

"No, you keep it," Steve said, and then there was nothing to say. They walked in silence.

"It's a lot of money," Dave said finally. When Steve didn't answer him, he added angrily, "I turned to you, Steve. I asked you, didn't I?"

"That man knew how much his boy wanted that cap," Steve said.

"Sure. But he recognized how much it was worth to us."

"No, you let him take it away from us," Steve blurted.

"That's unfair," Dave said. "Don't dare say that to me."

"I don't want to be like you," Steve muttered, and he darted across the road and walked along on the other side of the street.

"It's unfair," Dave said angrily, only now he didn't mean that Steve was unfair, he meant that what had happened in the prosperous Hudson home was unfair, and he didn't know quite why. He had been trapped, not just by Mr. Hudson, but by his own life. Across the road Steve was hurrying along with his head down, wanting to be alone. They walked most of the way home on opposite sides of the street, until Dave could stand it no longer. "Steve," he called, crossing the street. "It was very unfair. I mean, for you to say . . ." but Steve started to run. Dave walked as fast as he could and Steve was getting beyond him, and he felt embarrassed and suddenly he yelled, "Steve!" and he started to chase his son. He wanted to get hold of Steve and pound him, and he didn't know why. He gained on him, he gasped for breath and he almost got him by the shoulder. Turning, Steve saw his father's face in the street light and was terrified; he circled away, got to the house, and rushed in, yelling, "Mother!"

"Son, Son!" she cried, rushing from the kitchen. As soon as she threw her arms around Steve, shielding him, Dave's anger left him and he felt stupid. He walked past them into the kitchen.

"What happened?" she asked anxiously. "Have you both gone crazy? What did you do, Steve?"

"Nothing," he said sullenly.

"What did your father do?"

"We found the boy with my ball cap, and he let the boy's father take it from us."

"No, no," Dave protested. "Nobody pushed us around. The man didn't put anything over us." He felt tired and his face was burning. He told what had happened; then he slowly took the two ten-dollar bills out of his wallet and tossed them on the table and looked up guiltily at his wife.

It hurt him that she didn't pick up the money, and that she didn't rebuke him. "It is a lot of money, Son," she said slowly. "Your father was only trying to do what he knew was right, and it'll work out, and you'll understand." She was soothing Steve, but Dave knew she felt that she needed to be gentle with him, too, and he was ashamed.

When she went with Steve to his bedroom, Dave sat by himself. His son had contempt for him, he thought. His son, for the first time, had seen how easy it was for another man to handle him, and he had judged him and had wanted to walk alone on the other side of the street. He looked at the money and he hated the sight of it.

His wife returned to the kitchen, made a cup of tea, talked soothingly, and said it was incredible that he had forced the Hudson man to pay him twenty dollars for the cap, but all Dave could think of was Steve was scared of me.

Finally, he got up and went into Steve's room. The room was in darkness, but he could see the outline of Steve's body on the bed, and he sat down beside him and whispered, "Look, Son, it was a mistake. I know why. People like us — in circumstances where money can scare us. No, no," he said, feeling ashamed and shaking his head apologetically; he was taking the wrong way of showing the boy they were together; he was covering up his own failure. For the failure had been his, and it had come out of being so separated from his son that he had been blind to what was beyond price in a boy's life. He longed now to show Steve he could be with him from day to day. His hand went out hesitantly to Steve's shoulder. "Steve, look," he said eagerly. "The trouble was I didn't realize how much I enjoyed it that night at the ball park. If I had watched you playing for your own team — the kids around here say you could be a great pitcher. We could take that money and buy a new pitcher's glove for you, and a catcher's mitt. Steve, Steve, are you listening? I could catch you, work with you in the lane. Maybe I could be your coach ... watch you become a great pitcher." In the half-darkness he could see the boy's pale face turn to him.

Steve, who had never heard his father talk like this, was shy and wondering. All he knew was that his father, for the first time, wanted to be with him in his hopes and adventures. He said, "I guess you do know how important that cap was." His hand went out to his father's arm. "With that man the cap was — well it was just something he could buy, eh Dad?" Dave gripped his son's hand hard. The wonderful generosity of childhood — the price the boy was willing to pay to be able to count on his father's admiration and approval — made him feel humble, then strangely exalted.

QUESTIONS

It has been said that Morley Callaghan never gives us character, but rather, characteristics; never whole human beings, but rather, significant human feelings. He is not concerned with creating plot and event, but rather, with devising situations in which man's capacity for feeling can be explored, as can the cross-purposes and misunderstandings which separate human beings from each other.

1. How much do you know about each of the main characters in this story?

2. What is the role of the mother in the story?

3. Account for Dave Diamond's recurring feeling of guilt in his relations with his son.

4. Explain the "magical" properties of Eddie Condon's cap for Steve. Is it a thing of wonder and power only because Steve loves baseball? Or does it also represent some value which seems lacking in the shy boy's life?

5. What is the significance of the fact that Diamond takes off his hat in the elevator — and doesn't know why?

6. Contrast the motives of Hudson and Diamond in the "bargaining" scene.

7. Why is Diamond wrong — and short-sighted — when he thinks that his son recoiled from him when he "had seen how easy it was for another man to handle him"?

8. How, in the last scene, does the father return to the son, not the cap, but everything that the cap had represented and meant?

*Dorothy*

*Parker*

# Arrangement in black and white

*Dorothy Parker (b. 1893), American satirist, was educated at Miss Dana's school, Morristown, New Jersey, and the Blessed Sacrament Convent, New York City. From 1916 to 1917, she was dramatic critic for the magazine,* Vanity Fair. *In 1927, she became book critic for the* New Yorker *magazine, but resigned to become a free-lance writer after her first volume of verse,* Enough Rope, *1927, became a "best-seller". In 1928, she published a second book of verse,* Sunset Gun, *which was followed in 1930 by* Lament for the Living, *a collection of her short stories. Other works are* Death and Taxes *(1931),* Not So Deep as a Well *(1936), and* Here Lies *(1939). She collaborated with Ross Evans on one play,* The Court of Illyria *(1949), and with Arnaud d'Usseau on another,* Ladies of the Corridor *(1954). "Arrangement in Black and White" is a good example of her keen satirist's ear for dialogue, and it is reprinted from* The Portable Dorothy Parker *by Dorothy Parker (copyright 1927, 1944 by Dorothy Parker), by permission of The Viking Press, Inc.*

THE WOMAN with the pink velvet poppies twined round the assisted gold of her hair traversed the crowded room at an interesting gait combining a skip with a sidle, and clutched the lean arm of her host.

"Now I got you!" she said. "Now you can't get away!"

"Why, hello," said her host. "Well. How are you?"

"Oh, I'm finely," she said. "Just simply finely. Listen. I want you to do me the most terrible favour. Will you? Will you please? Pretty please?"

"What is it?" said her host.

"Listen," she said. "I want to meet Walter Williams. Honestly, I'm just simply crazy about that man. Oh, when he sings! When he sings those spirituals! Well, I said to Burton, 'It's a good thing for you Walter Williams is coloured,' I said, 'or you'd have lots of reason to be jealous.' I'd really love to meet him. I'd like to tell him I've heard him sing. Will you be an angel and introduce me to him?"

"Why, certainly," said her host. "I thought you'd met him. The party's for him. Where is he, anyway?"

"He's over there by the bookcase," she said. "Let's wait till those people get through talking to him. Well, I think you're simply marvellous, giving this perfectly marvellous party for him, and having him meet all these white people, and all. Isn't he terribly grateful?"

"I hope not," said her host.

"I think it's really terrible nice," she said. "I do. I don't see why on earth it isn't perfectly all right to meet coloured people. I haven't any feeling at all about it — not one single bit. Burton — oh, he's just the other way. Well, you know, he comes from Virginia, and you know how they are."

"Did he come tonight?" said her host.

"No, he couldn't," she said. "I'm a regular grass widow to-night. I told him when I left, 'There's no telling what I'll do,' I said. He was just so tired out, he couldn't move. Isn't it a shame?"

"Ah," said her host.

"Wait till I tell him I met Walter Williams!" she said. "He'll just about die. Oh, we have more arguments about coloured people. I talk to him like I don't know what, I get so excited. 'Oh, don't be so silly,' I say. But I must say for Burton, he's heaps broader-minded than lots of these Southerners. He's really aw-fully fond of coloured people. Well, he says himself, he wouldn't have white servants. And you know, he had this old coloured nurse, this regular old nigger mammy, and he just simply loves her. Why, every time he goes home, he goes out in the kitchen to see her. He does, really, to this day. All he says is, he says he hasn't got a word to say against coloured people as long as they keep their place. He's always doing things for them — giving them clothes and I don't know what all. The only thing he says, he says he wouldn't sit down at the table with one for a million dollars. 'Oh,' I say to him, 'you make me sick, talking like that.' I'm just terrible to him. Aren't I terrible?"

"Oh, no, no, no," said her host. "No, no."

"I am," she said. "I know I am. Poor Burton! Now, me, I don't feel that way at all. I haven't the slightest feeling about coloured people. Why, I'm just crazy about some of them. They're just like children — just as easy-going, and always singing and laughing and everything. Aren't they the happiest things you ever saw in your life? Honestly, it makes me laugh just to hear them. Oh, I like them. I really do. Well, now, listen, I have this coloured laundress, I've had her for years, and I'm devoted to her. She's a real character. And I want to tell you, I think of her as my friend. That's the way I think of her. As I say to Burton, 'Well, for Heaven's sakes, we're all human beings!' Aren't we?"

"Yes," said her host. "Yes, indeed."

"Now this Walter Williams," she said. "I think a man like that's a real artist. I do. I think he deserves an awful lot of credit. Goodness, I'm so crazy about music or anything, I don't care *what* colour he is. I honestly think if a person's an artist, nobody ought to have any feeling at all about meeting them. That's absolutely what I say to Burton. Don't you think I'm right?"

"Yes," said her host. "Oh, yes."

"That's the way I feel," she said. "I just can't understand people being narrow-minded. Why, I absolutely think it's a privilege to meet a man like Walter Williams. Yes, I do. I haven't any feeling at all. Well, my goodness, the good Lord made him, just the same as He did any of us. Didn't He?"

"Surely," said her host. "Yes, indeed."

"That's what I say," she said. "Oh, I get so furious when people are narrow-minded about coloured people. It's just all I can do not to say something. Of course, I do admit when you get a bad coloured man, they're simply terrible. But as I say to Burton, there are some bad white people, too, in this world. Aren't there?"

"I guess there are," said her host.

"Why, I'd really be glad to have a man like Walter Williams come to my house and sing for us, some time," she said. "Of course, I couldn't ask him on account of Burton, but I wouldn't have any feeling about it at all. Oh, can't he sing! Isn't it marvellous, the way they all have music in them? It just seems to be right *in* them. Come on, let's go on over and talk to him. Listen, what shall I do when I'm introduced? Ought I to shake hands? Or what?"

"Why, do whatever you want," said her host.

"I guess maybe I'd better," she said. "I wouldn't for the world have him think I had any feeling. I think I'd better shake hands, just the way I would with anybody else. That's just exactly what I'll do."

They reached the tall young Negro, standing by the bookcase. The host performed introductions; the Negro bowed.

"How do you do?" he said.

The woman with the pink velvet poppies extended her hand at the length of her arm and held it so for all the world to see, until the Negro took it, shook it, and gave it back to her.

"Oh, how do you do, Mr. Williams," she said. "Well, how do you do. I've just been saying, I've enjoyed your singing so awfully much. I've been to your concerts, and we have you on the phonograph and everything. Oh, I just enjoy it!"

She spoke with great distinctness, moving her lips meticulously, as if in parlance with the deaf.

"I'm so glad," he said.

"I'm just simply crazy about that 'Water Boy' thing you sing," she said. "Honestly, I can't get it out of my head. I have my husband nearly crazy, the way I go around humming it all the time. Oh, he looks just as black as the ace of — Well. Tell me, where on earth do you ever get all those songs of yours? How do you ever get hold of them?"

"Why," he said, "there are so many different ——"

"I should think you'd love singing them," she said. "It must be more fun. All those darling old spirituals – oh, I just love them! Well, what are you doing, now? Are you still keeping up your singing? Why don't you have another concert, some time?"

"I'm having one the sixteenth of this month," he said.

"Well, I'll be there," she said. "I'll be there, if I possibly can. You can count on me. Goodness, here comes a whole raft of people to talk to you. You're just a regular guest of honor! Oh, who's that girl in white? I've seen her some place."

"That's Katherine Burke," said her host.

"Good Heavens," she said, "is that Katherine Burke? Why, she looks entirely different off the stage. I thought she was much better-looking. I had no idea she was so terribly dark. Why, she looks almost like – Oh, I think she's a wonderful actress! Don't you think she's a wonderful actress, Mr. Williams? Oh, I think she's marvellous. Don't you?"

"Yes, I do," he said.

"Oh, I do, too," she said. "Just wonderful. Well, goodness, we must give someone else a chance to talk to the guest of honor. Now, don't forget, Mr. Williams, I'm going to be at that concert if I possibly can. I'll be there applauding like everything. And if I can't come, I'm going to tell everybody I know to go, anyway. Don't you forget!"

"I won't," he said. "Thank you so much."

The host took her arm and piloted her into the next room.

"Oh, my dear," she said. "I nearly died! Honestly, I give you my word, I nearly passed away. Did you hear that terrible break I made? I was just going to say Katherine Burke looked almost like a nigger. I just caught myself in time. Oh, do you think he noticed?"

"I don't believe so," said her host.

"Well, thank goodness," she said, "because I wouldn't have embarrassed him for anything. Why, he's awfully nice. Just as nice as he can be. Nice manners, and everything. You know, so many coloured people, you give them an inch, and they walk all over you. But he doesn't try any of that. Well, he's got more sense, I suppose. He's really nice. Don't you think so?"

"Yes," said her host.

"I liked him," she said. "I haven't any feeling at all because he's a coloured man. I felt just as natural as I would with anybody. Talked to him as naturally, and everything. But honestly, I could hardly keep a straight face. I kept thinking of Burton. Oh, wait till I tell Burton I called him 'Mister'!"

QUESTIONS

1. What comment about American society is Dorothy Parker making in "Arrangement in Black and White"?

2. (a) What does the writer want you to think of the following: (1) the woman, (2) the negro, and (3) the host?
(b) For each of the characters above, point out some details in the story that made you form these judgements of them.

3. You will probably agree that the laughter provoked by this story leaves a somewhat bitter aftertaste. Why?

4. This is a dramatic story — that is, the writer employs the methods available to the dramatist. Explain.

5. Note the strict economy in Dorothy Parker's narrative passages. Frequently in her compact stories, she begins with a sentence that accomplishes several purposes: (a) it begins to characterize the main person in the story, (b) it sets the scene by telling where the person is, and (c) it shows what he or she is doing. To what extent does she achieve these three purposes in the opening sentence of "Arrangement in Black and White"?

6. What do you consider to be the climax of the story? Justify your choice.

7. Explain the significance of the last sentence in the story.

8. The title, "Arrangement in Black and White", is at once obvious and subtle. What is the obvious meaning? What is another, subtler, meaning?

9. In what ways does this story resemble Charles Lamb's "Juke Judkins" (Part One)? In what ways is it different?

10. Compare this story with Morley Callaghan's "A Cap for Steve" as to theme, methods of revealing character, and handling of the climax.

*Val*

*Mulkerns*

# The world outside

*Val Mulkerns (b. 1925) was born in Dublin and educated at the Dominican College there. For a while she taught school in London, England, where she published her first novel,* A Time Outworn *(1950), which Frank O'Connor, one of Ireland's best contemporary writers, has said "is the most interesting and significant (novel) to have come out of Ireland in twenty-five years." Upon returning to Dublin she became assistant editor of an Irish magazine,* The Bell. *Her short stories and verse have been published in various magazines in the British Isles, and in Australia and the United States. "The World Outside" is reprinted by permission of the author.*

MOST OF THE CHILDREN were early that morning, creeping in subdued and stiff in the unaccustomed shoes, their faces and limbs shining from prolonged scrubbing. Some of the boys looked unusually ugly because of having had their hair savagely attacked with scissors and bowl the previous night by over-zealous mothers, but the girls were glossy and braided and comely, and looked much more confident than the boys, as if handling inspectors would not be much trouble to them. The school master scanned all the faces sharply, planning the traditional reshuffle. Something nervous and trusting in the general atmosphere prompted him to put them at ease, though he was jumpy enough himself.

"Tell me, is it the same crowd at all I have before me, or is it some swanky gang down from Dublin for the day?" he grinned at them in Irish, and a relieved pleased ripple of laughter went over the desks. "Let me see now, we'll have to have yourself in the front, Mary Mannion, to show off that brave red ribbon, and let you take yourself to the back desk, Tomas Peig where with God's help you'll get a chance to show the Inspector how to do fractions." The point was that Mary was easy on the eyes and utterly brainless, and Tomas Peig was a bright lad and back benchers were inevitably questioned. "We'll have you over by the window, Muiris, and our friend with the red head in the second row. Will you get those boots back on you this minute, Tadg, and I'll flay the hide off you if I see them anywhere except where they're meant to be. Do you think now that it was to decorate the floor for me that your mother went to Clifden last week and handed out a mint of money? No, Sir, well you may be sure the answer is No, Sir, and take heed of what I said to you, if you value that hide of yours." But as the reshuffling went on, they understood the unusual bantering humour for what it was, an effort to put them at ease, and their faces beamed gratefully back at him. They were being examined, and God knew what horrible things would happen to them if they failed to please the inspector, and here was Boozy, the decent man, and he with nothing to fear being a Master, soft as butter with them to drive away their nervousness.

"Now listen to me the lot of you. If he speaks to you in Irish don't answer him back in a blast of English just to show that you know it. Answer him in Irish. Now if he speaks to you in English, what are you to do, Mary Mannion?"

"Answer him in Irish, sir," said Mary with a bright confident smile. There was a gale of laughter, and Mary was prodded incredulously by her neighbours.

" 'Tis a professor of Logic we'll make out of you. If he speaks to you in English, what will *you* do, tell her, Martin Flaherty?"

"Answer him in English, sir."

"Right. Now keep that in your heads. The next thing to remember is if he asks the class in general a question and you think you know the answer, put up your hands. Don't be afraid. He won't eat you if you happen to be wrong. He's probably a fine, well-fed man. The only people whose hands I don't want to see up for anything are Mary Mannion and Micilin Sean Mullen, because they have a job keeping up with the best of us, and we'll give them a rest today. Next year with the help of God they'll be ready for anything. Do you hear that now, the pair of you?"

"Yes, sir." Micilin Sean was beaming with relief and Mary Mannion was sulking.

"Right. Now the next thing to remember is —" his eyes suddenly caught sight of a figure at the gate — "that he's coming up the path this minute, and let you keep as still as mice while I call the register." There were sighs and gasps and rapid intakes of breath all around, and then utter petrified silence, and everybody answering "*Annso, a Mhaighistear*" in an unrecognizable whisper.

Mr. Mulvey was gray and hunched and small, with heavy-lidded gloomy eyes and a mouth turning down hopelessly at the corners. A first glance, before he opened his mouth, suggested that his voice would be a sick wind among the reeds, but in fact it was big and jolly and when he laughed, which was frequently, you had the fantastic impression that some enchantment had been worked before your eyes and that this was certainly not the man who had walked into the room. It was difficult to say whether his life had taken the form of a victorious battle against his natural temperament, or whether it was only his appearance which belied him. His clothes were silver gray and faultlessly pressed, and he carried a neatly rolled black umbrella and a black brief-case.

As he stepped into the room out of the thickening rain, the children scraped to their feet and stood looking at him with dismay. They were more used to fat tweedy red-faced inspectors with patches of leather down their jackets. He shook hands with and spoke a few pleasant words to Mr. McGlynn, and then turned to the pupils with his incredible smile, which showed square healthy white teeth, slightly prominent, and produced numbers of answering smiles. He was delighted to see them all, absolutely delighted, and hoped to learn more this morning than he had ever done at school. Would they sit down now, and attend to Mr. McGlynn's lesson, and later on he'd have a chat with them. He sat down on the chair which had been placed for him near the window, opened his brief-case, and became again, in a moment, the gloomy little gray man who had entered the room. The schoolmaster finished calling the register, closed the book, and sent Mary Mannion across with it to the inspector. Then the lesson began, Geography. The large map of Europe behind the master's desk was covered by a map of Mexico, and as was his usual custom, he began by giving them a general impression of the country itself, the colour, the atmosphere, then something of its history. His words were alive and interesting, because omnivorous reading of everything from strictly technical works or anthropological works to things like Graham Greene's *The Lawless Roads* had produced complete familiarity. It happened to be Mexico today because that was the stage of the syllabus they had reached, but it was the same with everywhere, when he was sober, that is. The three maps which he drew with quick strokes, one of the physical regions, one of the climatic regions, and the third showing produce, were accurate and even beautiful with their lively blending colours. The class was set to work, an intricate business because of the different ages. Little working groups were put together, and a résumé of what in particular each had to tackle was given, and the older pupils were set some questions on the lesson.

All this time, the bent little depressed figure by the window appeared to be taking no notice. The register had been scrutinized and laid aside, and also some sample exercise books, and then he seemed to give all his attention to some private papers. The Arithmetic lesson went by, and the Irish grammar lesson, and then towards midday, when a rising wind was lashing the rain against the windows, he stood up and the transfiguring smile shone out.

"Well now, I suppose you're all fit for bed, after the work you've done this morning, what?" He drew the required laugh from them, and rubbed his small gray hands happily together. "But before we let you off home there are one or two things

which have been puzzling me for some time." He changed rapidly
to English. "Tell me, is Mexico in the Northern Hemisphere or
in the Southern Hemisphere?" The hands shot up, and so did
Mary Mannion's, but it was rapidly lowered. "I see my little
friend here with the red ribbon knows and doesn't know. Which
hemisphere is Mexico in, will you tell me now like the sound
woman you are?"

"The Southern Hemisphere, sir," said Mary Mannion with
superb confidence and a shake of the head. There were the inevitable gasps from the class, and Mr. Mulvey smiled still more
brilliantly.

"I don't think we all agree with you there, do we?" and there
was an enthusiastic chorus of "No sir!" "The last time I was in
Mexico," he went on, directly addressing Mary Mannion, who
was smiling engagingly at him, "it was in the Northern Hemisphere. Will you remember that, because I don't think it's moved
since then?"

"Yes, sir. No, sir," said Mary Mannion with another engaging
smile.

"Well now there's another thing that's been puzzling me. A
few weeks ago I went into the dining room of my house in Galway and two of the children had apples, nice big red ones. Sean
said, 'Daddy, I'll give you half mine,' and Maire said, 'I'll give
you three-eighths of mine, Daddy.' Now I thought a while before
I decided which I'd take, and I want you to think now. Which
was the more decent offer of the two, Sean's or Maire's?" The
hands went up slowly, three, four, six, then ten. "Difficult question to put to a poor simple father, wasn't it? How did I know
which to take?" Again he was speaking Irish.

"I'd have taken the both of them, sir," said Mary Mannion
in lamentable English, beside herself with the notice she had
achieved.

"Ni thuigim," said Mr. Mulvey, with another brilliant smile,
and then ignored her. "Well, will you tell me, the boy at the
back, there?"

Tomas Peig, to the schoolmaster's joy, got smartly to his feet,
held back his fair head and spoke up very clearly. "Sean's offer

was the one you should have taken, sir, because he was giving you four-eighths (or a half) and Maire was only giving you three-eighths."

"Splendid. If I had been as bright as you now, I wouldn't have done myself out of the eighth of a fine apple."

Before they had quite finished laughing, the inspector turned to the schoolmaster and said, "I think the best thing we can do now is to send them off home for the rest of the day because they're too clever for us."

When they had all filed out into the cloakroom in clattering happiness, Mr. Mulvey's gloomy gray eyes roamed for a while about the schoolmaster's face before the smile broke again and he held out his hand. "That was the only Geography lesson in Ireland that's ever interested me," he said. He glanced quickly again at the schoolmaster's qualifications listed on the sheet before him, and asked sharply: "What are you doing here? We could do with plenty more of your kind in the national schools throughout the country but — ?" He shrugged, half-smiling the question.

"It suits me here," Peter McGlynn said briefly, "I like it."

The inspector shrugged again. "If you ever wanted a change, my friend Dr. Linnane in Galway would jump at a man like you — preparing boys for University scholarships, that sort of thing."

"Thanks," the schoolmaster said without interest, "I'll remember if I ever decide to change. It's very kind of you."

"Nonsense," Mulvey replied, with an old-fashioned air, gathering his things together and fastening the brief-case. "You lived for some time in Mexico, I take it?"

"No. My Grand Tour took the form of a day trip to Liverpool. I never slept a night outside this country in my life."

"Remarkable. I taught, myself, for seven years in Mexico City and you brought it back into this classroom today, the heat, the filth, the colour, the indolence, the preposterous fascination of the place. It's remarkable."

"No," Peter McGlynn smiled, "it's Baedeker, and a studious youth, and Graham Greene and a trick of the tongue. You'll not refuse a bite of lunch with me in our one and only hostelry, Pats Flaherty's?"

"I will not," said the inspector warmly, "I spend my life having lunch with clerical managers and a man can do with a bit of civilization now and again."

Pats' wife had clearly taken some trouble to see that the catering arrangements of Ballyconnolly would stand up to inspection quite as well as the school. As soon as she had received the schoolmaster's order two days previously, she had set to work, scouring and polishing the little square room of the bar, hunting out her best lace tablecloth, unused since the previous inspector's visit, and fixing a formidable array of family photographs along the mantlepiece. Despite these, the warm, low-ceilinged little room with its scarlet geraniums and looped lace curtains was welcoming to the two men as they stepped in out of the bitter wild morning. The place was permeated by the fragrance of roasting fowl, stewed apples, and strong spirits, blending deliciously with the bitterness of turf smoke. Kate Pats Flaherty bustled busily in and out, talking all the time.

" 'Tis frozen and demented the pair of you must be with the hunger, now. Ah, sure I often heard it said a man that works with his brain needs twice the feeding of a man that works with his body, and why wouldn't he, indeed? There was a cousin of my own, Mr. Mulvey, sir, and there he is before ye on the mantlepiece with the white face there in the middle, and hadn't they got him starved in the college above in Dublin and he going in for a priest. Night and day he was at the books, God pity him, and he no more than a lad, and there wasn't he only out a priest a few months, and his brother not even married, when he took a delicacy and died on his poor mother, God between us and all harm. 'Twas a fright to the world the way she took it, bawling and crying every time she'd look at a priest for years after. There she is for you now, Mr. McGlynn, on the bend of the mantlepiece with the feathery hat down near her nose, but sure God is good and didn't the second lad, a fine big puck of a boy, go in for a priest after, and he's a curate below in Kerry now. Another sup of that soup, Mr. Mulvey, sir? Or the Master? Well now, I'll have that bird on the table before you'll be finished licking your lips. There he is to your north now, Mr. Mulvey, sir, with the fine soft plucks on him and the holy book in his hands. We had him here now, and you could have seen him only a few weeks ago, and there was never a lad like him for feeding, and wouldn't he need it, I ask you, and him not to be dying on us like his poor brother, God rest his soul." Half of this oration was in English and half in Irish, and during journeys to the kitchen and to the bar the rich strong voice came clearly back to her guests, of whom she expected and desired no response. It was only when the last course had been cleared away and the bottle of whiskey ordered by the schoolmaster was between them on the table, and the smoke from their cigarettes was rising to the low ceiling, that Kate Pats Flaherty drew the door behind her, put her head around it again and said: "I'll leave ye now to yourselves to talk to your heart's content and if there's any other thing in the world ye want, leave a screech out of ye and I'll hear it."

She went, and the door closed at last. In the brief satisfied silence the rain beat in gusty blasts against the window, and the wind swept down the chimney to set the turf leaping and blazing. The hunched gray man in the gray clothes was the first to speak, lifting the gloomy eyes that were flecked now with a faint humour.

"There's Ireland for you now, McGlynn, all of it. Unending rain rattling the windows, and inside a kindly woman boasting about her clerical relations, and two men drinking whiskey, and outside the rest of the world. If Michelangelo painted the Resurrection on her smoky ceiling she wouldn't give it a look or him a thank-you if her portly cousin His Reverence were within miles of the place. Once upon a time we exported scholars and culture to the Continent. Now we export nothing but beasts and priests, God help us." And there began one of those inevitable discussions on what's wrong with the country, that never end and are more common in Ireland than discussions on religion or sex. But before the well-worn tracks had been followed to within reach of their muddy end, the talk under the direction of Mr. Mulvey took a turn to Mexico, and from there to Spain where he had found his wife, the daughter of a Spaniard who had a ballet company in Mexico but who had left his daughter in Spain to be educated. In the warm half-forgotten enchantment of good whiskey on which the brain floated away like a dead flower and only the senses and the imagination were taut and alive, the schoolmaster felt the sun like the caressing tongue of some fantastic animal, at once savage and tender, and smelled the fruit piled high in the narrow streets, and the bitterness of cheap wine, shivered at the sudden white chill inside the vaulted Cathedrals where black-eyed women chattered and laughed before Mass began and felt no urge to leave their personalities like gifts outside the church door, at which filthy mewling beggars held out diseased limbs; he watched the cypresses shooting eager and dark into warm, star-filled air tingling with the music of De Falla to which a girl was dancing like a flame, twisting and writhing in the dark agony of exorcism; narrow martyred faces of El Greco floated in a golden mist beside the warm sensual beauties of Velasquez and in a time-less jumble of history real and imagined the sweet sane voice of a woman saint blended with the fat bass voice of a wandering peasant demanding an island of his master; and over it all, rising and falling like a sea of sound was the music of Albeniz, the *Iberia*, of which every note was as familiar as the sound of rain beating on gray stone.

He had no clear memory of when exactly the little gray in-spector left him, but only a vague impression of a warm handgrip and a voice urging him to visit the house in Galway to meet Maria, and look at some Spanish etchings and some Mexican carvings, and he vaguely remembered too standing at the door of Pats Flaherty's and watching the huddled gray figure disappearing through driving rain in the direction of his car, and then he re-membered turning back into the fire-broken shadows of the bar, the tang of spirits and turf-smoke in his nostrils, and his head bemused with sunlight.

QUESTIONS

1. To stimulate our curiosity and grip our imagination, a story need not have life and death urgency. Irish writers in particular can take a routine crisis in daily life and fill it with significance and even poetic beauty.

(a) What makes the basic situation in this story one which interests you?

(b) The first paragraph is admirably concise. Refer to it to show that Val Mulkerns has managed to include (1) background exposition, (2) comedy, (3) setting, (4) preliminary characterization, and (5) a suggestion of conflict.

2. (a) What relationship exists between the teacher and his pupils?

(b) Explain Val Mulkerns' method of making us aware of this relationship.

3. The arrival of Mr. Mulvey is itself a source of suspense. How does the author intensify it?

4. (a) Although we do not forget the inspector, there is a fairly long passage during which we see him only out of the corner of our eye. Where and how does the author focus our attention at this time?

(b) How does she use the inspector's re-entry into the class's activities to renew suspense?

(c) At what point does this tension relax into comedy?

5. The author has dropped us hints to explain McGlynn's lack of interest in teaching in more important schools. What are they?

6. (a) After the official inspectoral visit has ended, the story could lapse into anti-climax. How does the author maintain our interest?

(b) The final revelation of the inspector's personality in the last two paragraphs provides an unusual climax to the story. Explain.

7. What is your final evaluation of the character of (a) the inspector and (b) the teacher? Explain what touches of characterization have led you to these opinions.

*Katherine*

*Mansfield*

# Mr. Reginald Peacock's day

Katherine Mansfield *(1888-1923) was born in Wellington, New Zealand, and published her first short story at the age of nine. Her first volume of stories,* In a German Pension, *appeared in 1911. She collaborated with John Middleton Murry (the critic and editor whom she married) and the novelist D. H. Lawrence in the production of the magazine,* The Signature. *A victim of tuberculosis, she spent the last few years of her life in Switzerland and southern Europe. A fine literary critic as well as a sensitive poet, Katherine Mansfield achieved her major literary successes in the short-story form. Among her best volumes are* Prelude *(1918),* The Garden Party *(1922),* The Doves' Nest *(1923), and* Something Childish *(1924). Katherine Mansfield is generally acknowledged to be one of the great short story writers of this century. The following story is reprinted by permission of The Society of Authors as the literary representative of the Estate of the late Miss Mansfield.*

IF THERE WAS ONE THING that he hated more than another it was the way she had of waking him in the morning. She did it on purpose, of course. It was her way of establishing her grievance for the day, and he was not going to let her know how successful it was. But really, really, to wake a sensitive person like that was positively dangerous! It took him hours to get over it — simply hours. She came into the room buttoned up in an overall, with a handkerchief over her head — thereby proving that she had been up herself and slaving since dawn — and called in a low, warning voice: "Reginald!"

"Eh! What! What's that? What's the matter?"

"It's time to get up; it's half-past eight." And out she went, shutting the door quietly after her, to gloat over her triumph, he supposed.

He rolled over in the big bed, his heart still beating in quick, dull throbs, and with every throb he felt his energy escaping him, his — his inspiration for the day stifling under those thudding blows. It seemed that she took a malicious delight in making life more difficult for him than — Heaven knows — it was, by denying him his rights as an artist, by trying to drag him down to her level. What was the matter with her? What the hell did she want? Hadn't he three times as many pupils now as when they were first married, earned three times as much, paid for every stick and stone that they possessed, and now had begun to shell out for Adrian's kindergarten? ... And had he ever reproached her for not having a penny to her name? Never a word — never a sign! The truth was that once you married a woman she became insatiable, and the truth was that nothing was more fatal for an artist than marriage, at any rate until he was well over forty.... Why had he married her? He asked himself this question on an average about three times a day, but he never could answer it satisfactorily. She had caught him at a weak moment, when the first plunge into reality had bewildered and overwhelmed him for a time. Looking back, he saw a pathetic, youthful creature, half child, half wild untamed bird, totally incompetent to cope with bills and creditors and all the sordid details of existence. Well — she had done her best to clip his wings, if that was any satisfaction for her, and she could congratulate herself on the success of this early morning trick. One ought to wake exquisitely, reluctantly, he thought, slipping down in the warm bed. He began to imagine a series of enchanting scenes which ended with his latest, most charming pupil putting her bare, scented arms round his neck and covering him with her long, perfumed hair. "Awake, my love!" ...

As was his daily habit, while the bath water ran, Reginald Peacock tried his voice.

"When her mother tends her before the laughing mirror,
    Looping up her laces, tying up her hair,"
he sang, softly at first, listening to the quality, nursing his voice until he came to the third line:

"Often she thinks, were this wild thing wedded ..."
and upon the word "wedded" he burst into such a shout of triumph that the tooth-glass on the bathroom shelf trembled and even the bath tap seemed to gush stormy applause....

Well, there was nothing wrong with his voice, he thought, leaping into the bath and soaping his soft, pink body all over with a loofah shaped like a fish. He could fill Covent Garden with it! "*Wedded*," he shouted again, seizing the towel with a magnificent operatic gesture, and went on singing while he rubbed as though he had been Lohengrin tipped out by an unwary Swan and drying himself in the greatest haste before that tiresome Elsa came along....

Back in his bedroom, he pulled the blind up with a jerk, and standing upon the pale square of sunlight that lay upon the carpet like a sheet of cream blotting-paper, he began to do his exercises — deep breathing, bending forward and back, squatting like a frog and shooting out his legs — for if there was one thing he had a horror of it was of getting fat, and men in his profession had a dreadful tendency that way. However, there was no sign of it at present. He was, he decided, just right, just in good proportion. In fact, he could not help a thrill of satisfaction when he saw himself in the glass, dressed in a morning coat, dark grey trousers, grey socks and a black tie with a silver thread in it. Not that he was vain — he couldn't stand vain men — no; the sight of himself gave him a thrill of purely artistic satisfaction. "*Voilà tout!*" said he, passing his hand over his sleek hair.

That little, easy French phrase blown so lightly from his lips, like a whiff of smoke, reminded him that someone had asked him again, the evening before, if he was English. People seemed to find it impossible to believe that he hadn't some Southern blood. True, there was an emotional quality in his singing that had nothing of the John Bull in it. . . . The doorhandle rattled and turned round and round. Adrian's head popped through.

"Please, father, mother says breakfast is quite ready, please."

"Very well," said Reginald. Then, just as Adrian disappeared: "Adrian!"

"Yes, father."

"You haven't said 'good morning.' "

A few months ago Reginald had spent a week-end in a very aristocratic family, where the father received his little sons in the morning and shook hands with them. Reginald thought the practice charming, and introduced it immediately, but Adrian felt dreadfully silly at having to shake hands with his own father every morning. And why did his father always sort of sing to him instead of talk? . . .

In excellent temper, Reginald walked into the dining-room and sat down before a pile of letters, a copy of the *Times* and a little covered dish. He glanced at the letters and then at his breakfast. There were two thin slices of bacon and one egg.

"Don't you want any bacon?" he asked.

"No, I prefer a cold baked apple. I don't feel the need of bacon every morning."

Now, did she mean that there was no need for him to have bacon every morning, either, and that she grudged having to cook it for him?

"If you don't want to cook the breakfast," said he, "why don't you keep a servant? You know we can afford one, and you know how I loathe to see my wife doing the work. Simply because all the women we have had in the past have been failures and utterly upset my régime, and made it almost impossible for me to have any pupils here, you've given up trying to find a decent woman. It's not impossible to train a servant — is it? I mean, it doesn't require genius?"

"But I prefer to do the work myself; it makes life so much more peaceful. . . . Run along, Adrian darling, and get ready for school."

"Oh no, that's not it!" Reginald pretended to smile. "You do the work yourself, because, for some extraordinary reason, you love to humiliate me. Objectively, you may not know that, but, subjectively, it's the case." This last remark so delighted him that he cut open an envelope as gracefully as if he had been on the stage. . . .

"Dear Mr. Peacock,

I feel I cannot go to sleep until I have thanked you again for the wonderful joy your singing gave me this evening. Quite unforgettable. You make me wonder, as I have not wondered since I was a girl, if this is *all*. I mean, if this ordinary world is *all*. If there is not, perhaps, for those of us who understand, divine beauty and richness awaiting us if we only have the *courage* to see it. And to make it ours. . . . The house is so quiet. I wish you were here now that I might thank you in person. You are doing a great thing. You are teaching the world to escape from life!

Yours, most sincerely,

Aenone Fell.

P.S. – I am in every afternoon this week. . . ."

The letter was scrawled in violet ink on thick, handmade paper. Vanity, that bright bird, lifted its wings again, lifted them until he felt his breast would break.

"Oh well, don't let us quarrel," said he, and actually flung out a hand to his wife.

But she was not great enough to respond.

"I must hurry and take Adrian to school," said she. "Your room is quite ready for you."

Very well – very well – let there be open war between them! But he was hanged if he'd be the first to make it up again!

He walked up and down his room and was not calm again until he heard the outer door close upon Adrian and his wife. Of course, if this went on, he would have to make some other arrangement. That was obvious. Tied and bound like this, how could he help the world to escape from life? He opened the piano and looked up his pupils for the morning. Miss Betty Brittle, the Countess Wilkowska and Miss Marian Morrow. They were charming, all three.

Punctually at half-past ten the door-bell rang. He went to the door. Miss Betty Brittle was there, dressed in white, with her music in a blue silk case.

"I'm afraid I'm early," she said, blushing and shy, and she opened her big blue eyes very wide. "Am I?"

"Not at all, dear lady. I am only too charmed," said Reginald. "Won't you come in?"

"It's such a heavenly morning," said Miss Brittle. "I walked across the Park. The flowers were too marvellous."

"Well, think about them while you sing your exercises," said Reginald, sitting down at the piano. "It will give your voice colour and warmth."

Oh, what an enchanting idea! What a *genius* Mr. Peacock was. She parted her pretty lips and began to sing like a pansy.

"Very good, very good, indeed," said Reginald, playing chords that would waft a hardened criminal to heaven. "Make the notes round. Don't be afraid. Linger over them, breathe them like a perfume."

How pretty she looked, standing there in her white frock, her little blonde head tilted, showing her milky throat.

"Do you ever practise before a glass?" asked Reginald. "You ought to, you know; it makes the lips more flexible. Come over here."

They went over to the mirror and stood side by side.

"Now sing — moo-e-koo-e-oo-e-a!"

But she broke down and blushed more brightly than ever.

"Oh," she cried, "I can't. It makes me feel so silly. It makes me want to laugh. I do look so absurd!"

"No, you don't. Don't be afraid," said Reginald, but laughed, too, very kindly. "Now, try again!"

The lesson simply flew and Betty Brittle quite got over her shyness.

"When can I come again?" she asked, tying the music up again in the blue silk case. "I want to take as many lessons as I can just now. Oh, Mr. Peacock, I *do* enjoy them so much. May I come the day after to-morrow?"

"Dear lady, I shall be only too charmed," said Reginald, bowing her out.

Glorious girl! And when they had stood in front of the mirror, her white sleeve had just touched his black one. He could feel — yes, he could actually feel a warm, glowing spot, and he stroked it. She loved her lessons. His wife came in.

"Reginald, can you let me have some money? I must pay the dairy. And will you be in for dinner to-night?"

"Yes, you know I'm singing at Lord Timbuck's at half-past nine. Can you make me some clear soup with an egg in it?"

"Yes. And the money, Reginald. It's eight and sixpence."

"Surely that's very heavy — isn't it?"

"No, it's just what it ought to be. And Adrian must have milk."

There she was — off again. Now she was standing up for Adrian against him.

"I have not the slightest desire to deny my child a proper amount of milk," said he. "Here is ten shillings."

The door-bell rang. He went to the door.

"Oh," said the Countess Wilkowska, "the stairs. I have not a breath." And she put her hand over her heart as she followed him into the music-room. She was all in black, with a little black hat with a floating veil — violets in her bosom.

"Do not make me sing exercises to-day," she cried, throwing out her hands in her delightful foreign way. "No, to-day, I want only to sing songs. . . . And may I take off my violets? They fade so soon."

"They fade so soon — they fade so soon," played Reginald on the piano.

"May I put them here?" asked the Countess, dropping them in a little vase that stood in front of one of Reginald's photographs.

"Dear lady, I should be only too charmed!"

She began to sing, and all was well until she came to the phrase: "You love me. Yes, I *know* you love me!" Down dropped his hands from the keyboard, he wheeled round, facing her.

"No, no; that's not good enough. You can do better than that," cried Reginald ardently. "You must sing as if you were in love. Listen; let me try and show you." And he sang.

"Oh yes, yes. I see what you mean," stammered the little Countess. "May I try it again?"

"Certainly. Do not be afraid. Let yourself go. Confess yourself. Make proud surrender!" he called above the music. And she sang.

"Yes; better that time. But I still feel you are capable of more. Try it with me. There must be a kind of exultant defiance as well — don't you feel?" And they sang together. Ah! now she was sure she understood. "May I try once again?"

"You love me. Yes, I *know* you love me."

The lesson was over before that phrase was quite perfect. The little foreign hands trembled as they put the music together.

"And you are forgetting your violets," said Reginald softly.

"Yes, I think I will forget them," said the Countess, biting her underlip. What fascinating ways these foreign women have!

"And you will come to my house on Sunday and make music?" she asked.

"Dear lady, I shall be only too charmed!" said Reginald.

"Weep ye no more, sad fountains,
   Why need ye flow so fast?"

sang Miss Marion Morrow, but her eyes filled with tears and her chin trembled.

"Don't sing just now," said Reginald. "Let me play it for you." He played so softly.

"Is there anything the matter?" asked Reginald. "You're not quite happy this morning."

No, she wasn't; she was awfully miserable.

"You don't care to tell me what it is?"

It really was nothing particular. She had those moods sometimes when life seemed almost unbearable.

"Ah, I know," he said; "if I could only help!"

"But you do; you do! Oh, if it were not for my lessons I don't feel I could go on."

"Sit down in the arm-chair and smell the violets and let me sing to you. It will do you just as much good as a lesson."

Why weren't all men like Mr. Peacock?

"I wrote a poem after the concert last night — just about what I felt. Of course, it wasn't *personal*. May I send it to you?"

"Dear lady, I should be only too charmed!"

By the end of the afternoon he was quite tired and lay down on a sofa to rest his voice before dressing. The door of his room was open. He could hear Adrian and his wife talking in the dining-room.

"Do you know what that teapot reminds me of, mummy? It reminds me of a little sitting-down kitten."

"Does it, Mr. Absurdity?"

Reginald dozed. The telephone bell woke him.

"Aenone Fell is speaking. Mr. Peacock, I have just heard that you are singing at Lord Timbuck's to-night. Will you dine with me, and we can go on together afterwards?" And the words of his reply dropped like flowers down the telephone.

"Dear lady, I should be only too charmed."

What a triumphant evening! The little dinner *tête-à-tête* with Aenone Fell, the drive to Lord Timbuck's in her white motor-car, when she thanked him again for the unforgettable joy. Triumph upon triumph! And Lord Timbuck's champagne simply flowed.

"Have some more champagne, Peacock," said Lord Timbuck. Peacock, you notice — not Mr. Peacock — but Peacock, as if he were one of them. And wasn't he? He was an artist. He could sway them all. And wasn't he teaching them all to escape from life? How he sang! And he sang, as in a dream he saw their feathers and their flowers and their fans, offered to him, laid before him, like a huge bouquet.

"Have another glass of wine, Peacock."

"I could have any one I liked by lifting a finger," thought Peacock, positively staggering home.

But as he let himself into the dark flat his marvellous sense of elation began to ebb away. He turned up the light in the bedroom. His wife lay asleep, squeezed over to her side of the bed. He remembered suddenly how she had said when he had told her he was going out to dinner: "You might have let me know before!" And how he had answered: "Can't you possibly speak to me without offending against even good manners!" It was incredible, he thought, that she cared so little for him — incredible that she wasn't interested in the slightest in his triumphs and his artistic career. When so many women in her place would have given their eyes ... Yes, he knew it. ... Why not acknowledge it? ... And there she lay, an enemy, even in her sleep. ... Must it ever be thus? he thought, the champagne still working. Ah, if we only were friends, how much I could tell her now! About this evening; even about Timbuck's manner to me, and all that they said to me and so on and so on. If only I felt that she was here to come back to — that I could confide in her — and so on and so on.

In his emotion he pulled off his evening boot and simply hurled it in the corner. The noise woke his wife with a terrible start. She sat up, pushing back her hair. And he suddenly decided to have one more try to treat her as a friend, to tell her everything, to win her. Down he sat on the side of the bed and seized one of her hands. But of all those splendid things he had to say, not one could he utter. For some fiendish reason, the only words he could get out were: "Dear lady, I should be so charmed — so charmed!"

QUESTIONS

Although Katherine Mansfield tells this story in the third person (as though by an observer looking in from the outside), the story is nevertheless told entirely from the point of view of Mr. Reginald Peacock.

1. Why is the story from Mr. Peacock's point of view? Why not from his wife's?

2. If the story had been told in the first person, would the tone and point of the story have been the same? Would we have been able to judge Mr. Peacock as clearly if all the words had been his?

3. What does the author do in the opening paragraphs to make us distrust Mr. Peacock and "read between the lines" for a knowledge of what he is really like?

4. What do we get to know about his wife? We cannot accept Mr. Peacock's view of her. Why not?

5. What different things do we learn about Mr. Peacock during the series of music lessons?

6. What sort of man does Mr. Peacock believe himself to be? Why are we unable to agree with him?

7. At Lord Timbuck's party is Mr. Peacock *really* "one of them"?

8. Why, on his return from the party, does Peacock want to "confide" in his wife?

9. What is the significance, for the tone and point of the whole story, of "the only words he could get out: 'Dear lady, I should be so charmed — so charmed'?"

# Part three

*Clive Staples*
*Lewis*

# Right and wrong as a clue to the meaning of the universe

*Clive Staples Lewis (1898-1963) was born in Belfast, Ireland, and educated at Oxford. He has achieved an international reputation with major literary studies such as* The Allegory of Love *(1936),* A Preface to Paradise Lost *(1942), and* English Literature in the Sixteenth Century *(1954). Professor Lewis has reached a wide popular audience with fictional works such as* The Pilgrim's Regress *(1933) and* Out of the Silent Planet *(1938). Perhaps he is best known for his popular books on religious ideas and values. These include* The Screwtape Letters *(1942),* A Case for Christianity *(1942), and* Beyond Personality *(1944). Both in his fiction and non-fiction, Professor Lewis is deeply concerned with the meaning and place of religion in the modern world. The following talk is reprinted from* Broadcast Talks *by C. S. Lewis, by permission of the publisher, Geoffrey Bles, Ltd.*

EVERYONE HAS HEARD people quarrelling. Sometimes it sounds funny and sometimes it sounds merely unpleasant; but however it sounds, I believe we can learn something very important from listening to the kind of things they say. They say things like this: "That's my seat; I was here first" — "Leave him alone, he isn't doing you any harm" — "Why should you shove in first?" — "Give me a bit of your orange, I gave you a bit of mine" —

"How'd you like it if anyone did the same to you?" — "Come on, you promised." People say things like that every day, educated people as well as uneducated, and children as well as grown-ups. Now what interests me about all these remarks is that the man who makes them isn't just saying that the other man's behaviour doesn't happen to please him. He is appealing to some kind of standard of behaviour which he expects the other man to know about. And the other man very seldom replies, "To hell with your standard." Nearly always he tries to make out that what he has been doing doesn't really go against the standard, or that if it does there is some special excuse. He pretends there is some special reason in this particular case why the person who took the seat first should not keep it, or that things were quite different when he was given the bit of orange, or that something has turned up which lets him off keeping his promise. It looks, in fact, very much as if both parties had in mind some kind of Law or Rule of fair play or decent behaviour or morality or whatever you like to call it, about which they really agreed. And they have. If they hadn't, they might, of course, fight like animals, but they couldn't *quarrel* in the human sense of the word. Quarrelling means trying to show that the other man's in the wrong. And there'd be no sense in trying to do that unless you and he had some sort of agreement as to what Right and Wrong are; just as there'd be no sense in saying that a footballer had committed a foul unless there was some agreement about the rules of football.

Now this Law or Rule about Right and Wrong used to be called the Law of Nature. Nowadays, when we talk of the "laws of nature" we usually mean things like gravitation, or heredity, or the laws of chemistry. But when the older thinkers called the Law of Right and Wrong the Law of Nature, they really meant the Law of *Human* Nature. The idea was that, just as falling stones are governed by the law of gravitation and chemicals by chemical laws, so the creature called man also had *his* law — with this great difference, that the stone couldn't choose whether it obeyed the law of gravitation or not, but a man could choose either to obey the Law of Human Nature or to disobey it. They called it Law of Nature because they thought that every one knew it by nature and didn't need to be taught it. They didn't mean, of course, that you mightn't find an odd individual here and there who didn't know it, just as you find a few people who are colour-blind or have no ear for a tune. But taking the race as a whole, they thought that the human idea of Decent Behaviour was obvious to everyone. And I believe they were right. If they weren't, then all the things we say about this war are nonsense. What is the sense in saying the enemy are in the wrong unless Right is a real thing which the Germans at bottom know as well as we do and ought to practise? If they had no notion of what we mean by right, then, though we might still have to fight them, we could no more blame them for that than for the colour of their hair.

I know that some people say the idea of a Law of Nature or decent behaviour known to all men is unsound, because different civilizations and different ages have had quite different moralities. But they haven't. They have had only *slightly* different moralities. Just think what a *quite* different morality would mean. Think of a country where people were *admired* for running away in battle, or where a man felt *proud* of double-crossing all the people who had been kindest to him. You might just as well try to imagine a country where two and two made five. Men have differed as regards what people you ought to be unselfish to — whether it was only your own family, or your fellow countrymen, or everyone. But they have always agreed that you oughtn't to put yourself first. Selfishness has never been admired. Men have differed as to whether you should have one wife or four. But they have always agreed that you mustn't simply have any woman you liked.

But the most remarkable thing is this. Whenever you find a man who says he doesn't believe in a real Right and Wrong, you will find the same man going back on this a moment later. He may break his promise to you, but if you try breaking one to him he'll be complaining "It's not fair" before you can say Jack Robinson. A nation may say treaties don't matter; but then, next minute, they spoil their case by saying that the particular treaty they want to break was an unfair one. But if treaties don't matter, and if there's no such thing as Right and Wrong – in other words, if there is no Law of Nature – what is the difference between a fair treaty and an unfair one? Haven't they given away the fact that, whatever they say, they really know the Law of Nature just like anyone else?

It seems, then, we are forced to believe in a real Right and Wrong. People may be sometimes mistaken about them, just as people sometimes get their sums wrong; but they are not a matter of mere taste and opinion any more than the multiplication table. Now if we're agreed about that, I go on to my next point, which is this. None of us are really keeping the Law of Nature. If there are any exceptions among you, I apologise to them. They'd better switch on to another station, for nothing I'm going to say concerns them. And now, turning to the ordinary human beings who are left:

I hope you won't misunderstand what I'm going to say. I'm not preaching, and Heaven knows I'm not pretending that I'm better than anyone else. I'm only trying to call attention to a fact: the fact that this year, or this month, or, more likely, this very day, we have failed to practise ourselves the kind of behaviour we expect from other people. There may be all sorts of excuses for us. That time you were so unfair to the children was when you were very tired. That slightly shady business about the money – the one you've almost forgotten – came when you were very hard up. And what you promised to do for old So-an-so and have never done – well, you never would have promised if you'd known how frightfully busy you were going to be. And as for your behaviour to your wife (or husband), if I knew how irritating they could be, I wouldn't wonder at it – and who the dickens am I, anyway? I am just the same. That is to say, I don't succeed in keeping the Law of Nature very well, and the moment anyone tells me I'm not keeping it, there starts up in my mind a string of excuses as long as your arm. The question at the moment is not whether they are good excuses. The point is that they are one more proof of how deeply, whether we like it or not, we believe in the Law of Nature. If we didn't believe in decent behaviour, why should we be so anxious to make excuses for not having behaved decently? The truth is, we believe in decency so much — we feel the Rule or Law pressing on us so — that we can't bear to face the fact that we're breaking it, and consequently we try to shift the responsibility. For you notice that it's only for our bad behaviour that we find all these explanations. We put our *bad* temper down to being tired or worried or hungry; we put our good temper down to ourselves.

Well, those are the two points I wanted to make tonight. First, that human beings, all over the earth, have this curious idea that they *ought* to behave in a certain way, and can't really get rid of it. Secondly, that they don't in fact behave in that way. They know the Law of Nature; they break it. These two facts are the foundation of all clear thinking about ourselves and the universe we live in.

If they are the foundation, I had better stop to make that foundation firm before I go on. Some of the letters I have had from listeners show that a good many people find it difficult to understand just what this Law of Human Nature, or Moral Law, or Rule of Decent Behaviour is.

For example, some people write to me saying, "Isn't what you call the Moral Law simply our herd instinct and hasn't it been developed just like all our other instincts?" Now I don't deny that we may have a herd instinct: but that isn't what I mean by the Moral Law. We all know what it feels like to be prompted by instinct — by mother love, or sexual instinct, or the instinct for food. It means you feel a strong want or desire to act in a certain way. And, of course, we sometimes do feel just that sort of desire to help another person: and no doubt that desire is due to the herd instinct. But feeling a desire to help is quite different from feeling that you ought to help whether you want to or not. Supposing you hear a cry for help from a man in danger. You will probably feel two desires — one a desire to give help (due to your herd instinct), the other a desire to keep out of danger (due to the instinct for self-preservation). But you will find inside you, in addition to these two impulses, a third thing which tells you that you ought to follow the impulse to help, and suppress the impulse to run away. Now this thing that judges between two instincts, that decides which should be encouraged, can't itself be .either of them. You might as well say that the sheet of music which tells you, at a given moment, to play one note on the piano and not another, is itself one of the notes on the keyboard. The Moral Law is, so to speak, the tune we've got to play: our instincts are merely the keys.

Another way of seeing that the Moral Law is not simply one of our instincts is this. If two instincts are in conflict, and there is nothing in a creature's mind except those two instincts, obviously the stronger of the two must win. But at those moments when we are most conscious of the Moral Law, it usually seems to be telling us to side with the weaker of the two impulses. You probably *want* to be safe much more than you want to help the man who is drowning: but the Moral Law tells you to help him all the same. And doesn't it often tell us to try to make the right impulse stronger than it naturally is? I mean, we often feel it our duty to stimulate the herd instinct, by waking up our imaginations and arousing our pity and so on, so as to get up enough steam for doing the right thing. But surely we are not acting *from* instinct when we set about making an instinct stronger than it is? The thing that says to you, "Your herd instinct is asleep. Wake it up," can't itself *be* the herd instinct. The thing that tells you which note on the piano needs to be played louder can't itself be that note!

Here is a third way of seeing it. If the Moral Law was one of our instincts, we ought to be able to point to some one impulse inside us which was always what we call "good," always in agreement with the rule of right behaviour. But you can't. There is none of our impulses which the Moral Law won't sometimes tell us to suppress, and none which it won't sometimes tell us to encourage. It is a mistake to think that some of our impulses — say, mother love or patriotism — are good, and others, like sex or the fighting instinct, are bad. All we mean is that the occasions on which the fighting instinct or the sexual desire need to be restrained are rather more frequent than those for restraining mother love or patriotism. But there are situations in which it is the duty of a married man to encourage his sexual impulse and of a soldier to encourage the fighting instinct. There are also occasions on which a mother's love for her own children or a man's love for his own country have to be suppressed or they'll lead to unfairness towards other people's children or countries. Strictly speaking, there aren't such things as good and bad impulses. Think once again of a piano. It hasn't got two kinds of notes on it, the "right" notes and the "wrong" ones. Every single note is right at one time and wrong at another. The Moral Law isn't any one instinct or any set of instincts: it is something which makes a kind of tune (the tune we call goodness or right conduct) by directing the instincts.

By the way, this point is of great practical consequence. The most dangerous thing you can do is to take any one impulse of your own nature and set it up as the thing you ought to follow at all costs. There's not one of them which won't make us into devils if we set it up as an absolute guide. You might think love of humanity in general was safe, but it isn't. If you leave out justice you'll find yourself breaking agreements and faking evidence in trials "for the sake of humanity," and become in the end a cruel and treacherous man.

Other people write to me saying, "Isn't what you call the Moral Law just a social convention, something that is put into us by education?" I think there is a misunderstanding here. The people who ask that question are usually taking it for granted that if we have learned a thing from parents and teachers, then that thing must be merely a human invention. But, of course, that isn't so. We all learned the multiplication table at school. A child who grew up alone on a desert island wouldn't know it. But surely it doesn't follow that the multiplication table is simply a human convention, something human beings have made up for themselves and might have made different if they had liked? *Of course* we learn the Rule of Decent Behaviour from parents and teachers, as we learn everything else. But some of the things we learn are mere convention which might have been different — we learn to keep to the left of the road, but it might just as well have been the rule to keep to the right — and others of them, like

mathematics, are real truths. The question is which class the Law
of Human Nature belongs to.

There are two reasons for saying it belongs to the same class
as mathematics. The first is, as I said last time, that though there
are differences between the moral ideas of one time or country
and those of another, the differences aren't really very big — you
can recognize the same Law running through them all: whereas
mere conventions — like the rule of the road or the kind of
clothes people wear — differ completely. The other reason is
this. When you think about these differences between the morality of one people and another, do you think that the morality of
one people is ever better or worse than that of another? Have any
of the changes been improvements? If not, then of course there
could never be any moral progress. Progress means not just
changing, but changing for the better. If no set of moral ideas
were truer or better than any other there would be no sense in
preferring civilized morality to savage morality, or Christian
morality to Nazi morality. In fact, of course, we all do believe
that some moralities *are* better than others. We do believe that
some of the people who tried to change the moral ideas of their
own age were what we'd call Reformers or Pioneers — people
who understood morality better than their neighbours did. Very
well then. The moment you say that one set of moral ideas can
be better than another, you are, in fact, measuring them both by
a standard, saying that one of them conforms to that standard
more nearly than the other. But the standard that measures two
things is something different from either. You are, in fact, com-
paring them both with some Real Morality, admitting that there
is *really* such a thing as Right, independent of what people think,
and that some people's ideas get nearer to that real Right than
others. Or put it this way. If your moral ideas can be truer, and
those of the Nazis less true, there must be something — some Real
Morality — for them to be true *about*. The reason why your idea
of New York can be truer or less true than mine is that New
York is a real place, existing quite apart from what either of us
thinks. If when each of us said "New York," each meant merely
"The town I am imagining in my own head", how could one of

us have truer ideas than the other? There'd be no question of truth or falsehood at all. In the same way, if the Rule of Decent Behaviour meant simply "whatever each nation happens to approve", there'd be no sense in saying that any one nation had ever been more correct in its approval than any other; no sense in saying that the world could ever grow better or worse.

So you see that though the differences between people's ideas of Decent Behaviour often make you suspect that there is no real natural Law of Behaviour at all, yet the things we are bound to think about these differences really prove just the opposite. But one word before I end. I think that some listeners have been exaggerating the differences, because they have not distinguished between differences of morality and differences of belief about facts. For example, one listener wrote and said, "Three hundred years ago people in England were putting witches to death. Was that what you call the Rule of Human Nature or Right Conduct?" But surely the reason we don't execute witches is that we don't believe there are such things. If we did – if we really thought that there were people going about who had sold themselves to the devil and received supernatural powers from him in return and were using these powers to kill their neighbours or drive them mad or bring bad weather, surely we'd all agree that if anyone deserved the death penalty, then these filthy quislings did. There's no difference of moral principle here: the difference is simply about matter of fact. It may be a great advance in *knowledge* not to believe in witches: there's no moral advance in not executing them when you don't think they are there! You wouldn't call a man humane for ceasing to set mouse-traps if he did so because he believed there were no mice in the house.

I now go back to what I said at the end of the first talk, that there were two odd things about the human race. First, that they were haunted by the idea of a sort of behaviour they ought to practise, what you might call fair play, or decency, or morality, or the Law of Nature. Second, that they didn't in fact do so. Now some of you may wonder why I called this odd. It may seem to you the most natural thing in the world. In particular, you may have thought I was rather hard on the human race. After all, you may say, what I call breaking the Law of Right and Wrong or of Nature, only means that people aren't perfect. And why on earth should I expect them to be? Well, that would be a good answer if what I was trying to do was to fix the exact amount of blame which is due to us for not behaving as we expect others to behave. But that isn't my job at all. I'm not concerned at present with blame; I'm trying to find out truth. And from that point of view the very idea of something being imperfect, of its not being what it ought to be, has certain consequences.

If you take a thing like a stone or a tree, it is what it is and there's no sense in saying it ought to have been otherwise. Of course you may say a stone's "the wrong shape" if you want to use it for a rockery, or that a tree's a bad tree because it doesn't give you as much shade as you expected. But all you mean is that the stone or the tree doesn't happen to be convenient for some purpose of your own. You're not, except as a joke, blaming them for that. You really know that, given the weather and the soil, the tree *couldn't* have been any different. What we, from our point of view, call a "bad" tree is obeying the laws of its nature, just as much as a "good" one.

Now have you noticed what follows? It follows that what we usually call the laws of nature – the way weather works on a tree, for example – may not really be *laws* in the strict sense, but only in a manner of speaking. When you say that falling stones always obey the law of gravitation, isn't this much the same as saying that the law only means "what stones always do"? You don't really think that when a stone is let go, it suddenly remembers that it is under orders to fall to the ground! You mean only that, in fact, it *does* fall. In other words, you can't be sure that there is anything over and above the facts themselves, any law about what ought to happen, as distinct from what does happen. The laws of nature, as applied to stones or trees, may mean only "what Nature, in fact, does." But if you turn to the Law of Human Nature, the Law of Decent Behaviour, it's a different matter. That law certainly doesn't mean "what human beings, in fact, do"; for, as I said before, many of them don't obey this law at all, and none of them obey it completely. The law of gravity tells you what stones do if you drop them; but the Law of Human Nature tells you what human beings ought to do, and don't. In other words, when you're dealing with humans, something else comes in above and beyond the actual facts. You have the facts (how men do behave) and you also have something else (how they ought to behave). In the rest of the universe there needn't be anything but the facts. Electrons and molecules behave in a certain way, and certain results follow, and that *may* be the whole story.* But men behave in a certain way and that's not the whole story, for all the time you know that they ought to behave differently.

Now this is really so peculiar that one is tempted to try to explain it away. For instance, we might try to make out that when you say a man oughtn't to act as he does, you only mean the same as when you say that a stone's the wrong shape; namely, that what he's doing happens to be inconvenient to you. But that just isn't true. A man occupying the corner seat in the train because he got there first, and a man who slipped into it while my back was turned and removed my bag, are both equally inconvenient. But I blame the second man and don't blame the first. I'm not angry — except perhaps for a moment before I come to my senses — with a man who trips me up by accident; I am angry with a man who tries to trip me up even if he doesn't succeed. Yet the first has hurt me and the second hasn't. Sometimes the behaviour which I call bad is not inconvenient to me at all, but the very opposite. In war, each side may find a traitor on the other side very useful. But though they use him and pay him they regard him as human vermin. So you can't say that what we call decent behaviour in others is simply the behaviour that happens to be useful to us. And as for decent behaviour in ourselves, I suppose it's pretty obvious that it doesn't mean the behaviour that pays. It means things like being content with thirty shillings when you might have got three pounds, leaving a girl alone when you'd like to make love to her, staying in dangerous places when you

---

*I don't think it *is* the whole story, as you will see later. I mean that, as far as the argument has gone up to date, it *may* be.

could go somewhere safer, keeping promises you'd rather not keep, and telling the truth even when it makes you look a fool.

Some people say that though decent conduct doesn't mean what pays each particular person at a particular moment, still, it means what pays the human race as a whole; and that consequently there's no mystery about it. Human beings, after all, have some sense; they see that you can't have any real safety or happiness except in a society where every one plays fair, and it's because they see this that they try to behave decently. Now, of course, it's perfectly true that safety and happiness can only come from individuals, classes, and nations being honest and fair and kind to each other. It is one of the most important truths in the world. But as an explanation of why we feel as we do about Right and Wrong it just misses the point. If we ask, "Why ought I to be unselfish?" and you reply, "Because it is good for society," we may then ask, "Why should I care what's good for society except when it happens to pay *me* personally?" and then you'll have to say, "Because you ought to be unselfish" — which simply brings us back to where we started. You're saying what's true, but you're not getting any further. If a man asked what was the point of playing football, it wouldn't be much good saying, "in order to score goals", for trying to score goals is the game itself, not the reason for the game, and you'd really only be saying that football was football — which is true, but not worth saying. In the same way, if a man asks what is the point of behaving decently, it's no good replying, "in order to benefit society", for trying to benefit other people, in other words being unselfish, is one of the things decent behaviour consists in; all you're really saying is that decent behaviour is decent behaviour. You'd have said just as much if you'd stopped at the statement, "Men ought to be unselfish."

And that's just where I do stop. Men ought to be unselfish, ought to be fair. Not that men are unselfish, nor that they like being unselfish, but that they ought to be. The Moral Law, or Law of Human Nature, is not simply a fact about human behaviour in the same way as the Law of Gravitation is, or may be, simply a fact about how heavy objects behave. On the other hand, it's not a mere fancy, for we can't get rid of the idea, and most of the things we say and think about men would be reduced to nonsense if we did. And it's not simply a statement about how we should like men to behave for our own convenience; for the behaviour we call bad or unfair isn't exactly the same as the behaviour we find inconvenient, and may even be the opposite. Consequently, this Rule of Right and Wrong, or Law of Human Nature, or whatever you call it, must somehow or other be a real thing – a thing that's really there, not made up by ourselves. And yet it's not a fact in the ordinary sense, in the same way as our actual behaviour is a fact. It begins to look as if we'll have to admit that there's more than one kind of reality; that, in this particular case, there's something above and beyond the ordinary facts of men's behaviour, and yet quite definitely real – a real law, which none of us made, but which we find pressing on us.

Let us sum up what we have reached so far. In the case of stones and trees and things of that sort, what we call the Laws of Nature may not be anything except a way of speaking. When you say that nature is governed by certain laws, this may only mean that nature does, in fact, behave in a certain way. The so-called laws may not be anything real – anything above and beyond the actual facts which we observe. But in the case of Man, we saw that this won't do. The Law of Human Nature, or of Right and Wrong, must be something above and beyond the actual facts of human behaviour. In this case, besides the actual facts, you have something else – a real law which we didn't invent and which we know we ought to obey.

Tonight I want to consider what this tells us about the universe we live in. Ever since men were able to think, they've been wondering what this universe really is and how it came to be there. And, very roughly, two views have been held. First, there is what is called the materialist view. People who take that view think that matter and space just happen to exist, and always have existed, nobody knows why; and that the matter, behaving in certain fixed ways, has just happened, by a sort of fluke, to produce creatures like ourselves who are able to think. By one

chance in a thousand something hit our sun and made it produce
the planets; and by another thousandth chance the chemicals
necessary for life, and the right temperature, arose on one of
these planets, and so some of the matter on this earth came alive;
and then, by a very long series of chances, the living creatures
developed into things like us. The other view is the religious
view.* According to it, what is behind the universe is more like
a mind than it's like anything else we know. That is to say, it's
conscious, and has purposes, and prefers one thing to another.
And on this view it made the universe, partly for purposes we
don't know, but partly, at any rate, in order to produce creatures
like itself – I mean, like itself to the extent of having minds.
Please don't think that one of these views was held a long time
ago and that the other has gradually taken its place. Wherever
there have been thinking men both views turn up. And note this
too. You can't find out which view is the right one by science
in the ordinary sense. Science works by experiments. It watches
how things behave. Every scientific statement in the long run,
however complicated it looks, really means, "I pointed the tele-

---

*In order to keep this Talk short enough I mentioned only the Materialist view
and the Religious view. But to complete I ought to mention the In-Between
view called Life-Force philosophy, or Creative-Evolution, or Emergent Evolution. The wittiest expositions of it come in the works of Mr. G. B. Shaw, but
the most profound ones in those of Bergson. People who hold this view say that
the small variations by which life on this planet "evolved" from the lowest
forms to Man were not due to chance but to the "striving" or "purposiveness"
of a Life-Force. When people say this we must ask them whether by Life-Force
they mean something with a mind or not. If they do, then "a mind bringing
life into existence and leading it to perfection" is really a God, and their view
is thus identical with the Religious. If they don't, then what is the sense in
saying that something without a mind "strives" or has "purposes"? This seems
to me fatal to their view. One reason why many people find Creative Evolution so attractive is that it gives one much of the emotional comfort of believ-
ing in God and none of the less pleasant consequences. When you are feeling
fit and the sun is shining and you don't want to believe that the whole universe
is a mere mechanical dance of atoms, it's nice to be able to think of this great
mysterious Force rolling on through the centuries and carrying you on its
crest. If, on the other hand, you want to do something rather shabby, the Life-
Force being only a blind force, with no morals and no mind, will never interfere with you like that troublesome God we learned about when we were
children. The Life-Force is a sort of *tame* God. *You* can switch *it* on when
you want, but *it* won't bother *you*. All the thrills of religion and none of the
cost. Is the Life-Force the greatest achievement of wishful thinking the world
has yet seen?

scope to such and such a part of the sky at 2.20 a.m. on 15th January and saw so-and-so", or "I put some of this stuff in a pot and heated it to such-and-such a temperature and it did so-and-so." Don't think I'm saying anything against science: I'm only saying what its job is. And the more scientific a man is, the more (I believe) he'd agree with me that this is the job of science – and a very useful and necessary job it is too. But why anything comes to be there at all, and whether there's anything behind the things science observes – something of a different kind – this is not a scientific question. If there is "Something Behind", then either it will have to remain altogether unknown to men or else make itself known in some different way. The statement that there is any such thing, and the statement that there's no such thing, are neither of them statements that science can make. And real scientists don't usually make them. It's usually the journalists and popular novelists who have picked up a few odds and ends of half-baked science from textbooks who go in for them. After all, it's really a matter of common sense. Suppose science ever became complete so that it knew every single thing in the whole universe. Don't you see that the questions "Why is there a universe?" "Why does it go on as it does?" "Has it any meaning?" would remain just as they were?

Now the position would be quite hopeless but for this. There is one thing, and only one, in the whole universe which we know more about than we could learn from external observation. That one thing is Man. We don't merely observe men, we *are* men. In this case we have, so to speak, inside information; we're in the know. And because of that, we know that men find themselves under a moral law, which they didn't make, and can't quite forget even when they try, and which they know they ought to obey. Notice the following point. Anyone studying Man from the outside as we study electricity or cabbages, not knowing our language and consequently not able to get any inside knowledge from *us*, but merely observing what we did, would never get the slightest evidence that we had this moral law. How could he? for his observations would only show what we did, and the moral law is about what we ought to do. In the same way, if there *is*

anything above or behind the observed facts in the case of stones
or the weather, we, by studying them from outside, could never
hope to discover it.

The position of the question, then, is like this. We want to
know whether the universe simply happens to be what it is for
no reason or whether there is a power behind it that makes it what
it is. Since that power, if it exists, would be not one of the facts
but a reality which makes the facts, no mere observation of the
facts can find it. There's only one case in which we can know
whether there's anything more, namely our own case. And in that
one case we find there is. Or put it the other way round. If there
was a controlling power outside the universe, it could not show
itself to us as one of the facts inside the universe — no more than
the architect of a house could actually be a wall or staircase or
fireplace in that house. The only way in which we could expect
it to show itself would be inside *us* as an influence or a command
trying to get us to behave in a certain way. And that's just what
we do find inside us. Doesn't it begin to look, if I may say so,
very suspicious? In the only case where you can expect to get an
answer, the answer turns out to be yes; and in the other cases,
where you don't get an answer, you see *why* you don't. Suppose
someone asked me, when I see a man in blue uniform going down
the street leaving little paper packets at each house, why I suppose that they contain letters. I should reply, "Because whenever
he leaves a similar little packet for me I find it does contain a
letter." And if he then objected — "But you've never seen all
these letters which you think the other people are getting", I
should say, "Of course not, and I shouldn't expect to, because
they're not addressed to me. I'm explaining the packets I'm not
allowed to open by the ones I am allowed to open." It's the same
about this question. The only packet I'm allowed to open is Man.
When I do, especially when I open that particular man called
Myself, I find that I don't exist on my own, that I'm under a law;
that somebody or something wants me to behave in a certain way.
I don't, of course, think that if I could get inside a stone or a tree
I should find exactly the same thing, just as I don't think all the
other people in the street get the *same* letters as I do. I should

expect, for instance, to find that the stone *had* to obey the law of gravity — that whereas the sender of the letters merely tells me to do right, He *compels* the stone to obey the laws of its nature. But I should expect to find that there was, so to speak, a sender of letters in both cases, a Power behind the facts, a Director, a Guide.

Now don't think I'm going faster than I really am. I'm not yet within a hundred miles of the God of Christian theology. All I've got to is a Something which is directing the universe, and which appears in me as a law urging me to do right and making me feel responsible and uncomfortable when I do wrong. I think we have to assume it's more like a mind than it's like anything else we know — because after all the only other thing we know is matter and you can hardly imagine a bit of matter making a law. But, of course, it needn't be very like a mind, still less like a person. But one word of warning. There's been a great deal of soft soap talked about God for the last hundred years. That's not what I'm offering. You can cut all that out.

CRITIQUE AND QUESTIONS

In this Section we have three essays concerned with the problem of man's place in the universe and therefore, in some degree, with the meaning and purpose of human life. Bertrand Russell is a rationalist; that is, a man who seeks to understand man's origin and destiny by means of the faculty of reason alone. He studies the evidence as a lawyer would and thus scrutinizes the twisted argument of human history under the microscope of his own intellect; he calculates, as a social scientist would, the consequences of man's incredible forward leap in knowledge and power; he proposes, as an experimental scientist should, a working hypothesis for the control of the forces unleashed by man's inventive science. He is a rationalist and he is a naturalist, for nowhere does he admit the validity and effectualness of any human faculty other than reason; nowhere does he entertain even the possibility of a supernatural reality.

G. K. Chesterton and C. S. Lewis are both literary men, men who practise the imaginative life and are in awe of it. Both are deeply religious men, committed not to the possibility but to the certainty of supernatural reality. Both would agree with Bertrand Russell that the natural sciences cannot define and direct "the good life", cannot instil man with moral purpose, cannot in themselves make man at home in the universe. But neither would agree with Bertrand Russell that this purpose is to be discovered and fulfilled and man made secure and "at home" by means of still another science, still another concoction of human reason — "mass psychology".

Chesterton, in the essay included here, stops short of a religious statement of his case, although you may feel (and rightly) that a religious statement is at least implied. Chesterton is concerned in this instance, with the imaginative faculty, a faculty which is like an inner light strong enough to see through reason and beyond it. He is concerned with the artist's *capacity* for a kind of truth not available to the logical and science-making faculty at all. It should not be surprising that the world of nature and of men shines for him with a light never seen on sea or land — or in the pages of Bertrand Russell.

Note, too, the difference in style. Russell writes what has come to be the "normal" style of the clear-headed, knowledgeable, modern rationalist. The style is abstract rather than concrete. Arguments are advanced by generalization that sweep up whole centuries and continents in a single paragraph. The appeal is always to a view of nature and history and a kind of evidence which can be taken for granted among "educated" modern men. While the argument proceeds logically (Russell *is* a clear-headed man), it proceeds with the kind of easy confidence which suggests that there is not much need for argument at all. One need only *explain* and arrange the self-evident evidence to draw the inevitable conclusion.

There was a time (not so long ago) when the literary man could write with this easy confidence, could assume that his poetic or imaginative view of life would be immediately understood and approved. No more. Chesterton must stand us on our heads before he can assume that our feet stand on his kind of ground. He must seem to talk nonsense before he can make his kind of sense — the kind of sense we have lost these days, or are in danger of losing. And he cannot depend on abstract statement as though a bond of unquestioned ideas and values linked him comfortably with the average reader. He has to prick our skins with sharp images, provoke us with seemingly outrageous fantasy, turn us quite upside-down in order to look us in the eye. We must be treated like new-born babies, made naked, held by the feet head-downward, and slapped pink until the cry of the imagination bursts from our own lips and we are "delivered" from the old body of our blindness.

Chesterton's style is a strategy. So is the style of Lewis. He is writing on a topic (the law of nature) which, in ages gone by, was treated by religious writers and philosophers in language even more abstract (and confident) than the language of Russell's essay. In other ages (and until the nineteenth century), the preacher and the theologian could assume between himself and his audience, a set of shared assumptions about man's place in nature and society and about man's relation to the Deity. It could be taken for granted that there was a moral law meant to govern the affairs of men both private and public. It could be taken for granted that the law-giver was God Himself. Theologians, in the seventeenth and even in the eighteenth century, could afford to speculate, in legalistic and abstract terms, on the kind and degree of man's obligation under the moral law. In short, they could afford to generalize as sweepingly and as confidently as Russell does now, but, of course, on the basis of very different assumptions.

Lewis is writing (or rather talking) in an age which is some-times referred to as "the post-Christian age" — an age in which the religious thinker can no longer take it for granted that his audience shares his assumptions. Lewis cannot even be sure of the composition of his audience, for this is a *spoken* essay, in fact, a closely integrated series of short radio talks. Because he is talking — and talking into the anonymous air — he must be doubly careful of his style. Like an actor on a bare stage, he must use his words to make up for the lack of scenery. He *must* illustrate. He cannot be abstract. He talks from a bare stage to minds that may be as bare as it.

Notice how anxious he is to ground his ideas in the facts of every-day experience — games, business, the keyboard of a piano, mouse-traps, the weather, and the war which is being fought. Notice how each new idea is advanced cautiously, defined, illustrated, and questioned. Notice how much more precise and cautious he is than Russell. Notice how scrupulous he is not to assume, in advance, any agreement between the audience and himself. Notice how diligently he sums up his evidence and tests his foothold at each step before advancing to new and higher ground.

It would be presumptuous to paraphrase the thought of this essay. Lewis feels constrained to interpret himself as he goes. One must observe, however, that he insists that man's sense of what he *ought* to be and what he *ought* to do, cannot be explained away by rational, scientific evidence or argument. He concludes that the presence of a moral law inexplicable in natural terms can only be explained in supernatural terms. While he is a convinced Christian, Lewis is not here making a case for Christianity as such. He is rather arguing, on the basis of human experience, for the recognition of a law of conduct which, by its very nature, cannot be merely human in origin. The idea of a Law of Nature is pre-Christian and can be traced to the Stoic philosophers of the ancient world. It is compatible with a variety of religious beliefs, of which Christianity is one.

In this essay, then, Lewis does not pretend to proclaim a faith. Rather, he reasons his way to the very edge of realities which lie beyond the reach of human reason.

His reference, however, to "soft soap" in the very last paragraph of the essay seems to suggest that while faith gives a knowledge which reason cannot give, this knowledge will not be contrary to reason; and if it is true knowledge, it will not offend reason.

1. What is the difference between the two phrases, "Law of Nature" and "Laws of Nature"? (Note that Mr. Lewis upholds the first and Chesterton "deflates" the second.)

2. In what sense does the Law of Nature seem to apply to nations as well as to individuals? Why is it important for Lewis's argument that the Law does apply to very different nations and cultures?

3. Why cannot the Law be explained in terms of instinct? Social convention?

4. Was the burning of witches in accordance with the Law of Nature?

5. Why does the author think it impossible to explain the Law of Nature in terms of self-interest?

6. What is the author's conception of the function and value of science? What are thought to be the limits of science?

7. What is meant by the Materialist view of the universe? The Religious view? The In-Between view?

8. How does an acceptance of the moral Law of Nature affect one's view of the meaning of the universe?

*Robertson*

*Davies*

# Remember Creatore

*Robertson Davies (b. 1913) was born in Thamesville, Ontario
and studied at Queen's University (Kingston) and Oxford. After
a brief career as actor in the Old Vic Repertory Theatre (and
teacher in the Old Vic School), Mr. Davies returned to Canada
and, until his appointment as Master of Massey College in the
University of Toronto (1961), was the editor of the* Peter-
borough Examiner. *Students of the theatre prize his first book,*
Shakespear's Boy Actors *(1939). His plays include* Eros at
Breakfast and other plays *(1949),* Fortune My Foe *(1949),*
At My Heart's Core *(1950),* A Jig for a Gypsy *(1954),*
Hunting Stuart *(1955), and* A Voice from the Attic *(1960).*
*He has published three novels,* Tempest-Tost *(1951),*
Leaven of Malice *(1954), and* A Mixture of Frailties *(1958).*
The Diary of Samuel Marchbanks *(1947) and* Table-Talk
of Samuel Marchbanks *(1949), are vehicles of witty comment
on life and art. Mr. Davies is also widely known for his essays
and reviews. "Remember Creatore" is reprinted by permission
of the author.*

MY FIRST CLEAR MEMORY of the Canadian National Exhibition is
of seeing Signor Creatore eat his dinner.

Although I cannot have been more than six years old at the
time I had definite ideas about genius, and especially about musi-

cal genius. One did not expect a genius to behave like other men in any respect; the divine afflatus, with which geniuses were filled, permitted of nothing that was common-place. Geniuses were also notably idiosyncratic in the matter of hair. I had heard Creatore draw ravishing music from his concert band during the afternoon, and I looked forward with delight to his evening performance; his hair fell to his shoulders in glistening black ringlets; his manner of eating could only be described as vivacious gormandizing. Plainly the man was a genius, and I watched him with such awe that I was barely able to eat.

Other boys went to the CNE to see automobiles, or to haunt the Midway, or to collect samples of food in the Pure Food exhibits, or to gape at effigies of the Prince of Wales, modelled in creamery butter. I went to hear bands. My father paid occasional visits to the Press Building, and one of my brothers took a queer interest in a dingy little building where paintings were hung; but what real business would a family of Welsh extraction have at such an affair as the CNE except to listen to the bands? In our household music was not a hobby or a pastime; it was one of life's chief preoccupations. My father sang and played the flute and directed a choir; my mother sang and played the piano; one of my brothers sang and wrought manfully with the cornet. I sang myself — a piece which began:

A little pink rose in my garden grew,
The prettiest rose of them all;
'Twas kissed by the sun and caressed by the Jew ...

"By the dew," the voice of authority would say. But next time the Jew would be sure to get into it, and I saw no harm in him. After all, was not Mendelssohn, an effigy of whom sat upon the piano top, a Jew? To a boy reared thus, what could the CNE offer to touch its bands?

At the time of my earliest acquaintance with the CNE my musical taste lacked chastity. It was chastened later by a Scottish music master, and reached a fine peak of virginal austerity when I was about 21. Of late years it has begun to grow a little blowsy, and there are times when I feel that I could relish one of

Creatore's band concerts again. He liked richly emotional music, and to it he brought his own fine endowment of sentiment. It is many years since I heard music played as melodramatically as it was played by his band. Rossini, von Suppé, Auber — these were musicians whose works he played. But it was in Verdi that he showed his strength.

His rendition of the Miserere from *Il Trovatore* was a masterly piece of showmanship. Before it was played there would be a short pause while the principal cornet player left the bandstand, and removed himself to a considerable distance, in the darkness (for this was inescapably a piece for the evening concert). The dreary howling of the monks was heard, and the plaint of Leonora, and then, magically,

Ah, I have sighed to rest me,
Deep in the quiet grave —

It was the principal cornet, personating the imprisoned Manrico, far away in the darkness. It would have drawn tears from a brazen image. When it was over Signor Creatore was forced to bow again and again.

There were other bands, of course, chiefly English bands from the Guards regiments and a few lay bands, like the Besses o' the Barn. These bands played in a style quite different from that which Creatore displayed so magnificently, and they played different music. I even heard an American band — naval, I think — on one occasion, but did not care for it, as both the vigorous emotionalism of the Italian, and what I may call the imperial grandeur of the English bands were lacking.

One of the great tests of a band, of course, was its manner of playing *God Save the King*. Creatore sought to astound his hearers by running the emotional gamut in this piece of 14 bars. He began sadly and very softly, as though His Majesty were on his last legs and prayer unavailing; then he plucked up hope, then he exulted, then he blared in triumph. It was exhausting, glorious, and took twice as much time as the English bands required to play the same piece. The English did it with effortless superiority, as though to say: "We have frequently played this air in the presence of the King-Emperor and have reason to believe that he was perfectly satisfied." The American band gave an impression that every man was treacherously muttering the words of *My Country 'Tis of Thee* into his instrument; which was, of course, intolerable. I have probably misjudged this band, for like most children I was a patriotic bigot.

Music played an important part, also, in the nightly spectacle which was held before the grandstand. Here one was likely to be confronted with a choir of one thousand voices, which sang slowly and carefully, much as one understands the ancient Roman hydraulus, or water organ, to have been played; like the hydraulus, too, its sound could be heard for approximately 60 miles. Nero was fond of the hydraulus, and Nero would have liked the CNE choir. I preferred the clowns who rescued furniture from a burning house, and tumbled out of upstairs windows with pianos in their arms. I did not care for the policemen who rode their horses in a seemingly interminable gyration called a Musical Ride, for it did not appear to me to be sufficiently musical, and it was obvious that as a ride it was giving no pleasure to anyone. But the fireworks with which the performance came to an end were superb; they rejoiced the eye as Creatore had feasted the ear.

In the recollections of many of my Canadian contemporaries the Midway plays a prominent part, but it is not so with me. I recall a journey through something which was called a House of Mirth, and I remember that the final mirthful burst consisted of being shot down a chute into the arms of two large, sweaty men, who stood on one's feet. This was probably very merry for middle-aged women, but I did not like it. Nor did I care for the sad-faced monkeys who were strapped into tiny motor cars and whizzed rapidly round a track. I liked to gape at giants, dwarfs, and malformed persons; but this was considered, quite rightly, to be a displeasing characteristic in a child and was not encouraged. My curiosity was in no way cruel. Deviations from the commonplace attracted me strongly, as they still do; and to me the hermaphrodite and the living skeleton were interesting for the same reason as was Creatore, or the resplendent Guardsmen of the bands — because such people did not often come my way and I hoped that they might impart some great revelation to me, some insight which would help me to a clearer understanding of the world about me. There are people, I know, who refuse to believe that children ever think in this way, but my remembrance on this point is clear and, I believe, honest.

Because the Toronto Saturnalia played so important a part in my early life I did not quickly grasp the possibility, when I was living abroad at a later time, that foreigners might not have heard of it. Every country of any size has, I now believe, some similar jamboree which it solemnly believes to be the finest exhibition of its kind on earth. I have spoken of the CNE to Frenchmen and they have not been impressed; they prefer to talk about occasional Paris expositions which are, they assure me, very large and very gay. Englishmen are unsatisfactory in the same way; they assume that the CNE is an inferior Wembley. Australians seem to think that the CNE must be a mild Canadian version of the Melbourne Show. I have talked eloquently about the great age of the CNE and of its remarkable place in our national life, but I have found that even Westerners do not fully believe me. And here and there I have discovered disaffected and contumacious persons who call it (pretending afterward that it was a slip of the tongue) "the Toronto Fair." I suppose one has to be born and bred in Eastern Canada to understand the true and abiding inwardness, the mystical essence, of the CNE; one must have attended it as a child.

My most recent visit to the CNE was during its last epiphany before it was suspended because of the war. I had hoped for a band, but there was none which could engage my attention. Lily Pons was there, but I have an unreasonable prejudice against listening to singers while standing in a restless crowd. The pageant before the grandstand lacked theme and clowns. The whole show was showing the strain of war. But even in such reduced circumstances it had something of its old magic, and I was not sorry that I had gone. I shall go again. I will never be one of those zealots who sleep on the ground outside the main gates for a week before the Exhibition opens, in order to be the first inside; but I shall go from time to time, and if I ever get my Cloak of Invisibility I shall go quite often.

There are people who maintain that one may achieve invisibility for a time by eating fern seed. I may try it this year, and drop in for a few hours at the CNE. My desire to be invisible is simply explained: I want to watch people closely without attracting their attention, and I have never mastered the trick of doing this which detectives are said to possess. When I stare at someone, he stiffens, glares about him till he finds me, and stares in return. Sometimes he makes personal remarks. Yet I mean him no harm, and my intent gaze implies no criticism. When I stare at women their necks grow red and they nudge their escorts. When I stare at children they weep. My staring is innocent of evil intention, however. I merely want to see what people are doing, and if possible to divine what they think about it. The CNE is an ideal spot for this pursuit, and when I was a child I could stare to my heart's content and no one noticed me. I long to recover once again this most precious of the gifts of childhood.

If, therefore, I should partially materialize at your side when you are visiting the CNE this year, apparent yet transparent, and staring with the intensity of a hypnotist, you will know that the effect of the fern seed is beginning to wear off.

QUESTIONS

Recollections of the events of one's childhood are apt to seem merely sentimental when recounted to others. The trick is somehow not to get drowned in the past which suddenly bubbles up in the memory as though it were really present. Nor must the writer, as adult, allow himself to dissolve backwards into the child. The past must be present, but not present; the man, boy, yet not boy.

1. In what ways and by what means does Robertson Davies avoid the sentimental in this essay?

2. What is done in the opening paragraphs to keep you constantly aware of the adult as well as the child, of the distance between past and present?

3. How is this control of distance confirmed by the paragraph on the author's musical taste, and by his amusing distinction between Italian, British, and Canadian bands?

4. What is the significance of the author's remarks about "honest" recollection just after his description of the midway? And why is there a paragraph on what Frenchmen and Australians and Britishers think of the CNE?

5. What is the role of the "fern seed" and "The Cloak of Invisibility" in holding past and present together and yet apart, in the playful embrace of the future?

*Bertrand*

*Russell*

# The science to save us from science

*Bertrand Russell (1872-1970) was born in Wales. A grandson of the great Victorian statesman, Lord John Russell, he is a member of one of England's most distinguished families. Educated at Trinity College, Cambridge, he first won attention with the* Principia Mathematica *(1910-13), in collaboration with Alfred North Whitehead. As a philosopher, he has had a major influence on contemporary thought and he has ventured forcefully into the discussion of politics, morals, and education. Among his major publications are:* Mysticism and Logic *(1914),* Skeptical Essays *(1928),* The Scientific Outlook *(1931),* A History of Western Philosophy *(1945), and* The Impact of Science on Society *(1951). The following essay appeared in* Great Essays in Science, *edited by Martin Gardner and published by Pocket Books, Inc.*

SINCE THE BEGINNING of the seventeenth century scientific discovery and invention have advanced at a continually increasing rate. This fact has made the last three hundred and fifty years profoundly different from all previous ages. The gulf separating man from his past has widened from generation to generation, and finally from decade to decade. A reflective person, meditating on the extinction of trilobites, dinosaurs and mammoths, is driven to ask himself some very disquieting questions. Can our species endure so rapid a change? Can the habits which insured survival in a comparatively stable past still suffice amid the kaleidoscopic scenery of our time? And, if not, will it be possible to change ancient patterns of behavior as quickly as the inventors change our material environment? No one knows the answer, but it is possible to survey probabilities, and to form some hypotheses as to the alternative directions that human development may take.

The first question is: Will scientific advance continue to grow more and more rapid, or will it reach a maximum speed and then begin to slow down?

The discovery of scientific method required genius, but its utilization requires only talent. An intelligent young scientist, if he gets a job giving access to a good laboratory, can be pretty certain of finding out something of interest, and may stumble upon some new fact of immense importance. Science, which was still a rebellious force in the early seventeenth century, is now integrated with the life of the community by the support of governments and universities. And as its importance becomes more evident, the number of people employed in scientific research continually increases. It would seem to follow that, so long as social and economic conditions do not become adverse, we may expect the rate of scientific advance to be maintained, and even increased, until some new limiting factor intervenes.

It might be suggested that, in time, the amount of knowledge needed before a new discovery could be made would become so great as to absorb all the best years of a scientist's life, so that by the time he reached the frontier of knowledge he would be senile. I suppose this may happen some day, but that day is certainly very distant. In the first place, methods of teaching improve. Plato thought that students in his academy would have to spend ten years learning what was then known of mathematics; nowadays any mathematically minded schoolboy learns much more mathematics in a year.

In the second place, with increasing specialization, it is possible to reach the frontier of knowledge along a narrow path, involving much less labor than a broad highway. In the third place, the frontier is not a circle but an irregular contour, in some places not far from the center. Mendel's epoch-making discovery required little previous knowledge; what it needed was a life of elegant leisure spent in a garden. Radio-activity was discovered by the fact that some specimens of pitchblende were unexpectedly found to have photographed themselves in the dark. I do not think, therefore, that purely intellectual reasons will slow up scientific advances for a very long time to come.

There is another reason for expecting scientific advance to continue, and that is that it increasingly attracts the best brains. Leonardo da Vinci was equally pre-eminent in art and science, but it was from art that he derived his greatest fame. A man of similar endowments living at the present day would almost certainly hold some post which would require his giving all his time to science; if his politics were orthodox, he would probably be engaged in devising the hydrogen bomb, which our age would consider more useful than his pictures. The artist, alas, has not the status that he once had. Renaissance princes might compete for Michelangelo; modern states compete for nuclear physicists.

There are considerations of quite a different sort which might lead to an expectation of scientific retrogression. It may be held that science itself generates explosive forces which will, sooner or later, make it impossible to preserve the kind of society in which science can flourish. This is a large and different question, to which no confident answer can be given. It is a very important question, which deserves to be examined. Let us therefore see what is to be said about it.

Industrialism, which is in the main a product of science, has provided a certain way of life and a certain outlook on the world. In America and Britain, the oldest industrial countries, this outlook and this way of life have come gradually, and the population has been able to adjust itself to them without any violent breach of continuity. These countries, accordingly, did not develop dangerous psychological stresses. Those who preferred the old ways could remain on the land, while the more adventurous could migrate to the new centres of industry. There they found pioneers who were compatriots, who shared in the main the general outlook of their neighbors. The only protests came from men like Carlyle and Ruskin, whom everybody at once praised and disregarded.

It was a very different matter when industrialism and science, as well-developed systems, burst violently upon countries hitherto ignorant of both, especially since they came as something foreign, demanding imitation of enemies and disruption of ancient national habits. In varying degrees this shock has been endured by Germany, Russia, Japan, India, and the natives of Africa. Everywhere it has caused and is causing upheavals of one sort or another, of which as yet no one can foresee the end.

The earliest important result of the impact of industrialism on Germans was the Communist Manifesto. We think of this now as the Bible of one of the two powerful groups into which the world is divided, but it is worth while to think back to its origin in 1848. It then shows itself as an expression of admiring horror by two young university students from a pleasant and peaceful cathedral city, brought roughly and without intellectual preparation into the hurly-burly of Manchester competition.

Germany, before Bismarck had "educated" it, was a deeply religious country, with a quiet, exceptional sense of public duty. Competition, which the British regarded as essential to efficiency, and which Darwin elevated to an almost cosmic dignity, shocked the Germans, to whom service to the state seemed the obviously right moral ideal. It was therefore natural that they should fit industrialism into a framework of nationalism or socialism. The Nazis combined both. The somewhat insane and frantic character of German industrialism and the policies it inspired is due to its foreign origin and its sudden advent.

Marx's doctrine was suited to countries where industrialism was new. The German Social Democrats abandoned his dogmas when their country became industrially adult. But by that time Russia was where Germany had been in 1848, and it was natural that Marxism should find a new home. Stalin, with great skill, has combined the new revolutionary creed with the traditional belief in "Holy Russia" and the "Little Father." This is as yet the most notable example of the arrival of science in an environment that is not ripe for it. China bids fair to follow suit.

Japan, like Germany, combined modern technique with worship of the state. Educated Japanese abandoned as much of their ancient way of life as was necessary in order to secure industrial and military efficiency. Sudden change produced collective hysteria, leading to insane visions of world power unrestrained by traditional pieties.

These various forms of madness — communism, nazism, Japanese imperialism — are the natural result of the impact of science on nations with a strong pre-scientific culture. The effects in Asia are still at an early stage. The effects upon the native races of Africa have hardly begun. It is therefore unlikely that the world will recover sanity in the near future.

The future of science — nay more, the future of mankind — depends upon whether it will be possible to restrain these various collective hysterias until the populations concerned have had time to adjust themselves to the new scientific environment. If such adjustment proves impossible, civilized society will disappear, and science will be only a dim memory. In the Dark Ages science was not distinguished from sorcery, and it is not impossible that a new Dark Ages may revive this point of view.

The danger is not remote; it threatens within the next few years. But I am not now concerned with such immediate issues. I am concerned with the wider question: Can a society based, as ours is, on science and scientific technique, have the sort of stability that many societies had in the past, or is it bound to develop explosive forces that will destroy it? This question takes us beyond the sphere of science into that of ethics and moral codes and the imaginative understanding of mass psychology. This last is a matter which political theorists have quite unduly neglected.

Let us begin with moral codes. I will illustrate the problem by a somewhat trivial illustration. There are those who think it wicked to smoke tobacco, but they are mostly people untouched by science. Those whose outlook has been strongly influenced by science usually take the view that smoking is neither a vice nor a virtue. But when I visited a Nobel works, where rivers of nitroglycerine flowed like water, I had to leave all matches at the entrance, and it was obvious that to smoke inside the works would be an act of appalling wickedness.

This instance illustrates two points: first, that a scientific outlook tends to make some parts of traditional moral codes appear superstitious and irrational; second, that by creating a new environment science creates new duties, which may happen to coincide with those that have been discarded. A world containing hydrogen bombs is like one containing rivers of nitro-glycerine; actions elsewhere harmless may become dangerous in the highest degree. We need therefore, in a scientific world, a somewhat different moral code from the one inherited from the past. But to give a new moral code sufficient compulsive force to restrain actions formerly considered harmless is not easy, and cannot possibly be achieved in a day.

As regards ethics, what is important is to realize the new dangers and to consider what ethical outlook will do most to diminish them. The most important new facts are that the world is more unified than it used to be, and that communities at war with each other have more power of inflicting mutual disaster than at any former time. The question of power has a new importance. Science has enormously increased human power, but has not increased it without limit. The increase of power brings an increase of responsibility; it brings also a danger of arrogant self-assertion, which can only be averted by continuing to remember that man is not omnipotent.

The most influential sciences, hitherto, have been physics and chemistry; biology is just beginning to rival them. But before very long psychology and especially mass psychology, will be recognized as the most important of all sciences from the standpoint of human welfare. It is obvious that populations have dominant moods, which change from time to time according to their circumstances. Each mood has a corresponding ethic. Nelson inculcated these ethical principles on midshipmen: to tell the truth, to shoot straight, and to hate a Frenchman as you would the devil. This last was chiefly because the English were angry with France for intervening on the side of America; Shakespeare's Henry V says:

*If it be a sin to covet honour,*
*I am the most offending soul alive.*

This is the ethical sentiment that goes with aggressive imperialism: "honour" is proportional to the number of harmless people you slaughter. A great many sins may be excused under the name of "patriotism." On the other hand complete powerlessness suggests humility and submission as the greatest virtues; hence the vogue of stoicism in the Roman Empire and of Methodism among the English poor in the early nineteenth century. When, however, there is a chance of successful revolt, fierce vindictive justice suddenly becomes the dominant ethical principle.

In the past, the only recognized way of inculcating moral precepts has been by preaching. But this method has very definite limitations: it is notorious that, on the average, sons of clergy are not morally superior to other people. When science has mastered this field, quite different methods will be adopted. It will be known what circumstances generate what moods, and what moods incline men to what ethical systems. Governments will then decide what sort of morality their subjects are to have and their subjects will adopt what the Government favours, but will do so under the impression that they are exercising free will. This may sound unduly cynical, but that is only because we are not yet accustomed to applying science to the human mind. Science has powers for evil, not only physically, but mentally: the hydrogen bomb can kill the body, and government propaganda (as in Russia) can kill the mind.

In view of the terrifying power that science is conferring on governments, it is necessary that those who control governments should have enlightened and intelligent ideals, since otherwise they can lead mankind to disaster.

I call an ideal "intelligent" when it is possible to approximate to it by pursuing it. This is by no means sufficient as an ethical criterion, but it is a test by which many aims can be condemned. It cannot be supposed that Hitler desired the fate which he brought upon his country and himself, and yet it was pretty certain that this would be the result of his arrogance. Therefore the ideal of *Deutschland über Alles* can be condemned as unintelligent. (I do not mean to suggest that this is its only defect.) Spain, France, Germany, and Russia have successively sought world dominion; three of them have endured defeat in consequence, but their fate has not inspired wisdom.

Whether science — and indeed civilization in general — can long survive depends upon psychology, that is to say, it depends upon what human beings desire. The human beings concerned are rulers in totalitarian countries, and the mass of men and women in democracies. Political passions determine political conduct much more directly than is often supposed. If men desire victory more than cooperation, they will think victory possible.

But if hatred so dominates them that they are more anxious to see their enemies killed than to keep their own children alive, they will discover all kinds of "noble" reasons in favor of war. If they resent inferiority or wish to preserve superiority, they will have the sentiments that promote the class war. If they are bored beyond a point, they will welcome excitement even of a painful kind.

Such sentiments, when widespread, determine the policies and decisions of nations. Science can, if rulers so desire, create sentiments which will avert disaster and facilitate cooperation. At present there are powerful rulers who have no such wish. But the possibility exists, and science can be just as potent for good as for evil. It is not science, however, which will determine how science is used.

Science, by itself, cannot supply us with an ethic. It can show us how to achieve a given end, and it may show us that some ends cannot be achieved. But among ends that can be achieved our choice must be decided by other than purely scientific considerations. If a man were to say, "I hate the human race, and I think it would be a good thing if it were exterminated", we could say, "Well, my dear sir, let us begin the process with you." But this is hardly argument, and no amount of science could prove such a man mistaken.

But all who are not lunatics are agreed about certain things: That it is better to be alive than dead, better to be adequately fed than starved, better to be free than a slave. Many people desire those things only for themselves and their friends; they are quite content that their enemies should suffer. These people can be refuted by science: Mankind has become so much one family that we cannot insure our own prosperity except by insuring that of everyone else. If you wish to be happy yourself, you must resign yourself to seeing others also happy.

Whether science can continue, and whether, while it continues, it can do more good than harm, depends upon the capacity of mankind to learn this simple lesson. Perhaps it is necessary that all should learn it, but it must be learned by all who have great power, and among those some still have a long way to go.

QUESTIONS

1. Bertrand Russell asks three questions in the first paragraph of this essay. How is each question answered in the development of the essay?

2. Why is each question of crucial importance for us now?

3. What reasons does the author give to support his conviction that science will continue to advance?

4. In what different ways has modern society been affected by science?

5. How does the author explain the emergence in our time of Communism, Nazism, and Japanese Imperialism?

6. Why does the author believe that new moral codes have to be devised to fit the needs of a scientific world?

7. How does he attempt to argue that all "moral codes" and "ethical sentiments" are the temporary creations of particular times and needs? Note his examples.

8. What values and ideals does Bertrand Russell believe to be permanent and unchanging?

9. How are these ideals and values to be preserved? What *is* the science which can save us from science?

10. Would Russell's faith in reason and the principles of psychology satisfy William Faulkner (Part One)? Hugh MacLennan (Part One)? C. S. Lewis (Part Three)? What has Russell left out of the reasonable medicine he has prepared for us?

*Gilbert Keith*

*Chesterton*

# The logic of elfland

---

*Gilbert Keith Chesterton (1874-1936) was born at Campden Hill, London, England, and educated at St. Paul's School and the Slade School of Art. One of the great wits of his time and a superb literary stylist, he published, with almost equal success, poetry, light essays, literary criticism, and fiction. His Father Brown detective stories are still widely popular, and his critical studies of the great Victorian,* Robert Browning *(1903), and* Charles Dickens *(1906), contain brilliant insights, as does his study of* Chaucer *(1932). He was received into the Roman Catholic Church in 1922 and became one of that Church's most compelling champions. Of his many writings,* St. Francis of Assisi *(1923) and* The Everlasting Man *(1925) are perhaps the most memorable. For many present-day readers, his reputation rests on the dazzling play of mind revealed in the best essays and poems. "The Logic of Elfland" is reprinted from Mr. Chesterton's* Orthodoxy *by permission of the publisher, The Bodley Head, Ltd.*

---

MY FIRST AND LAST PHILOSOPHY, that which I believe in with unbroken certainty, I learnt in the nursery. I generally learnt it from a nurse; that is, from the solemn and star-appointed priestess at once of democracy and tradition. The things I believed most then, the things I believe most now, are the things called fairy tales. They seem to me to be the entirely reasonable things. They are not fantasies: compared with them other things are fantastic. Compared with them religion and rationalism are both abnormal, though religion is abnormally right and rationalism abnormally wrong. Fairyland is nothing but the sunny country of common sense. It is not earth that judges heaven, but heaven that judges earth; so for me at least it was not earth that criticised elfland, but elfland that criticised the earth. I knew the magic beanstalk before I had tasted beans; I was sure of the Man in the Moon before I was certain of the moon. This was at one with all popular tradition. Modern minor poets are naturalists, and talk about the bush or the brook; but the singers of the old epics and fables were supernaturalists, and talked about the gods of brook and bush. That is what the moderns mean when they say that the ancients did not "appreciate Nature", because they said that Nature was divine. Old nurses do not tell children about the grass, but about the fairies that dance on the grass; and the old Greeks could not see the trees for the dryads.

But I deal here with what ethic and philosophy come from being fed on fairy tales. If I were describing them in detail I could note many noble and healthy principles that arise from them. There is the chivalrous lesson of *Jack the Giant Killer;* that giants should be killed because they are gigantic. It is a manly mutiny against pride as such. For the rebel is older than all the kingdoms, and the Jacobin has more tradition than the Jacobite. There is the lesson of *Cinderella,* which is the same as that of the Magnificat — *exaltavit humiles.* There is the great lesson of *Beauty and the Beast;* that a thing must be loved *before* it is lovable. There is the terrible allegory of the *Sleeping Beauty*, which tells how the human creature was blessed with all birthday gifts, yet cursed with death; and how death also may perhaps be softened to a sleep. But I am not concerned with any of the separate statutes of elfland, but with the whole spirit of its law, which I learnt before I could speak, and shall retain when I cannot write. I am concerned with a certain way of looking at life, which was created in me by the fairy tales, but has since been meekly ratified by the mere facts.

It might be stated this way. There are certain sequences or developments (cases of one thing following another), which are, in the true sense of the word, reasonable. They are, in the true sense of the word, necessary. Such are mathematical and merely logical sequences. We in fairyland (who are the most reasonable of all creatures) admit that reason and that necessity. For instance, if the Ugly Sisters are older than Cinderella, it is (in an iron and awful sense) *necessary* that Cinderella is younger than the Ugly Sisters. There is no getting out of it. Haeckel may talk as much fatalism about that fact as he pleases: it really must be. If Jack is the son of a miller, a miller is the father of Jack. Cold reason decrees it from her awful throne: and we in fairyland submit. If the three brothers all ride horses, there are six animals and eighteen legs involved: that is true rationalism, and fairyland is full of it. But as I put my head over the hedge of the elves and began to take notice of the natural world, I observed an extraordinary thing. I observed that learned men in spectacles were talking of the actual things that happened — dawn and death and so on — as if *they* were rational and inevitable. They talked as if the fact that trees bear fruit were just as *necessary* as the fact that two and one trees make three. But it is not. There is an enormous difference by the test of fairyland; which is the test of the imagination. You cannot *imagine* two and one not making three. But you can easily imagine trees not growing fruit; you can imagine them growing golden candlesticks or tigers hanging on by the tail. These men in spectacles spoke much of a man named Newton, who was hit by an apple, and who discovered a law. But they could not be got to see the distinction between a true law, a law of reason, and the mere fact of apples falling. If the apple hit Newton's nose, Newton's nose hit the apple. That is a true necessity: because we cannot conceive the one occurring without the other. But we can quite well conceive the apple not falling on his nose; we can fancy it flying ardently through the air to hit some other nose, of which it had a more definite dislike. We have always in our fairy tales kept this sharp distinction between the science of mental relations, in which there really are laws, and the science of physical facts, in which there are no laws, but only weird repetitions. We believe in bodily miracles, but not in mental impossibilities. We believe that a Beanstalk climbed up to Heaven; but that does not at all confuse our convictions on the philosophical question of how many beans make five.

Here is the peculiar perfection of tone and truth in the nursery tales. The man of science says, "Cut the stalk, and the apple will fall"; but he says it calmly, as if the one idea really led up to the other. The witch in the fairy tale says, "Blow the horn, and the ogre's castle will fall"; but she does not say it as if it were something in which the effect obviously arose out of the cause. Doubtless she has given the advice to many champions, and has seen many castles fall, but she does not lose either her wonder or her reason. She does not muddle her head until it imagines a necessary mental connection between a horn and a falling tower. But the scientific men do muddle their heads, until they imagine a necessary mental connection between an apple leaving the tree and an apple reaching the ground. They do really talk as if they had found not only a set of marvellous facts, but a truth connecting those facts. They do talk as if the connection of two strange things physically connected them philosophically. They feel that because one incomprehensible thing constantly follows another incomprehensible thing the two together somehow make up a comprehensible thing. Two black riddles make a white answer.

In fairyland we avoid the word "law"; but in the land of science they are singularly fond of it. Thus they will call some interesting conjecture about how forgotten folks pronounced the alphabet, Grimm's Law. But Grimm's Law is far less intellectual than Grimm's Fairy Tales. The tales are, at any rate, certainly tales; while the law is not a law. A law implies that we know the nature of the generalisation and enactment; not merely that we have noticed some of the effects. If there is a law that pick-pockets shall go to prison, it implies that there is an imaginable mental connection between the idea of prison and the idea of picking pockets. And we know what the idea is. We can say why we take liberty from a man who takes liberties. But we cannot say why an egg can turn into a chicken any more than we can say why a bear could turn into a fairy prince. As *ideas*, the egg and the chicken are further off each other than the bear and the prince; for no egg in itself suggests a chicken, whereas some princes do suggest bears. Granted, then, that certain transformations do happen, it is essential that we should regard them in the philosophic manner of fairy tales, not in the unphilosophic manner of science and the "Laws of Nature." When we are asked why eggs turn to birds or fruits fall in autumn, we must answer exactly as the fairy godmother would answer if Cinderella asked her why mice turned to horses or her clothes fell from her at twelve o'clock. We must answer that it is *magic*. It is not a "law", for we do not understand its general formula. It is not a necessity, for though we can count on it happening practically, we have no right to say that it must always happen. It is no argument for unalterable law (as Huxley fancied) that we count on the ordinary course of things. We do not count on it; we bet on it. We risk the remote possibility of a miracle as we do that of a poisoned pancake or a world-destroying comet. We leave it out of account, not because it is a miracle, and therefore an impossibility, but because it is a miracle, and therefore an exception. All the terms used in the science books, "law," "necessity," "order," "tendency," and so on, are really unintellectual, because they assume an inner synthesis which we do not possess. The only words that ever satisfied me as describing Nature are the terms used in the fairy books, "charm," "spell," "enchantment." They express the arbitrariness of the fact and its mystery. A tree grows fruit because it is a *magic* tree. Water runs downhill because it is bewitched. The sun shines because it is bewitched.

I deny altogether that this is fantastic or even mystical. We may have some mysticism later on; but this fairy-tale language about things is simply rational and agnostic. It is the only way I can express in words my clear and definite perception that one thing is quite distinct from another; that there is no logical connection between flying and laying eggs. It is the man who talks about "a law" that he has never seen who is the mystic. Nay, the ordinary scientific man is strictly a sentimentalist. He is a sentimentalist in this essential sense, that he is soaked and swept away by mere associations. He has so often seen birds fly and lay eggs that he feels as if there must be some dreamy, tender connection between the two ideas, whereas there is none. A forlorn lover might be unable to dissociate the moon from lost love; so the materialist is unable to dissociate the moon from the tide. In both cases there is no connection, except that one has seen them together. A sentimentalist might shed tears at the smell of apple-blossom, because, by a dark association of his own, it reminded him of his boyhood. So the materialist professor (though he conceals his tears) is yet a sentimentalist, because, by a dark association of his own, apple-blossoms remind him of apples. But the cool rationalist from fairyland does not see why, in the abstract, the apple tree should not grow crimson tulips; it sometimes does in his country.

This elementary wonder, however, is not a mere fancy derived from the fairy tales; on the contrary, all the fire of the fairy tales is derived from this. Just as we all like love tales because there is an instinct of sex, we all like astonishing tales because they touch the nerve of the ancient instinct of astonishment. This is proved by the fact that when we are very young children we do not need fairy tales: we only need tales. Mere life is interesting enough. A child of seven is excited by being told that Tommy opened a door and saw a dragon. But a child of three is excited by being told that Tommy opened a door. Boys like romantic tales; but babies like realistic tales — because they find them romantic. In fact, a baby is about the only person, I should think, to whom a modern realistic novel could be read without boring him. This proves that even nursery tales only echo an almost pre-natal leap of interest and amazement. These tales say that apples were golden only to refresh the forgotten moment when we found that they were green. They make rivers run with wine only to make us remember, for one wild moment, that they run with water. I have said that this is wholly reasonable and even agnostic. And, indeed, on this point I am all for the higher agnosticism; its better name is Ignorance. We have all read in scientific books, and, indeed, in all romances, the story of the man who has forgotten his name. This man walks about the streets and can see and appreciate everything; only he cannot remember who he is.

Well, every man is that man in the story. Every man has forgotten who he is. One may understand the cosmos, but never the ego; the self is more distant than any star. Thou shalt love the Lord thy God; but thou shalt not know thyself. We are all under the same mental calamity; we have all forgotten our names. We have all forgotten what we really are. All that we call common sense and rationality and practicality and positivism only means that for certain dead levels of our life we forget that we have forgotten. All that we call spirit and art and ecstasy only means that for one awful instant we remember that we forget.

QUESTIONS

1. What immediately suggests that Chesterton's view of reality is wholly unlike Bertrand Russell's? In other words, what human faculty does Chesterton stress which Bertrand Russell completely ignores?

2. What does the author mean by the *spirit* of the law of elfland?

3. Why does the author seem to object to the "law" of cause and effect? Why does he prefer the term "magic" to "law"? Why does he call the scientist a "sentimentalist" (like "the forlorn lover") and the imaginative man a "cool rationalist"?

4. Chesterton's playful, fanciful tone is deceptive — deliberately so. The reader allows himself to be charmed by an almost child-like (never childish) play of thought. And then, suddenly, we know that this is not play (or not *just* play). Where — and how — does the author reveal that he is in dead earnest — that his elfland *is* real?

5. What does he mean by saying that "the self is more distant than any star"?

6. Would Chesterton not say that Bertrand Russell, his scientists, and his mass psychologists are men who have forgotten what they really are? Why?

7. Are the views of Bertrand Russell and G. K. Chesterton wholly incompatible?

*Gilbert*

*Highet*

# Henry Fowler: modern English usage

*Gilbert Highet (b. 1906), teacher, essayist and critic, was born and educated in Glasgow, Scotland. After graduating from Glasgow University in 1928, he did further study at Oxford and lectured there in Classics until 1938, when he came to Columbia University, New York. His academic career was interrupted from 1941 to 1946 by a period of military service with the British army, but after being demobilised he returned to Columbia, where he is now Anthon Professor of the Latin Language and Literature. He has become widely known through his broadcast talks, later collected as essays in* People, Places and Books *(1953),* A Clerk at Oxenford *(1954), and through his position on the editorial board of* The Book of the Month Club. *Some of his other books dealing with classical authors and ideas are* The Classical Tradition *(1949),* Juvenal the Satirist *(1954),* The Migration of Ideas *(1954) and* Poets in a Landscape *(1957). His essay on Fowler is typical of his interest in language and his respect for those who use it well. This essay is reprinted from* People, Places, and Books *by Gilbert Highet (copyright 1953 by Gilbert Highet), by permission of Oxford University Press, Inc.*

READING BOOKS is a pleasure. But if it is a pleasure to read books, it is also a pleasure to talk about them. I suppose it is a way of reliving the pleasure the book gave us originally, when we first ate it and digested it. Gourmets, like Brillat-Savarin, do the same with meals which have been cooked and served to them long ago. The difference is that the gourmet has a diminishing pleasure, as time wears on. People who talk about books have a perpetual pleasure, and often an increasing pleasure as their taste grows finer, their memory richer.

There are not too many books which give us such pleasure. When we meet them, we recommend them to one another. One of my perennial favorites is *Modern English Usage*, by Henry Fowler, published in 1926, and still a heavy seller. I bought it first in 1929, when I went up to Oxford, and I am now on my second copy. It was, I believe, a standby of the late Alexander Woollcott; Harold Ross of *The New Yorker* was devoted to it; and one of the most battered copies I have ever seen was on the desk of the editor of a famous newspaper — he told me he used it every day, and sometimes every hour.

Before we look at this remarkable book, who was its author, Fowler himself? He was a strange fellow. He was one of those eccentrics who seem to be a special product of England — not the wild surrealist eccentrics, but the logical eccentrics, who decide exactly what to do in a large number of situations, do it with relentless consistency, and omit to notice that logical behaviour often looks perfectly crazy to the rest of the world. He was rather like the White Knight in *Alice,* except that the Knight was ineffective while Fowler was ferociously efficient. If you had seen a little man with bright red cheeks, a great pointed beard, and a perfectly bald head, running briskly through the streets of London to bathe in the Serpentine (at least once breaking the ice to do so); or if you had seen him working at his proofs while sitting outside his cottage in the Channel Islands in a November sea-mist, wearing football shorts and a jersey (or should it be a guernsey?), you would have recognized one of the long line of English eccentrics which begins with Chaucer and is still flourishing in the person of Mr. Churchill.

Fowler was nearly seventy when the book came out: for he was born almost a century ago now, in 1858. He went to one of the private schools which the English persist in calling public schools (it was Rugby), and then on to Oxford, where he was at Balliol College and had a mediocre record. He spent the first seventeen years of his working life as a schoolmaster at Sedbergh; and he was apparently rather bad: the reverse of Mr. Chips. The boys called him "Joey Stinker" because he smoked heavily. He had no distinguished pupils; he was too shy to teach well; all this period of his life was a failure which prepared him for his later success.

He gave up teaching at the age of forty-one, and went back to London to try free-lancing — for, like so many of the Englishmen we hear of in the nineteenth century, he had a private income: not much, but he was passing rich on £120 a year. After some time, the Oxford University Press learned of his undoubted talents and his wide knowledge of literature; and he was engaged to work upon the great *Oxford English Dictionary*, which thereafter became the focus of his life. (This makes him a fairly direct descendant of that other eccentric, Dr. Samuel Johnson.) In 1911, he brought out, as a by-product, a pocket dictionary which was not, like the big one, historically arranged, but straightforward and contemporary: *The Concise Oxford Dictionary of Current English.*

In the first World War he volunteered for ordinary service, at the age of fifty-seven (I *said* he was eccentric). He disguised his age as the acceptable one of forty-four. And, characteristically, he protested violently when he was not sent into the combat zone but kept unloading and guarding stores at a rear-area seaport. Finally he fell ill and was invalided out; his beloved brother Francis, who had worked with him and joined up with him, died of TB contracted in service. *Modern English Usage* was planned by the two, writing together, and is dedicated by Fowler to the memory of his brother.

He returned to civilian life and went on working on the *Oxford Dictionary*, writing a number of articles for specialist periodicals about the proper use of language, the avoidance of pedantry, and other subjects dear to his heart and his sharp, uncompromising, commonsensical mind. As the result of all the second twenty years of his career, *Modern English Usage* came out in 1926, was well received, and has been selling well ever since. He was astounded at the fan-mail which he got from all over the world, arguing, agreeing, contradicting, suggesting, admiring, or simply begging. A convict in a prison in California wrote and asked him for a free copy "to prepare him for a literary career when he had served his time". The man Fowler died in 1933, but the book — and this is the chief reason why people try to write good books — has gone on living.

And now, what about the book itself? *Modern English Usage* is set out like a dictionary; and indeed its full title is *A Dictionary of Modern English Usage*. But it gives much less information than a dictionary: hardly any derivations, no explanations of easy words, no attempt at completeness. In fact, it is a book about difficult and disputable words, habits, and groupings of words. Most of the information is given in short paragraphs. Let us look up one, and see how it works. What does *garble* mean? I am never quite sure myself. I should say a garbled story was a confused and unintelligible story, wouldn't you? Fowler will know, and he will tell us. Here he is:

> **garble.** The original meaning is to sift, to sort into sizes with a view to using the best or rejecting the worst. The modern transferred sense is to subject a set of facts, evidence, a report, a speech, &c., to such a process of sifting as results in presenting all of it that supports the impression one wishes to give of it & deliberately omitting all that makes against or qualifies this. **Garbling** stops short of falsification and misquotation, but not of misrepresentation; a garbled account is partial in both senses.

That is not quite typical of Fowler's style. His sentences are usually shorter, and more cutting. But it does give a fine impression of his clear, logical mind, and of his talent for conveying the maximum information without pedantry or waste of energy.

The paragraph also shows pretty clearly what the uses of the book are. Fowler had two chief aims in view. One was to help people who were vague or confused about the true meanings of words and the neatest and most exact methods of expression. Ought we to avoid a split infinitive at all costs? Is it necessary to

say something like this: "The four powers have combined to
forbid flatly hostilities" — because we are afraid of saying "to
flatly forbid hostilities"? Fowler will argue it out, and make it
clear to us.* The other purpose of his book was to prevent the
corruption of our language by the intrusion of clumsy, careless,
slipshod, or ignorant words and phrases. In speaking and writing,
as in other things, we acquire bad habits very easily, and soon
become unaware of them. They spread from one man to another,
then from one generation to another; they can infect a whole
epoch, and ruin what might have been forceful speech and convincing books. The only way to avoid such habits is constant
vigilance; and Fowler's work is a permanent warning.

The information is given in these short pithy paragraphs. The
warnings are mainly conveyed in longer articles. It is really delightful to read them, for they combine lucid thinking with pungent expression, and at their best they have the same style and
finish as a well-played game of chess. Very often Fowler gathers
a large variety of roughly similar mistakes together under a common heading, disposes of them all in one article, and then has only
to refer to it to convince his readers. To take an easy example, I
suppose we all remember the phrase coined by a late President:
*back to normalcy*. And I suppose most of us have felt uneasy
about it, perhaps without knowing exactly why. *Normalcy* ... it
sounds wrong. Look it up in Fowler, and you will know what is
wrong with it. He refers to his article on *Hybrid Derivatives*.
Turn to that article. It begins:

> Hybrid derivatives are words formed from a stem or word belong-
> ing to one language by applying to it a suffix or prefix belonging to
> another. It will be convenient to class with these the words, abor-
> tions rather than hybrids, in which all the elements belong indeed
> to one language, but are so put together as to outrage that language's
> principles of formation ... It will not be possible here to lay down
> rules for word-formation, which is a complicated business; but a
> few remarks on some of [these] words may perhaps instil caution,
> & a conviction that word-making, like other manufactures, should
> be done by those who know how to do it.

*See his article on *Split Infinitive*.

Well, that still does not tell us what is wrong with *back to normalcy*. But it shows us in which direction we should think. There is something wrong with the way the word is formed. *Normal* and *-cy* will not go together. Fowler does not tell us what is right — although a glance at the big Dictionary will show us. But he sets us to calculating. *Normalness?* No. *Normaltude?* No, no, no. But there is a formation which we do use; *abnormality;* and *formality;* and *legality.* That's it: *back to normality.*

There are two principles which govern language. One is usage: what most people say. The other is logic: what makes sense, what is consistent. Sometimes the two conflict, and then Fowler will use common sense and advise which we should follow. Often they agree, and then he will show us why. What he has — very briefly — shown us how to do is what we all do most of the time. Listen to two schoolboys talking about the behavior of a third. One will say, "That's stupid. That's real stupidity!" The other will add, "It's just plain dumbness" — he won't say, "dumbity." The first will go on, "It's just idiocy" — not "idiotness." Sometimes he will say *idiotcy;* and then, if he is wise, he will look up Fowler, who says

idiocy, -tcy. The - t - is wrong.*

Well, that is how Fowler works, and it is a pleasure to watch him working. He had a pretty sure touch, because he knew a great deal. He had an enormous store of information about the English language which he had gathered while working on the Dictionary. You see, what people sometimes forget about language is that it exists not only in space but in time. Spanish, for example, is not only the language which is spoken from the Pyrenées to the Straits of Gibraltar and from the Mexican frontier to Cape Horn (excepting Brazil and some enclaves). It is also the language in which Cervantes wrote his great novel and Góngora his astonishing pastoral poems; and although these books were born in the seventeenth century they are still alive, people still read them, they still matter, they still affect the language quite as much as what people say *now*, in *one district*. Similarly, when

*It is wrong because we don't say *vacantcy* or *advocatecy*.

Fowler met a problem in English, he asked himself not only what people were saying in 1910 or 1920, but also what they had written in the books which were still valid.

Here is a modern instance. During the last war the American government was putting out a phrase-book for soldiers who were to occupy a foreign country. One of the phrases was "I was laying on the bed." The language experts objected, and said that the correct American English was not that, but "I was lying on the bed." The compilers of the book replied that 90 per cent of the GIs who would use the book always said, "I was laying on the bed."

Who was right?

Fowler states the facts first, as he knew them from his reading. Lay means "put to rest", lie means "be at rest." One is transitive, the other in intransitive. But then he adds, "Confusion between the words lay and lie is very common in uneducated talk."

In fact, broad usage — the custom of our language as represented in its books for centuries and in the speech of educated people always — says, "I was lying on the bed." But the temporary usage of this single group of speakers at one time says "I was laying on the bed"; and since the Army book was being written only for that one purpose and time, it was right. Otherwise, wrong.

Fowler knew his historic English books well; he also knew contemporary writing well. He seems to have read all the daily and weekly papers and all the magazines, and to have clipped them for examples of good and bad writing. If he had put in only the horrors, the monstrous sentences which *The New Yorker* prints under headings like BLOCK THAT METAPHOR!, then his book would be rather painful to read. He really has some monsters, like this —

Recognition is given to it by no matter whom it is displayed.

And this:

Speculation on the subject of the constitution of the British representation at the Washington inauguration of the League of Nations . . .

But usually, when there is a problem, he not only prints what is wrong and analyses it to show why it is wrong, but provides the alternative that should have been chosen. He does the work of a good copy editor, but explains it, too: for instance, take this sentence of gobbledygook:

> As to how far such reinforcements are available, this is quite another matter.

Fowler says, "omit 'as to' and 'this' ":

> How far such reinforcements are available is quite another matter.

(He adds, "The writer has chosen to get out of the room by a fire-escape when the door was open.")

There are not many people who can write such a level-headed book on a subject which they know very well, practise very effectively, and worry about. (Fortified by Mr. Fowler's defense of the habit, I have just ended a sentence with a preposition.)

He has his faults, as all strong writers and teachers have. His prejudices, however, are not irritating. In particular, he was not biased against American English. He realized that it was simply a different form, both in time and in space. He could scarcely foresee the present era, when the two languages — partly as a result of the last war, partly because of the movies and magazines, and partly also because of the sharing of experiences and modes of thought — are crossing each other's frontiers. I have heard my American friends using slang which I thought was purely English, and South-Eastern English at that; and I have seen bold Americanisms on the austere pages of the *Times Literary Supplement*.

Fowler's chief fault was that he did not realize how fertile a living language like English still is, and how it can be expanded, remade, revitalized by the effort of strongly imaginative people and adventurous talkers and writers. He lived too much alone, and too much with old books, and too much away from the ordinary working man, to know that. It would have done him good to spend a year in the Yorkshire factories, or in the deep

South of the United States. He would have revised his views of the creative powers of our language if he had talked to the Negro mother who, when asked by the census-taker how old her children were, said: "I has one lap baby, one crawler, one porch chile, and one yard young 'un."

But his principal aim was not to encourage innovation, but to prevent degeneration and to promote flexibility, grace, and directness. Like Ernest Renan, he felt that a badly constructed sentence meant a badly formed thought, a truth ill conceived. He was not a creator. He was a teacher and a doctor. He loved our language when it was well spoken and well written. He hated the people who deform it by carelessness and ignorance: in the same way a doctor hates the men who pollute the public water supply or who sell decaying food. Therefore his book is really a draught of medicine — not sweet, not bitter, but astringent and cleansing. It is a good book because it is good for us, all of us, who speak, and write, and think.

QUESTIONS

1. Although the essay opens with enthusiastic comments about books, much of it is a character study of one man. How do you account for this emphasis?

2. The author says of Henry Fowler: "He was a strange fellow." Examine paragraphs 3 to 7, and explain how Highet persuades us to accept this evaluation.

3. (a) What were Henry Fowler's two chief aims in writing *Modern English Usage*?
   (b) What does the essayist consider to be the greatest virtues of this book?
   (c) How does he make these qualities clear to us?

4. Gilbert Highet's style, though learned, always seems colloquial and friendly. How does he achieve this effect? In your answer refer to passages that illustrate (a) his wide reading, and (b) his conversational tone.

5. (a) For what purpose does Highet refer to the grammatical controversy over a sentence in the American army's phrase-book? (b) Do you agree with the conclusion that he arrives at in this dispute? Explain your reasoning.

6. In this essay Gilbert Highet tells us a great deal about Henry Fowler; indirectly he also tells us much about himself. What impressions do you get of the essayist's personality? What gave you these impressions?

7. The essay ends as it began -- with an interestingly developed metaphor. Explain why each of these metaphors is apt, and in what way they are related.

*George*
*Orwell*

# Down the mine

—————

*George Orwell (1903-1950), English essayist and novelist whose real name was Eric Blair, was born in India and educated in England. After serving in the Burma and Indian Imperial Police from 1922 to 1928, he returned to Europe, where he earned his living as a teacher and later as an assistant in a book shop. In 1937, he was badly wounded while fighting in Spain for the Republicans. Following the Second World War, he wrote for several journals and published his two most famous works:* Animal Farm *(1945) and* Nineteen Eighty-Four *(1949). Some of his other books are* Burmese Days *(1934),* Homage to Catalonia *(1938), and* Inside the Whale *(1940). The following essay, a chapter in* The Road to Wigan Pier *(1937), illustrates Orwell's passionate conviction that he is his brother's keeper. This essay is reprinted by permission of Martin Secker and Warburg, Ltd.*

—————

OUR CIVILIZATION, *pace* Chesterton, is founded on coal, more completely than one realizes until one stops to think about it. The machines that keep us alive, and the machines that make machines, are all directly or indirectly dependent upon coal. In the metabolism of the Western world the coal-miner is second in importance only to the man who ploughs the soil. He is a sort of caryatid upon whose shoulders nearly everything that is not grimy is supported. For this reason the actual process by which coal is extracted is well worth watching, if you get the chance and are willing to take the trouble.

When you go down a coal-mine it is important to try and get to the coal face when the "fillers" are at work. This is not easy, because when the mine is working visitors are a nuisance and are not encouraged, but if you go at any other time, it is possible to come away with a totally wrong impression. On a Sunday, for instance, a mine seems almost peaceful. The time to go there is when the machines are roaring and the air is black with coal dust, and when you can actually see what the miners have to do. At those times the place is like hell, or at any rate like my own mental picture of hell. Most of the things one imagines in hell are there – heat, noise, confusion, darkness, foul air, and, above all, unbearably cramped space. Everything except the fire, for there is no fire down there except the feeble beams of Davy lamps and electric torches which scarcely penetrate the clouds of coal dust.

When you have finally got there – and getting there is a job in itself: I will explain that in a moment – you crawl through the last line of pit props and see opposite you a shiny black wall three or four feet high. This is the coal face. Overhead is the smooth ceiling made by the rock from which the coal has been cut; underneath is the rock again, so that the gallery you are in is only as high as the ledge of coal itself, probably not much more than a yard. The first impression of all, overmastering everything else for a while, is the frightful, deafening din from the conveyor belt which carries the coal away. You cannot see very far, because the fog of coal dust throws back the beam of your lamp, but you can see on either side of you the line of half-naked kneeling men, one to every four or five yards, driving their shovels under the fallen coal and flinging it swiftly over their left shoulders. They are feeding it on to the conveyor belt, a moving rubber belt a couple of feet wide which runs a yard or two behind them. Down this belt a glittering river of coal races constantly. In a big mine it is carrying away several tons of coal every minute. It bears it off to some place in the main roads where it is shot into tubs holding half a ton, and thence dragged to the cages and hoisted to the outer air.

It is impossible to watch the "fillers" at work without feeling a pang of envy for their toughness. It is a dreadful job that they do, an almost superhuman job by the standard of an ordinary person. For they are not only shifting monstrous quantities of coal, they are also doing it in a position that doubles or trebles the work. They have got to remain kneeling all the while – they could hardly rise from their knees without hitting the ceiling – and you can easily see by trying it what a tremendous effort this means. Shovelling is comparatively easy when you are standing up, because you can use your knee and thigh to drive the shovel along; kneeling down, the whole of the strain is thrown upon your arm and belly muscles. And the other conditions do not exactly make things easier. There is the heat – it varies, but in some mines it is suffocating – and the coal dust that stuffs up your throat and nostrils and collects along your eyelids, and the un-ending rattle of the conveyor belt, which in that confined space is rather like the rattle of a machine gun. But the fillers look and work as though they were made of iron. They really do look like iron – hammered iron statues – under the smooth coat of coal dust which clings to them from head to foot. It is only when you see miners down the mine and naked that you realize what splendid men they are. Most of them are small (big men are at a disadvantage in that job) but nearly all of them have the most noble bodies; wide shoulders tapering to slender supple waists, and small pronounced buttocks and sinewy thighs, with not an ounce of waste flesh anywhere. In the hotter mines they wear only a pair of thin drawers, clogs and knee-pads; in the hottest mines of all, only the clogs and knee-pads. You can hardly tell by the look of them whether they are young or old. They may be any age up to sixty or even sixty-five, but when they are black and naked they all look alike. No one could do their work who had not a young man's body, and a figure fit for a guardsman at that; just a few pounds of extra flesh on the waist-line, and the constant bending would be impossible. You can never forget that spectacle once you have seen it – the line of bowed, kneeling figures, sooty black all over, driving their huge shovels under the coal with stupendous force and speed. They are on the job for seven and a half hours, theoretically without a break, for there is no time "off". Actually they snatch a quarter of an hour or so at some time during the shift to eat the food they have brought with them, usually a hunk of bread and dripping and a bottle of cold tea. The first time I was watching the "fillers" at work I put my hand upon some dreadful slimy thing among the coal dust. It was a chewed quid of tobacco. Nearly all the miners chew tobacco, which is said to be good against thirst.

Probably you have to go down several coal-mines before you can get much grasp of the processes that are going on round you. This is chiefly because the mere effort of getting from place to place makes it difficult to notice anything else. In some ways it is even disappointing, or at least is unlike what you have expected. You get into the cage, which is a steel box about as wide as a telephone box and two or three times as long. It holds ten men, but they pack it like pilchards in a tin, and a tall man cannot stand upright in it. The steel door shuts upon you, and somebody working the winding gear above drops you into the void. You have the usual momentary qualm in your belly and a bursting sensation in the ears, but not much sensation of movement till you get near the bottom, when the cage slows down so abruptly that you could swear it is going upwards again. In the middle of the run the cage probably touches sixty miles an hour; in some of the deeper mines it touches even more. When you crawl out at the bottom you are perhaps four hundred yards underground. That is to say you have a tolerable-sized mountain on top of you; hundreds of yards of solid rock, bones of extinct beasts, subsoil, flints, roots of growing things, green grass and cows grazing on it – all this suspended over your head and held back only by wooden props as thick as the calf of your leg. But because of the speed at which the cage has brought you down, and the complete blackness through which you have travelled, you hardly feel yourself deeper down than you would at the bottom of the Piccadilly tube.

What *is* surprising, on the other hand, is the immense horizontal distances that have to be travelled underground. Before I had been down a mine I had vaguely imagined the miner stepping out of the cage and getting to work on a ledge of coal a few yards away. I had not realized that before he even gets to work he may have had to creep along passages as long as from London Bridge to Oxford Circus. In the beginning, of course, a mine shaft is sunk somewhere near a seam of coal. But as that seam is worked out and fresh seams are followed up, the workings get further and further from the pit bottom. If it is a mile from the pit bottom to the coal face, that is probably an average distance; three miles is a fairly normal one; there are even said to be a few mines where it is as much as five miles. But these distances bear no relation to distances above ground. For in all that mile or three miles as it may be, there is hardly anywhere outside the main road, and not many places even there, where a man can stand upright.

You do not notice the effect of this till you have gone a few hundred yards. You start off, stooping slightly, down the dim-lit gallery, eight or ten feet wide and about five high, with the walls built up with slabs of shale, like the stone walls in Derbyshire. Every yard or two there are wooden props holding up the beams and girders; some of the girders have buckled into fantastic curves under which you have to duck. Usually it is bad going underfoot — thick dust or jagged chunks of shale, and in some mines where there is water it is as mucky as a farm-yard. Also there is the track for the coal tubs, like a miniature railway track with sleepers a foot or two apart, which is tiresome to walk on. Everything is grey with shale dust; there is a dusty fiery smell which seems to be the same in all mines. You see mysterious machines of which you never learn the purpose, and bundles of tools slung together on wires, and sometimes mice darting away from the beam of the lamps. They are surprisingly common, especially in mines where there are or have been horses. It would be interesting to know how they got there in the first place; possibly by falling down the shaft — for they say a mouse can fall any distance uninjured, owing to its surface area being so large relative to its weight. You press yourself against the wall to make way for lines of tubs jolting slowly towards the shaft, drawn by an endless steel cable operated from the surface. You creep through sacking curtains and thick wooden doors which, when they are opened, let out fierce blasts of air. These doors are an important part of the ventilation system. The exhausted air is sucked out of one shaft by means of fans, and the fresh air enters the other of its own accord. But if left to itself the air will take the shortest way round, leaving the deeper workings unventilated; so all the short cuts have to be partitioned off.

At the start to walk stooping is rather a joke, but it is a joke that soon wears off. I am handicapped by being exceptionally tall, but when the roof falls to four feet or less it is a tough job for anybody except a dwarf or a child. You not only have to bend double, you have also got to keep your head up all the while so as to see the beams and girders and dodge them when they come. You have, therefore, a constant crick in the neck, but this is nothing to the pain in your knees and thighs. After half a mile it becomes (I am not exaggerating) an unbearable agony. You begin to wonder whether you will ever get to the end — still more, how on earth you are going to get back. Your pace grows slower and slower. You come to a stretch of a couple of hundred yards where it is all exceptionally low and you have to work yourself along in a squatting position. Then suddenly the roof opens out to a mysterious height — scene of an old fall of rock, probably — and for twenty whole yards you can stand upright. The relief is overwhelming. But after this is another low stretch of a hundred yards and then a succession of beams which you have to crawl under. You go down on all fours; even this is a relief after the squatting business. But when you come to the end of the beams and try to get up again, you find that your knees have temporarily struck work and refuse to lift you. You call a halt, ignominiously, and say that you would like to rest for a minute or two. Your guide (a miner) is sympathetic. He knows that your muscles are not the same as his. "Only another four hundred yards," he says encouragingly; you feel that he might as well say another four hundred miles. But finally you do somehow creep as far as the coal face. You have gone a mile and taken the best part of an hour; a miner would do it in not much more than twenty minutes. Having got there, you have to sprawl in the coal dust and get your strength back for several minutes before you can even watch the work in progress with any kind of intelligence.

Coming back is worse than going, not only because you are already tired out but because the journey back to the shaft is slightly uphill. You get through the low places at the speed of a tortoise, and you have no shame now about calling a halt when your knees give way. Even the lamp you are carrying becomes a nuisance and probably when you stumble you drop it; whereupon, if it is a Davy lamp, it goes out. Ducking the beams becomes more and more of an effort, and sometimes you forget to duck. You try walking head down as the miners do, and then you bang your backbone. Even the miners bang their backbones fairly often. This is the reason why in very hot mines, where it is necessary to go about half naked, most of the miners have what they call "buttons down the back" — that is, a permanent scab on each vertebra. When the track is down hill the miners sometimes fit their clogs, which are hollow underneath, on to the trolley rails and slide down. In mines where the "travelling" is very bad all the miners carry sticks about two and a half feet long, hollowed out below the handle. In normal places you keep your hand on top of the stick and in the low places you slide your hand down into the hollow. These sticks are a great help, and the wooden crash-helmets — a comparatively recent invention — are a godsend. They look like a French or Italian steel helmet, but they are made of some kind of pith and very light, and so strong that you can take a violent blow on the head without feeling it. When finally you get back to the surface you have been perhaps three hours underground and travelled two miles, and you are more exhausted than you would be by a twenty-five-mile walk above ground. For a week afterwards your thighs are so stiff that coming downstairs is quite a difficult feat; you have to work your way down in a peculiar sidelong manner, without bending the knees. Your miner friends notice the stiffness of your walk and chaff you about it. ("How'd ta like to work down pit, eh?" etc.) Yet even a miner who has been long away from work — from illness, for instance – when he comes back to the pit, suffers badly for the first few days.

It may seem that I am exaggerating, though no one who has been down an old-fashioned pit (most of the pits in England are old-fashioned) and actually gone as far as the coal face, is likely to say so. But what I want to emphasize is this. Here is this frightful business of crawling to and fro, which to any normal person is a hard day's work in itself; and it is not part of the miner's work at all, it is merely an extra, like the City man's daily ride in the Tube. The miner does that journey to and fro, and sandwiched in between there are seven and a half hours of savage work. I have never travelled much more than a mile to the coal face; but often it is three miles, in which case I and most people other than coal-miners would never get there at all. This is the kind of point that one is always liable to miss. When you think of the coal-mine you think of depth, heat, darkness, blackened figures hacking at walls of coal; you don't think, necessarily, of those miles of creeping to and fro. There is the question of time, also. A miner's working shift of seven and a half hours does not sound very long, but one has got to add on to it at least an hour a day for "travelling", more often two hours and sometimes three. Of course, the "travelling" is not technically work and the miner is not paid for it; but it is as like work as makes no difference. It is easy to say that miners don't mind all this. Certainly, it is not the same for them as it would be for you or me. They have done it since childhood, they have the right muscles hardened, and they can move to and fro underground with a startling and rather horrible agility. A miner puts his head down and runs, with a long swinging stride, through places where I can only stagger. At the workings you see them on all fours, skipping round the pit props almost like dogs. But it is quite a mistake to think that they enjoy it. I have talked about this to scores of miners and they all admit that the "travelling" is hard work; in any case when you hear them discussing a pit among themselves the "travelling" is always one of the things they discuss. It is said that a shift always returns from work faster than it goes; nevertheless the miners all say that it is the coming away after a hard day's work, that is especially irksome. It is part of their work and they are equal to it, but certainly it is an effort. It is comparable, perhaps, to climbing a smallish mountain before and after your day's work.

When you have been down in two or three pits you begin to get some grasp of the processes that are going on underground. (I ought to say, by the way, that I know nothing whatever about the technical side of mining: I am merely describing what I have seen.) Coal lies in thin seams between enormous layers of rock, so that essentially the process of getting it out is like scooping the central layer from a Neapolitan ice. In the old days the miners used to cut straight into the coal with pick and crowbar — a very slow job because coal, when lying in its virgin state, is almost as hard as rock. Nowadays the preliminary work is done by an electrically-driven coal-cutter, which in principle is an immensely tough and powerful band-saw, running horizontally instead of vertically, with teeth a couple of inches long and half an inch or an inch thick. It can move backwards or forwards on its own power, and the men operating it can rotate it this way or that. Incidentally it makes one of the most awful noises I have ever heard, and sends forth clouds of coal dust which make it impossible to see more than two to three feet and almost impossible to breathe. The machine travels along the coal face cutting into the base of the coal and undermining it to the depth of five feet or five feet and a half; after this it is comparatively easy to extract the coal to the depth to which it has been undermined. Where it is "difficult gettin'", however, it has also to be loosened with explosives. A man with an electric drill, like a rather small version of the drills used in street-mending, bores holes at intervals in the coal, inserts blasting powder, plugs it with clay, goes round the corner if there is one handy (he is supposed to retire to twenty-five yards distance) and touches off the charge with an electric current. This is not intended to bring the coal out, only to loosen it. Occasionally, of course, the charge is too powerful, and then it not only brings the coal out but brings the roof down as well.

After the blasting has been done the "fillers" can tumble the coal out, break it up and shovel it on to the conveyor belt. It comes out first in monstrous boulders which may weigh anything up to twenty tons. The conveyor belt shoots it on to tubs, and the tubs are shoved into the main road and hitched on to an endlessly revolving steel cable which drags them to the cage. Then they are hoisted, and at the surface the coal is sorted by being run over screens, and if necessary is washed as well. As far as possible the "dirt" — the shale, that is — is used for making the roads below. All that cannot be used is sent to the surface and dumped; hence the monstrous "dirt-heaps", like hideous grey mountains, which are the characteristic scenery of the coal areas. When the coal has been extracted to the depth to which the machine has cut, the coal face has advanced by five feet. Fresh props are put in to hold up the newly exposed roof, and during the next shift the conveyor belt is taken to pieces, moved five feet forward and re-assembled. As far as possible the three operations of cutting, blasting and extraction are done in three separate shifts, the cutting in the afternoon, the blasting at night (there is a law, not always kept, that forbids its being done when other men are working near by), and the "filling" in the morning shift, which lasts from six in the morning until half past one.

Even when you watch the process of coal-extraction you probably only watch it for a short time, and it is not until you begin making a few calculations that you realize what a stupendous task the "fillers" are performing. Normally each man has to clear a space four or five yards wide. The cutter has undermined the coal to the depth of five feet, so that if the seam of coal is three or four feet high, each man has to cut out, break up and load on to the belt something between seven and twelve cubic yards of coal. This is to say, taking a cubic yard as weighing twenty-seven hundred-weight, that each man is shifting coal at a speed approaching two tons an hour. I have just enough experience of pick and shovel work to be able to grasp what this means. When I am digging trenches in my garden, if I shift two tons of earth during the afternoon, I feel that I have earned my tea. But earth is tractable stuff compared with coal, and I don't have to work kneeling down, a thousand feet underground, in suffocating heat and swallowing coal dust with every breath I take; nor do I have to walk a mile bent double before I begin. The miner's job would be as much beyond my power as it would be to perform on a flying trapeze or to win the Grand National. I am not a manual labourer and please God I never shall be one, but there are some kinds of manual work that I could do if I had to. At a pitch I could be a tolerable road-sweeper or an inefficient gardener or even a tenth-rate farm hand. But by no conceivable amount of effort or training could I become a coal-miner; the work would kill me in a few weeks.

Watching coal-miners at work, you realize momentarily what different universes people inhabit. Down there where coal is dug is a sort of world apart which one can quite easily go through life without ever hearing about. Probably a majority of people would even prefer not to hear about it. Yet it is the absolutely necessary counterpart of our world above. Practically everything we do, from eating an ice to crossing the Atlantic, and from baking a loaf to writing a novel, involves the use of coal, directly or indirectly. For all the arts of peace coal is needed; if war breaks out it is needed all the more. In time of revolution the miner must go on working or the revolution must stop, for revolution as much as reaction needs coal. Whatever may be happening on the surface, the hacking and shovelling have got to continue without a pause, or at any rate without pausing for more than a few weeks at the most. In order that Hitler may march the goose-step, that the Pope may denounce Bolshevism, that the cricket crowds may assemble at Lords, that the poets may scratch one another's backs, coal has got to be forthcoming. But on the whole we are not aware of it; we all know that we "must have coal", but we seldom or never remember what coal-getting involves. Here am I sitting writing in front of my comfortable coal fire. It is April but I still need a fire. Once a fortnight the coal cart drives up to the door and men in leather jerkins carry the coal indoors in stout sacks smelling of tar and shoot it clanking into the coal-hole under the stairs. It is only very rarely, when I make a definite mental effort, that I connect this coal with that far-off labour in the mines. It is just "coal" — something that I have got to have; black stuff that arrives mysteriously from nowhere in particular, like manna except that you have to pay for it. You could quite easily drive a car right across the north of England and never once remember that hundreds of feet below the road you are on, the miners are hacking at the coal. Yet in a sense it is the miners who are driving your car forward. Their lamp-lit world down there is as necessary to the daylight world above as the root is to the flower.

It is not long since conditions in the mines were worse than they are now. There are still living a few very old women who in their youth have worked underground, with the harness round their waists, and a chain that passed between their legs, crawling on all fours and dragging tubs of coal. They used to go on doing this even when they were pregnant. And even now, if coal could not be produced without pregnant women dragging it to and fro, I fancy we should let them do it rather than deprive ourselves of coal. But most of the time, of course, we should prefer to forget that they were doing it. It is so with all types of manual work; it keeps us alive, and we are oblivious of its existence. More than anyone else, perhaps, the miner can stand as the type of the manual worker, not only because his work is so exaggeratedly awful, but also because it is so vitally necessary and yet so remote from our experience, so invisible, as it were, that we are capable of forgetting it as we forget the blood in our veins. In a way it is even humiliating to watch coal-miners working. It raises in you a momentary doubt about your own status as an "intellectual" and a superior person generally. For it is brought home to you, at least while you are watching, that it is only because miners sweat their guts out that superior persons can remain superior. You and I and the editor of the *Times Lit. Supp.*, and the poets and the Archbishop of Canterbury and Comrade X, author of *Marxism for Infants* — all of us *really* owe the comparative decency of our lives to poor drudges underground, blackened to the eyes, with their throats full of coal dust, driving their shovels forward with arms and belly muscles of steel.

QUESTIONS

1. Orwell states that Western civilization depends upon coal and that "for this reason the actual process by which coal is extracted is well worth watching." However, this theme is secondary to his attitude towards the miners themselves.

(a) What is this attitude?

(b) In what parts of the essay does this attitude appear most clearly?

(c) The last two paragraphs powerfully restate the author's two main themes. Explain why these paragraphs make a strong conclusion to the essay.

2. If you have read this essay carefully, you will have formed a strong *visual* impression of a British coal miner.

(a) In your own words and, if possible, without re-reading the essay, describe him.

(b) What impressions of the coal-miner's *character* does the author give you?

(c) Look back over the essay, and bracket in the margin of the text the passages which support your answers to (a) and (b).

3. The most obvious sequence of events for Orwell to use in this narrative of his personal experience would be as follows:

(1) Arriving at the pit-head

(2) Descending the shaft

(3) Travelling to the coal face

(4) Working at the coal face

(a) What order does Orwell actually use?

(b) Suggest reasons why he uses this order.

4. In another essay, "Politics and the English Language", Orwell asserts: "A scrupulous writer in every sentence that he writes will ask himself at least four questions, thus: What am I trying to say? What words will express it? What image or idiom will make it clearer? Is this image fresh enough to have an effect? And he will probably ask himself two more: Could I have put it more shortly? Have I said anything that is avoidably ugly?" Pick out what you con-

sider is an interesting paragraph in this essay and answer the following:

(a) What topic does this paragraph develop? – or as Orwell puts it – what is he trying to say?

(b) Quote an image that he uses to make his meaning clearer. Assuming that this image is fresh enough to have an effect, what effect does it produce? Write a brief comment on the paragraph in answer to the author's last two questions.

5. One theme in Orwell's tragic novel, *Nineteen Eighty-Four*, is that man is capable of the most cunning cruelty to his fellow man – capable of keeping him enslaved under appalling physical conditions, and capable of manipulating his mind so that he ceases to be human and becomes merely a mechanically responding machine. To what extent is this theme foreshadowed in "Down the Mine"?

David Herbert

Lawrence

# The rocking-horse winner

David Herbert Lawrence (1885-1930) was born in the village of
Eastwood, Nottinghamshire, the gifted son of a coal miner.
His mother, a school teacher, encouraged him in his studies.
At fifteen he earned a teacher's certificate and later taught school
at Croydon. A prolific artist, he wrote poems, essays, short
stories, and novels, but it was as a writer of prose fiction that he
made his name famous. Some of his novels are Sons and Lovers
(1913), The Rainbow (1915), Women in Love (1920), Aaron's
Rod (1922), The Pluméd Serpent (1926), and Lady Chatterley's
Lover (1928). His short stories are collected in a volume entitled,
The Tales of D. H. Lawrence (1934). Throughout his work
runs the thought that human beings have within them deep,
instinctive forces which may bring them happiness, but which
modern society stifles. The reader may easily see how "The
Rocking-Horse Winner" is related to this theme. This story is
reprinted from The Complete Short Stories, Volume III, by
D. H. Lawrence, published by Messrs. William Heinemann, Ltd.,
by permission of Laurence Pollinger, Ltd. and the Estate of
the late Mrs. Frieda Lawrence.

THERE WAS A WOMAN who was beautiful, who started with all the
advantages, yet she had no luck. She married for love, and the
love turned to dust. She had bonny children, yet she felt they

had been thrust upon her, and she could not love them. They looked at her coldly, as if they were finding fault with her. And hurriedly she felt she must cover up some fault in herself. Yet what it was that she must cover up she never knew. Nevertheless, when her children were present, she always felt the centre of her heart go hard. This troubled her, and in her manner she was all the more gentle and anxious for her children, as if she loved them very much. Only she herself knew that at the centre of her heart was a hard little place that could not feel love, no, not for anybody. Everybody else said of her: "She is such a good mother. She adores her children." Only she herself, and her children themselves, knew it was not so. They read it in each other's eyes.

There were a boy and two little girls. They lived in a pleasant house, with a garden, and they had discreet servants, and felt themselves superior to anyone in the neighbourhood.

Although they lived in style, they felt always an anxiety in the house. There was never enough money. The mother had a small income, and the father had a small income, but not nearly enough for the social position which they had to keep up. The father went in to town to some office. But though he had good prospects, these prospects never materialized. There was always the grinding sense of the shortage of money, though the style was always kept up.

At last the mother said, "I will see if I can't make something." But she did not know where to begin. She racked her brains, and tried this thing and the other, but could not find anything successful. The failure made deep lines come into her face. Her children were growing up, they would have to go to school. There must be more money, there must be more money. The father, who was always very handsome and expensive in his tastes, seemed as if he never *would* be able to do anything worth doing. And the mother, who had a great belief in herself, did not succeed any better, and her tastes were just as expensive.

And so the house came to be haunted by the unspoken phrase: *There must be more money! There must be more money!* The children could hear it all the time, though nobody said it aloud.

They heard it at Christmas, when the expensive and splendid toys filled the nursery. Behind the shining modern rocking-horse, behind the smart doll's-house, a voice would start whispering: "There *must* be more money! There *must* be more money!" And the children would stop playing, to listen for a moment. They would look into each other's eyes, to see if they had all heard. And each one saw in the eyes of the other two that they too had heard. "There *must* be more money! There *must* be more money!"

It came whispering from the springs of the still-swaying rocking-horse, and even the horse, bending his wooden, champing head, heard it. The big doll, sitting so pink and smirking in her new pram could hear it quite plainly, and seemed to be smirking all the more self-consciously because of it. The foolish puppy, too, that took the place of the teddy-bear, he was looking so extraordinarily foolish for no other reason but that he heard the secret whisper all over the house: "There *must* be more money!"

Yet nobody ever said it aloud. The whisper was everywhere, and therefore no one spoke it. Just as no one ever says: "We are breathing!" in spite of the fact that breath is coming and going all the time.

"Mother," said the boy Paul one day, "why don't we keep a car of our own? Why do we always use uncle's, or else a taxi?"

"Because we're the poor members of the family," said the mother.

"But why *are* we, mother?"

"Well — I suppose," she said slowly and bitterly, "it's because your father has no luck."

The boy was silent for some time.

"Is luck money, mother?" he asked, rather timidly.

"No, Paul. Not quite. It's what causes you to have money."

"Oh!" said Paul vaguely. "I thought when Uncle Oscar said *filthy lucker*, it meant money."

"*Filthy lucre* does mean money," said the mother. "But it's lucre, not luck."

"Oh!" said the boy. "Then what *is* luck, mother?"

"It's what causes you to have money. If you're lucky you have money. That's why it's better to be born lucky than rich. If you're rich, you may lose your money. But if you're lucky, you will always get more money."

"Oh! Will you? And is father not lucky?"

"Very unlucky, I should say," she said bitterly.

The boy watched her with unsure eyes.

"Why?" he asked.

"I don't know. Nobody ever knows why one person is lucky and another unlucky."

"Don't they? Nobody at all? Does *nobody* know?"

"Perhaps God. But He never tells."

"He ought to, then. And aren't you lucky either, mother?"

"I can't be, if I married an unlucky husband."

"But by yourself, aren't you?"

"I used to think I was, before I married. Now I think I am very unlucky indeed."

"Why?"

"Well — never mind! Perhaps I'm not really," she said.

The child looked at her, to see if she meant it. But he saw, by the lines of her mouth, that she was only trying to hide something from him.

"Well, anyhow," he said stoutly, "I'm a lucky person."

"Why?" said his mother, with a sudden laugh.

He stared at her. He didn't even know why he had said it.

"God told me," he asserted, brazening it out.

"I hope He did, dear!" she said, again with a laugh, but rather bitter.

"He did, mother!"

"Excellent!" said the mother, using one of her husband's exclamations.

The boy saw she did not believe him; or rather, that she paid no attention to his assertion. This angered him somewhere, and made him want to compel her attention.

He went off by himself, vaguely, in a childish way, seeking for the clue to "luck". Absorbed, taking no heed of other people, he went about with a sort of stealth, seeking inwardly for luck. He wanted luck, he wanted it, he wanted it. When the two girls were playing dolls in the nursery, he would sit on his big rocking-horse, charging madly into space, with a frenzy that made the little girls peer at him uneasily. Wildly the horse careered, the waving dark hair of the boy tossed, his eyes had a strange glare in them. The little girls dared not speak to him.

When he had ridden to the end of his mad little journey, he climbed down and stood in front of his rocking-horse, staring fixedly into its lowered face. Its red mouth was slightly open, its big eye was wide and glassy-bright.

"Now!" he would silently command the snorting steed. "Now, take me to where there is luck! Now take me!"

And he would slash the horse on the neck with the little whip he had asked Uncle Oscar for. He *knew* the horse could take him to where there was luck, if only he forced it. So he would mount again, and start on his furious ride, hoping at last to get there. He knew he could get there.

"You'll break your horse, Paul!" said the nurse.

"He's always riding like that! I wish he'd leave off!" said his elder sister Joan.

But he only glared down on them in silence. Nurse gave him up. She could make nothing of him. Anyhow he was growing beyond her.

One day his mother and his Uncle Oscar came in when he was on one of his furious rides. He did not speak to them.

"Hallo, you young jockey! Riding a winner?" said his uncle.

"Aren't you growing too big for a rocking-horse? You're not a very little boy any longer, you know," said his mother.

But Paul only gave a blue glare from his big, rather close-set eyes. He would speak to nobody when he was in full tilt. His mother watched him with an anxious expression on her face.

At last he suddenly stopped forcing his horse into the mechanical gallop, and slid down.

"Well, I got there!" he announced fiercely, his blue eyes still flaring, and his sturdy long legs straddling apart.

"Where did you get to?" asked his mother.

"Where I wanted to go," he flared back at her.

"That's right, son!" said Uncle Oscar. "Don't you stop till you get there. What's the horse's name?"

"He doesn't have a name," said the boy.

"Gets on without all right?" asked the uncle.

"Well, he has different names. He was called Sansovino last week."

"Sansovino, eh? Won the Ascot. How did you know his name?"

"He always talks about horse-races with Bassett," said Joan.

The uncle was delighted to find that his small nephew was posted with all the racing news. Bassett, the young gardener, who had been wounded in the left foot in the war and had got his present job through Oscar Cresswell, whose batman he had been, was a perfect blade of the "turf." He lived in the racing events, and the small boy lived with him.

Oscar Cresswell got it all from Bassett.

"Master Paul comes and asks me, so I can't do more than tell him, sir," said Bassett, his face terribly serious, as if he were speaking of religious matters.

"And does he ever put anything on a horse he fancies?"

"Well — I don't want to give him away — he's a young sport, a fine sport, sir. Would you mind asking him himself? He sort of takes a pleasure in it, and perhaps he'd feel I was giving him away, sir, if you don't mind."

Bassett was serious as a church.

The uncle went back to his nephew, and took him off for a ride in the car.

"Say, Paul, old man, do you ever put anything on a horse?" the uncle asked.

The boy watched the handsome man closely.

"Why, do you think I oughtn't to?" he parried.

"Not a bit of it! I thought perhaps you might give me a tip for the Lincoln."

The car sped on into the country going down to Uncle Oscar's place in Hampshire.

"Honour bright?" said the nephew.

"Honour bright, son!" said the uncle.

"Well, then, Daffodil."

"Daffodil! I doubt it, sonny. What about Mirza?"

"I only know the winner," said the boy. "That's Daffodil."

"Daffodil, eh?"

There was a pause. Daffodil was an obscure horse comparatively.

"Uncle!"

"Yes, son?"

"You won't let it go any further, will you? I promised Bassett."

"Bassett be damned, old man! What's he got to do with it?"

"We're partners. We've been partners from the first. Uncle, he lent me my first five shillings, which I lost. I promised him, honour bright, it was only between me and him; only you gave me that ten-shilling note I started winning with, so I thought you were lucky. You won't let it go any further, will you?"

The boy gazed at his uncle from those big, hot, blue eyes, set rather close together. The uncle stirred and laughed uneasily.

"Right you are, son! I'll keep your tip private. Daffodil, eh? How much are you putting on him?"

"All except twenty pounds," said the boy. "I keep that in reserve."

The uncle thought it a good joke.

"You keep twenty pounds in reserve, do you, you young romancer? What are you betting, then?"

"I'm betting three hundred," said the boy gravely. "But it's between you and me, Uncle Oscar! Honour bright?"

The uncle burst into a roar of laughter.

"It's between you and me all right, you young Nat Gould," he said, laughing. "But where's your three hundred?"

"Bassett keeps it for me. We're partners."

"You are, are you! And what is Bassett putting on Daffodil?"

"He won't go quite as high as I do, I expect. Perhaps he'll go a hundred and fifty."

"What, pennies?" laughed the uncle.

"Pounds," said the child, with a surprised look at his uncle. "Bassett keeps a bigger reserve than I do."

Between wonder and amusement Uncle Oscar was silent. He

pursued the matter no further, but he determined to take his nephew with him to the Lincoln races.

"Now, son," he said, "I'm putting twenty on Mirza, and I'll put five for you on any horse you fancy. What's your pick?"

"Daffodil, uncle."

"No, not the fiver on Daffodil!"

"I should if it was my own fiver," said the child.

"Good! Good! Right you are! A fiver for me and a fiver for you on Daffodil."

The child had never been to a race-meeting before, and his eyes were blue fire. He pursed his mouth tight, and watched. A Frenchman just in front had put his money on Lancelot. Wild with excitement, he flayed his arms up and down, yelling *"Lancelot! Lancelot!"* in his French accent.

Daffodil came in first, Lancelot second, Mirza third. The child, flushed and with eyes blazing, was curiously serene. His uncle brought him four five-pound notes, four to one.

"What am I to do with these?" he cried, waving them before the boy's eyes.

"I suppose we'll talk to Bassett," said the boy. "I expect I have fifteen hundred now; and twenty in reserve; and this twenty."

His uncle studied him for some moments.

"Look here, son!" he said. "You're not serious about Bassett and that fifteen hundred, are you?"

"Yes, I am. But it's between you and me, uncle. Honour bright!"

"Honour bright all right, son! But I must talk to Bassett."

"If you'd like to be a partner, uncle, with Bassett and me, we could all be partners. Only, you'd have to promise, honour bright, uncle, not to let it go beyond us three. Bassett and I are lucky, and you must be lucky, because it was your ten shillings I started winning with. . . ."

Uncle Oscar took both Bassett and Paul into Richmond Park for an afternoon, and there they talked.

"It's like this, you see, sir," Bassett said. "Master Paul would get me talking about racing events, spinning yarns, you know, sir. And he was always keen on knowing if I'd made or if I'd lost.

It's about a year since, now, that I put five shillings on Blush of Dawn for him: and we lost. Then the luck turned, with that ten shillings he had from you: that we put on Singhalese. And since that time, it's been pretty steady, all things considering. What do you say, Master Paul?"

"We're all right when we're sure," said Paul. "It's when we're not quite sure that we go down."

"Oh, but we're careful then," said Bassett.

"But when are you *sure?*" smiled Uncle Oscar.

"It's Master Paul, sir," said Bassett, in a secret, religious voice. "It's as if he had it from heaven. Like Daffodil, now, for the Lincoln. That was as sure as eggs."

"Did you put anything on Daffodil?" asked Oscar Cresswell.

"Yes, sir. I made my bit."

"And my nephew?"

Bassett was obstinately silent, looking at Paul.

"I made twelve hundred, didn't I, Bassett? I told uncle I was putting three hundred on Daffodil."

"That's right," said Bassett, nodding.

"But where's the money?" asked the uncle.

"I keep it safe locked up, sir. Master Paul he can have it any minute he likes to ask for it."

"What, fifteen hundred pounds?"

"And twenty! And *forty*, that is, with the twenty he made on the course."

"It's amazing!" said the uncle.

"If Master Paul offers you to be partners, sir, I would, if I were you: if you'll excuse me," said Bassett.

Oscar Cresswell thought about it.

"I'll see the money," he said.

They drove home again, and, sure enough, Bassett came round to the garden-house with fifteen hundred pounds in notes. The twenty pounds reserve was left with Joe Glee, in the Turf Commission deposit.

"You see, it's all right, uncle, when I'm *sure!* Then we go strong, for all we're worth. Don't we, Bassett?"

"We do that, Master Paul."

"And when are you sure?" said the uncle, laughing.

"Oh, well, sometimes I'm *absolutely* sure, like about Daffodil," said the boy; "and sometimes I have an idea; and sometimes I haven't even an idea, have I, Bassett? Then we're careful, because we mostly go down."

"You do, do you! And when you're sure, like about Daffodil, what makes you sure, sonny?"

"Oh, well, I don't know," said the boy uneasily. "I'm sure, you know, uncle; that's all."

"It's as if he had it from heaven, sir," Bassett reiterated.

"I should say so!" said the uncle.

But he became a partner. And when the Leger was coming on Paul was "sure" about Lively Spark, which was a quite inconsiderable horse. The boy insisted on putting a thousand on the horse, Bassett went for five hundred, and Oscar Cresswell two hundred. Lively Spark came in first, and the betting had been ten to one against him. Paul had made ten thousand.

"You see," he said, "I was absolutely sure of him."

Even Oscar Cresswell had cleared two thousand.

"Look here, son," he said, "this sort of thing makes me nervous."

"It needn't, uncle! Perhaps I shan't be sure again for a long time."

"But what are you going to do with your money?" asked the uncle.

"Of course," said the boy, "I started it for mother. She said she had no luck, because father is unlucky, so I thought if I was lucky, it might stop whispering."

"What might stop whispering?"

"Our house. I *hate* our house for whispering."

"What does it whisper?"

"Why — why" — the boy fidgeted — "why, I don't know. But it's always short of money, you know, uncle."

"I know it, son, I know it."

"You know people send mother writs, don't you, uncle?"

"I'm afraid I do," said the uncle.

"And then the house whispers, like people laughing at you behind your back. It's awful, that is! I thought if I was lucky ——"

"You might stop it," added the uncle.

The boy watched him with big blue eyes, that had an uncanny cold fire in them, and he said never a word.

"Well, then!" said the uncle. "What are we doing?"

"I shouldn't like mother to know I was lucky," said the boy.

"Why not, son?"

"She'd stop me."

"I don't think she would."

"Oh!" — and the boy writhed in an odd way — "I *don't* want her to know, uncle."

"All right, son! We'll manage it without her knowing."

They managed it very easily. Paul, at the other's suggestion, handed over five thousand pounds to his uncle, who deposited it with the family lawyer, who was then to inform Paul's mother that a relative had put five thousand pounds into his hands, which sum was to be paid out a thousand pounds at a time, on the mother's birthday, for the next five years.

"So she'll have a birthday present of a thousand pounds for five successive years," said Uncle Oscar. "I hope it won't make it all the harder for her later."

Paul's mother had her birthday in November. The house had been "whispering" worse than ever lately, and, even in spite of his luck, Paul could not bear up against it. He was very anxious to see the effect of the birthday letter, telling his mother about the thousand pounds.

When there were no visitors, Paul now took his meals with his parents, as he was beyond the nursery control. His mother went into town nearly every day. She had discovered that she had an odd knack of sketching furs and dress materials, so she worked secretly in the studio of a friend who was the chief "artist" for the leading drapers. She drew the figures of ladies in furs and ladies in silk and sequins for the newspaper advertisements. This young woman artist earned several thousand pounds a year, but Paul's mother only made several hundreds, and she was again dissatisfied. She so wanted to be first in something, and she did not succeed, even in making sketches for drapery advertisements.

She was down to breakfast on the morning of her birthday. Paul watched her face as she read her letters. He knew the lawyer's letter. As his mother read it, her face hardened and became more expressionless. Then a cold, determined look came on her mouth. She hid the letter under the pile of others, and said not a word about it.

"Didn't you have anything nice in the post for your birthday, mother?" said Paul.

"Quite moderately nice," she said, her voice cold and absent.

She went away to town without saying more.

But in the afternoon Uncle Oscar appeared. He said Paul's mother had had a long interview with the lawyer, asking if the whole five thousand could not be advanced at once, as she was in debt.

"What do you think, uncle?" said the boy.

"I leave it to you, son."

"Oh, let her have it, then! We can get some more with the other," said the boy.

"A bird in the hand is worth two in the bush, laddie!" said Uncle Oscar.

"But I'm sure to *know* for the Grand National; or the Lincolnshire; or else the Derby. I'm sure to know for *one* of them," said Paul.

So Uncle Oscar signed the agreement, and Paul's mother touched the whole five thousand. Then something very curious happened. The voices in the house suddenly went mad, like a chorus of frogs on a spring evening. There were certain new furnishings, and Paul had a tutor. He was *really* going to Eton, his father's school, in the following autumn. There were flowers in the winter, and a blossoming of the luxury Paul's mother had been used to. And yet the voices in the house, behind the sprays of mimosa and almond-blossom, and from under the piles of iridescent cushions, simply trilled and screamed in a sort of ecstasy: "There *must* be more money! Oh-h-h; there *must* be more money. Oh, now, now-w! Now-w-w — there *must* be more money! — more than ever! More than ever!"

It frightened Paul terribly. He studied away at his Latin and Greek with his tutors. But his intense hours were spent with Bassett. The Grand National had gone by: he had not "known," and had lost a hundred pounds. Summer was at hand. He was in agony for the Lincoln. But even for the Lincoln he didn't "know," and he lost fifty pounds. He became wild-eyed and strange, as if something were going to explode in him.

"Let it alone, son! Don't you bother about it!" urged Uncle Oscar. But it was as if the boy couldn't really hear what his uncle was saying.

"I've got to know for the Derby! I've got to know for the Derby!" the child reiterated, his big blue eyes blazing with a sort of madness.

His mother noticed how overwrought he was.

"You'd better go to the seaside. Wouldn't you like to go now to the seaside, instead of waiting? I think you'd better," she said, looking down at him anxiously, her heart curiously heavy because of him.

But the child lifted his uncanny blue eyes.

"I couldn't possibly go before the Derby, mother!" he said. "I couldn't possibly!"

"Why not?" she said her voice becoming heavy when she was opposed. "Why not? You can still go from the seaside to see the Derby with your Uncle Oscar, if that's what you wish. No need for you to wait here. Besides, I think you care too much about these races. It's a bad sign. My family has been a gambling family, and you won't know till you grow up how much damage it has done. But it has done damage. I shall have to send Bassett away, and ask Uncle Oscar not to talk racing to you, unless you promise to be reasonable about it: go away to the seaside and forget it. You're all nerves!"

"I'll do what you like, mother, so long as you don't send me away till after the Derby," the boy said.

"Send you away from where? Just from this house?"

"Yes," he said, gazing at her.

"Why, you curious child, what makes you care about this house so much, suddenly? I never knew you loved it."

He gazed at her without speaking. He had a secret within a secret, something he had not divulged, even to Bassett or to his Uncle Oscar.

But his mother, after standing undecided and a little bit sullen for some moments, said:

"Very well, then! Don't go to the seaside till after the Derby, if you don't wish it. But promise me you won't let your nerves go to pieces. Promise you won't think so much about horse-racing and *events*, as you call them!"

"Oh, no," said the boy casually. "I won't think much about them, mother. You needn't worry. I wouldn't worry, mother, if I were you."

"If you were me and I were you," said his mother, "I wonder what we *should* do!"

"But you know you needn't worry, mother, don't you?" the boy repeated.

"I should be awfully glad to know it," she said wearily.

"Oh, well, you *can*, you know. I mean, you *ought* to know you needn't worry," he insisted.

"Ought I? Then I'll see about it," she said.

Paul's secret of secrets was his wooden horse, that which had no name. Since he was emancipated from a nurse and a nursery-governess, he had had his rocking-horse removed to his own bedroom at the top of the house.

"Surely, you're too big for a rocking-horse!" his mother had remonstrated.

"Well, you see, mother, till I can have a *real* horse, I like to have *some* sort of animal about," had been his quaint answer.

"Do you feel he keeps you company?" she laughed.

"Oh, yes! He's very good, he always keeps me company, when I'm there," said Paul.

So the horse, rather shabby, stood in an arrested prance in the boy's bedroom.

The Derby was drawing near, and the boy grew more and more tense. He hardly heard what was spoken to him, he was very frail, and his eyes were really uncanny. His mother had sudden strange seizures of uneasiness about him. Sometimes, for half an hour, she would feel a sudden anxiety about him that was almost anguish. She wanted to rush to him at once, and know he was safe.

Two nights before the Derby, she was at a big party in town, when one of her rushes of anxiety about her boy, her first-born, gripped her heart till she could hardly speak. She fought with the feeling, might and main, for she believed in common sense. But it was too strong. She had to leave the dance and go downstairs to telephone to the country. The children's nursery-governess was terribly surprised and startled at being rung up in the night.

"Are the children all right, Miss Wilmot?"

"Oh, yes, they are quite all right."

"Master Paul? Is he all right?"

"He went to bed as right as a trivet. Shall I run up and look at him?"

"No," said Paul's mother reluctantly. "No! Don't trouble. It's all right. Don't sit up. We shall be home fairly soon." She did not want her son's privacy intruded upon.

"Very good," said the governess.

It was about one o'clock when Paul's mother and father drove up to their house. All was still. Paul's mother went to her room and slipped off her white fur cloak. She had told her maid not to wait up for her. She heard her husband downstairs, mixing a whisky and soda.

And then, because of the strange anxiety at her heart, she stole upstairs to her son's room. Noiselessly she went along the upper corridor. Was there a faint noise? What was it?

She stood, with arrested muscles, outside his door, listening. There was a strange, heavy, and yet not loud noise. Her heart stood still. It was a soundless noise, yet rushing and powerful. Something huge, in violet, hushed motion. What was it? What in God's name was it? She ought to know. She felt that she knew the noise. She knew what it was.

Yet she could not place it. She couldn't say what it was. And on and on it went, like a madness.

Softly, frozen with anxiety and fear, she turned the door-handle.

The room was dark. Yet in the space near the window, she heard and saw something plunging to and fro. She gazed in fear and amazement.

Then suddenly she switched on the light, and saw her son, in his green pyjamas, madly surging on the rocking-horse. The blaze of light suddenly lit him up, as he urged the wooden horse, and lit her up, as she stood, blonde, in her dress of pale green and crystal, in the doorway.

"Paul!" she cried. "Whatever are you doing?"

"It's Malabar!" he screamed, in a powerful strange voice. "It's Malabar!"

His eyes blazed at her for one strange and senseless second, as he ceased urging his wooden horse. Then he fell with a crash to the ground, and she, all her tormented motherhood flooding upon her, rushed to gather him up.

But he was unconscious, and unconscious he remained, with some brain-fever. He talked and tossed, and his mother sat stonily by his side.

"Malabar! It's Malabar! Bassett, Bassett, I *know!* It's Malabar!"

So the child cried, trying to get up and urge the rocking-horse that gave him his inspiration.

"What does he mean by Malabar?" asked the heart-frozen mother.

"I don't know," said the father stonily.

"What does he mean by Malabar?" she asked her brother Oscar.

"It's one of the horses running for the Derby," was the answer.

And, in spite of himself, Oscar Cresswell spoke to Bassett, and himself put a thousand on Malabar: at fourteen to one.

The third day of the illness was critical: they were waiting for a change. The boy, with his rather long, curly hair, was tossing ceaselessly on the pillow. He neither slept nor regained consciousness, and his eyes were like blue stones. His mother sat, feeling her heart had gone, turned actually into a stone.

In the evening, Oscar Cresswell did not come, but Bassett sent a message, saying could he come up for one moment, just one moment? Paul's mother was very angry at the intrusion, but on second thoughts she agreed. The boy was the same. Perhaps Bassett might bring him to consciousness.

The gardener, a shortish fellow with a little brown moustache, and sharp little brown eyes, tiptoed into the room, touched his imaginary cap to Paul's mother, and stole to the bedside, staring with glittering, smallish eyes at the tossing, dying child.

"Master Paul!" he whispered. "Master Paul! Malabar came in first all right, a clean win. I did as you told me. You've made over seventy thousand pounds, you have; you've got over eighty thousand. Malabar came in all right, Master Paul."

"Malabar! Malabar! Did I say Malabar, mother? Did I say Malabar? Do you think I'm lucky, mother? I knew Malabar, didn't I? Over eighty thousand pounds! I knew, didn't I know I knew? Malabar came in all right. If I ride my horse till I'm sure, then I tell you, Bassett, you can go as high as you like. Did you go for all you were worth, Bassett?"

"I went a thousand on it, Master Paul."

"I never told you, mother, that if I can ride my horse, and *get there*, then I'm absolutely sure — oh, absolutely! Mother, did I ever tell you? I *am* lucky!"

"No, you never did," said the mother.

But the boy died in the night.

And even as he lay dead, his mother heard her brother's voice saying to her: "My God, Hester, you're eighty-odd thousand to the good, and a poor devil of a son to the bad. But, poor devil, poor devil, he's best gone out of a life where he rides his rocking-horse to find a winner."

CRITIQUE AND QUESTIONS

Lawrence felt that the modern scrambling for money was draining man of his noblest instincts. This story carries a powerful message for members of any society in which getting and displaying mechanical luxuries seem urgently important. The suppression of a basic human instinct is a matter for sorrow, and the opening paragraph establishes the haunting tone of sadness that Lawrence maintains throughout the story. The woman, who is nameless until the last paragraph, knows that her heart has a little lifeless core that renders her incapable of love. If this core really were dead and she could not love, the story would lose some of its pathos; but the conclusion, although it sustains this image of a dead centre to her heart — "His mother sat, feeling her heart had gone, turned actually into stone" — demonstrates that her love has been merely entranced, frozen into a sleep of years. Ironically, it is the cold touch of her child's death that re-awakens in this sleeping beauty her power to love: "Then he fell with a crash to the ground and she, all her tormented motherhood flooding upon her, rushed to gather him up."

The opening words of the story read like a fairy tale. "There was a woman who was beautiful, who started with all the advantages, yet she had no luck." This simple style is appropriate, for like a fairy tale, "The Rocking-Horse Winner" is a mixture of realism and the supernatural and like a fairy tale, it teaches a lesson. At first it seems as if Lawrence is going to give us the moral directly. He approaches his lesson by *explaining* the opening situation, *telling* us about the loveless relationship of the children and the parents rather than *showing* us dramatically through action and dialogue. He sums up the family's history of bad luck, introduces the voices that trouble the children with the whisper, "There must be more money", and tells us of the rocking-horse that makes its appearance as one of the many expensive Christmas gifts which the parents cannot afford, but buy because "the style was always kept up". The rocking-horse is the link between the sinister realm of the super-natural and the world of ordinary reality; Lawrence prepares us to accept its later terrifying significance by endowing it with aware-ness when it first appears: "... even the horse, bending his wooden, champing head, heard it ... 'There must be more money!' "

But after this exposition and summary, notice that Lawrence at once begins to dramatize what he has previously merely explained. Sometimes Lawrence is criticized for preaching in his novels and stories rather than working out his themes artistically through his characters and events. Whether or not this criticism applies to "The Rocking-Horse Winner", you must decide for yourself. At least it is clear that he uses the dramatic technique extensively. The woman's unappeased hunger for money and the boy's pathetic desire to be "lucky" are made clear dramatically through dialogue. The scene ends with Paul's stout assertion, unconsciously ironic when we consider what happens later, "Well, anyhow . . . I'm a lucky person." Thus Paul hurls defiance at the dark gods presiding over human greed. The plot has begun.

Immediately Lawrence hints at the sinister influence of the horse in Paul's quest for money. In order to think, he sits upon his horse, "charging madly into space, with a frenzy that made the little girls peer at him uneasily." Through the uneasiness of the little girls and through the eerie description of Paul's appearance as he rides, we are prepared for the later mystical communion between the boy and his horse. There are repeated references to the unnatural brilliance of the boy's eyes. In his relationship with the horse, he becomes transformed, a cruel little priest hating his oracle and demanding a prophecy with hysterical urgency, " 'Now, take me to where there is luck! Now take me!' and he would slash the horse on the neck with the little whip he had asked uncle Oscar for." Lawrence seems to be saying that the forces driving human beings to seek money are cruel and pervert the instinct of love.

This reference to the whip skilfully implicates uncle Oscar in the parents' guilt for Paul's eventual death and makes a neat transition into the next passage of dialogue. Uncle Oscar's first words are highly significant and, considering Paul's fate, ironic. "Hullo young jockey! Riding a winner?" Their conversation sounds natural and convincing. Very economically it shows the uncle's easy-going camaraderie with Paul; it hints at, though does not make explicit, Paul's method of predicting a winner; and it introduces the fourth main character in the story, the gardener, Bassett. Bassett, less jocular than the uncle, appears to sense from the first that the boy's success in racing is more than natural. His face is as "serious as a church", and he describes Paul's interest in racing "as if he were speaking of religious matters". If you look back over the story, you will see that Lawrence has Bassett repeat the idea that the boy's uncanny gift is supernatural. He senses some of the truth, but not the entire, sinister truth.

The uncle joins the partnership and the partnership flourishes. In this part of the story it is rewarding to pay particular attention to the way Lawrence builds up suspense. We have the anxious feeling that no good can come of this weird enterprise. How does Lawrence achieve this effect? He does it partly through several skilful touches of dialogue and description which an attentive re-reading will uncover, but the crisis by which he intensifies the suspense is, of course, Paul's inability to pick a winner after he has released almost all his previous winnings to his mother. Under this sudden shower of unexpected wealth, the house blossoms into luxurious new furnishings. Lawrence uses this part of the story to emphasize his theme, though he does it dramatically, not through preaching. The voices, far from being stilled, "suddenly went mad, like a chorus of frogs on a spring evening ... 'There *must* be more money! Oh-h-h; there *must* be more money. Oh, now, now-w! Now-w-w — there *must* be more money! — more than ever! More than ever!' " Paul becomes frightened. He loses on the Grand National, then on the Lincoln. The references to the wildness in Paul's eyes increase; even his mother notices the change in him. The pace of the story accelerates towards the climax. Not only is Paul unable to predict a winner for the Derby, but his mother threatens to remove him to the seaside, away from the house, away from the rocking-horse which now resides in his bedroom at the top of the house. Tension is further increased by Lawrence's description of the boy's appearance: "... he was very frail and his eyes were really uncanny", and by the mother's mounting concern: "Sometimes for half an hour she would feel a sudden anxiety about him that was almost anguish."

The climax begins by concentrating the reader's attention on the mother's fears and her apprehensive behaviour at a party two nights before the Derby. She telephones home and is temporarily reassured. But at last, an apprehensive conviction that he is in danger drives her back to her house. The final meeting of mother and son in the attic is a scene in blinding greenish light, ended by the mournfully prophetic trumpet call of the Derby winner's name. Re-read this scene and notice how Lawrence leads up to it with a series of short sentences like anguished breathing, how he focuses attention first on the boy and then on the mother, how he lengthens the final passage so that it soars up to the mother's exclamation and the boy's single, strident cry. And consider why Lawrence chose the name, "Malabar", instead of, say, "Sea-Biscuit" or "Runabout".

The dark powers have permitted the child to pry from them the name of the winner that will put the distraught mother "eighty odd thousand to the good". But the pale horse has thrown its rider. The *dénouement* tells us what we suspect must follow — that the boy dies. What the mother's thoughts are about her latest shower of gold, Lawrence leaves to our horrified imagination.

1. Lawrence was a passionately moral writer with a philosophic conviction to impress upon his reader. Express concisely the important ideas you think he was trying to communicate in "The Rocking-Horse Winner".

2. "Even if you disregard its moral lesson, 'The Rocking-Horse Winner' can stand examination as a skilfully told horror story in which there is a subtle blending of the natural and the supernatural." Discuss the validity of this opinion.

3. In order to make the story plausible, the writer must have us believe that Paul is an extremely sensitive boy with a streak of fanaticism. How does Lawrence persuade us that Paul had these qualities?

4. Refer to the story to illustrate the various techniques by which the author makes us aware of the woman's chief character traits. Consider the use of dialogue, description of her behaviour, and the author's direct exposition.

5. The mother's attitude toward her son undergoes a development during the story. Describe her first attitude and trace the changes in this attitude referring to significant passages in the story.

James
Joyce

# Araby

---

*James Joyce (1882-1941) was born in Dublin, Ireland, and educated at the Dublin Royal University. A rebellious spirit, highly critical of the cultural, religious, and social life of Ireland, Joyce spent his adult life in Continental Europe. His sensitive and incisive volume of short stories,* Dubliners, *appeared in 1914; and a play,* The Exiles, *appeared in 1918. The three novels,* A Portrait of the Artist as a Young Man *(1916),* Ulysses *(1922), and* Finnegans Wake *(1939), ascend a rising scale of technical complexity and difficulty. There are critics who contend that Joyce is the greatest novelist of our age; there are others who fear that he has damaged the novel form by asking too much of it — and of his readers. There is no question, however, but that he has exerted a deep influence on the craft of fiction in our time. Unlike the later works, Joyce's early stories are clear in style and simple, lyrical, and haunting in effect. "Araby" is reprinted from* Dubliners *(all rights reserved) by permission of The Viking Press, Inc.*

---

NORTH RICHMOND STREET, being blind, was a quiet street except at the hour when the Christian Brothers' School set the boys free. An uninhabited house of two storeys stood at the blind end, detached from its neighbours in a square ground. The other houses of the street, conscious of decent lives within them, gazed at one another with brown imperturbable faces.

The former tenant of our house, a priest, had died in the back drawing-room. Air, musty from having been long enclosed, hung in all the rooms, and the waste room behind the kitchen was littered with old useless papers. Among these I found a few paper-covered books, the pages of which were curled and damp: *The Abbot*, by Walter Scott, *The Devout Communicant* and *The Memoirs of Vidocq*. I liked the last best because its leaves were yellow. The wild garden behind the house contained a central apple-tree and a few straggling bushes under one of which I found the late tenant's rusty bicycle-pump. He had been a very charitable priest; in his will he had left all his money to institutions and the furniture of his house to his sister.

When the short days of winter came dusk fell before we had well eaten our dinners. When we met in the street the houses had grown sombre. The space of sky above us was the colour of everchanging violet and towards it the lamps of the street lifted their feeble lanterns. The cold air stung us and we played till our bodies glowed. Our shouts echoed in the silent street. The career of our play brought us through the dark muddy lanes behind the houses where we ran the gauntlet of the rough tribes from the cottages, to the back doors of the dark dripping gardens where odours arose from the ashpits, to the dark odorous stables where a coachman smoothed and combed the horse or shook music from the buckled harness. When we returned to the street light from the kitchen windows had filled the areas. If my uncle was seen turning the corner we hid in the shadow until we had seen him safely housed. Or if Mangan's sister came out on the doorstep to call her brother in to his tea we watched her from our shadow peer up and down the street. We waited to see whether she would remain or go in and, if she remained, we left our shadow and walked up to Mangan's steps resignedly. She was waiting for us, her figure defined by the light from the half-opened door. Her brother always teased her before he obeyed and I stood by the railings looking at her. Her dress swung as she moved her body and the soft rope of her hair tossed from side to side.

Every morning I lay on the floor in the front parlour watching her door. The blind was pulled down to within an inch of the sash so that I could not be seen. When she came out on the doorstep my heart leaped. I ran to the hall, seized my books and followed her. I kept her brown figure always in my eye and, when we came near the point at which our ways diverged, I quickened my pace and passed her. This happened morning after morning. I had never spoken to her, except for a few casual words, and yet her name was like a summons to all my foolish blood.

Her image accompanied me even in places the most hostile to romance. On Saturday evenings when my aunt went marketing I had to go to carry some of the parcels. We walked through the flaring streets, jostled by drunken men and bargaining women, amid the curses of labourers, the shrill litanies of shop-boys who stood on guard by the barrels of pigs' cheeks, the nasal chanting of street-singers, who sang a *come-all-you* about O'Donovan Rossa, or a ballad about the troubles in our native land. These noises converged in a single sensation of life for me: I imagined that I bore my chalice safely through a throng of foes. Her name sprang to my lips at moments in strange prayers and praises which I myself did not understand. My eyes were often full of tears (I could not tell why) and at times a flood from my heart seemed to pour itself out into my bosom. I thought little of the future. I did not know whether I would ever speak to her or not or, if I spoke to her, how I could tell her of my confused adoration. But my body was like a harp and her words and gestures were like fingers running upon the wires.

One evening I went into the back drawing-room in which the priest had died. It was a dark rainy evening and there was no sound in the house. Through one of the broken panes I heard the rain impinge upon the earth, the fine incessant needles of water playing in the sodden beds. Some distant lamp or lighted window gleamed below me. I was thankful that I could see so little. All my senses seemed to desire to veil themselves, and, feeling that I was about to slip from them, I pressed the palms of my hands together until they trembled, murmuring: *"O love! O love!"* many times.

At last she spoke to me. When she addressed the first words to me I was so confused that I did not know what to answer. She asked me was I going to *Araby*. I forgot whether I answered yes or no. It would be a splendid bazaar, she said she would love to go.

"And why can't you?" I asked.

While she spoke she turned a silver bracelet round and round her wrist. She could not go, she said, because there would be a retreat that week in her convent. Her brother and two other boys were fighting for their caps and I was alone at the railings. She held one of the spikes, bowing her head towards me. The light from the lamp opposite our door caught the white curve of her neck, lit up her hair that rested there and, falling, lit up the hand upon the railing. It fell over one side of her dress and caught the white border of a petticoat, just visible as she stood at ease.

"It's well for you," she said.

"If I go," I said, "I will bring you something."

What innumerable follies laid waste my waking and sleeping thoughts after that evening! I wished to annihilate the tedious intervening days. I chafed against the work of school. At night in my bedroom and by day in the classroom her image came between me and the page I strove to read. The syllables of the word *Araby* were called to me through the silence in which my soul luxuriated and cast an Eastern enchantment over me. I asked for leave to go to the bazaar on Saturday night. My aunt was surprised and hoped it was not some Freemason affair. I answered few questions in class. I watched my master's face pass from amiability to sternness; he hoped I was not beginning to idle. I could not call my wandering thoughts together. I had hardly any patience with the serious work of life which, now that it stood between me and my desire, seemed to me child's play, ugly monotonous child's play.

On Saturday morning I reminded my uncle that I wished to go to the bazaar in the evening. He was fussing at the hallstand, looking for the hatbrush, and answered me curtly:

"Yes, boy, I know."

As he was in the hall I could not go into the front parlour and lie at the window. I left the house in bad humour and walked slowly towards the school. The air was pitilessly raw and already my heart misgave me.

When I came home to dinner my uncle had not yet been home. Still it was early. I sat staring at the clock for some time and, when its ticking began to irritate me, I left the room. I mounted the staircase and gained the upper part of the house. The high cold empty gloomy rooms liberated me and I went from room to room singing. From the front window I saw my companions playing below in the street. Their cries reached me weakened and indistinct and, leaning my forehead against the cool glass, I looked over at the dark house where she lived. I may have stood there for an hour, seeing nothing but the brown-clad figure cast by my imagination, touched discreetly by the lamplight at the curved neck, at the hand upon the railings and at the border below the dress.

When I came downstairs again I found Mrs. Mercer sitting at the fire. She was an old garrulous woman, a pawnbroker's widow, who collected used stamps for some pious purpose. I had to endure the gossip of the tea-table. The meal was prolonged beyond an hour and still my uncle did not come. Mrs. Mercer stood up to go: she was sorry she couldn't wait any longer, but it was after eight o'clock and she did not like to be out late, as the night air was bad for her. When she had gone I began to walk up and down the room, clenching my fists. My aunt said:

"I'm afraid you may put off your bazaar for this night of Our Lord."

At nine o'clock I heard my uncle's latchkey in the halldoor. I heard him talking to himself and heard the hallstand rocking when it had received the weight of the overcoat. I could interpret these signs. When he was midway through his dinner I asked him to give me the money to go to the bazaar. He had forgotten.

"The people are in bed and after their first sleep now," he said.

I did not smile. My aunt said to him energetically:

"Can't you give him the money and let him go? You've kept him late enough as it is."

My uncle said he was very sorry he had forgotten. He said he believed in the old saying: "All work and no play makes Jack a

dull boy." He asked me where I was going and, when I had told
him a second time he asked me did I know *The Arab's Farewell
to his Steed.* When I left the kitchen he was about to recite the
opening lines of the piece to my aunt.

I held a florin tightly in my hand as I strode down Buckingham
Street towards the station. The sight of the streets thronged with
buyers and glaring with gas recalled to me the purpose of my
journey. I took my seat in a third-class carriage of a deserted
train. After an intolerable delay the train moved out of the station
slowly. It crept onward among ruinous houses and over the
twinkling river. At Westland Row Station a crowd of people
pressed to the carriage doors; but the porters moved them back,
saying that it was a special train for the bazaar. I remained alone
in the bare carriage. In a few minutes the train drew up beside
an improvised wooden platform. I passed out on to the road and
saw by the lighted dial of a clock that it was ten minutes to ten.
In front of me was a large building which displayed the magical
name.

I could not find any sixpenny entrance and, fearing that the
bazaar would be closed, I passed in quickly through a turnstile,
handing a shilling to a weary-looking man. I found myself in a
big hall girdled at half its height by a gallery. Nearly all the stalls
were closed and the greater part of the hall was in darkness. I
recognized a silence like that which pervades a church after a
service. I walked into the centre of the bazaar timidly. A few
people were gathered about the stalls which were still open.
Before a curtain, over which the words *Café Chantant* were
written in coloured lamps, two men were counting money on
a salver. I listened to the fall of the coins.

Remembering with difficulty why I had come I went over to
one of the stalls and examined porcelain vases and flowered tea-
sets. At the door of the stall a young lady was talking and laughing with two young gentlemen. I remarked their English accents
and listened vaguely to their conversation.

"O, I never said such a thing!"

"O, but you did!"

"O, but I didn't!"

"Didn't she say that?"

"Yes. I heard her."

"O, there's a . . . fib!"

Observing me the young lady came over and asked me did I wish to buy anything. The tone of her voice was not encouraging; she seemed to have spoken to me out of a sense of duty. I looked humbly at the great jars that stood like eastern guards at either side of the dark entrance to the stall and murmured:

"No, thank you."

The young lady changed the position of one of the vases and went back to the two young men. They began to talk of the same subject. Once or twice the young lady glanced at me over her shoulder.

I lingered before her stall, though I knew my stay was useless, to make my interest in her wares seem the more real. Then I turned away slowly and walked down the middle of the bazaar. I allowed the two pennies to fall against the sixpence in my pocket. I heard a voice call from one end of the gallery that the light was out. The upper part of the hall was now completely dark.

Gazing up into the darkness I saw myself as a creature driven and derided by vanity; and my eyes burned with anguish and anger.

QUESTIONS

The short stories of James Joyce (and indeed his larger and later works) are lyrics rather than tales. It is important in reading "Araby" to linger over the qualities of image, mood, and tempo.

1. If you were asked to reduce this story to pure narrative (to a succession of events), what would you have to strike out?

2. Could this story have been written as effectively in the third person?

3. What is the value, for the mood of the story, of the opening descriptive paragraphs — the sombre light, the deserted house, the dead

priest and his books, the cold, the silence, and the "dark dripping gardens"?

4. What do we find out about the girl? Why, for the purposes of the story, is it unnecessary to tell us more about her?

5. Why is there so little talk between the boy and the girl?

6. Where and by what means does the author present the boy in love as isolated, alone, and shut in upon himself (even when he is not physically alone)? Why this emphasis upon isolation?

7. Contrast the meaning of the bazaar in prospect with the drab reality of the bazaar in fact.

8. What purpose is served by having the boy arrive late at the bazaar and leave empty-handed?

9. Why does the story begin and end in darkness? At what points in the story does light appear? Why?

*Thomas*

*Raddall*

# Pax Britannica

―――――――――――――

*Thomas Raddall (b. 1903), novelist and historian, was born in England, but came to Halifax, Nova Scotia, with his parents in 1913. At the age of fifteen, he left school to enlist as a wireless operator, and from 1918 to 1922, served as a radio officer, both at sea and at stations along the Nova Scotia coast. Later he settled in Liverpool, Nova Scotia, working as a bookkeeper and contributing short stories to various magazines. Since 1938, he has lived entirely by his pen. His first published collection of short stories was* The Pied Piper of Dipper Creek *(1939). Some of his novels are* His Majesty's Yankees *(1942),* Roger Sudden *(1945),* Pride's Fancy *(1946),* The Nymph and the Lamp *(1950),* Tidefall *(1953),* The Wings of Night *(1956) and* The Governor's Lady *(1960). He has also published historical works, including* Halifax, Warden of the North *(1948) and* The Path of Destiny *(1957). His historical stories vividly suggest the hazards of pioneer life in early Nova Scotia. The following story is reprinted with the author's permission.*

―――――――――――――

IN THE BEGINNING the site of our town was a low wooded slope beside a tidal river in a most lonely stretch of the Nova Scotia coast. Not exactly lonely, for the river ran fifty or sixty miles into the peninsula and made a very easy highway for the canoes of the Micmacs, a people hostile to intruders, especially those who spoke the English tongue. In the fighting for Acadie the Micmacs, blood allies of the French, had played a bloody part. But in the end they were out-matched by frontier fighters as ruthless and as cunning as themselves. One of these was Silas Bradford, the founder of our town.

Bradford is a fascinating figure even now. He must have fascinated his contemporaries. Who else could have led them away from the peace and security of Cape Cod, the home of their pilgrim fathers, to settle in this Indian-haunted wilderness which the English called Nova Scotia, the French called Acadie, and which the Micmacs were quite sure was Megumaage? He had come first to the peninsula in 1745 and joined that amazing army of raw New England militia which conquered Louisbourg. Afterwards he and his company of rangers remained in the peninsula to curb the raids of the Micmacs. The regiment of British regulars at Annapolis were helpless outside their palisades. When Halifax was founded in '49 its garrison was little better off. The white inhabitants of the province were almost entirely French in blood and hostile in sentiment — and closely allied to the Micmacs in all ways.

And so for years the ranger companies under men like Bradford carried on a single-handed war against the savages. Of that struggle perhaps the less said the better; a merciless business conducted by canoe and afoot in the wilderness, dependent always on surprise for success — a long and hungry journey in utter stealth, a sudden volley of shots and yells, a closing rush with the tomahawks rising and falling, and the little circular patches of skin and hair dripping red from the belts. Both sides had their victories.

Sometimes the scalps were traded for blankets and hatchets in the French posts toward Quebec, a currency as good as *louis d'or*. Sometimes they went to Halifax for the British governor's bounty — any price from £5 to £50, depending on the circumstances, and no questions asked. A patch of clotted hair might be a man's, a woman's or a child's — who could tell? A bloody chapter....

When the British made the second and final conquest of Louisbourg in 1758, Silas Bradford was there with his armed sloop and his rangers, an amphibious company very useful in the coastal creeks and in the forest about the town. Young Wolfe, the brigadier with the red hair and the absurd chin, was even then fermenting plans for Quebec in the following year, and bespoke, amongst many things, Silas, his rangers, and his sloop. The rangers went to Quebec, and it was one of them who first pointed out to Wolfe that now famous path up the cliff before the Plains of Abraham. But Silas himself had other plans.

In the destruction of Louisbourg he foresaw the final overthrow of the French empire in America. The time was ripe for a matter he had cherished many years, a settlement of his own people in the promised land. He went back to Cape Cod, the place of his birth, and his old neighbours flocked to hear him. The itch for new settlement was strong in all New England. The vast lands to the west, so far from the sea, had no charm for these fishermen sons of the pilgrims. It was the peninsula of Nova Scotia they saw in all their dreams, a great wharf thrusting out toward the cod banks.

Pious men, these, singing psalms through their noses precisely as they talked, for they were Yankees of the Yankees, gaunt powerful men with nutcracker faces and shrewd eyes, who drank much rum and feared nobody but a God who was always very near and talked through his nose to them.

"A fine place to dry fish and handy the Banks," Bradford told them. "We'd ha' moved our families there long since if 'tweren't for the French and Injuns."

"They say there's good farmland along Fundy Bay," said Increase Nickerson. "Cleared and diked by the 'Cajun people that was took off in '55. To be had now for the takin'."

"That's for farmers," Bradford snorted. "We're fishermen, us Cape-Codders. That Nova Scotia province must always depend in the main upon the fishery, and the south and east coast is the place for it — handy the Banks, an easy run to Halifax or Boston, and none o' that Fundy tide, where your harbour goes out to sea twice a day and leaves your vessel on her beam ends in the mud."

He spread a map before them and thrust a thick finger at the inlet where our town now stands. "There's Kebamkoogwek. Meanin', The-River-has-a-Bar-at-its-Mouth."

"Humph!" they said.

"Ah, but the river scours a channel in the bar, with twenty feet good water on common tides and a goodish bit more on the springs. What d'ye want? It's schooners you've got, not seventy-fours. Within the bar the river takes a turn to the west and there's a tidal pool, sheltered from all winds. That's the place for us. A brook runs off the hillside big enough to turn a sawmill, grist-mill, anything ye want. The whole land's a forest that's never heard the sound of an axe — shipbuildin' timber growin' by the waterside — and there's a salmon fishery in the river mouth good for a thousand barrels a season."

"Then why didn't the French settle the place?" demanded Micah Daggett.

Bradford grunted. "Farmers! They'd no real taste for the sea. The French must have their hands and feet in the dirt always. Well, there's more rock than dirt at Kebamkoogwek."

Then Judah Merricombe spoke the question in all their minds. "What about the Injuns?"

"Look'ee here," Silas Bradford said. "In my father's time they hanged women for witches at Salem. 'Cause why? 'Cause they were afeared o' what they didn't know. So 'tis with people don't know Injuns. Injuns ain't a danger but to men that's afraid o' the shadows in the forest. 'Tell you I've been in those parts nigh fifteen year, fightin' Injuns their own way, and beat 'em at it. D'ye know what they call me? Mel-ke-ga — Strong Fist, that is. Ay, and they've other names for me, come to that. Noo-je-na-be-de-ga — The Slayer — and after we drove out the 'Cajun French and burnt their farms it was Pe-jis-to-wa-ya-luk — He-Smokes-Them-Out. D'ye think they'd provoke me lightly? I tell you I was trained in a rough school that held the only good Injuns were the dead 'uns. Strike, strike first, and strike hard — that's the secret, and waste no time on words. *They* know. I'm not saying this to boast."

"We must have room for the flakes to spread and dry our fish,"

Judah objected. "Means an almighty big stockade for a few men and boys to guard when we're off to the Banks."

"Are ye men or what?" Silas Bradford cried. "I'll have no stockade about me. We'll build our settlement as if 'twas on Cape Cod, for look'ee here, a stockade's a bad thing. People inside come to think upon it as the limit o' their world. The savages see it that way too. I'll have none of it."

"We've got wives and younkers to think of," Amos Harding said.

"Ease your minds, then. The Injuns have wives and younkers too. They've learned their lesson. Wrote in blood, it was. Besides, they're a scattered, wanderin', shiftless people. The mad priest Le Loutre managed to gather a few hundred *kenaps* now and again, wi' the promise o' blankets and arms and some trumpery for their women; but he never held 'em long, 'specially after they'd got mauled in a fight or two. Besides, Le Loutre is gone now. His bishop at Quebec disowned him and sent Father Maillard to preach peace amongst the tribes. Ye've nothing to fear but your own fancies. Words! Words! Great God, I am no talking man. D'ye want to go or not?"

"People's goin' to Nova Scotia from all New England," Increase Nickerson said.

"Us too, then," Amos Harding said, "afore someone gets to Kebamkoogwek ahead of us."

So they agreed and formed a Committee of Proprietors, in the New England fashion (in Old England they would have called themselves a Company of Adventurers), and came to Kebamkoogwek in the summer of 1759, when Wolfe was hammering at the gates of Quebec. Sixteen schooners lay in the tidal pool above the bar. Women stared over the low bulwarks at the forest where the axes rang; quiet, unsmiling Cape Cod women in heavy homespun gowns, relieved by a bright handkerchief about the shoulders; the hard-working, child-bearing pioneer women who married at sixteen, were middle-aged at twenty-eight, and very often dead at thirty-five.

Each settler had a measured strip of water-front with all the land that lay behind it, and so our town began as a procession of clearings along the shore, linked by a rough track where the yoked oxen struggled to haul sleds (they had no wagons) amongst the boulders and the stumps. The first homes were crude log huts with puncheon floors, stone-slab hearths and chimneys of clay moulded over sticks.

But Silas Bradford built himself a proper house at the very start. He was rich in the light of those times. The Nova Scotia governors had paid him well for his sloop and his services: and in the background, in the dark scalp-hunting years . . . well, the prices had been good and paid in gold. He brought his material ready-sawn from Boston, beams of red pine, oak posts and joists, white pine scantlings, planks and clapboards, spruce flooring, windows of real glass, doors — he forgot nothing, not even the bricks for the chimneys, nor the great slab of mahogany for the mantelpiece in the parlour, nor the delft tiles for the hearth. A provident man.

It was strange to him that the others clung so to the sea in their building, as if it were a refuge to be kept at hand. Silas chose his land deliberately at the north skirt of the settlement, at the edge of the forest where the river flowed down from the mysterious interior. As for the town street, he scorned the track that clung thus to the harbourside and cut out a road running straight up the slope into the forest, and built his house to face it, calling it Wolfe Street after his old commander, and so it is known to this day.

They wanted to call their settlement Newport, because it was just that; but someone pointed out that there was a Newport in Rhode Island, founded by Antinomians from Massachusetts Bay, and therefore not quite respectable, and Bradford said bluntly, "Call it Oldport and be done with it. It's old enough. The Injuns say their great god Glooskap camped here when the world was young."

And Oldport it was, and is.

They saw a few Indians in the Fall, canoes stealing up-river in the dusk, hugging the far side of the pool; but there was nothing to fear from these furtive wanderers. Oldport kept a musket over its mantelpiece, ready to hand, and let defence go at that. The first winter was hard. They still tell tales of it in our town. The river froze, and the tidal pool as well, and the great mass of ice in the pool rose and fell with the tide, breaking along the shores, swaying its tremendous weight against the banks with the winds, freezing again on the slack.

The makeshift wharves of that first summer were crushed to matchwood, and some of the vessels sank at their moorings. Food ran short. They had relied on the hunting, and the hunting that year was poor. For fresh meat they snared white hares in the frozen swamps. Flour was a luxury. Chiefly they lived on cod-fish caught and dried the previous year, and on smoked salmon and old ship-biscuit. They suffered a disease which may have been scurvy or a form of beri-beri, but which they considered a malady of the country. Yet they hung on. An enduring people.

As soon as the ice was out of the river they patched their vessels and set out for the fishery on which their lives and fortunes depended, leaving the boys and old men to get firewood for the women. They felt their town secure. Had not Silas Bradford said so, and wasn't he there, the grim strong man, to face whatever problems might arise?

A few days after they sailed for the Banks, Ichabod Limard came rattling at Bradford's door, the stout oak door fetched all the way from Boston. Ichabod was a tall pale youth from the Maine backwoods, where he had been scalped with a number of other unfortunates in one of the French-Indian raids. His coarse yellow hair stopped at a patch of pink skin on the top of his head, crudely circular like the tonsure of a monk, where the scalp had healed. The muscles of his face had gone slack, as the muscles of scalped heads do, so that his features dripped downward like soft wax, a mass of thick wrinkles and heavy jowls, with the eyes peering light blue through the slits. His mind had warped, too.

Silas opened the door and the poor half-wit stood gibbering in the warmth of the Bradford kitchen, in his torn and patched drab homespun breeches and grey woollen stockings, a coarse linsey shirt and ragged blue coat. There was still much snow in the shadow of the woods but where the sun fell the ground was bare,

with greasy mud in the hollows. Ichabod's moosehide moccasins
soiled the hooked rug on the kitchen floor.

"Injuns?" Silas said. "Well, what of it?"

Mrs. Bradford turned an inquiring eye. She itched to order
this filthy ragamuffin out of doors — messing her clean floor! —
but she was vaguely alarmed.

"All the men away at the fishing," she murmured, as if Silas
did not know. She was a little afraid of Silas, a grim man, and
touchy on some subjects. She had asked him once, soon after
they were married, if he had ever scalped a woman — a tactless
question.

He answered abruptly, "Be still, woman." His grey eyes had
gone hard and cold, like the ice in the edge of the woods. She
folded her hands and said no more. He took a musket from the
moose-horns over the mantel, poured a stiff charge from the
powder-horn hanging on the wall, measured it with the ramrod,
poured a little more, thrust home a wad, two balls, another wad.
He examined the gun-flint, primed the gun, nodded, and leaned
the musket against a chair.

He exchanged his shoes for a pair of moccasins and pulled on
a shirt of caribou hide, his ranger shirt, the sleeves fringed from
wrist to shoulder with dangling leather points. His old ranger
cap of raccoon fur hung on a nail, its glossy tail dangling. For
some queer whim he rejected it and put on his thrice-cocked blue
Boston hat, his ship hat, crisp and stained with salt, one peak torn
by the flying grape at Louisbourg. It gave him a certain air of
authority, perhaps, that the fur cap lacked.

He slipped a tomahawk in his belt, slung on powder-horn and
bullet pouch, caught up the musket and was gone, all in a potent
silence. Mrs. Bradford saw him step across the stones and stumps
of "Wolfe Street" and vanish amongst the pines, moving like a
lean cat in his moccasins. Silas struck back upon the ridge and
followed it for a mile in the bare hardwoods on the south side of
the crest, where the spring sun had melted the snow and his
moccasins left no tracks. Then he turned toward the river.

On the north slope, where the April sun never fell, the snow
lay deep and crusted in the green gloom of tall pines and hem-

locks. He wished he had brought his snowshoes but the crust
bore him well enough. A fool's journey, he told himself. The
poor half-wit had seen half a dozen peaceful hunters and multi-
plied them by four. He was always seeing Injuns.

Silas perceived the camp smoke now, and moved more cautiously. From the bare branch of a great oak on a spur of the ridge
he looked straight down upon the camp, fifteen wigwams or
more, some in the edge of the woods, the rest pitched on a flat
of dead grass at the riverside. Children moved about the fires, a
few curs slept in the sun. Beside one of the fires a group of young
squaws were playing *al-tes-ta-kun*. They used a platter finely
carved from knurl of maple, tossing the little bone discs and
catching them expertly. At each throw they bent forward, heads
together, watching the fall of the discs, counting those with the
lucky mark uppermost, and the spillikins they used for forfeit
passed from hand to hand.

Their caribou-hide smocks and leggings were soiled with the
grease and soot of winter fires. They wore fillets of red cloth
about their heads but the long black hair flittered about their
shoulders with their rocking movements. The rattle of dice and
the giggling laughter came up very clearly to the man in the oak.
They were keeping no watch. Were these people peaceable or
simply ignoring the presence of the white settlement just below,
knowing its impotence? There was no sign of men or canoes.
That was ominous.

Silas descended the tree carefully and walked down to the
camp. The snow crust held firmly to the very edge of the trees
but in the sunny wild meadow by the river the brown grass was
bare. He stood there in plain sight with the musket in the crook
of his arm. For a long time he remained thus, a statue in a shaft
of sunlight through the trees. The young squaws were intent on
their game. An older woman came from a wigwam, waddling
toward the river with a brass pot in her hand. She saw Bradford
and froze at once. They stared at each other.

One or two of the players looked up, regarding the woman
curiously, and followed her stiff gaze to the man in the edge of
the woods. Then the whole camp was watching him, even the

children, all in utter silence. The curs, sensing trouble, roused from their slumbers and snarled, but like the women, they were awed by this still intruder.

"*Kway!*" said Bradford in his strong voice. "Greeting!"

They did not answer. All those black eyes were wide and frightened.

"Where are my Meeg-a-Mahg brothers?"

Again silence.

Bradford said softly, "I see that my daughters have no tongues and I am sad, for my warriors take the hair of silent women."

A young squaw spoke hurriedly. "*Wis-ko-ma-ya-sa* — they have gone to hunt moose."

"My daughter lies! I see the rock where my brothers have been grinding paint. They have taken the canoes. Do the Meeg-a-Magh paint for the hunt? Do they hunt moose in canoes? *Tal-sut-um-un* — how does it sound to thee?" He could see wrinkled female faces peering from the wigwam flaps. One spoke.

"There is one canoe, an old one. Behold, it is in the bushes by the river."

Silas gestured fiercely. "Take it then, and fetch my brothers. I would have talk with them."

"They would not come," the old woman said sullenly.

"Tell them Pe-jis-to-wa-ya-luk stands in their camp, my daughter. They will come." None moved. The old woman withdrew, frightened, into the wigwam. Silas turned his cold eyes to the hesitating young squaws.

"What pleasure shall the young men find in the arms of dead women? Who is to shelter the child when the wigwam burns? Go, while there is time!"

Two ran to a clump of alders on the bank and put off in a canoe, an old thing with gunwales chipped and splintered on hard portages, the sides a mass of bark patches and daubs of black gum. They paddled rapidly downstream and disappeared around the bend.

A long wait. Bradford said no more. The women watched him beadily. After a time they began to steal glances into the woods at his back. He had expected that. The warriors would land their canoes below the point and creep through the woods to see what was afoot before showing themselves. His position there was awkward, for he dared not take his eyes from the women. They were as quick with a tomahawk as any of their men.

He stepped over to the group of young women silent about the forgotten game, and squatted where he could watch them and the woods, with the musket across his knees. They shrank away from him, and he said quietly, "*Won-to-ko-de* — it is peace." In swift side-glances he kept an eye on the river but nothing came around the bend. From the woods came the cry of the loon; not the maniacal laughter but the long call, three minor notes, a mournful sound.

He murmured, "The loon has no feet for branches, my daughters. Call my brothers to the fire. I wish to make talk."

A young matron — he had noticed her anxious gaze toward the staring children — stood up quickly and flung back her head, pouring the loon's wild laughter from her throat. In a moment, magically, an Indian stood in the open at the edge of the meadow. There was no movement, no sound. He materialized. The *kenap* wore nothing but a leather breech-clout and moccasins. His round Micmac face was streaked with red and orange paint. His brown body shone with bear grease. The coarse black hair was gathered on the top of his head with a thong — the Micmacs did not shave the head leaving nothing but a scalp-lock like the continental tribes — and a single eagle feather was thrust through the knot. He carried an ancient French firelock and a glittering steel tomahawk. A stone tobacco pipe was slung about his neck by a thong.

"*Won-to-ko-de*," called Bradford, without rising. They could not shoot him where he sat without risking the squaws. The warrior advanced boldly and squatted facing the white man at a safe distance, just beyond the reach of a tomahawk. He stank of sweat and rancid bear grease. Evidently the return had been made in some haste. Bradford found some grim humour in the thought of the other *kenaps*, stripped and painted for war, cooling their sweat now in the icy gloom of the trees, with the snow crust under their feet — perhaps beneath their bellies. They could not stay there long. They were tough, but not as tough as that.

Silas called out in his ringing voice toward the trees, "Ho! Is thy sagamore afraid, my brothers, that he send a *kenap* to make his talk? What medicine is this?"

Instantly the bushes parted and a tall Indian stepped into the sunlight. Like the other he was stripped to breech-clout and moccasins; but the moccasins were gaudy with rows of coloured trade beads, a pewter crucifix hung from a thin brass chain about his neck, and he wore on his head a silver-laced cocked hat of the kind worn by French officers at Louisbourg and Quebec.

The sagamore was painted more elaborately than his *kenap*. A black stripe encircled mouth and nose, overlaid with stripes of red ochre, and his eye-sockets were flaring scarlet cups. He carried a fine fowling-piece with a chased silver lock-plate. Silas stood up as he approached. They dropped their guns carefully and held up their right hands.

"Kway!"

"Kway!"

"I am called Kwemoo, the Loon," said the sagamore calmly.

"I greet thee, O Loon. Men call me Strong Fist. I have other names."

The fierce black eyes gleamed in their scarlet sockets. "The trees of the forest know the fame of Strong Fist. Ayah! His medicine is all-powerful. Did I not fire a ball at him by the waters of Tawopskek ten summers gone? And did not the Strong Fist brush it aside? Ayah! This thing I saw!"

Silas remembered that, an ambush almost in the shadow of Fort Anne. He had been shifting his tomahawk from the right hand to the left, and the ball glanced from the moving blade.

"Behold, I come to make talk with my brother," he said smoothly, "and find none but squaws and children in his camp. Have my brothers made war medicine?" A rhetorical question. War medicine was plain on their faces.

"Behold," retorted the sagamore, "we have watched my white brother's village and saw none but squaws and children. Where are the white warriors?"

The inevitable question! They had seen the weakness of the town. Still, The Slayer's bold appearance in their camp puzzled them, as he intended it should. Silas hoped that his famous presence there amongst their women and children would poison their spirit with precisely the same fear he knew himself. A subtle notion. Yet he was not a subtle man, and felt a sickening doubt of his ability to accomplish what he wished.

There was no blinking the uncomfortable facts. The Loon was no petty patriarch. These painted *kenaps* were the advance patrol of a tribe moving down the river from the winter hunting grounds in the interior, a pack of human wolves, lean and famished after the hard months in the snow. Ordinarily they would scatter up and down the coast in little fishing camps for the summer; but Oldport, a shining new temptation, lay between them and the sea. The thought of the defenceless settlement weighed on Silas like a stone. He cursed his blind confidence. This was what came of trusting other things than guns! For the first time in his life he faced a situation in which words were the only possible weapons, and heard a mocking laughter ringing out of all the past. This was Silas Bradford, the fighting man who believed in nothing else, who left the talking to men with a taste for it and held them in contempt — even the founder of Halifax, the man Cornwallis, whom he had liked otherwise.

He seemed to see Cornwallis now, treating patiently with petty chiefs who stank the council room and shed lice on the carpet, nursing their self-respect, sending them away with gifts, seeing that the guard presented arms as they passed, striving for the goodwill of those savage ragamuffins — Cornwallis the aristocrat, with a fleet in the harbour and regiments at his beck! To Captain Silas Bradford of the rangers all that smacked of cowardice, a paltry compromise with evil. Words! Words! Words, when any sound man knew the only good Injuns were the dead ones!

Now, suddenly, he saw what lay behind that madness. The Englishman had looked forward to a time — to this time — when small settlements would spring up along the coast, impossible to garrison, dependent for their prosperity, indeed their existence, upon the goodwill of the savages. But all that was past and far away. What words could serve now, here in this wild meadow, in the presence of these staring squaws, the wooden-faced *kenap* and his chief, the menace lurking in the trees and moving down the river?

The Micmacs had a smattering of bastard French but no English at all. Silas spoke Micmac well, but he had no respect for it, a grunting tongue that crammed a sentence into a single word and again took half a minute's gutturals to express what an Englishman could say in a second. In Micmac oratory the circuitous approach was the only decent way to the subject, you talked in circles, in rhetorical questions, in queer flowery figures of speech. They had a weakness for eloquence and could be swayed, as Le Loutre had swayed them against the English. Could he, the man who did not believe in words, talk them out of their war paint when they knew their own strength and surmised his weakness?

But did they know his weakness? The sagamore kept darting a suspicious gaze across the river, and staring toward the high pines at the top of the ridge. It dawned upon Bradford suddenly that the Indians, noting the absence of white men in the town, suspected a trick, an ambush — more, a raid upon their camp. His presence there was proof of it. He had deceived the squaws with some such pretence but he was astonished that the warriors should believe it also. How long before they guessed the truth?

"Why have my white brothers made their village at Kebamkoogwek?" demanded the sagamore harshly. "The river is ours, O Strong Fist. These are our hunting-grounds."

"We do not want your hunting-grounds, O Kwemoo, for we are ship-men who must go upon the Big Water for fish. We want only peace in this place."

The sagamore grunted, "Behold, long ago when I was a young man we made a peace with the English. Was it not broken? Behold, ten summers gone I went to Chebuktook with other sagamores of the Meeg-a-Mahg and Maliseet peoples and made peace with the English again. Did we not make our totems upon the white bark? Did not the English sagamores make theirs in the name of their great sagamore Joj across the Big Water? Did we not bury the hatchet? Who dug it up again? Konwallich turned you and your leather-shirts upon us. He gave you gold for scalps of our people."

"Not before the Meeg-a-Mahg broke the peace," insisted Bradford vigorously. "Who took the hair of his red-coats outside the palisades of Chebuktook? At Tawopskek? Was not this in the Meeg-a-Mahg country? Men do not scalp themselves."

"It was done at the Otter's bidding," muttered the sagamore sullenly.

"Ayah! There is much blood upon the hands of Le Loutre. Now he is gone. So be it. The English now are at Quebec, O Kwemoo. Louisbourg is no more. There is no stone upon another."

"Onontio has strong medicine," said The Loon doubtfully.

By this name the Algonkin tribes knew the king of France.

"The medicine of the great sagamore Joj is stronger. Behold, the French have gone from all the Meeg-a-Mahg country. Did we not take them away in our ships? Did not we burn their villages?"

"The snow melts in the spring sun, O Strong Fist. But is there not another winter and another snow?"

Silas was getting nowhere, and meanwhile the rest of the war party had been slipping from the chill woods into the sunlight. Some stood tense in the edge of the meadow, watching the silent green mass of the hillside. The rest grouped themselves about the speakers. The rustle of moccasins behind him tried Bradford's nerves in a new and painful manner, his ears strained for the whistle of the descending tomahawk, all instinct crying out, urging him to leap aside and make a fight for it. But he stood motionless with thumbs hooked in his belt, steadying knee and hand and eye, serving a bitter apprenticeship in the strange art of diplomacy.

All the *kenaps* were stripped, greased and painted for war. He counted twenty-three. Their ribs and the powerful ropes of muscle stood forth in the brown hairless skin — it had been a hard and hungry winter but there was no weakness in them. All were armed with good steel tomahawks and guns of various worth. One young *kenap* had in his belt a matchlock pistol with a huge butt beautifully chased, a thing of unguessed age. At every waist dangled one or two crooked-knives, made from scraps of metal on the old savage pattern, with short blades and large curved hafts, and sheaths of leather ornamented with beads and dyed porcupine quills. Some wore necklaces of bear teeth which, like the grease on their bodies, were supposed to give them the strength of Moween. Others had tobacco pipes slung about their necks. All had powder horns and bullet pouches. Bradford wondered what they contained after a winter's hunting.

One of the *kenaps* spoke up boastfully. "The Meeg-a-Mahg will drive the English into the Big Water. Then Onontio will return to his brothers."

He had a villainous squint. Silas stabbed a finger at him.

"*Ankaptaan!* Behold! He looks two ways and sees only his nose, and that he calls Onontio!"

The shadow of a smile passed over the tall sagamore's face. Silas turned to him, but included them all in the wave of his big hand. Out of his aching fear for the women and children in the town below, his memories of Cornwallis, his own half-anger, half-remorse — out of these and yet from nowhere that he understood, the words he wanted rushed to his mouth at last.

"O my brothers, this is thy hunting-ground, and the river is thy path between winter and summer. So be it. My people have made their village where the river meets the tide, for though they must live upon the earth like other men their living lies in the Big Water. So be it. The land is wide, the Big Water is wide, and all we are very small. The great wigwam of the sky covers us alike, and the stars look down upon us, and all we are very small. When the young moon comes, a virgin upon her back, does she not shine upon us all? When she has met her lord the sun beneath the world and returned ripe to the sky again, does she not shine upon us all? Who does the sun warm in spring? Who does he burn in summer? Behold, when the wild goose flies southward in the fall of the year his wings fan up the cold wind from the north, and does not the north wind blow upon us all? The snow — is it deeper for my brothers than for me? Does the fire warm one man more than another? The hunting is poor, and behold, you hunger.

The fishing is poor, and behold, we hunger. Is it not the same hunger?"

"*We-la-boog-wa,*" grunted the sagamore. "These are good words."

"Behold, my brothers, He-who-looks-at-his-nose talked of war. It is easy to talk of war. Squaws, children can talk of war. But when the blood flows, what talk can put it back? Behold, the Meeg-a-Mahg are mighty warriors. The French are mighty warriors. The English are mighty warriors. Have they not proved themselves, all through the time of our fathers and our own? And is the hunting better? Are there more fish in the Big Water? The smoke in the wigwam — does it smart the eye less because a new scalp dries upon the pole? There is a time for war and we have had much war. The death-cry of the warrior has silenced the birds in the forest. The wailing of the squaws is as the east wind in the reeds. Is there no time for peace?"

"These are the words of a coward," the squinting *kenap* said.

"My brother cannot see beyond his nose. How brave is that?"

The young squaws giggled. The *kenap* scowled.

"Behold, how handsome is this man, my daughters! What one among thee would not take him to her arms? That one is surely blind of an eye and cannot see from the other!"

The squaws laughed aloud now. The young braves stirred uneasily. The white man was goading He-who-looks-at-his-nose deliberately. The young men were keen for war, yet they feared to speak, for they were proud and the white man had a barbed tongue, and the laughter of squaws was a clinging thing. All this the white man knew.

The squinting *kenap* sprang, swinging high the tomahawk, and Bradford stepped forward swiftly and struck him full in the face with that ham-like fist, a tremendous buffet. The *kenap* lay on his back with the blood spurting from mouth and nostrils.

"Ayah!" murmured the squaws. "Truly this is Strong Fist."

"He wanted blood," Bradford said quietly. "He has it. Let him suck well on it. Behold, I have come amongst ye alone. Is there fear in my heart then? Yet I talk peace! And I speak for all the English here upon the river. Is there fear in these words?"

"There is no fear in the English," said the tall chief gravely, "if they are all like thee and thy leather-shirts, O Strong Fist. I have known them many moons, and the blood of the Meeg-a-Mahg flowed wherever they went. They kept their faces high and had the heart of Moween the bear. The forest was their pathway, the river their drinking-pot, they took the war path in the summer heat and in the winter snow, and there was no staying them. These things we know. But how are we to know if Strong Fist means these words of peace?" And saying this the sagamore turned and cast a meaning glance toward the forest on the ridge.

Silas put forth a hand toward the ridge, as if a regiment of his leather-shirts were there concealed. "O Kwemoo, there is one way to know, the ancient way, the only way. Let us bury the hatchet together — here! — and may the curse of all the evil spirits in the sky, the forest, the rivers, and the sea fall upon him who breaks the peace!"

The *kenaps* drew back a little, uneasy at this invocation of evil. All the superstition in their bones had come awake. There was a silence. He-who-looks-at-his-nose lay like a dead man, eyes closed, blood oozing slowly from his nostrils and drying in thick dribbles over the paint upon his cheeks. The children stared at him, fascinated.

The Loon spoke suddenly. "O Strong Fist, these are good words. Let us bury the hatchet as you say." His intent black eyes regarding his own fine weapon reluctantly, then flicked to the shining steel in Bradford's belt. Silas considered swiftly.

"O Kwemoo, the burial of the hatchet is a custom of the ancient time. Let us then bury *koon-da-wa-se*, a stone hatchet, as the ancient people did."

The Micmacs had long since discarded stone weapons, but some of the finer specimens were preserved as keepsakes, he knew well. The sagamore made an imperious gesture to one of the squaws. She trotted away to a wigwam and brought out a tomahawk of the olden time. The head was of a dark stone like nothing Silas had seen in Nova Scotia, taken in some far war perhaps, or passed through the tribes in the way of trade. Its edge was much broken.

"Behold," The Loon said doubtfully, "our children have played with this thing upon the rocks. Is this good medicine?"

This or nothing, Silas thought. Aloud he cried, holding the thing high, "Behold, my brothers! Is not the edge broken? So does the hatchet grow dull with much war! Have we not taken it from the hands of children? So do the fathers bury the hatchet, that the children may live in peace!"

He flung the tomahawk out over the river, and it went looping end over end and disappeared in a small feather of spray.

"*Talaak?* Why?" asked the sagamore, astonished.

"That no man dig it up again! Let there be peace between our peoples till the rivers run dry and vanish from the earth. Is it well?"

"It is well," they chanted.

The Loon turned his bright black gaze to the still woods on the ridge.

"Let my white brother now call his *kenaps* to the stream, that we may wash our faces together in the custom."

"O Loon," Bradford said softly, "there are no warriors. They have gone in their great canoes to fish far out upon the Big Water. See!"

He poured forth the long yowling war-whoop of the Mohawks that his rangers had made their own. There was no answer from the hillside. Nothing moved. The woods lay breathless under the beat of the sunshine — breathless and empty.

Two or three warriors of the Meeg-a-Mahg came to their feet fingering hatchets, muttering that Strong Fist had tricked them into peace. The sagamore rebuked them sternly.

"O fools, the hatchet has been buried. So be it. Strong Fist has the heart of a bear. Behold, he came alone into our midst and with his naked hand smote down He-who-looks-at-his-nose. What one of you would go into the English village with naked hands? Let such a one say if there be shame in peace between brave men!"

With an immense dignity he strode to the river's edge and fell upon his knees, washing the war-paint from his face. The others followed, silently, and the unpainted Bradford knelt beside them and went through the ritual, drenching face and beard. The squaws withdrew in haste to the wigwams, for it was not good that women should look upon these things. Where the *al-tes-ta-kun* players had sat the fire was dying. A thin wisp rose blue from the embers straight into the April sky. The smitten *kenap* lay a little distance away, making snoring sounds. His nose was broken.

The dice lay in the maple-wood platter where the squaws had dropped them, in a litter of the forfeit-spillikins. A warrior returning from the stream scattered them contemptuously with a sweep of his moccasin. The men formed a wide circle, squatting about the thin smoulder of the fire, with Bradford at The Loon's right hand. A stone pipe was fitted with a reed and its bowl was filled with the harsh tobacco of the Meeg-a-Mahg — leaves of the wild *ta-ma-wa* mixed with shreds of willow bark. The sagamore lit it with a coal and sucked in a great whiff, closing his eyes and letting the smoke curl slowly from his nostrils. He passed the pipe to Bradford.

The pipe went round the circle, was filled, was passed again. Thus they sat for hours, in a profound silence, while the sun dropped down the sky and the squaws whispered together in the wigwams. And so it was that with the coming of the dusk there came upon our river and our town a peace — a peace that never was broken.

QUESTIONS

1. The first third of the story is mostly preparatory, with a long passage of dialogue sandwiched between two passages of exposition and summary. Explain what Raddall accomplishes in this part, considering setting, characterization, and plot.

2. (a) At what point does the author introduce the emergency which provides conflict for this story?
   (b) Why is Ichabod Limard described in such detail?

3. The incident in which Bradford observes the Micmac women leaves the reader with the illusion of actually seeing what is going on.

The same is true of the scene when the warriors arrive. How does the author achieve this sharp visual focus?

4. (a) What qualities of Bradford's character is the author bringing out by means of the dialogue with the squaws?

(b) Even though the Micmac men are not present, this is a tense scene. Why?

5. At the beginning of the story Silas Bradford is a remote and forbidding figure, seen always from the outside. But from the time he enters the Indian encampment, the author permits us more and more to know what is going on in his mind. What are the advantages of this technique of narration in this part of the story?

6. Earlier, when speaking to the New Englanders, Bradford said, "Strike, strike first, and strike hard — that's the secret, and waste no time on words."

(a) How does the author relate this attitude to the flashback in which Bradford recalls Cornwallis' diplomacy with the Indian chiefs?

(b) How is it related to his ordeal in the Micmac camp?

(c) What moment would you regard as the peak of this long climactic incident? Explain your reasoning.

*Sinclair*

*Ross*

# One's a heifer

*Sinclair Ross (b. 1908), author of one novel,* As for Me and My
House *(1941), and many short stories, was born in Saskatchewan
near Prince Albert. His parents were prairie homesteaders. In
1924 he became a bank teller and subsequently worked in several
Saskatchewan towns before being transferred to Winnipeg.
During the Second World War, he served in Europe with the
Royal Canadian Ordnance Corps. At present he lives in Montreal.
Most of his stories appeared originally in* Queen's Quarterly.
*"One's a Heifer" was first printed in* Canadian Accent, *a Penguin
publication. This story represents one of Ross's recurrent
themes — the psychological effects of living on a prairie home-
stead — and is here reprinted by permission of the author.*

MY UNCLE WAS LAID UP that winter with sciatica, so when the
blizzard stopped and still two of the yearlings hadn't come home
with the other cattle, Aunt Ellen said I'd better saddle Tim and
start out looking for them.

"Then maybe I'll not be back tonight," I told her firmly.
"Likely they've drifted as far as the sandhills. There's no use
coming home without them."

I was thirteen, and had never been away like that all night before, but, busy with the breakfast, Aunt Ellen said yes, that
sounded sensible enough, and while I ate, hunted up a dollar in
silver for my meals.

"Most people wouldn't take it from a lad, but they're strangers up towards the hills. Bring it out independent-like, but don't insist too much. They're more likely to grudge you a feed of oats for Tim."

After breakfast I had to undress again, and put on two suits of underwear and two pairs of thick, home-knitted stockings. It was a clear, bitter morning. After the storm the drifts lay clean and unbroken to the horizon. Distant farm-buildings stood out distinct against the prairie as if the thin sharp atmosphere were a magnifying glass. As I started off Aunt Ellen peered cautiously out of the door a moment through a cloud of steam, and waved a red and white checkered dish-towel. I didn't wave back, but conscious of her uneasiness rode erect, as jaunty as the sheepskin and two suits of underwear would permit.

We took the road straight south about three miles. The calves, I reasoned, would have by this time found their way home if the blizzard hadn't carried them at least that far. Then we started catercornering across fields, riding over to straw-stacks where we could see cattle sheltering, calling at farmhouses to ask had they seen any strays. "Yearlings," I said each time politely. "Red with white spots and faces. The same almost except that one's a heifer and the other isn't."

Nobody had seen them. There was a crust on the snow not quite hard enough to carry Tim, and despite the cold his flanks and shoulders soon were steaming. He walked with his head down, and sometimes, taking my sympathy for granted, drew up a minute for breath.

My spirits, too, began to flag. The deadly cold and the flat white silent miles of prairie asserted themselves like a disapproving presence. The cattle round the straw-stacks stared when we rode up as if we were intruders. The fields stared, and the sky stared. People shivered in their doorways, and said they'd seen no strays.

At about one o'clock we stopped at a farmhouse for dinner. It was a single oat sheaf half thistles for Tim, and fried eggs and bread and tea for me. Crops had been poor that year, they apologized, and though they shook their heads when I brought out my money I saw the woman's eyes light greedily a second, as if her instincts of hospitality were struggling hard against some urgent need. We too, I said, had had poor crops lately. That was why it was so important that I find the calves.

We rested an hour, then went on again. "Yearlings," I kept on describing them. "Red with white spots and faces. The same except that one's a heifer and the other isn't."

Still no one had seen them, still it was cold, still Tim protested what a fool I was.

The country began to roll a little. A few miles ahead I could see the first low line of sandhills. "They'll be there for sure," I said aloud, more to encourage myself than Tim. "Keeping straight to the road it won't take a quarter as long to get home again."

But home now seemed a long way off. A thin white sheet of cloud spread across the sky, and though there had been no warmth in the sun the fields looked colder and bleaker without the glitter on the snow. Straw-stacks were fewer here, as if the land were poor, and every house we stopped at seemed more dilapidated than the one before.

A nagging wind rose as the afternoon wore on. Dogs yelped and bayed at us, and sometimes from the hills, like the signal of our approach, there was a thin, wavering howl of a coyote. I began to dread the miles home again almost as much as those still ahead. There were so many cattle straggling across the fields, so many yearlings just like ours. I saw them for sure a dozen times, and as often choked my disappointment down and clicked Tim on again.

And at last I really saw them. It was nearly dusk, and along with fifteen or twenty other cattle they were making their way towards some buildings that lay huddled at the foot of the sandhills. They passed in single file less than fifty yards away, but when I pricked Tim forward to turn them back he floundered in a snowed-in water-cut. By the time we were out they were a little distance ahead, and on account of the drifts it was impossible to put on a spurt of speed and pass them. All we could do was take our place at the end of the file, and proceed at their pace towards the buildings.

It was about half a mile. As we drew near I debated with Tim whether we should ask to spend the night or start off right away for home. We were hungry and tired, but it was a poor, shiftless-looking place. The yard was littered with old wagons and machinery; the house was scarcely distinguishable from the stables. Darkness was beginning to close in, but there was no light in the windows.

Then as we crossed the yard we heard a shout, "Stay where you are," and a man came running towards us from the stable. He was tall and ungainly, and, instead of the short sheepskin that most farmers wear, had on a long black overcoat nearly to his feet. He seized Tim's bridle when he reached us, and glared for a minute as if he were going to pull me out of the saddle. "I told you to stay out," he said in a harsh, excited voice. "You heard me, didn't you? What do you want coming round here anyway?"

I steeled myself and said, "Our two calves."

The muscles of his face were drawn together threateningly, but close to him like this and looking straight into his eyes I felt that for all their fierce look there was something about them wavering and uneasy. "The two red ones with the white faces," I continued. "They've just gone into the shed over there with yours. If you'll give me a hand getting them out again I'll start for home now right away."

He peered at me a minute, let go the bridle, then clutched it again. "They're all mine," he countered. "I was over by the gate. I watched them coming in."

His voice was harsh and thick. The strange wavering look in his eyes steadied itself for a minute to a dare. I forced myself to meet it and insisted, "I saw them back a piece in the field. They're ours all right. Let me go over a minute and I'll show you."

With a crafty tilt of his head he leered, "You didn't see any calves. And now, if you know what's good for you, you'll be on your way."

"You're trying to steal them," I flared rashly. "I'll go home and get my uncle and the police after you – then you'll see whether they're our calves or not."

My threat seemed to impress him a little. With a shifty glance in the direction of the stable he said, "All right, come along and look them over. Then maybe you'll be satisfied." But all the way across the yard he kept his hand on Tim's bridle, and at the shed made me wait a few minutes while he went inside.

The cattle shed was a lean-to on the horse stable. It was plain enough: he was hiding the calves before letting me inside to look around. While waiting for him, however, I had time to realize that he was a lot bigger and stronger than I was, and that it might be prudent just to keep my eyes open, and not give him too much insolence.

He reappeared carrying a smoky lantern. "All right," he said pleasantly enough, "come in and look around. Will your horse stand, or do you want to tie him?"

We put Tim in an empty stall in the horse stable, then went through a narrow doorway with a bar across it to the cattle shed. Just as I expected, our calves weren't there. There were two red ones with white markings that he tried to make me believe were the ones I had seen, but, positive I hadn't been mistaken, I shook my head and glanced at the doorway we had just come through. It was narrow, but not too narrow. He read my expression and said, "You think they're in there. Come on, then, and look around."

The horse stable consisted of two rows of open stalls with a passage down the centre like an aisle. At the far end were two box-stalls, one with a sick colt in it, the other closed. They were both boarded up to the ceiling, so that you could see inside them only through the doors. Again he read my expression, and with a nod towards the closed one said, "It's just a kind of harness room now. Up till a year ago I kept a stallion."

But he spoke furtively, and seemed anxious to get me away from that end of the stable. His smoky lantern threw great swaying shadows over us; and the deep clefts and triangles of shadow on his face sent a little chill through me, and made me think what a dark and evil face it was.

I was afraid, but not too afraid. "If it's just a harness room," I said recklessly, "why not let me see inside? Then I'll be satisfied and believe you."

He wheeled at my question, and sidled over swiftly to the stall. He stood in front of the door, crouched down a little, the lantern in front of him like a shield. There was a sudden stillness through the stable as we faced each other. Behind the light from his lantern the darkness hovered vast and sinister. It seemed to hold its breath, to watch and listen. I felt a clutch of fear now at my throat, but I didn't move. My eyes were fixed on him so intently that he seemed to lose substance, to loom up close a moment, then recede. At last he disappeared completely, and there was only the lantern like a hard hypnotic eye.

It held me. It held me rooted, against my will. I wanted to run from the stable, but I wanted even more to see inside the stall. And yet I was afraid to see inside the stall. So afraid that it was a relief when at last he gave a shame-faced laugh and said, "There's a hole in the floor — that's why I keep the door closed. If you didn't know, you might step into it — twist your foot. That's what happened to one of my horses a while ago."

I nodded as if I believed him, and went back tractably to Tim. But regaining control of myself as I tried the saddle girths, beginning to feel that my fear had been unwarranted, I looked up and said, "It's ten miles home, and we've been riding hard all day. If we could stay a while — have something to eat, and then get started —"

The wavering light came into his eyes again. He held the lantern up to see me better, such a long, intent scrutiny that it seemed he must discover my designs. But he gave a nod finally, as if reassured, brought oats and hay for Tim, and suggested, companionably, "After supper we can have a game of checkers."

Then, as if I were a grown-up, he put out his hand and said, "My name is Arthur Vickers."

Inside the house, rid of his hat and coat, he looked less forbidding. He had a white nervous face, thin lips, a large straight nose, and deep uneasy eyes. When the lamp was lit I fancied I could still see the wavering expression in them, and decided it was what you called a guilty look.

"You won't think much of it," he said apologetically, following my glance around the room. "I ought to be getting things cleaned up again. Come over to the stove. Supper won't take long."

It was a large, low-ceilinged room that for the first moment or two struck me more like a shed or granary than a house. The table in the centre was littered with tools and harness. On a rusty cook-stove were two big steaming pots of bran. Next to the stove stood a grindstone, then a white iron bed covered with coats and horse blankets. At the end opposite the bed, weasel and coyote skins were drying. There were guns and traps on the wall, a horse collar, a pair of rubber boots. The floor was bare and grimy. Ashes were littered around the stove. In a corner squatted a live owl with a broken wing.

He walked back and forth a few times looking helplessly at the disorder, then cleared off the table and lifted the pots of bran to the back of the stove. "I've been mending harness," he explained. "You get careless, living alone like this. It takes a woman anyway."

My presence, apparently, was making him take stock of the room. He picked up a broom and swept for a minute, made an ineffective attempt to straighten the blankets on the bed, brought another lamp out of a cupboard and lit it. There was an ungainly haste to all his movements. He started unbuckling my sheepskin for me, then turned away suddenly to take off his own coat. "Now we'll have supper," he said with an effort at self-possession. "Coffee and beans is all I can give you — maybe a little molasses."

I replied diplomatically that that sounded pretty good. It didn't seem right, accepting hospitality this way from a man trying to steal your calves, but theft, I reflected, surely justified deceit. I held my hands out to the warmth and asked if I could help.

There was a kettle of plain navy beans already cooked. He dipped out enough for our supper into a frying pan, and on top laid rashers of fat salt pork. While I watched that they didn't burn he rinsed off a few dishes. Then he set out sugar and canned milk, butter, molasses, and dark heavy biscuits that he had baked himself the day before. He kept glancing at me so apologetically all the while that I leaned over and sniffed the beans, and said at home I ate a lot of them.

"It takes a woman," he repeated as we sat down to the table. "I don't often have anyone here to eat with me. If I'd known, I'd have cleaned things up a little."

I was too intent on my plateful of beans to answer. All through the meal he sat watching me, but made no further attempts at conversation. Hungry as I was, I noticed that the wavering, uneasy look was still in his eyes. A guilty look, I told myself again, and wondered what I was going to do to get the calves away. I finished my coffee and he continued:

"It's worse even than this in the summer. No time for meals — and the heat and flies. Last summer I had a girl cooking for a few weeks, but it didn't last. Just a cow she was — just a big stupid cow — and she wanted to stay on. There's a family of them back in the hills. I had to send her home."

I wondered should I suggest starting now, or ask to spend the night. Maybe when he's asleep, I thought, I can slip out of the house and get away with the calves. He went on, "You don't know how bad it is sometimes. Weeks on end and no one to talk to. You're not yourself — you're not sure what you're going to say or do."

I remembered hearing my uncle talk about a man who had gone crazy living alone. And this fellow Vickers had queer eyes all right. And there was the live owl over in the corner, and the grindstone standing right beside the bed. "Maybe I'd better go now," I decided aloud. "Tim'll be rested, and it's ten miles home."

But he said no, it was colder now, with the wind getting stronger, and seemed so kindly and concerned that I half forgot my fears. "Likely he's just starting to go crazy," I told myself, "and it's only by staying that I'll have a chance to get the calves away."

When the table was cleared and the dishes washed he said he would go out and bed down the stable for the night. I picked up my sheepskin to go with him, but he told me sharply to stay inside. Just for a minute he looked crafty and forbidding as when I first rode up on Tim, and to allay his suspicions I nodded compliantly and put my sheepskin down again. It was better like that anyway, I decided. In a few minutes I could follow him, and perhaps, taking advantage of the shadows and his smoky lantern, make my way to the box-stall unobserved.

But when I reached the stable he had closed the door after him and hooked it from the inside. I walked round a while, tried to slip in by way of the cattle shed, and then had to go back to the house. I went with a vague feeling of relief again. There was still time, I told myself, and it would be safer anyway when he was sleeping.

So that it would be easier to keep from falling asleep myself I planned to suggest coffee again just before we went to bed. I knew that the guest didn't ordinarily suggest such things, but it was no time to remember manners when there was someone trying to steal your calves.

When he came in from the stable we played checkers. I was no match for him, but to encourage me he repeatedly let me win. "It's a long time now since I've had a chance to play," he kept on saying, trying to convince me that his short-sighted moves weren't intentional. "Sometimes I used to ask her to play, but I had to tell her every move to make. If she didn't win she'd upset the board and go off and sulk."

"My aunt is a little like that too," I said. "She cheats sometimes when we're playing cribbage — and, when I catch her, says her eyes aren't good."

"Women talk too much ever to make good checker players. It takes concentration. This one, though, couldn't even talk like anybody else."

After my long day in the cold I was starting to yawn already. He noticed it, and spoke in a rapid, earnest voice, as if afraid I might lose interest soon and want to go to bed. It was important for me too to stay awake, so I crowned a king and said, "Why don't you get someone, then, to stay with you?"

"Too many of them want to do that." His face darkened a

little, almost as if warning me. "Too many of the kind you'll never get rid of again. She did, last summer when she was here. I had to put her out."

There was silence for a minute, his eyes flashing, and wanting to placate him I suggested, "She liked you, maybe."

He laughed a moment, harshly. "She liked me all right. Just two weeks ago she came back — walked over with an old suitcase and said she was going to stay. It was cold at home, and she had to work too hard, and she didn't mind even if I couldn't pay her wages."

I was getting sleepier. To keep awake I sat on the edge of the chair where it was uncomfortable and said, "Hadn't you asked her to come?"

His eyes narrowed. "I'd had trouble enough getting rid of her the first time. There were six of them at home, and she said her father thought it time that someone married her."

"Then she must be a funny one," I said. "Everyone knows that the man's supposed to ask the girl."

My remark seemed to please him. "I told you didn't I?" he said, straightening a little, jumping two of my men. "She was so stupid that at checkers she'd forget whether she was black or red."

We stopped playing now. I glanced at the owl in the corner and the ashes littered on the floor, and thought that keeping her would maybe have been a good idea after all. He read it in my face and said, "I used to think that too sometimes. I used to look at her and think nobody knew now anyway and that she'd maybe do. You need a woman on a farm all right. And night after night she'd be sitting there where you are — right there where you are, looking at me, not even trying to play —"

The fire was low, and we could hear the wind. "But then I'd go up in the hills, away from her for a while, and start thinking back the way things used to be, and it wasn't right even for the sake of your meals ready and your house kept clean. When she came back I tried to tell her that, but all the family are the same, and I realized it wasn't any use. There's nothing you can do when you're up against that sort of thing. The mother talks just like a child of ten. When she sees you coming she runs and hides. There are six of them, and it's come out in every one."

It was getting cold, but I couldn't bring myself to go over to the stove. There was the same stillness now as when he was standing at the box-stall door. And I felt the same illogical fear, the same powerlessness to move. It was the way his voice lowered, the glassy, cold look in his eyes. The rest of his face disappeared; all I could see were his eyes. And they filled me with a vague and overpowering dread. My voice gone a whisper on me, I asked, "And when you wouldn't marry her — what happened then?"

He remained motionless a moment, as if answering silently; then with an unexpected laugh like a breaking dish said, "Why, nothing happened. I just told her she couldn't stay. I went to town for a few days — and when I came back she was gone."

"Has she been back to bother you since?" I asked.

He made a little silo of checkers. "No — she took her suitcase with her."

To remind him that the fire was going down I went over to the stove and stood warming myself. He raked the coals with the lifter and put in poplar, two split pieces for a base and a thick round log on top. I yawned again. He said maybe I'd like to go to bed now, and I shivered and asked him could I have a drink of coffee first. While it boiled he stood stirring the two big pots of bran. The trouble with coffee, I realized, was that it would keep him from getting sleepy too.

I undressed finally and got into bed, but he blew out only one of the lamps, and sat on playing checkers with himself. I dozed a while, then sat up with a start, afraid it was morning already and that I'd lost my chance to get the calves away. He came over and looked at me a minute, then gently pushed my shoulders back on the pillow. "Why don't you come to bed too?" I asked, and he said, "Later I will — I don't feel sleepy yet."

It was like that all night. I kept dozing on and off, wakening in a fright each time to find him still there sitting at his checker board. He would raise his head sharply when I stirred, then tiptoe over to the bed and stand close to me listening till satisfied again I was asleep. The owl kept wakening too. It was down in the corner still where the lamplight scarcely reached, and I could see its eyes go on and off like yellow bulbs. The wind whistled drearily around the house. The blankets smelled like an old granary. He suspected what I was planning to do, evidently, and was staying awake to make sure I didn't get outside.

Each time I dozed I dreamed I was on Tim again. The calves were in sight, but far ahead of us, and with the drifts so deep we couldn't overtake them. Then instead of Tim it was the grindstone I was straddling, and that was the reason, not the drifts, that we weren't making better progress.

I wondered what would happen to the calves if I didn't get away with them. My uncle had sciatica, and it would be at least a day before I could be home and back again with some of the neighbours. By then Vickers might have butchered the calves, or driven them up to a hiding place in the hills where we'd never find them. There was the possibility, too, that Aunt Ellen and the neighbours wouldn't believe me. I dozed and woke – dozed and woke – always he was sitting at the checker board. I could hear the dry tinny ticking of an alarm clock, but from where I was lying couldn't see it. He seemed to be listening to it too. The wind would sometimes creak the house, and then he would give a start and sit rigid a moment with his eyes fixed on the window. It was always the window, as if there was nothing he was afraid of that could reach him by the door.

Most of the time he played checkers with himself, moving his lips, muttering words I couldn't hear, but once I woke to find him staring fixedly across the table as if he had a partner sitting there. His hands were clenched in front of him, there was a sharp, metallic glitter in his eyes. I lay transfixed, unbreathing. His eyes as I watched seemed to dilate, to brighten, to harden like a bird's. For a long time he sat contracted, motionless, as if gathering himself to strike, then furtively he slid his hand an inch or two along the table towards some checkers that were piled beside the board. It was as if he were reaching for a weapon, as if his invisible partner were an enemy. He clutched the checkers, slipped slowly from his chair and straightened. His movements were sure, stealthy, silent like a cat's. His face had taken on a desperate, contorted look. As he raised his hand the tension was unbearable.

It was a long time — a long time watching him the way you watch a finger tightening slowly in the trigger of a gun — and then suddenly wrenching himself to action he hurled the checkers with such vicious fury that they struck the wall in front of him and clattered back across the room.

And everything was quiet again. I started a little, mumbled to myself as if half-awakened, lay quite still. But he seemed to have forgotten me, and after standing limp and dazed a minute got down on his knees and started looking for the checkers. When he had them all, he put more wood in the stove, then returned quietly to the table and sat down. We were alone again; everything was exactly as before. I relaxed gradually, telling myself that he'd just been seeing things.

The next time I woke he was sitting with his head sunk forward on the table. It looked as if he had fallen asleep at last, and huddling alert among the bed-clothes I decided to watch a minute to make sure, then dress and try to slip out to the stable.

While I watched, I planned exactly every movement I was going to make. Rehearsing it in my mind as carefully as if I were actually doing it, I climbed out of bed, put on my clothes, tiptoed stealthily to the door and slipped outside. By this time, though, I was getting drowsy, and relaxing among the blankets I decided that for safety's sake I should rehearse it still again. I rehearsed it four times altogether, and the fourth time dreamed that I hurried on successfully to the stable.

I fumbled with the door a while, then went inside and felt my way through the darkness to the box-stall. There was a bright light suddenly and the owl was sitting over the door with his yellow eyes like a pair of lanterns. The calves, he told me, were in the other stall with the sick colt. I looked and they were there all right, but Tim came up and said it might be better not to start for home till morning. He reminded me that I hadn't paid for his feed or my own supper yet, and that if I slipped off this way it would mean that I was stealing, too. I agreed, realizing now that it wasn't the calves I was looking for after all, and that I still had to see inside the stall that was guarded by the owl. "Wait here," Tim said, "I'll tell you if he flies away," and without further questioning I lay down in the straw and went to sleep again ... When I woke coffee and beans were on the stove already, and though the lamp was still lit I could tell by the window that it was nearly morning.

We were silent during breakfast. Two or three times I caught him watching me, and it seemed his eyes were shiftier than before. After his sleepless night he looked tired and haggard. He left the table while I was still eating and fed raw rabbit to the owl, then came back and drank another cup of coffee. He had been friendly and communicative the night before, but now, just as when he first came running out of the stable in his long black coat, his expression was sullen and resentful. I began to feel that he was in a hurry to be rid of me.

I took my time, however, racking my brains to outwit him still and get the calves away. It looked pretty hopeless now, his eyes on me so suspiciously, my imagination at low ebb. Even if I did get inside the box-stall to see the calves — was he going to stand back then and let me start off home with them? Might it not more likely frighten him, make him do something desperate, so that I couldn't reach my uncle or the police? There was the owl over in the corner, the grindstone by the bed. And with such a queer fellow you could never tell. You could never tell, and you had to think about your own skin too. So I said politely, "Thank you, Mr. Vickers, for letting me stay all night," and remembering what Tim had told me took out my dollar's worth of silver.

He gave a short dry laugh and wouldn't take it. "Maybe you'll come back," he said, "and next time stay longer. We'll go shooting up in the hills if you like — and I'll make a trip to town for things so that we can have better meals. You need company sometimes for a change. There's been no one here now quite a while."

His face softened again as he spoke. There was an expression in his eyes as if he wished that I could stay on now. It puzzled me. I wanted to be indignant, and it was impossible. He held my sheepskin for me while I put it on, and tied the scarf around the collar with a solicitude and determination equal to Aunt Ellen's. And then he gave his short dry laugh again, and hoped I'd find my calves all right.

He had been out to the stable before I was awake, and Tim was ready for me, fed and saddled. But I delayed a few minutes, pretending to be interested in his horses and the sick colt. It would be worth something after all, I realized, to get just a glimpse of the calves. Aunt Ellen was going to be sceptical enough of my story as it was. It could only confirm her doubts to hear me say I hadn't seen the calves in the box-stall, and was just pretty sure that they were there.

So I went from stall to stall, stroking the horses and making comparisons with the ones we had at home. The door, I noticed, he had left wide open, ready for me to lead out Tim. He was walking up and down the aisle, telling me which horses were quiet, which to be careful of. I came to a nervous chestnut mare, and realized she was my only chance.

She crushed her hips against the side of the stall as I slipped up to her manger, almost pinning me, then gave her head a toss and pulled back hard on the halter shank. The shank, I noticed, was tied with an easy slip-knot that the right twist and a sharp tug would undo in half a second. And the door was wide open, ready for me to lead out Tim — and standing as she was with her body across the stall diagonally, I was for the moment screened from sight.

It happened quickly. There wasn't time to think of consequences. I just pulled the knot, in the same instant struck the mare across the nose. With a snort she threw herself backwards, almost trampling Vickers, then flung up her head to keep from tripping on the shank and plunged outside.

It worked as I hoped it would. "Quick," Vickers yelled to me, "the gate's open — try and head her off" — but instead I just waited till he himself was gone, then fairly flew to the box-stall.

The door was fastened with two tight-fitting slide-bolts, one so high that I could scarcely reach it standing on my toes. It wouldn't yield. The head of the pin was small and round, and the whiffle-tree kept glancing off. I was too terrified to pause a moment and take careful aim.

Terrified of the stall though, not of Vickers. Terrified of the stall, yet compelled by a frantic need to get inside. For the moment I had forgotten Vickers, forgotten even the danger of his catching me. I worked blindly, helplessly, as if I were confined and smothering. For a moment I yielded to panic, dropped the piece of whiffle-tree and started kicking at the door. Then, collected again, I forced back the lower bolt, and picking up the whiffle-tree tried to pry the door out a little at the bottom. But I had wasted too much time. Just as I dropped to my knees to peer through the opening Vickers seized me. I struggled to my feet and fought a moment, but it was such a hard, strangling clutch at my throat that I felt myself go limp and blind. In desperation then I kicked him, and with a blow like a reflex he sent me staggering to the floor.

But it wasn't the blow that frightened me. It was the fierce, wild light in his eyes.

Stunned as I was, I looked up and saw him watching me, and, sick with terror, made a bolt for Tim. I untied him with hands that moved incredibly, galvanized for escape. I knew now for sure that Vickers was crazy. He followed me outside, and, just as I mounted, seized Tim again by the bridle. For a second or two it made me crazy too. Gathering up the free ends of the rein I lashed him hard across the face. He let go of the bridle, and, frightened and excited too now, Tim made a dash across the yard and out of the gate. Deep as the snow was, I kept him galloping for half a mile, pommelling him with my fists, kicking my heels against his sides. Then of his own accord he drew up short for breath, and I looked around to see whether Vickers was following. He wasn't — there was only the snow and the hills, his buildings a lonely little smudge against the whiteness — and the relief was like a stick pulled out that's been holding up tomato vines or peas. I slumped across the saddle weakly, and till Tim started on again lay there whimpering like a baby.

We were home by noon. We didn't have to cross fields or stop at houses now, and there had been teams on the road packing down the snow so that Tim could trot part of the way and even canter. I put him in the stable without taking time to tie or unbridle him, and ran to the house to tell Aunt Ellen. But I was still frightened, cold and a little hysterical, and it was a while before she could understand how everything had happened. She was silent a minute, indulgent, then helping me off with my sheepskin said kindly, "You'd better forget about it now, and come over and get warm. The calves came home themselves yesterday. Just about an hour after you set out."

I looked up at her. "But the stall, then — just because I wanted to look inside he knocked me down — and if it wasn't the calves in there —"

She didn't answer. She was busy building up the fire and looking at the stew.

QUESTIONS

1. Although the boy's mistake makes us hesitant to jump to a hasty conclusion, what explanation are we tempted to offer for Vickers' secretiveness?

2. Stories with surprise endings always invite a second reading to see whether the author has built up logically to the surprise, or whether he has cheated and suddenly introduced an implausible trick. What preparation does Ross make in the earlier part of the story so that in the *dénouement* we will believe it to be possible that the boy could have been completely sure and yet wrong in his identification of the two calves?

3. The boy's visit with Vickers is the heart of the story. In this part, the author must furnish us with the evidence for a later startling conclusion, and keep us in increasing suspense. By referring to the events of this visit, point out (a) How Ross creates and develops suspense and (b) How he prepares us for the conclusion that he intends us to reach in the *dénouement*.

4. The author makes frequent reference to the wounded owl and the grindstone by the bed. What reasons might he have for including these in the story?

5. Some of Sinclair Ross's other prairie stories leave the impression of a people bound in poverty to a grudging land. Considering relevant passages of description, dialogue, and action, discuss to what extent "One's a Heifer" has this effect?

6. Like "By the Waters of Babylon" (p. 237), this story concerns an adolescent boy who has a profoundly disturbing experience. Both stories include a journey which terminates in a revelation. Compare these two stories further as to similarities and differences in characterization, structure, and effect.

*Somerset*

*Maugham*

# Mr. Know-All

---

*Somerset Maugham (b. 1874) was born in Paris and educated at*
*Heidelberg and St. Thomas's Hospital, London. A great*
*wanderer (he has been several times around the world and has*
*lived for extensive periods in the South Seas, Spain, and the*
*United States), Maugham has drawn in his work on his knowledge*
*of many peoples and many places. His first successful play,*
My Lady Frederick, *appeared in 1907. His fame as a novelist*
*was firmly established with* Of Human Bondage *(1915), a*
*largely autobiographical tale based on his experiences as a medical*
*student in London. Among his important novels are* The Moon
and Sixpence *(1919),* The Painted Veil *(1925),* Cakes and Ale
*(1930),* The Narrow Corner *(1932), and* The Razor's Edge
*(1944). Perhaps his best plays are* The Circle *(1921) and* The
Letter *(1927). "Mr. Know-All" is reprinted from* Cosmopolitans
*by permission of William Heinemann Ltd., Doubleday and*
*Company, Inc., and the author.*

---

I WAS PREPARED to dislike Max Kelada even before I knew him.
The war had just finished and the passenger traffic in the ocean-
going liners was heavy. Accommodation was very hard to get
and you had to put up with whatever the agents chose to offer
you. You could not hope for a cabin to yourself and I was thank-

ful to be given one in which there were only two berths. But when I was told the name of my companion my heart sank. It suggested closed port-holes and the night air rigidly excluded. It was bad enough to share a cabin for fourteen days with anyone (I was going from San Francisco to Yokohama), but I should have looked upon it with less dismay if my fellow-passenger's name had been Smith or Brown.

When I went on board I found Mr. Kelada's luggage already below. I did not like the look of it; there were too many labels on the suitcases, and the wardrobe trunk was too big. He had unpacked his toilet things, and I observed that he was a patron of the excellent Monsieur Coty; for I saw on the washing-stand his scent, his hair-wash and his brilliantine. Mr. Kelada's brushes, ebony with his monogram in gold, would have been all the better for a scrub. I did not at all like Mr. Kelada. I made my way into the smoking-room. I called for a pack of cards and began to play patience. I had scarcely started before a man came up to me and asked me if he was right in thinking my name was so-and-so.

"I am Mr. Kelada," he added, with a smile that showed a row of flashing teeth, and sat down.

"Oh, yes, we're sharing a cabin, I think."

"Bit of luck, I call it. You never know who you're going to be put in with. I was jolly glad when I heard you were English. I'm all for us English sticking together when we're abroad, if you understand what I mean."

I blinked.

"Are you English?" I asked, perhaps tactlessly.

"Rather. You don't think I look like an American, do you? British to the backbone, that's what I am."

To prove it, Mr. Kelada took out of his pocket a passport and airily waved it under my nose.

King George has many strange subjects. Mr. Kelada was short and of a sturdy build, clean-shaven and dark-skinned, with a fleshy, hooked nose and very large, lustrous and liquid eyes. His long black hair was sleek and curly. He spoke with a fluency in which there was nothing English and his gestures were exuberant. I felt pretty sure that a closer inspection of that British passport

would have betrayed the fact that Mr. Kelada was born under a
bluer sky than is generally seen in England.

"What will you have?" he asked me.

I looked at him doubtfully. Prohibition was in force and to all
appearances the ship was bone-dry. When I am not thirsty I do
not know which I dislike more, ginger-ale or lemon-squash. But
Mr. Kelada flashed an oriental smile at me.

"Whisky and soda or a dry Martini, you have only to say the
word."

From each of his hip-pockets he fished a flask and laid them on
the table before me. I chose the Martini, and calling the steward
he ordered a tumbler of ice and a couple of glasses.

"A very good cocktail," I said.

"Well, there are plenty more where that came from, and if
you've got any friends on board, you tell them you've got a pal
who's got all the liquor in the world."

Mr. Kelada was chatty. He talked of New York and of San
Francisco. He discussed plays, pictures, and politics. He was
patriotic. The Union Jack is an impressive piece of drapery, but
when it is flourished by a gentleman from Alexandria or Beirut,
I cannot but feel that it loses somewhat in dignity. Mr. Kelada
was familiar. I do not wish to put on airs, but I cannot help feeling that it is seemly in a total stranger to put mister before my
name when he addresses me. Mr. Kelada, doubtless to set me at
my ease, used no such formality. I did not like Mr. Kelada. I had
put aside the cards when he sat down, but now, thinking that for
this first occasion our conversation had lasted long enough, I
went on with my game.

"The three on the four," said Mr. Kelada.

There is nothing more exasperating when you are playing
patience than to be told where to put the card you have turned
up before you have had a chance to look for yourself.

"It's coming out, it's coming out," he cried. "The ten on the
knave."

With rage and hatred in my heart I finished. Then he seized
the pack.

"Do you like card tricks?"

"No, I hate card tricks," I answered.

"Well, I'll just show you this one."

He showed me three. Then I said I would go down to the dining-room and get my seat at table.

"Oh, that's all right," he said. "I've already taken a seat for you. I thought that as we were in the same state-room we might just as well sit at the same table."

I did not like Mr. Kelada.

I not only shared a cabin with him and ate three meals a day at the same table, but I could not walk round the deck without his joining me. It was impossible to snub him. It never occurred to him that he was not wanted. He was certain that you were as glad to see him as he was to see you. In your own house you might have kicked him downstairs and slammed the door in his face without the suspicion dawning on him that he was not a welcome visitor. He was a good mixer, and in three days knew everyone on board. He ran everything. He managed the sweeps, conducted the auctions, collected money for prizes at the sports, got up quoit and golf matches, organised the concert and arranged the fancy dress ball. He was everywhere and always. He was certainly the best-hated man in the ship. We called him Mr. Know-All, even to his face. He took it as a compliment. But it was at meal times that he was most intolerable. For the better part of an hour then he had us at his mercy. He was hearty, jovial, loquacious and argumentative. He knew everything better than anybody else, and it was an affront to his overweening vanity that you should disagree with him. He would not drop a subject, however unimportant, till he had brought you round to his way of thinking. The possibility that he could be mistaken never occurred to him. He was the chap who knew. We sat at the doctor's table. Mr. Kelada would certainly have had it all his own way, for the doctor was lazy and I was frigidly indifferent, except for a man called Ramsay who sat there also. He was as dogmatic as Mr. Kelada and resented bitterly the Levantine's cocksureness. The discussions they had were acrimonious and interminable.

Ramsay was in the American Consular Service, and was stationed at Kobe. He was a great heavy fellow from the Middle

West, with loose fat under a tight skin, and he bulged out of his ready-made clothes. He was on his way back to resume his post, having been on a flying visit to New York to fetch his wife, who had been spending a year at home. Mrs. Ramsay was a very pretty little thing, with pleasant manners and a sense of humour. The Consular Service is ill paid, and she was dressed always very simply; but she knew how to wear her clothes. She achieved an effect of quiet distinction. I should not have paid any particular attention to her but that she possessed a quality that may be common enough in women, but nowadays is not obvious in their demeanour. You could not look at her without being struck by her modesty. It shone in her like a flower on a coat.

One evening at dinner the conversation by chance drifted to the subject of pearls. There had been in the papers a good deal of talk about the culture pearls which the cunning Japanese were making, and the doctor remarked that they must inevitably diminish the value of real ones. They were very good already; they would soon be perfect. Mr. Kelada, as was his habit, rushed the new topic. He told us all that was to be known about pearls. I do not believe Ramsay knew anything about them at all, but he could not resist the opportunity to have a fling at the Levantine, and in five minutes we were in the middle of a heated argument. I had seen Mr. Kelada vehement and voluble before, but never so voluble and vehement as now. At last something that Ramsay said stung him, for he thumped the table and shouted:

"Well, I ought to know what I am talking about. I'm going to Japan just to look into this Japanese pearl business. I'm in the trade and there's not a man in it who won't tell you that what I say about pearls goes. I know all the best pearls in the world and what I don't know about pearls isn't worth knowing."

Here was news for us, for Mr. Kelada, with all his loquacity, had never told anyone what his business was. We only knew vaguely that he was going to Japan on some commercial errand. He looked round the table triumphantly.

"They'll never be able to get a culture pearl that an expert like me can't tell with half an eye." He pointed to a chain that Mrs. Ramsay wore. "You take my word for it, Mrs. Ramsay, that chain you're wearing will never be worth a cent less than it is now."

Mrs. Ramsay in her modest way flushed a little and slipped the chain inside her dress. Ramsay leaned forward. He gave us all a look and a smile flickered in his eyes.

"That's a pretty chain of Mrs. Ramsay's, isn't it?"

"I noticed it at once," answered Mr. Kelada. "Gee, I said to myself, those are pearls all right."

"I didn't buy it myself, of course. I'd be interested to know how much you think it cost."

"Oh, in the trade somewhere round fifteen thousand dollars. But if it was bought on Fifth Avenue I shouldn't be surprised to hear that anything up to thirty thousand was paid for it."

Ramsay smiled grimly.

"You'll be surprised to hear that Mrs. Ramsay bought that string at a department store the day before we left New York, for eighteen dollars."

Mr. Kelada flushed.

"Rot. It's not only real, but it's as fine a string for its size as I've ever seen."

"Will you bet on it? I'll bet you a hundred dollars it's imitation."

"Done."

"Oh, Elmer, you can't bet on a certainty," said Mrs. Ramsay. She had a little smile on her lips and her tone was gently deprecating.

"Can't I? If I get a chance of easy money like that I should be all sorts of a fool not to take it."

"But how can it be proved?" she continued. "It's only my word against Mr. Kelada's."

"Let me look at the chain, and if it's imitation I'll tell you quickly enough. I can afford to lose a hundred dollars," said Mr. Kelada.

"Take it off, dear. Let the gentleman look at it as much as he wants."

Mrs. Ramsay hesitated a moment. She put her hands to the clasp.

"I can't undo it," she said. "Mr. Kelada will just have to take my word for it."

I had a sudden suspicion that something unfortunate was about to occur, but I could think of nothing to say.

Ramsay jumped up.

"I'll undo it."

He handed the chain to Mr. Kelada. The Levantine took a magnifying glass from his pocket and closely examined it. A smile of triumph spread over his smooth and swarthy face. He handed back the chain. He was about to speak. Suddenly he caught sight of Mrs. Ramsay's face. It was so white that she looked as though she were about to faint. She was staring at him with wide and terrified eyes. They held a desperate appeal; it was so clear that I wondered why her husband did not see it.

Mr. Kelada stopped with his mouth open. He flushed deeply. You could almost *see* the effort he was making over himself.

"I was mistaken," he said. "It's a very good imitation, but of course as soon as I looked through my glass I saw that it wasn't real. I think eighteen dollars is just about as much as the damned thing's worth."

He took out his pocket-book and from it a hundred-dollar note. He handed it to Ramsay without a word.

"Perhaps that'll teach you not to be so cocksure another time, my young friend," said Ramsay as he took the note.

I noticed that Mr. Kelada's hands were trembling.

The story spread over the ship as stories do, and he had to put up with a good deal of chaff that evening. It was a fine joke that Mr. Know-All had been caught out. But Mrs. Ramsay retired to her state-room with a headache.

Next morning I got up and began to shave. Mr. Kelada lay on his bed smoking a cigarette. Suddenly there was a small scraping sound and I saw a letter pushed under the door. I opened the door and looked out. There was nobody there. I picked up the letter and saw that it was addressed to Max Kelada. The name was written in block letters. I handed it to him.

"Who's this from?" He opened it. "Oh!"

He took out of the envelope, not a letter, but a hundred-dollar note. He looked at me and again he reddened. He tore the envelope into little bits and gave them to me.

"Do you mind just throwing them out of the port-hole?"

I did as he asked, and then I looked at him with a smile.

"No one likes being made to look a perfect damned fool," he said.

"Were the pearls real?"

"If I had a pretty little wife I shouldn't let her spend a year in New York while I stayed at Kobe," said he.

At that moment I did not entirely dislike Mr. Kelada. He reached out for his pocket-book and carefully put in it the hundred-dollar note.

QUESTIONS

Somerset Maugham, unlike James Joyce, D. H. Lawrence, and Morley Callaghan, works in the old tradition of *the story as story*. He makes the most of plot situation and the "twist", the unexpected reversal which suddenly turns all the tables, converts the villains into heroes and reveals depths of guilt in the seemingly innocent.

1. Why, at the beginning and before having met him, does the narrator dislike Kelada?

2. How does the author induce you to accept the narrator's opinion of Kelada?

3. Why does Kelada pass himself off as an Englishman?

4. How does the author make it seem plausible that Ramsay should engage Kelada in a heated argument?

5. What quality in Mrs. Ramsay does the narrator stress?

6. Kelada's generous behaviour towards Mrs. Ramsay is, of course, the "twist" towards which the whole story has moved. Does this behaviour throw a new light on what has gone before? Does it change your view of the narrator? Of the other passengers? Has Kelada been misunderstood and therefore misrepresented? Do any of his previous acts and attitudes now take on a different significance?

7. Do you feel that the author has tricked you unfairly? Or despite the surprise "twist" do you feel that the conclusion is convincing and fair to the facts of the story as they have been given to you?

8. By treating Mrs. Ramsay's infidelity as a mere incident in the revelation of Kelada's unexpected compassion, has the author weakened or compromised the moral implications of the story?

9. Is Kelada's charity towards Mrs. Ramsay the sign and seal of a larger charity towards her — and the forgiveness of sin?

10. Is the story merely clever, without serious moral implications of any kind, to be enjoyed as one enjoys a game in which the underdog wins a surprising victory in the last minute of play?

*Edward Morgan*

*Forster*

# The machine stops

---

*Edward Morgan Forster (b. 1879) was educated at Cambridge.
With only a handful of books to his credit, he has, nevertheless,
won recognition as one of the finest novelists of the twentieth
century. In addition to two volumes of short stories,* The Celestial
Omnibus *(1923) and* The Eternal Moment *(1928), Forster has
published five novels:* Where Angels Fear to Tread *(1905),*
The Longest Journey *(1907),* A Room with a View *(1908),*
Howard's End *(1910), and* A Passage to India *(1924).*
*Mr. Forster is also a shrewd critic of the novel form and has
exerted an influence as an essayist, reviewer, and broadcaster.
Opera lovers will remember that he wrote the libretto for
Benjamin Britten's* Billy Budd. *"The Machine Stops" is from*
The Eternal Moment And Other Stories *by E. M. Forster
(copyright 1928 by Harcourt, Brace & World, Inc.; renewed,
1956, by E. M. Forster) and is reprinted here by permission of
the publisher.*

---

## 1. *The Air-Ship*

IMAGINE, if you can, a small room, hexagonal in shape, like the
cell of a bee. It is lighted neither by window nor by lamp, yet it
is filled with a soft radiance. There are no apertures for ventilation, yet the air is fresh. There are no musical instruments, and
yet, at the moment that my meditation opens, this room is

throbbing with melodious sounds. An arm-chair is in the centre, by its side a reading-desk — that is all the furniture. And in the arm-chair there sits a swaddled lump of flesh — a woman, about five feet high, with a face as white as a fungus. It is to her that the little room belongs.

An electric bell rang.

The woman touched a switch and the music was silent.

"I suppose I must see who it is," she thought, and set her chair in motion. The chair, like the music, was worked by machinery, and it rolled her to the other side of the room, where the bell still rang importunately.

"Who is it?" she called. Her voice was irritable, for she had been interrupted often since the music began. She knew several thousand people; in certain directions human intercourse had advanced enormously.

But when she listened into the receiver, her white face wrinkled into smiles, and she said:

"Very well. Let us talk, I will isolate myself. I do not expect anything important will happen for the next five minutes — for I can give you fully five minutes, Kuno. Then I must deliver my lecture on 'Music during the Australian Period'. "

She touched the isolation knob, so that no one else could speak to her. Then she touched the lighting apparatus, and the little room was plunged into darkness.

"Be quick!" she called, her irritation returning. "Be quick, Kuno; here I am in the dark wasting my time."

But it was fully fifteen seconds before the round plate that she held in her hands began to glow. A faint blue light shot across it, darkening to purple, and presently she could see the image of her son, who lived on the other side of the earth, and he could see her.

"Kuno, how slow you are."

He smiled gravely.

"I really believe you enjoy dawdling."

"I have called you before, mother, but you were always busy or isolated. I have something particular to say."

"What is it, dearest boy? Be quick. Why could you not send it by pneumatic post?"

"Because I prefer saying such a thing. I want —"

"Well?"

"I want you to come and see me."

Vashti watched his face in the blue plate.

"But I can see you!" she exclaimed. "What more do you want?"

"I want to see you not through the Machine," said Kuno. "I want to speak to you not through the wearisome Machine."

"Oh, hush!" said his mother, vaguely shocked. "You mustn't say anything against the Machine."

"Why not?"

"One mustn't."

"You talk as if a god had made the Machine," cried the other. "I believe that you pray to it when you are unhappy. Men made it, do not forget that. Great men, but men. The Machine is much, but it is not everything. I see something like you in this plate, but I do not see you. I hear something like you through this telephone, but I do not hear you. That is why I want you to come. Come and stop with me. Pay me a visit, so that we can meet face to face, and talk about the hopes that are in my mind."

She replied that she could scarcely spare the time for a visit.

"The air-ship barely takes two days to fly between me and you."

"I dislike air-ships."

"Why?"

"I dislike seeing the horrible brown earth, and the sea, and the stars when it is dark. I get no ideas in an air-ship."

"I do not get them anywhere else."

"What kind of ideas can the air give you?"

He paused for an instant.

"Do you not know four big stars that form an oblong, and three stars close together in the middle of the oblong, and hanging from these stars, three other stars?"

"No, I do not. I dislike the stars. But did they give you an idea? How interesting; tell me."

"I had an idea that they were like a man."

"I do not understand."

"The four big stars are the man's shoulders and his knees. The three stars in the middle are like the belts that men wore once, and the three stars hanging are like a sword."

"A sword?"

"Men carried swords about with them, to kill animals and other men."

"It does not strike me as a very good idea, but it is certainly original. When did it come to you first?"

"In the air-ship —" He broke off and she fancied that he looked sad. She could not be sure, for the Machine did not transmit nuances of expression. It only gave a general idea of people — an idea that was good enough for all practical purposes, Vashti thought. The imponderable bloom, declared by a discredited philosophy to be the actual essence of intercourse, was rightly ignored by the Machine, just as the imponderable bloom of the grape was ignored by the manufacturers of artificial fruit. Something "good enough" had long since been accepted by our race.

"The truth is," he continued, "that I want to see these stars again. They are curious stars. I want to see them not from the air-ship, but from the surface of the earth, as our ancestors did, thousands of years ago. I want to visit the surface of the earth."

She was shocked again.

"Mother, you must come, if only to explain to me what is the harm of visiting the surface of the earth."

"No harm," she replied, controlling herself. "But no advantage. The surface of the earth is only dust and mud, no life remains on it, and you would need a respirator, or the cold of the outer air would kill you. One dies immediately in the outer air."

"I know; of course I shall take all precautions."

"And besides —"

"Well?"

She considered, and chose her words with care. Her son had a queer temper, and she wished to dissuade him from the expedition.

"It is contrary to the spirit of the age," she asserted.

"Do you mean by that, contrary to the Machine?"

"In a sense, but —"

His image in the blue plate faded.

"Kuno!"

He had isolated himself.

For a moment Vashti felt lonely.

Then she generated the light, and the sight of her room, flooded with radiance and studded with electric buttons, revived her. There were buttons and switches everywhere — buttons to call for food, for music, for clothing. There was the hot-bath button, by pressure of which a basin of (imitation) marble rose out of the floor, filled to the brim with a warm deodorized liquid. There was the cold-bath button. There was the button that produced literature. And there were of course the buttons by which she communicated with her friends. The room, though it contained nothing, was in touch with all that she cared for in the world.

Vashti's next move was to turn off the isolation-switch, and all the accumulations of the last three minutes burst upon her. The room was filled with the noise of bells, and speaking-tubes. What was the new food like? Could she recommend it? Had she had any ideas lately? Might one tell her one's own ideas? Would she make an engagement to visit the public nurseries at an early date? — say this day month.

To most of these questions she replied with irritation — a growing quality in that accelerated age. She said that the new food was horrible. That she could not visit the public nurseries through press of engagements. That she had no ideas of her own but had just been told one — that four stars and three in the middle were like a man: she doubted there was much in it. Then she switched off her correspondents, for it was time to deliver her lecture on Australian music.

The clumsy system of public gatherings had been long since abandoned; neither Vashti nor her audience stirred from their rooms. Seated in her arm-chair she spoke, while they in their arm-chairs heard her, fairly well, and saw her, fairly well. She opened with a humorous account of music in the pre-Mongolian epoch, and went on to describe the great outburst of song that followed the Chinese conquest. Remote and primeval as were the methods of I-San-So and the Brisbane school, she yet felt (she said) that study of them might repay the musician of today: they had freshness; they had, above all, ideas.

Her lecture, which lasted ten minutes, was well received, and at its conclusion she and many of her audience listened to a lecture on the sea; there were ideas to be got from the sea; the speaker had donned a respirator and visited it lately. Then she fed, talked to many friends, had a bath, talked again, and summoned her bed.

The bed was not to her liking. It was too large, and she had a feeling for a small bed. Complaint was useless, for beds were of the same dimension all over the world, and to have had an alternative size would have involved vast alterations in the Machine. Vashti isolated herself – it was necessary, for neither day nor night existed under the ground – and reviewed all that had happened since she had summoned the bed last. Ideas? Scarcely any. Events – was Kuno's invitation an event?

By her side, on the little reading-desk, was a survival from the ages of litter – one book. This was the Book of the Machine. In it were instructions against every possible contingency. If she was hot or cold or dyspeptic or at loss for a word, she went to the book, and it told her which button to press. The Central Committee published it. In accordance with a growing habit, it was richly bound.

Sitting up in the bed, she took it reverently in her hands. She glanced round the glowing room as if some one might be watching her. Then, half ashamed, half joyful, she murmured "O Machine! O Machine!" and raised the volume to her lips. Thrice she kissed it, thrice inclined her head, thrice she felt the delirium of acquiescence. Her ritual performed, she turned to page 1367, which gave the times of the departure of the air-ships from the island in the southern hemisphere, under whose soil she lived, to the island in the northern hemisphere, whereunder lived her son.

She thought, "I have not the time."

She made the room dark and slept; she awoke and made the room light; she ate and exchanged ideas with her friends, and listened to music and attended lectures; she made the room dark and slept. Above her, beneath her, and around her, the Machine hummed eternally; she did not notice the noise, for she had been born with it in her ears. The earth, carrying her, hummed as it sped through silence, turning her now to the invisible sun, now to the invisible stars. She awoke and made the room light.

"Kuno!"

"I will not talk to you," he answered, "until you come."

"Have you been on the surface of the earth since we spoke last?"

His image faded.

Again she consulted the book. She became very nervous and lay back in her chair palpitating. Think of her as without teeth or hair. Presently she directed the chair to the wall, and pressed an unfamiliar button. The wall swung apart slowly. Through the opening she saw a tunnel that curved slightly, so that its goal was not visible. Should she go to see her son, here was the beginning of the journey.

Of course she knew all about the communication-system. There was nothing mysterious in it. She would summon a car and it would fly with her down the tunnel until it reached the lift that communicated with the air-ship station: the system had been in use for many, many years, long before the universal establishment of the Machine. And of course she had studied the civilization that had immediately preceded her own — the civilization that had mistaken the functions of the system, and had used it for bringing people to things, instead of for bringing things to people. Those funny old days, when men went for change of air instead of changing the air in their rooms! And yet — she was frightened of the tunnel: she had not seen it since her last child was born. It curved — but not quite as she remembered; it was brilliant — but not quite as brilliant as a lecturer had suggested. Vashti was seized with the terrors of direct experience. She shrank back into the room, and the wall closed up again.

"Kuno," she said, "I cannot come to see you. I am not well."

Immediately an enormous apparatus fell on to her out of the ceiling, a thermometer was automatically inserted between her lips, a stethoscope was automatically laid upon her heart. She lay powerless. Cool pads soothed her forehead. Kuno had telegraphed to her doctor.

So the human passions still blundered up and down in the

Machine. Vashti drank the medicine that the doctor projected into her mouth, and the machinery retired into the ceiling. The voice of Kuno was heard asking how she felt.

"Better." Then with irritation: "But why do you not come to me instead?"

"Because I cannot leave this place."

"Why?"

"Because, any moment, something tremendous may happen."

"Have you been on the surface of the earth yet?"

"Not yet."

"Then what is it?"

"I will not tell you through the Machine."

She resumed her life.

But she thought of Kuno as a baby, his birth, his removal to the public nurseries, her one visit to him there, his visits to her — visits which stopped when the Machine had assigned him a room on the other side of the earth. "Parents, duties of," said the Book of the Machine, "cease at the moment of birth. P. 422327483." True, but there was something special about Kuno — indeed there had been something special about all her children — and, after all, she must brave the journey if he desired it. And "something tremendous might happen." What did that mean? The nonsense of a youthful man, no doubt, but she must go. Again she pressed the unfamiliar button, again the wall swung back, and she saw the tunnel that curved out of sight. Clasping the Book, she rose, tottered on to the platform, and summoned the car. Her room closed behind her: the journey to the northern hemisphere had begun.

Of course it was perfectly easy. The car approached and in it she found arm-chairs exactly like her own. When she signalled, it stopped, and she tottered into the lift. One other passenger was in the lift, the first fellow creature she had seen face to face for months. Few travelled in these days, for, thanks to the advance of science, the earth was exactly alike all over. Rapid intercourse, from which the previous civilization had hoped so much, had ended by defeating itself. What was the good of going to Pekin when it was just like Shrewsbury? Why return to Shrewsbury when it would be just like Pekin? Men seldom moved their bodies; all unrest was concentrated in the soul.

The air-ship service was a relic from the former age. It was kept up, because it was easier to keep it up than to stop it or to diminish it, but it now far exceeded the wants of the population. Vessel after vessel would rise from the vomitories of Rye or of Christchurch (I use the antique names), would sail into the crowded sky, and would draw up at the wharves of the south — empty. So nicely adjusted was the system, so independent of meteorology, that the sky, whether calm or cloudy, resembled a vast kaleidoscope whereon the same patterns periodically recurred. The ship on which Vashti sailed started now at sunset, now at dawn. But always, as it passed above Rheims, it would neighbour the ship that served between Helsingfors and the Brazils, and, every third time it surmounted the Alps, the fleet of Palermo would cross its track behind. Night and day, wind and storm, tide and earthquake, impeded man no longer. He had harnessed Leviathan. All the old literature, with its praise of Nature, and its fear of Nature, rang false as the prattle of a child.

Yet as Vashti saw the vast flank of the ship, stained with exposure to the outer air, her horror of direct experience returned. It was not quite like the air-ship in the cinematophote. For one thing it smelt — not strongly or unpleasantly, but it did smell, and with her eyes shut she should have known that a new thing was close to her. Then she had to walk to it from the lift, had to submit to glances from the other passengers. The man in front dropped his Book — no great matter, but it disquieted them all. In the rooms, if the Book was dropped, the floor raised it mechanically, but the gangway to the air-ship was not so prepared, and the sacred volume lay motionless. They stopped — the thing was unforeseen — and the man, instead of picking up his property, felt the muscles of his arm to see how they had failed him. Then some one actually said with direct utterance: "We shall be late" — and they trooped on board, Vashti treading on the pages as she did so.

Inside, her anxiety increased. The arrangements were old-fashioned and rough. There was even a female attendant, to whom she would have to announce her wants during the voyage.

Of course a revolving platform ran the length of the boat, but she was expected to walk from it to her cabin. Some cabins were better than others, and she did not get the best. She thought the attendant had been unfair, and spasms of rage shook her. The glass valves had closed, she could not go back. She saw, at the end of the vestibule, the lift in which she had ascended going quietly up and down, empty. Beneath those corridors of shining tiles were rooms, tier below tier, reaching far into the earth, and in each room there sat a human being, eating, or sleeping, or producing ideas. And buried deep in the hive was her own room. Vashti was afraid.

"O Machine! O Machine!" she murmured, and caressed her Book, and was comforted.

Then the sides of the vestibule seemed to melt together, as do the passages that we see in dreams, the lift vanished, the Book that had been dropped slid to the left and vanished, polished tiles rushed by like a stream of water, there was a slight jar, and the air-ship, issuing from its tunnel, soared above the waters of a tropical ocean.

It was night. For a moment she saw the coast of Sumatra edged by the phosphorescence of waves, and crowned by lighthouses, still sending forth their disregarded beams. These also vanished, and only the stars distracted her. They were not motionless, but swayed to and fro above her head, thronging out of one skylight into another, as if the universe and not the air-ship was careening. And, as often happens on clear nights, they seemed now to be in perspective, now on a plane; now piled tier beyond tier into the infinite heavens, now concealing infinity, a roof limiting for ever the visions of men. In either case they seemed intolerable. "Are we to travel in the dark?" called the passengers angrily, and the attendant, who had been careless, generated the light, and pulled down the blinds of pliable metal. When the air-ships had been built, the desire to look direct at things still lingered in the world. Hence the extraordinary number of sky-lights and windows, and the proportionate discomfort to those who were civilized and refined. Even in Vashti's cabin one star peeped through a flaw in the blind, and after a few hours' uneasy slumber, she was disturbed by an unfamiliar glow, which was the dawn.

Quick as the ship had sped westwards, the earth had rolled eastwards quicker still, and had dragged back Vashti and her companions towards the sun. Science could prolong the night, but only for a little, and those high hopes of neutralizing the earth's diurnal revolution had passed, together with hopes that were possibly higher. To "keep pace with the sun," or even to outstrip it, had been the aim of the civilization preceding this. Racing aeroplanes had been built for the purpose, capable of enormous speed, and steered by the greatest intellects of the epoch. Round the globe they went, round and round, westward, westward, round and round, amidst humanity's applause. In vain. The globe went eastward quicker still, horrible accidents occurred, and the Committee of the Machine, at the time rising into prominence, declared the pursuit illegal, unmechanical, and punishable by Homelessness.

Of Homelessness more will be said later.

Doubtless the Committee was right. Yet the attempt to "defeat the sun" aroused the last common interest that our race experienced about the heavenly bodies, or indeed about anything. It was the last time that men were compacted by thinking of a power outside the world. The sun had conquered, yet it was the end of his spiritual dominion. Dawn, midday, twilight, the zodiacal path, touched neither men's lives nor their hearts, and science retreated into the ground, to concentrate herself upon problems that she was certain of solving.

So when Vashti found her cabin invaded by a rosy finger of light, she was annoyed, and tried to adjust the blind. But the blind flew up altogether, and she saw through the skylight small pink clouds, swaying against a background of blue, and as the sun crept higher, its radiance entered direct, brimming down the wall, like a golden sea. It rose and fell with the air-ship's motion, just as waves rise and fall, but it advanced steadily, as a tide advances. Unless she was careful, it would strike her face. A spasm of horror shook her and she rang for the attendant. The attendant too was horrified, but she could do nothing; it was not her place to mend the blind. She could only suggest that the lady should change her cabin, which she accordingly prepared to do.

People were almost exactly alike all over the world, but the attendant of the air-ship, perhaps owing to her exceptional duties, had grown a little out of the common. She had often to address passengers with direct speech, and this had given her a certain roughness and originality of manner. When Vashti swerved away from the sunbeams with a cry, she behaved barbarically — she put out her hand to steady her.

"How dare you!" exclaimed the passenger. "You forget yourself!"

The woman was confused, and apologized for not having let her fall. People never touched one another. The custom had become obsolete, owing to the Machine.

"Where are we now?" asked Vashti haughtily.

"We are over Asia," said the attendant, anxious to be polite.

"Asia?"

"You must excuse my common way of speaking. I have got into the habit of calling places over which I pass by their unmechanical names."

"Oh, I remember Asia. The Mongols came from it."

"Beneath us, in the open air, stood a city that was once called Simla."

"Have you ever heard of the Mongols and of the Brisbane school?"

"No."

"Brisbane also stood in the open air."

"Those mountains to the right — let me show you them." She pushed back a metal blind. The main chain of the Himalayas was revealed. "They were once called the Roof of the World, those mountains."

"What a foolish name!"

"You must remember that, before the dawn of civilization, they seemed to be an impenetrable wall that touched the stars. It was supposed that no one but the gods could exist above their summits. How we have advanced, thanks to the Machine!"

"How we have advanced, thanks to the Machine!" said Vashti.

"How we have advanced, thanks to the Machine!" echoed the passenger who had dropped his Book the night before, and who was standing in the passage.

"And that white stuff in the cracks? — what is it?"

"I have forgotten its name."

"Cover the window, please. These mountains give me no ideas."

The northern aspect of the Himalayas was in deep shadow: on the Indian slope the sun had just prevailed. The forests had been destroyed during the literature epoch for the purpose of making newspaper-pulp, but the snows were awakening to their morning glory, and clouds still hung on the breasts of Kinchinjunga. In the plain were seen the ruins of cities, with diminished rivers creeping by their walls, and by the sides of these were sometimes the signs of vomitories, marking the cities of today. Over the whole prospect air-ships rushed, crossing and intercrossing with incredible *aplomb*, and rising nonchalantly when they desired to escape the perturbations of the lower atmosphere and to traverse the Roof of the World.

"We have indeed advanced, thanks to the Machine," repeated the attendant, and hid the Himalayas behind a metal blind.

The day dragged wearily forward. The passengers sat each in his cabin, avoiding one another with an almost physical repulsion and longing to be once more under the surface of the earth. There were eight or ten of them, mostly young males, sent out from the public nurseries to inhabit the rooms of those who had died in various parts of the earth. The man who had dropped his Book was on the homeward journey. He had been sent to Sumatra for the purpose of propagating the race. Vashti alone was travelling by her private will.

At midday she took a second glance at the earth. The air-ship was crossing another range of mountains, but she could see little, owing to clouds. Masses of black rock hovered below her, and merged indistinctly into grey. Their shapes were fantastic; one of them resembled a prostrate man.

"No ideas here," murmured Vashti, and hid the Caucasus behind a metal blind.

In the evening she looked again. They were crossing a golden sea, in which lay many small islands and one peninsula.

She repeated, "No ideas here," and hid Greece behind a metal blind.

## 2. *The Mending Apparatus*

By a vestibule, by a lift, by a tubular railway, by a platform, by a sliding door — by reversing all the steps of her departure did Vashti arrive at her son's room, which exactly resembled her own. She might well declare that the visit was superfluous. The buttons, the knobs, the reading-desk with the Book, the temperature, the atmosphere, the illumination — all were exactly the same. And if Kuno himself, flesh of her flesh, stood close beside her at last, what profit was there in that? She was too well-bred to shake him by the hand.

Averting her eyes, she spoke as follows:

"Here I am. I have had the most terrible journey and greatly retarded the development of my soul. It is not worth it, Kuno, it is not worth it. My time is too precious. The sunlight almost touched me, and I have met with the rudest people. I can only stop a few minutes. Say what you want to say, and then I must return."

"I have been threatened with Homelessness," said Kuno.

She looked at him now.

"I have been threatened with Homelessness, and I could not tell you such a thing through the Machine."

Homelessness means death. The victim is exposed to the air, which kills him.

"I have been outside since I spoke to you last. The tremendous thing has happened, and they have discovered me."

"But why shouldn't you go outside!" she exclaimed. "It is perfectly legal, perfectly mechanical, to visit the surface of the earth. I have lately been to a lecture on the sea; there is no objection to that; one simply summons a respirator and gets an Egression-permit. It is not the kind of thing that spiritually-minded people do, and I begged you not to do it, but there is no legal objection to it."

"I did not get an Egression-permit."

"Then how did you get out?"

"I found out a way of my own."

The phrase conveyed no meaning to her, and he had to repeat it.

"A way of your own?" she whispered. "But that would be wrong."

"Why?"

The question shocked her beyond measure.

"You are beginning to worship the Machine," he said coldly. "You think it irreligious of me to have found out a way of my own. It was just what the Committee thought, when they threatened me with Homelessness."

At this she grew angry. "I worship nothing!" she cried. "I am most advanced. I don't think you irreligious, for there is no such thing as religion left. All the fear and the superstition that existed once have been destroyed by the Machine. I only meant that to find out a way of your own was — Besides, there is no new way out."

"So it is always supposed."

"Except through the vomitories, for which one must have an Egression-permit, it is impossible to get out. The Book says so."

"Well, the Book's wrong, for I have been out on my feet."

For Kuno was possessed of a certain physical strength.

By these days it was a demerit to be muscular. Each infant was examined at birth, and all who promised undue strength were destroyed. Humanitarians may protest, but it would have been no true kindness to let an athlete live; he would never have been happy in that state of life to which the Machine had called him; he would have yearned for trees to climb, rivers to bathe in, meadows and hills against which he might measure his body. Man must be adapted to his surroundings, must he not? In the dawn of the world our weakly must be exposed on Mount Taygetus, in its twilight our strong will suffer euthanasia, that the Machine may progress, that the Machine may progress, that the Machine may progress eternally.

"You know that we have lost the sense of space. We say 'space is annihilated', but we have annihilated not space, but the sense thereof. We have lost a part of ourselves. I determined to recover it, and I began by walking up and down the platform of the railway outside my room. Up and down, until I was tired, and so did recapture the meaning of 'Near' and 'Far'. 'Near' is a place to which I can get quickly *on my feet*, not a place to which the train or the air-ship will take me quickly. 'Far' is a place to which I cannot get quickly on my feet; the vomitory is 'far', though I could be there in thirty-eight seconds by summoning the train. Man is the measure. That was my first lesson. Man's feet are the measure for distance, his hands are the measure for ownership, his body is the measure for all that is lovable and desirable and strong. Then I went further: it was then that I called to you for the first time, and you would not come.

"This city, as you know, is built deep beneath the surface of the earth, with only the vomitories protruding. Having paced the platform outside my own room, I took the lift to the next platform and paced that also, and so with each in turn, until I came to the topmost, above which begins the earth. All the platforms were exactly alike, and all that I gained by visiting them was to develop my sense of space and my muscles. I think I should have been content with this – it is not a little thing – but as I walked and brooded, it occurred to me that our cities had been built in the days when men still breathed the outer air, and that there had been ventilation shafts for the workmen. I could think of nothing but these ventilation shafts. Had they been destroyed by all the food-tubes and medicine-tubes and music-tubes that the Machine has evolved lately? Or did traces of them remain? One thing was certain. If I came upon them anywhere, it would be in the railway-tunnels of the topmost story. Everywhere else, all space was accounted for.

"I am telling my story quickly, but don't think that I was not a coward or that your answers never depressed me. It is not the proper thing, it is not mechanical, it is not decent to walk along a railway-tunnel. I did not fear that I might tread upon a live rail and be killed. I feared something far more intangible – doing what was not contemplated by the Machine. Then I said to myself, 'Man is the measure,' and I went, and after many visits I found an opening.

"The tunnels, of course, were lighted. Everything is light, artificial light; darkness is the exception. So when I saw a black gap in the tiles, I knew that it was an exception, and rejoiced. I put in my arm — I could put in no more at first — and waved it round and round in ecstasy. I loosened another tile, and put in my head, and shouted into the darkness: 'I am coming, I shall do it yet,' and my voice reverberated down endless passages. I seemed to hear the spirits of those dead workmen who had returned each evening to the starlight and to their wives, and all the generations who had lived in the open air called back to me, 'You will do it yet, you are coming.' "

He paused, and, absurd as he was, his last words moved her. For Kuno had lately asked to be a father, and his request had been refused by the Committee. His was not a type that the Machine desired to hand on.

"Then a train passed. It brushed by me, but I thrust my head and arms into the hole. I had done enough for one day, so I crawled back to the platform, went down in the lift, and summoned my bed. Ah, what dreams! And again I called you, and again you refused."

She shook her head and said:

"Don't. Don't talk of these terrible things. You make me miserable. You are throwing civilization away."

"But I had got back the sense of space and a man cannot rest then. I determined to get in at the hole and climb the shaft. And so I exercised my arms. Day after day I went through ridiculous movements, until my flesh ached, and I could hang by my hands and hold the pillow of my bed outstretched for many minutes. Then I summoned a respirator, and started.

"It was easy at first. The mortar had somehow rotted, and I soon pushed some more tiles in, and clambered after them into the darkness, and the spirits of the dead comforted me. I don't know what I mean by that. I just say what I felt. I felt, for the first time, that a protest had been lodged against corruption, and that even as the dead were comforting me, so I was comforting the unborn. I felt that humanity existed, and that it existed without clothes. How can I possibly explain this? It was naked, humanity seemed naked, and all these tubes and buttons and machineries neither came into the world with us, nor will they follow us out, nor do they matter supremely while we are here. Had I been strong, I would have torn off every garment I had, and gone out into the outer air unswaddled. But this is not for me, nor perhaps for my generation. I climbed with my respirator and my hygienic clothes and my dietetic tabloids! Better thus than not at all.

"There was a ladder, made of some primeval metal. The light from the railway fell upon its lowest rungs, and I saw that it led straight upwards out of the rubble at the bottom of the shaft. Perhaps our ancestors ran up and down it a dozen times daily, in their building. As I climbed, the rough edges cut through my gloves so that my hands bled. The light helped me for a little, and then came darkness and, worse still, silence which pierced my ears like a sword. The Machine hums! Did you know that? Its hum penetrates our blood, and may even guide our thoughts. Who knows! I was getting beyond its power. Then I thought: 'This silence means that I am doing wrong.' But I heard voices in the silence, and again they strengthened me." He laughed. "I had need of them. The next moment I cracked my head against something."

She sighed.

"I had reached one of those pneumatic stoppers that defend us from the outer air. You may have noticed them on the air-ship. Pitch dark, my feet on the rungs of an invisible ladder, my hands cut; I cannot explain how I lived through this part, but the voices still comforted me, and I felt for fastenings. The stopper, I suppose, was about eight feet across. I passed my hand over it as far as I could reach. It was perfectly smooth. I felt it almost to the centre. Not quite to the centre, for my arm was too short. Then the voice said: 'Jump. It is worth it. There may be a handle in the centre, and you may catch hold of it and so come to us your own way. And if there is no handle, so that you may fall and are dashed to pieces — it is still worth it: you will still come to us your own way.' So I jumped. There was a handle, and —"

He paused. Tears gathered in his mother's eyes. She knew that he was fated. If he did not die today he would die tomorrow. There was not room for such a person in the world. And with her pity disgust mingled. She was ashamed at having borne such a son, she who had always been so respectable and so full of ideas. Was he really the little boy to whom she had taught the use of his stops and buttons, and to whom she had given his first lessons in the Book? The very hair that disfigured his lip showed that he was reverting to some savage type. On atavism the Machine can have no mercy.

"There was a handle, and I did catch it. I hung tranced over the darkness and heard the hum of these workings as the last whisper in a dying dream. All the things I had cared about and all the people I had spoken to through tubes appeared infinitely little. Meanwhile the handle revolved. My weight had set something in motion and I span slowly, and then —

"I cannot describe it. I was lying with my face to the sunshine. Blood poured from my nose and ears and I heard a tremendous roaring. The stopper, with me clinging to it, had simply been blown out of the earth, and the air that we make down here was escaping through the vent into the air above. It burst up like a fountain. I crawled back to it — for the upper air hurts — and, as it were, I took great sips from the edge. My respirator had flown goodness knows where, my clothes were torn. I just lay with my lips close to the hole, and I sipped until the bleeding stopped. You can imagine nothing so curious. This hollow in the grass — I will speak of it in a minute, — the sun shining into it, not brilliantly but through marbled clouds, — the peace, the nonchalance, the sense of space, and, brushing my cheek, the roaring fountain of our artificial air! Soon I spied my respirator, bobbing up and down in the current high above my head, and higher still were many air-ships. But no one ever looks out of air-ships, and in my case they could not have picked me up. There I was, stranded. The sun shone a little way down the shaft, and revealed the topmost rung of the ladder, but it was hopeless trying to reach it. I should either have been tossed up again by the escape, or else have fallen in, and died. I could only lie on the grass, sipping and sipping, and from time to time glancing around me.

"I knew that I was in Wessex, for I had taken care to go to a lecture on the subject before starting. Wessex lies above the room in which we are talking now. It was once an important state. Its kings held all the southern coast from the Andredswald to Cornwall, while the Wansdyke protected them on the north, running over the high ground. The lecturer was only concerned with the rise of Wessex, so I do not know how long it remained an international power, nor would the knowledge have assisted me. To tell the truth I could do nothing but laugh, during this part. There was I, with a pneumatic stopper by my side and a respirator bobbing over my head, imprisoned, all three of us, in a grassgrown hollow that was edged with fern."

Then he grew grave again.

"Lucky for me that it was a hollow. For the air began to fall back into it and to fill it as water fills a bowl. I could crawl about. Presently I stood. I breathed a mixture, in which the air that hurts pre-dominated whenever I tried to climb the sides. This was not so bad. I had not lost my tabloids and remained ridiculously cheerful, and as for the Machine, I forgot about it altogether. My one aim now was to get to the top, where the ferns were, and to view whatever objects lay beyond.

"I rushed to the slope. The new air was still too bitter for me and I came rolling back, after a momentary vision of something grey. The sun grew very feeble, and I remembered that he was in Scorpio — I had been to a lecture on that too. If the sun is in Scorpio and you are in Wessex, it means that you must be as quick as you can, or it will get too dark. (This is the first bit of useful information I have ever got from a lecture, and I expect it will be the last.) It made me try frantically to breathe the new air, and to advance as far as I dared out of my pond. The hollow filled so slowly. At times I thought that the fountain played with less vigour. My respirator seemed to dance nearer the earth; the roar was decreasing."

He broke off.

"I don't think this is interesting you. The rest will interest you even less. There are no ideas in it, and I wish that I had not troubled you to come. We are too different, mother."

She told him to continue.

"It was evening before I climbed the bank. The sun had very nearly slipped out of the sky by this time, and I could not get a good view. You, who have just crossed the Roof of the World, will not want to hear an account of the little hills that I saw — low colourless hills. But to me they were living and the turf that covered them was a skin, under which their muscles rippled, and I felt that those hills had called with incalculable force to men in the past, and that men had loved them. Now they sleep — perhaps for ever. They commune with humanity in dreams. Happy the man, happy the woman, who awakes the hills of Wessex. For though they sleep, they will never die."

His voice rose passionately.

"Cannot you see, cannot all your lecturers see, that it is we who are dying, and that down here the only thing that really lives is the Machine? We created the Machine, to do our will, but we cannot make it do our will now. It has robbed us of the sense of space and of the sense of touch, it has blurred every human relation and narrowed down love to a carnal act, it has paralyzed our bodies and our wills, and now it compels us to worship it. The Machine develops — but not on our lines. The Machine proceeds — but not to our goal. We only exist as the blood corpuscles that course through its arteries, and if it could work without us, it would let us die. Oh, I have no remedy — or, at least, only one — to tell men again and again that I have seen the hills of Wessex as Aelfrid saw them when he overthrew the Danes.

"So the sun set. I forgot to mention that a belt of mist lay between my hill and other hills, and that it was the colour of pearl."

He broke off for the second time.

"Go on," said his mother wearily.

He shook his head.

"Go on. Nothing that you say can distress me now. I am hardened."

"I had meant to tell you the rest, but I cannot: I know that I cannot: good-bye."

Vashti stood irresolute. All her nerves were tingling with his blasphemies. But she was also inquisitive.

"This is unfair," she complained. "You have called me across the world to hear your story, and hear it I will. Tell me – as briefly as possible, for this is a disastrous waste of time – tell me how you returned to civilization."

"Oh – that!" he said, starting. "You would like to hear about civilization. Certainly. Had I got to where my respirator fell down?"

"No – but I understand everything now. You put on your respirator, and managed to walk along the surface of the earth to a vomitory, and there your conduct was reported to the Central Committee."

"By no means."

He passed his hand over his forehead, as if dispelling some strong impression. Then, resuming his narrative, he warmed to it again.

"My respirator fell about sunset. I had mentioned that the fountain seemed feebler, had I not?"

"Yes."

"About sunset, it let the respirator fall. As I said, I had entirely forgotten about the Machine, and I paid no great attention at the time, being occupied with other things. I had my pool of air, into which I could dip when the outer keenness became intolerable, and which would possibly remain for days, provided that no wind sprang up to disperse it. Not until it was too late, did I realize what the stoppage of the escape implied. You see – the gap in the tunnel had been mended: the Mending Apparatus; the Mending Apparatus was after me.

"One other warning I had, but I neglected it. The sky at night was clearer than it had been in the day, and the moon, which was about half the sky behind the sun, shone into the dell at moments quite brightly. I was in my usual place – on the boundary between the two atmospheres – when I thought I saw something dark move across the bottom of the dell, and vanish into the shaft.

In my folly, I ran down. I bent over and listened, and I thought I heard a faint scraping noise in the depths.

"At this — but it was too late — I took alarm. I determined to put on my respirator and to walk right out of the dell. But my respirator had gone. I knew exactly where it had fallen — between the stopper and the aperture — and I could even feel the mark that it had made in the turf. It had gone, and I realized that something evil was at work, and I had better escape to the other air, and, if I must die, die running towards the cloud that had been the colour of a pearl. I never started. Out of the shaft — it is too horrible. A worm, a long white worm, had crawled out of the shaft and was gliding over the moonlit grass.

"I screamed. I did everything that I should not have done. I stamped upon the creature instead of flying from it, and it at once curled round the ankle. Then we fought. The worm let me run all over the dell, but edged up my leg as I ran. 'Help!' I cried. (That part is too awful. It belongs to the part that you will never know.) 'Help!' I cried. (Why cannot we suffer in silence?) 'Help!' I cried. Then my feet were wound together, I fell, I was dragged away from the dear ferns and the living hills, and past the great metal stopper (I can tell you this part), and I thought it might save me again if I caught hold of the handle. It also was enwrapped, it also. Oh, the whole dell was full of the things. They were searching it in all directions, they were denuding it, and the white snouts of others peeped out of the hole, ready if needed. Everything that could be moved they brought — brushwood, bundles of fern, everything, and down we all went intertwined into hell. The last things that I saw, ere the stopper closed after us, were certain stars, and I felt that a man of my sort lived in the sky. For I did fight, I fought till the very end, and it was only my head hitting against the ladder that quieted me. I woke up in this room. The worms had vanished. I was surrounded by artificial air, artificial light, artificial peace, and my friends were calling to me down speaking-tubes to know whether I had come across any new ideas lately."

Here his story ended. Discussion of it was impossible, and Vashti turned to go.

"It will end in Homelessness," she said quietly.

"I wish it would," retorted Kuno.

"The Machine has been most merciful."

"I prefer the mercy of God."

"By that superstitious phrase, do you mean that you could live in the outer air?"

"Yes."

"Have you ever seen, round the vomitories, the bones of those who were extruded after the Great Rebellion?"

"Yes."

"They were left where they perished for our edification. A few crawled away, but they perished, too — who can doubt it? And so with the Homeless of our own day. The surface of the earth supports life no longer."

"Indeed."

"Ferns and a little grass may survive, but all higher forms have perished. Has any air-ship detected them?"

"No."

"Has any lecturer dealt with them?"

"No."

"Then why this obstinacy?"

"Because I have seen them," he exploded.

"Seen *what?*"

"Because I have seen her in the twilight — because she came to my help when I called — because she, too, was entangled by the worms, and, luckier than I, was killed by one of them piercing her throat."

He was mad. Vashti departed, nor, in the troubles that followed, did she ever see his face again.

## 3. *The Homeless*

During the years that followed Kuno's escapade, two important developments took place in the Machine. On the surface they were revolutionary, but in either case men's minds had been prepared beforehand, and they did but express tendencies that were latent already.

The first of these was the abolition of respirators.

Advanced thinkers, like Vashti, had always held it foolish to visit the surface of the earth. Air-ships might be necessary, but what was the good of going out for mere curiosity and crawling along for a mile or two in a terrestrial motor? The habit was vulgar and perhaps faintly improper: it was unproductive of ideas, and had no connection with the habits that really mattered. So respirators were abolished, and with them, of course, the terrestrial motors, and except for a few lecturers, who complained that they were debarred access to their subject-matter, the development was accepted quietly. Those who still wanted to know what the earth was like had after all only to listen to some gramophone, or to look into some cinematophote. And even the lecturers acquiesced when they found that a lecture on the sea was none the less stimulating when compiled out of other lectures that had already been delivered on the same subject. "Beware of first-hand ideas!" exclaimed one of the most advanced of them. "First-hand ideas do not really exist. They are but the physical impressions produced by love and fear, and on this gross foundation who could erect a philosophy? Let your ideas be second-hand, and if possible tenth-hand, for then they will be far removed from the disturbing element — direct observation. Do not learn anything about this subject of mine — the French Revolution. Learn instead what I think that Enicharmon thought Urizen thought Gutch thought Ho-Yung thought Chi-Bo-Sing thought Lafcadio Hearn thought Carlyle thought Mirabeau said about the French Revolution. Through the medium of these eight great minds, the blood that was shed at Paris and the windows that were broken at Versailles will be clarified to an idea which you may employ most profitably in your daily lives. But be sure that the intermediates are many and varied, for in history one authority exists to counteract another. Urizen must counteract the skepticism of Ho-Yung and Enicharmon, I must myself counteract the impetuosity of Gutch. You who listen to me are in a better position to judge about the French Revolution than I am. Your descendants will be even in a better position than you, for they will learn what you think I think, and yet another intermediate will be added to the chain. And in time" — his voice rose — "there will come a generation that has got beyond facts, beyond impressions, a generation absolutely colourless, a generation

*seraphically free*
*From taint of personality,*

which will see the French Revolution not as it happened, nor as they would like it to have happened, but as it would have happened, had it taken place in the days of the Machine."

Tremendous applause greeted this lecture, which did but voice a feeling already latent in the minds of men — a feeling that terrestrial facts must be ignored, and that the abolition of respirators was a positive gain. It was even suggested that air-ships should be abolished too. This was not done, because air-ships had somehow worked themselves into the Machine's system. But year by year they were used less, and mentioned less by thoughtful men.

The second great development was the re-establishment of religion.

This, too, had been voiced in the celebrated lecture. No one could mistake the reverent tone in which the peroration had concluded, and it awakened a responsive echo in the heart of each. Those who had long worshipped silently, now began to talk. They described the strange feeling of peace that came over them when they handled the Book of the Machine, the pleasure that it was to repeat certain numerals out of it, however little meaning those numerals conveyed to the outward ear, the ecstasy of touching a button, however unimportant, or of ringing an electric bell, however superfluously.

"The Machine," they exclaimed, "feeds us and clothes us and houses us; through it we speak to one another, through it we see one another, in it we have our being. The Machine is the friend of ideas and the enemy of superstition: the Machine is omnipotent, eternal; blessed is the Machine." And before long this allocution was printed on the first page of the Book, and in subsequent editions the ritual swelled into a complicated system of praise and prayer. The word "religion" was sedulously avoided, and in theory the Machine was still the creation and the implement of man. But in practice all, save a few retrogrades, worshipped it as divine. Nor was it worshipped in unity. One believer would be chiefly impressed by the blue optic plates, through which he saw other believers; another by the mending apparatus, which sinful Kuno had compared to worms; another by the lifts, another by the Book. And each would pray to this or that, and ask it to intercede for him with the Machine as a whole. Persecution — that also was present. It did not break out, for reasons that will be set forward shortly. But it was latent, and all who did not accept the minimum known as "undenominational Mechanism" lived in danger of Homelessness, which means death, as we know.

To attribute these two great developments to the Central Committee, is to take a very narrow view of civilization. The Central Committee announced the developments, it is true, but they were no more the cause of them than were the kings of the imperialistic period the cause of war. Rather did they yield to some invincible pressure, which came no one knew whither, and which, when gratified, was succeeded by some new pressure equally invincible. To such a state of affairs it is convenient to give the name of progress. No one confessed the Machine was out of hand. Year by year it was served with increased efficiency and decreased intelligence. The better a man knew his own duties upon it, the less he understood the duties of his neighbour, and in all the world there was not one who understood the monster as a whole. Those master brains had perished. They had left full directions, it is true, and their successors had each of them mastered a portion of those directions. But Humanity, in its desire for comfort, had overreached itself. It had exploited the riches of nature too far. Quietly and complacently, it was sinking into decadence, and progress had come to mean the progress of the Machine.

As for Vashti, her life went peacefully forward until the final disaster. She made her room dark and slept; she awoke and made the room light. She lectured and attended lectures. She exchanged ideas with her innumerable friends and believed she was growing more spiritual. At times a friend was granted Euthanasia, and left his or her room for the homelessness that is beyond all human conception. Vashti did not much mind. After an unsuccessful lecture, she would sometimes ask for Euthanasia herself. But the death-rate was not permitted to exceed the birth-rate, and the Machine had hitherto refused it to her.

The troubles began quietly, long before she was conscious of them.

One day she was astonished at receiving a message from her son. They never communicated, having nothing in common, and she had only heard indirectly that he was still alive, and had been transferred from the northern hemisphere, where he had behaved so mischievously, to the southern — indeed, to a room not far from her own.

"Does he want me to visit him?" she thought. "Never again, never. And I have not the time."

No, it was madness of another kind.

He refused to visualize his face upon the blue plate, and speaking out of the darkness with solemnity said:

"The Machine stops."

"What do you say?"

"The Machine is stopping. I know it, I know the signs."

She burst into a peal of laughter. He heard her and was angry, and they spoke no more.

"Can you imagine anything more absurd?" she cried to a friend. "A man who was my son believes that the Machine is stopping. It would be impious if it was not mad."

"The Machine is stopping?" her friend replied. "What does that mean? The phrase conveys nothing to me."

"Nor to me."

"He does not refer, I suppose, to the trouble there has been lately with the music?"

"Oh no, of course not. Let us talk about music."

"Have you complained to the authorities?"

"Yes, and they say it wants mending, and referred me to the Committee of the Mending Apparatus. I complained of those curious gasping sighs that disfigure the symphonies of the Brisbane school. They sound like someone in pain. The Committee of the Mending Apparatus say that it shall be remedied shortly."

Obscurely worried, she resumed her life. For one thing, the defect in the music irritated her. For another thing, she could not forget Kuno's speech. If he had known that the music was out of repair — he could not know it, for he detested music — if he had known that it was wrong, "the Machine stops" was exactly the venomous sort of remark he would have made. Of course he had made it at a venture, but the coincidence annoyed her, and she spoke with some petulance to the Committee of the Mending Apparatus.

They replied, as before, that the defect would be set right shortly.

"Shortly! At once!" she retorted. "Why should I be worried by imperfect music? Things are always put right at once. If you do not mend it at once, I shall complain to the Central Committee."

"No personal complaints are received by the Central Committee," the Committee of the Mending Apparatus replied.

"Through whom am I to make my complaint, then?"

"Through us."

"I complain then."

"Your complaint shall be forwarded in its turn."

"Have others complained?"

This question was unmechanical, and the Committee of the Mending Apparatus refused to answer it.

"It is too bad!" she exclaimed to another of her friends. "There never was such an unfortunate woman as myself. I can never be sure of my music now. It gets worse and worse each time I summon it."

"I too have my troubles," the friend replied. "Sometimes my ideas are interrupted by a slight jarring noise."

"What is it?"

"I do not know whether it is inside my head, or inside the wall."

"Complain, in either case."

"I have complained, and my complaint will be forwarded in its turn to the Central Committee."

Time passed, and they resented the defects no longer. The defects had not been remedied, but the human tissues in that latter day had become so subservient, that they readily adapted themselves to every caprice of the Machine. The sigh at the crisis of the Brisbane symphony no longer irritated Vashti; she accepted it as part of the melody. The jarring noise, whether in the head or in the wall, was no longer resented by her friend. And so with the mouldy artificial fruit, so with the bath water that began to stink, so with the defective rhymes that the poetry machine had taken to emit. All were bitterly complained of at first, and then acquiesced in and forgotten. Things went from bad to worse un-challenged.

It was otherwise with the failure of the sleeping apparatus. That was a more serious stoppage. There came a day when over the whole world — in Sumatra, in Wessex, in the innumerable cities of Courland and Brazil — the beds, when summoned by their tired owners, failed to appear. It may seem a ludicrous matter, but from it we may date the collapse of humanity. The Committee responsible for the failure was assailed by complain-ants, whom it referred, as usual, to the Committee of the Mending Apparatus, who in its turn assured them that their complaints would be forwarded to the Central Committee. But the discontent grew, for mankind was not yet sufficiently adaptable to do with-out sleeping.

"Some one is meddling with the Machine —" they began.

"Some one is trying to make himself king, to reintroduce the personal element."

"Punish that man with Homelessness."

"To the rescue! Avenge the Machine! Avenge the Machine!"

"War! Kill the man!"

But the Committee of the Mending Apparatus now came for-ward, and allayed the panic with well-chosen words. It confessed that the Mending Apparatus was itself in need of repair.

The effect of this frank confession was admirable.

"Of course," said a famous lecturer — he of the French Revo-lution, who gilded each new decay with splendour — "of course we shall not press our complaints now. The Mending Apparatus has treated us so well in the past that we all sympathize with it, and will wait patiently for its recovery. In its own good time it will resume its duties. Meanwhile let us do without our beds, our tabloids, our other little wants. Such, I feel sure, would be the wish of the Machine."

Thousands of miles away his audience applauded. The Machine still linked them. Under the seas, beneath the roots of the mountains, ran the wires through which they saw and heard, the enormous eyes and ears that were their heritage, and the hum of many workings clothed their thoughts in one garment of subserviency. Only the old and the sick remained ungrateful, for it was rumoured that Euthanasia, too, was out of order, and the pain had reappeared among men.

It became difficult to read. A blight entered the atmosphere and dulled its luminosity. At times Vashti could scarcely see across her room. The air, too, was foul. Loud were the complaints, impotent the remedies, heroic the tone of the lecturer as he cried: "Courage, courage! What matter so long as the Machine goes on? To it the darkness and the light are one." And though things improved again after a time, the old brilliancy was never recaptured, and humanity never recovered from its entrance into twilight. There was an hysterical talk of "measures", of "provisional dictatorship", and the inhabitants of Sumatra were asked to familiarize themselves with the workings of the central power station, the said power station being situated in France. But for the most part panic reigned, and men spent their strength praying to their Books, tangible proofs of the Machine's omnipotence. There were gradations of terror – at times came rumours of hope – the Mending Apparatus was almost mended – the enemies of the Machine had been got under – new "nerve-centres" were evolving which would do the work even more magnificently than before. But there came a day when, without the slightest warning, without any previous hint of feebleness, the entire communication-system broke down, all over the world, and the world, as they understood it, ended.

Vashti was lecturing at the time and her earlier remarks had been punctuated with applause. As she proceeded the audience became silent, and at the conclusion there was no sound. Somewhat displeased, she called to a friend who was a specialist in sympathy. No sound: doubtless the friend was sleeping. And so with the next friend whom she tried to summon, and so with the next, until she remembered Kuno's cryptic remark, "The Machine stops."

The phrase still conveyed nothing. If Eternity was stopping it would of course be set going shortly.

For example, there was still a little light and air — the atmosphere had improved a few hours previously. There was still the Book, and while there was the Book there was security.

Then she broke down, for with the cessation of activity came an unexpected terror — silence.

She had never known silence, and the coming of it nearly killed her — it did kill many thousands of people outright. Ever since her birth she had been surrounded by the steady hum. It was to the ear what artificial air was to the lungs, and agonizing pains shot across her head. And scarcely knowing what she did, she stumbled forward and pressed the unfamiliar button, the one that opened the door of her cell.

Now the door of the cell worked on a simple hinge of its own. It was not connected with the central power station, dying far away in France. It opened, rousing immoderate hopes in Vashti, for she thought that the Machine had been mended. It opened, and she saw the dim tunnel that curved far away towards freedom. One look, and then she shrank back. For the tunnel was full of people — she was almost the last in that city to have taken alarm.

People at any time repelled her, and these were nightmares from her worst dreams. People were crawling about, people were screaming, whimpering, gasping for breath, touching each other, vanishing in the dark, and ever and anon being pushed off the platform on to the live rail. Some were fighting round the electric bells, trying to summon trains which could not be summoned. Others were yelling for Euthanasia or for respirators, or blaspheming the Machine. Others stood at the doors of their cells fearing, like herself, either to stop in them or to leave them. And behind all the uproar was silence — the silence which is the voice of the earth and of the generations who have gone.

No — it was worse than solitude. She closed the door again and sat down to wait for the end. The disintegration went on, accompanied by horrible cracks and rumbling. The valves that restrained the Medical Apparatus must have been weakened, for it ruptured and hung hideously from the ceiling. The floor heaved and fell and flung her from her chair. A tube oozed towards her serpent fashion. And at last the final horror approached — light began to ebb, and she knew that civilization's long day was closing.

She whirled round, praying to be saved from this, at any rate, kissing the Book, pressing button after button. The uproar outside was increasing, and even penetrated the wall. Slowly the brilliancy of her cell was dimmed, the reflections faded from her metal switches. Now she could not see the reading stand, now not the Book, though she held it in her hand. Light followed the flight of sound, air was following light, and the original void returned to the cavern from which it had been so long excluded. Vashti continued to whirl, like the devotees of an earlier religion, screaming, praying, striking at the buttons with bleeding hands.

It was thus that she opened her prison and escaped — escaped in the spirit: at least so it seems to me, ere my meditation closes. That she escapes in the body — I cannot perceive that. She struck, by chance, the switch that released the door, and the rush of foul air on her skin, the loud throbbing whispers in her ears, told her that she was facing the tunnel again, and the tremendous platform on which she had seen men fighting. They were not fighting now. Only the whispers remained, and the little whimpering groans. They were dying by hundreds out in the dark.

She burst into tears.

Tears answered her.

They wept for humanity, those two, not for themselves. They could not bear that this should be the end. Ere silence was completed their hearts were opened, and they knew what had been important on the earth. Man, the flower of all flesh, the noblest of all creatures visible, man who had once made god in his image, and had mirrored his strength on the constellations, beautiful naked man was dying, strangled in the garments that he had woven. Century after century had he toiled, and here was his reward. Truly the garment had seemed heavenly at first, shot with the colours of culture, sewn with the threads of self-denial. And heavenly it had been so long as it was a garment and no more, so long as man could shed it at will and live by the essence that is his soul, and the essence, equally divine, that is his body. The sin against the body — it was for that they wept in chief; the centuries of wrong against the muscles and the nerves, and those five portals by which we can alone apprehend — glozing it over with talk of evolution, until the body was white pap, the home of ideas as colourless, last sloshy stirrings of a spirit that had grasped the stars.

"Where are you?" she sobbed.

His voice in the darkness said, "Here."

"Is there any hope, Kuno?"

"None for us."

"Where are you?"

She crawled towards him over the bodies of the dead. His blood spurted over her hands.

"Quicker," he gasped, "I am dying — but we touch, we talk, not through the Machine."

He kissed her.

"We have come back to our own. We die, but we have recaptured life, as it was in Wessex, when Aelfrid overthrew the Danes. We know what they know outside, they who dwelt in the cloud that is the colour of a pearl."

"But, Kuno, is it true? Are there still men on the surface of the earth? Is this — this tunnel, this poisoned darkness — really not the end?"

He replied:

"I have seen them, spoken to them, loved them. They are hiding in the mist and the ferns until our civilization stops. To-day they are the Homeless — to-morrow —"

"Oh, to-morrow — some fool will start the Machine again, to-morrow."

"Never," said Kuno, "never. Humanity has learnt its lesson."

As he spoke, the whole city was broken like a honeycomb. An air-ship had sailed in through the vomitory into a ruined wharf.

It crashed downwards, exploding as it went, rending gallery after gallery with its wings of steel. For a moment they saw the nations of the dead, and, before they joined them, scraps of the untainted sky.

QUESTIONS

The artist (whether he be poet, painter, novelist or dramatist) frequently looks askance at the proud triumphs of science in our time. In works ranging from Aldous Huxley's novel, *Brave New World*, to Charlie Chaplin's film, *Modern Times*, the artist-as-prophet has sought to warn against our very success. Are we to be enslaved by the same machinery we have invented to serve us? Is it possible that in conquering nature we are in danger of destroying ourselves? E. M. Forster's "The Machine Stops", in the guise of "science fiction", is a prophetic parable. And it is a warning.

1. Describe the kind of world in which Vashti and Kuno live.

2. In what respects does it resemble our modern scientific world? In other words, how does the world of the story "make contact" with our own world?

3. What has happened to the physical nature of man in this "brave new world" of scientific convenience? Why?

4. Is there anything strange in the relation of mother and son? Is E. M. Forster merely exaggerating a tendency in human relations already discernible in modern life and in the state of the modern family?

5. What happens to the spirit of man in the perfect world of the machine?

6. What is the view of and the feeling for external nature in the machine world? Of past history?

7. What is the significance of The Book? Of prayers to The Machine?

8. Explain Kuno's revolt and his mother's disapproval of this revolt.

9. What is the Mending Apparatus? Why does it appear in the shape of the "worm" which drags Kuno into "hell"?

10. How, despite the catastrophe, does the author avoid pessimism and turn the tale into a "meditation" and a warning?

# Notes

---

p. 5   *Sir Joseph Barcroft:*   an English physiologist (1872-1947). He was world famous for his research on the circulatory and nervous systems. However, Kaempffert is mistaken in referring to him as a Nobel prize-winner.

p. 6   *Neanderthalers and Cro-Magnons:*   two types of early man who lived 30,000 to 100,000 years ago. Neanderthal man was short and heavily built. Cro-Magnon man, who superseded him, was taller and is generally believed to have been more closely related to modern man.

p. 6   *Wells:*   H. G. Wells. See biographical note on page 95.

p. 7   *the piece of work that Hamlet held up for admiration:*   in Shakespeare's tragedy, *Hamlet*, see Hamlet's speech to Rosencrantz and Guildenstern (Act II, Scene ii) beginning, "I will tell you why …"

p. 11   *summum bonum:*   a Latin phrase meaning *the highest good.*

p. 11   *Sir James Jeans:*   English mathematician, physicist and astronomer (1877-1946) whose vivid writings made science intelligible to the layman.

REMEMBRANCE DAY, 2010 A.D.

p. 18   *The Love-Hate*      MacLennan's ironic compound developed
        *Syndrome:*          from *syndrome*, a term in pathology
                             meaning *a group of symptoms typical of
                             a distinctive disease.*

ON JARGON

p. 28   *sub silentio:*      Latin for *in silence,* or *under cover of
                             silence.*

p. 28   *de diem in diem:*   a Latin phrase meaning *from day to day.*

p. 28   *cui bono?*          a Latin phrase from Cicero, *for whose
                             benefit is it?*

p. 28   *Babu:*              a Hindu clerk who writes English with
                             only slight knowledge of English idiom.

p. 31   *yclept:*            archaic word meaning *called* or *named.*

p. 31   *casus:*             Latin, literally, *a falling down;* by exten-
                             sion it came to mean *an occasion, an
                             opportunity,* or even *an adverse event,
                             a misfortune.*

p. 33   λόγος:               a Greek word for *speech, discourse,* or
                             *reason.*

JUKE JUDKINS

p. 40   *Vauxhall:*          a kind of parkland pleasure resort to
                             which admission was charged. Situated
                             in London on the south bank of the
                             Thames, it was in existence from the
                             1660's to 1859.

p. 42   *St. Michael's:*     a variety of orange then popular in
                             London.

THE FIRE

p. 60    *The New Utopia:* a novel by H. G. Wells (see page 95),
         published in 1905.


MR. ARCULARIS

p. 65    *Cavalleria*        a popular and tuneful opera first per-
         *Rusticana:*        formed in Rome in 1890 and composed
                             by Pietro Mascagni (1863-1945).

p. 67    *Plato:*            a Greek philosopher (c.428-c.348 B.C.),
                             author of *The Dialogues,* whose thought,
                             together with Aristotle's, set the direction
                             of philosophy for over two thousand
                             years.

p. 67    *Kipling:*          Rudyard Kipling (1865-1936) is a
                             British fiction writer and poet best
                             remembered for his stories of India and
                             his ballads of army life.

p. 67    *The Odyssey:*      one of the two epic poems attributed to
                             Homer.

p. 75    *the Hound of*      poem written by Francis Thompson
         *Heaven:*           (1859-1907), describing Christ's pursuit
                             of the human soul.

p. 80    *the Battle of*     a battle fought in 9 A.D. near Minden
         *Teutoburg Forest:* in Westphalia. Roman legions were
                             defeated by Germanic tribesmen. The
                             battle marks the end of Rome's invinci-
                             bility.


THE SECRET LIFE OF WALTER MITTY

p. 88    *hydroplane:*       Walter may be imagining a large flying
                             boat, or possibly a dirigible.

p. 89   *Obstreosis:*         Like the other medical-sounding terms,
                              this is the garbled concoction of Walter's
                              imagination.

p. 89   *Coreopsis:*          a yellow flower, in shape somewhat like
                              a daisy — a rather comical misuse in this
                              context.

p. 92   *Von Richtman's*      In 1939, Walter would, of course, have
        *circus:*             his images of war formed by films and
                              books about World War I. Von Richtman
                              might be inspired by the German air-ace,
                              Baron Manfred von Richthofen (1892-
                              1918), who shot down 80 planes. The
                              squadron of a German flyer was often
                              referred to as his circus.

THE DOOR IN THE WALL

p. 97   *West Kensington:* a district adjacent to Kensington, which
                           is a borough of London located on the
                           north side of the Thames, west of the
                           heart of the City. All the place names
                           mentioned in the story are in the same
                           general area.

p. 109  *the whip:*        a member of a  political  party in
                           Parliament whose duty it is to secure
                           the attendance of members of that party
                           on the occasion of an important division.

THE FIRING SQUAD

p. 119  *AWL:*             absent without leave. The seriousness of
                           this offence depends upon the length
                           and circumstances of the period of
                           absence.

PAUL'S CASE

p. 142 *four-in-hand:*     a tie of the period.

p. 144 *Raffelli:*     Jean Raffelli (1850-1924), French painter and sculptor, well known for his vivid painting of Paris streets.

p. 147 *John Calvin:*     a Protestant theologian (1509-1564) and a founder of Puritan beliefs. He emphasized thrift, industry, and sobriety.

p. 147 *Cordelia Street:*     Cordelia is the tragic heroine in Shakespeare's *King Lear*. She dies by strangulation in the last act. Probably Willa Cather used the name for this connotation.

p. 154 *Tiffany's:*     a fashionable jewellery store.

p. 154 *Waldorf:*     one of New York's most luxurious hotels.

MY REMARKABLE UNCLE

p. 169 *Manitoba:*     created a province in 1870. In the 1880's, the period referred to in this essay, its population doubled.

p. 169 *Portage Avenue:*     an historic main street of Winnipeg.

p. 170 *John Norquay:*     (1841-1889) son of prairie pioneers, he was elected in 1870 to the first Legislative Assembly of Manitoba and was premier of the province from 1878 to 1887.

p. 173 *Coppermine River:*     a river 525 miles long in the Mackenzie district of the Northwest Territories, flowing northwest into the Arctic Ocean.

MAN IN SOCIETY

p. 178   *Auschwitz:*        a Nazi concentration camp in Poland
                            during the Second World War and
                            notorious for the practice of bestial
                            torture.

p. 179   *Albert Einstein:*   (1879-1955) one of the greatest of all
                            theoretical mathematicians whose insights
                            led ultimately to the manufacture of the
                            atomic bomb. *Niels Bohr* (1885-    )
                            and *J. Franck* (1882-    ) made notable
                            contributions to atomic and electronic
                            science.

p. 179   *Hiroshima and*     Japanese cities desolated by American
         *Nagasaki:*          atomic bombs at the close of the Second
                            World War.

p. 179   *Wolfenden*         a report completed and presented by a
         *Report:*            Committee of the British Parliament in
                            1960. It recommended that certain moral
                            offences which caused no injury to
                            other persons be removed from the
                            Criminal Code.

p. 180   *James Clerk*       a British physicist (1831-1879), who was
         *Maxwell:*           a pioneer in the study of electricity.
                            His work, *Electricity and Magnetism*
                            (1873), is one of the milestones of the
                            development of modern science

p. 180   **Karl Friedrich**   (1777-1855) known as "the Prince of
         *Gauss:*             Mathematicians". He opened the way to
                            important developments in modern
                            mathematics and physical science.

p. 180   *Sir Isaac Newton:* a British mathematician, experimental
                            scientist, and philosopher (1642-1727),
                            whose principles have dominated the
                            natural sciences until our own time.

| | | |
|---|---|---|
| p. 180 | *Archimedes:* | a Greek mathematician and inventor (C. 287-212 B.C.), who was one of the most original and fruitful minds in the history of man. |
| p. 182 | *Malthusian:* | Thomas Robert Malthus (1766-1834) was an economist who argued that population increases in geometric ratio while food supplies increase only in arithmetical ratio. Therefore war, famine, and disease are seen as necessary checks to the growth of world population. |

AMERICAN SLANG

| | | |
|---|---|---|
| p. 194 | *George H. McKnight:* | a linguist. Mencken is quoting from McKnight's book, *English Words and Their Background.* For a complete account of Mencken's other sources of quotation see the full chapter, "American Slang", in his learned work, *The American Language.* |

ON BEING FOUND OUT

| | | |
|---|---|---|
| p. 201 | *coram populo:* | Latin for *in public.* |
| p. 202 | *Dr. Lincolnsinn:* | a man of law, called after one of the four Inns of Court which have the power of calling to the bar. |
| p. 202 | *Peccavi:* | Latin phrase meaning *I have sinned.* |
| p. 202 | *Siste tandem carnifex:* | Latin sentence meaning *Desist, villain!* |
| p. 203 | *Jack Ketch:* | an English executioner (d. 1686). "Jack Ketch" became the "trade name" of public hangmen in England for the next two centuries. |

p. 205  κτῆμα ἐς ἀεί  Greek for *a possession forever.*

p. 206  *Dies irae:*  Latin, *day of wrath — the Last Judgment.*

p. 206  *"Oh, Mr. Bar-*  Bardolph is a comic but unscrupulous
        *dolph! . . . that*  character in Shakespeare's history plays.
        *there pyx*  In *Henry V* he is condemned to death for
        *business!":*  stealing a pyx, the box containing the
        wafer which is consecrated at Mass to be
        carried to the sick. Doll Tearsheet and
        Mrs. Quickly are friends of Bardolph.

EAST AND WEST

p. 214  *Ram Mohan Roy:*  an Indian religious and social reformer
        (1774-1833). He began a movement
        which in 1831 resulted in the abolition of
        *suttee,* the Hindu ceremony in which the
        widow sacrificed herself on the funeral
        pyre of her dead husband.

p. 215  *Akbar:*  a Moslem emperor of India (1542-1605).
        Although he conquered Hindu territories,
        he established an era of religious and
        racial tolerance.

p. 217  *a great*  Tagore may be referring to Gautama,
        *personality:*  the Buddha (563-483 B.C.), an Indian
        religious leader whose teachings spread
        throughout the East and today form one
        of the world's great religions.

p. 218  *"Never the twain*  from the first line of "The Ballad of East
        *shall meet.":*  and West" by Rudyard Kipling. The
        complete line is, "Oh, East is East, and
        West is West, and never the twain shall
        meet."

THE WORLD OUTSIDE

p. 274  *Annso a*  Gaelic, meaning *Good morning, teacher,*
        *Mhaighistear:*

p. 276  *Ni thuigim:*  a Gaelic sentence, *I don't understand.*

p. 277  *Baedeker:*  now almost a synonym for *guide book.*
Karl Baedeker (1801-1859) began the
publication.

p. 280  *De Falla:*  a Spanish impressionist composer (1876-
1946).

p. 280  *El Greco:*  (1548-1614) born in Greece, practised
his art in Spain. His painting is a fine
expression of the mystical fervour of the
Spanish Counter-Reformation.

p. 280  *Velasquez:*  a Spanish painter (1599-1660), noted for
his realistic and sensuous portraits of the
Spanish court and royal family.

p. 280  *Albeniz:*  a Spanish composer and pianist (1860-
1909). One of his well-known piano
works is the *Iberia.*


MR. REGINALD PEACOCK'S DAY

p. 284  *Covent Garden:*  Covent Garden Theatre, London,
England, first opened in 1732 and is the
home of the leading English opera and
ballet companies. The present theatre is
the third on this site.

p. 284  *Lohengrin:*  the famous opera by Richard Wagner
first produced at Weimar, Germany, in
1850. In the first Act, Lohengrin, an
unknown knight, comes to rescue Elsa, a
damsel in distress. He sails down the river
in a boat drawn by a swan. The swan is
later revealed to be the distressed damsel's
brother, Gottfried, the rightful heir to
the land, who had been enchanted into

this shape by wicked spirits. He is released, and all live happily ever after.

RIGHT AND WRONG AS A CLUE TO THE
MEANING OF THE UNIVERSE

p. 303   *quislings:*        or collaborators, after Major Vidkun
                            Quisling, a Norwegian who headed a pro-
                            Nazi government in conquered Norway
                            during World War II. A similar quisling
                            government was headed in France by
                            Marshal Pétain after the fall of France.

p. 308   *G. B. Shaw:*      an Irish playwright and critic (1856-
                            1950) noted for his non-conformist ideas
                            on politics, philosophy, and religion.

p. 308   *Bergson:*         Henri Bergson (1859-1941) was a French
                            philosopher whose most influential book,
                            *Creative Evolution,* was published in
                            1907 and translated into English in 1911.

REMEMBER CREATORE

p. 316   *Creatore:*        the director of a famous Italian brass band
                            that toured North American exhibitions
                            and fairs in the 1920's and early 1930's.

p. 317   *Mendelssohn:*     Felix Mendelssohn (1809-1847) was one
                            of the great German composers of the
                            nineteenth century. He wrote distin-
                            guished music in all the forms except
                            opera.

p. 318   *Rossini:*         Gioacchino Rossini (1792-1868) was an
                            Italian composer of opera, best known for
                            *The Barber of Seville* (1816) and *William
                            Tell* (1829).

p. 318   *von Suppé:*       Franz von Suppé (1819-1895) lived most
                            of his life in Vienna and is remembered

for his overtures, *Light Cavalry* and *Poet and Peasant.*

p. 318   *Auber:*       Daniel François Esprit Auber (1782-1871) was a popular composer of operas whose best known works are *Masaniello* and *Fra Diavolo.*

p. 318   *Il Trovatore:*       the opera by Giuseppe Verdi, was first produced at Rome in 1853. The *Miserere (Lord have mercy on us)* is a chant sung in the last Act before the prison in which Manrico, the hero of the tale, awaits execution.

p. 320   *Wembley:*       the site of the British Empire Exhibition of 1924-25.

THE SCIENCE TO SAVE US
FROM SCIENCE

p. 325   *Mendel:*       Gregor Johann Mendel (1822-1884) was the discoverer of the first laws of heredity.

p. 325   *Michelangelo:*       the great sculptor and painter (1475-1564) whose works are regarded as the summit of the Italian Renaissance.

p. 326   *Carlyle:*       Thomas Carlyle (1795-1881) was a British essayist, historian, and philosopher. *Sartor Resartus* and *The French Revolution* are among his major works.

p. 326   *Ruskin:*       John Ruskin (1819-1900) was both an art critic and social theorist. *Modern Painters* and *Unto This Last* are representative works.

p. 326   *the Communist Manifesto:*       a treatise calling for the overthrow of the capitalist system was written by Karl

Marx (1818-1883) and Friedrich
Engels (1820-1895) in 1847.

p. 326 *Manchester
competition:*

refers to the kind of practice advocated
in the nineteenth century by the so-
called Manchester School of economics.
The School believed in unrestricted economic activity and was opposed to all
forms of state control or interference.

p. 326 *Darwin:*

Charles Darwin (1809-1882) published
his *The Origin of Species* in 1859 and
in it propounded his theory of evolution.

p. 327 *Nobel:*

Alfred Nobel (1833-1896) developed
and manufactured high explosives. The
Nobel plant is near Stockholm, Sweden.

p. 328 *Nelson:*

Horatio Nelson (1758-1805) was the
victor of Trafalgar (October 21, 1805),
a decisive naval battle in Britain's war
with Napoleon.

p. 329 *stoicism:*

the Stoics were a school of philosophers
founded by Zeno at the end of the
fourth century B.C. Stoicism identified
wisdom with virtue.

p. 329 *Methodism:*

a Christian movement founded in the
eighteenth century in England by John
and Charles Wesley and George White-
field. It places strong emphasis on
personal religious experience and con-
version.

p. 330 *Deutschland
über alles:*

*Germany above all else:* the title and first
line of the German national anthem,
used here as a symbol of German attempts
at world conquest.

THE LOGIC OF ELFLAND

p. 334   *Jacobin:*   the name of a political club at the time of the French Revolution. The name came to be used to describe people of extreme political views.

p. 334   *Jacobite:*   the name given to supporters of James II after the Revolution of 1688 and later used to denote supporters of the exiled House of Stuart after the accession of George I.

p. 334   *Magnificat:*   from the Song of the Virgin Mary (St. Luke 1.46). "My soul doth magnify the Lord . . . He . . . hath exalted the humble and the meek."

p. 335   *Haeckel:*   Ernst Haeckel (1834-1919) was a German biologist who advocated a doctrine of evolution which denied any distinction between spirit and matter. In his view, spiritual nature evolves from physical nature.

p. 335   *Newton:*   see note for "Man in Society" by C. P. Snow.

p. 336   *Grimm's Law:*   a scientific account of sound changes in the older Indo-germanic, Low and High German languages. The "Law maker" was Jakob Ludwig Karl Grimm (1785-1863).

HENRY FOWLER:
MODERN ENGLISH USAGE

p. 341   *Brillat-Savarin:*   French gourmet (1755-1826), author of *Physiologie du Goût*, a work on gastronomy.

p. 341    *Harold Ross:*        originator of *The New Yorker* magazine
                                and for many years its chief editor.

p. 341    *the White Knight*    a character in Lewis Carroll's *Through*
          *in Alice:*           *the Looking-glass.* Although he gallantly
                                rescued Alice, he was highly unpractical.

p. 342    *Mr. Chips:*          a schoolmaster in James Hilton's novel,
                                *Goodbye Mr. Chips.* He was much
                                loved by his students.

p. 342    *Dr. Samuel*         English man of letters (1709-1784) and
          *Johnson:*            author of the famous *Dictionary of the*
                                *English Language* (1755).

p. 344    *the phrase coined*   Warren Harding, President of the
          *by a late Presi-*    United States from 1921 to 1923, had
          *dent:*               as his campaign slogan in 1920, *Back to*
                                *Normalcy.*

p. 345    *Cervantes:*          a Spanish writer (1547-1616), author of
                                the classic, *Don Quixote.*

p. 345    *Góngora:*            a Spanish lyric poet (1561-1627).

p. 347    *Times Literary*      the *Times* is a London daily paper,
          *Supplement:*         founded in 1785. The *Literary Supple-*
                                *ment* is a related weekly publication
                                featuring literary articles and reviews.

p. 348    *Ernest Renan:*       a French critic and author (1823-1892),
                                most famous for his biography of Christ,
                                *La Vie de Jésus.*


DOWN THE MINE

p. 350    *pace:*               the ablative form of the Latin word for
                                *peace (pax).* It is used in announcing a
                                contrary opinion. Here it has the mean-
                                ing, *with all deference to you, Chester-*

*ton.* Chesterton, an ardent Roman Catholic, would contend that civilization
rested on spiritual values. (See Chesterton's essay, "The Logic of Elfland",
p. 331, which refutes the philosophy of
common sense materialism.)

p. 351  *Davy lamps:*  a safety lamp for miners, invented by Sir
Humphry Davy in 1817. The flame is
surrounded by wire gauze in order to
prevent contact with explosive gases
outside the lamp.

p. 352  *clogs:*  heavy wooden-soled boots worn by the
miners.

p. 353  *the Piccadilly*  that section of the London subway
*Tube:*  beneath the district of Piccadilly.

p. 354  *from London*  a distance of about three miles.
*Bridge to Oxford*
*Circus:*

p. 357  *the City man's*  the City, although a relatively small
*daily ride in the*  central portion of London, is its financial
*Tube:*  heart. Each morning, thousands travel
to it by subway.

ARABY

p. 386  *Walter Scott:*  Sir Walter Scott (1771-1832), a Scottish
poet and novelist, published *The Abbott*
in 1820.

p. 386  *The Devout*  was a popular devotional manual.
*Communicant:*

p. 386  *The Memoirs*  François Eugene Vidocq (1775-1857),
*of Vidocq:*  after a period of association with Parisian
criminals, rose to the rank of chief of

the detective branch of the Paris police.
The *Memoirs* (published in 1828) are
believed not to have been written by
Vidocq but unquestionably draw on his
experiences.

p. 388  *Freemason:*    a member of an ancient society which
was originally a craft or guild of
workers in a substance called freestone.
Modern Masonic lodges emphasize a
strong moral code and the practice of
mutual help. The rituals of the Order
are secret, but membership is openly
professed. The Roman Catholic Church
since the eighteenth century has forbidden its communicants to be members
of the Masonic Order.

p. 390  *The Arab's*    a poem by Caroline Norton (1808-1877),
*Farewell to*    a grand-daughter of Richard Brindsley
*His Steed:*    Sheridan.

PAX BRITANNICA

p. 394  *Silas Bradford:*    drawn from the character of Captain
Silvanus Cobb, one of the founders of
Liverpool, Nova Scotia, who commanded
a company of Goreham's Rangers in the
long war with the Indians.

p. 394  *'Cajun people:*    Nickerson's pronunciation of *Acadian
people.* In 1755 the British expelled from
Nova Scotia the French colonials, or
Acadians, who had refused to swear
allegiance to the British monarch.

p. 396  *seventy-fours:*    a seventy-four was a ship carrying
seventy-four guns.

p. 397  *Le Loutre:*    Le Loutre and Maillard are the actual
names of two missionary priests. Le
Loutre inspired the Indians in their raids
against the English-speaking settlers in
Nova Scotia. Although he was eventually
recalled to France, his sinister influence
helped lead to the expulsion of the
Acadians. Father Maillard was much
gentler. He lived with the Indians, enduring the hardships of their wandering life
and finally persuading them to send their
chiefs to Halifax to make peace.

p. 397  *Father Maillard:*   see note above.

p. 398  *puncheon floors:*  floors made of timbers that have been
only partly smoothed.

p. 398  *Oldport:*    actually Liverpool, Nova Scotia.

p. 400  *grape:*    small cast-iron balls strongly connected
together to form a charge for cannon.

p. 406  *sagamore Joj:*   George II, king of Great Britain.

ONE'S A HEIFER

p. 429  *whiffle-tree:*   a cross-bar on a wagon or carriage, which
is fixed across the head of the shafts, and
to which the traces are attached.

MR. KNOW-ALL

p. 433  *Coty:*    the name of a Parisian firm famous for its
perfume.

p. 436  *Levantine:*    an inhabitant of the Levant, approximately the area of present-day Lebanon.

THE MACHINE STOPS

p. 445  *the pre-*                     the subsequent passage suggests that
        *Mongolian epoch:*  Australia and New Zealand, the area of
                            the world where Vashti lives, had long
                            ago been over-run in an Oriental invasion.

p. 455  *Mount Taygetus:*  in Sparta. The Spartans left sickly infants
                           there to die of exposure.

p. 460  *Wessex:*          ancient Saxon kingdom dating from the
                           sixth century A.D. Originally in the south
                           of England, its boundaries grew until by
                           the middle of the tenth century its kings
                           ruled all of England.

p. 465  *Lafcadio*         Lafcadio Hearn (1850-1904),Irish-Greek
        *Hearn ...*        writer who wrote on subjects ranging
        *Carlyle ...*      from the French Revolution to Japanese
        *Mirabeau:*        culture; Thomas Carlyle (see note for
                           "The Science to Save Us From Science"
                           by Bertrand Russell.); Honoré Mirabeau
                           (1749-1791), French revolutionist and
                           statesman who helped precipitate the
                           revolution of 1789. The names preceding
                           these are fictitious.

9  10  11  12  13  14  15  Bry  76  75  74  73  72  71  70